LITERATURE OF THE
WOMEN'S SUFFRAGE CAMPAIGN IN ENGLAND

LITERATURE OF THE WOMEN'S SUFFRAGE CAMPAIGN IN ENGLAND

EDITED BY

CAROLYN CHRISTENSEN NELSON

broadview press

Canadian Cataloguing in Publication Data

Literature of the women's suffrage campaign in England / edited by Carolyn Christensen Nelson

Includes bibliographical references.
ISBN 1-55111-511-5

1. Feminism – England – Literary collections. 2. Women – England – Literary collections. 3. Feminism and literature – England. I. Nelson, Carolyn Christensen.

PR1111.F453L47 2004   820.8'0355   C2004-900696-7

Broadview Press, Ltd. is an independent, international publishing house, incorporated in 1985. Broadview believes in shared ownership, both with its employees and with the general public; since the year 2000 Broadview shares have been traded publicly on the Toronto Venture Exchange under the symbol BDP.

We welcome any comments and suggestions regarding any aspect of our publications—please feel free to contact us at the addresses below, or at broadview@broadviewpress.com / www.broadviewpress.com

North America
Post Office Box 1243, Peterborough, Ontario, Canada K9J 7H5
3576 California Road, Orchard Park, NY 14127
Tel: (705) 743-8990; Fax: (705) 743-8353;
e-mail: customerservice@broadviewpress.com

UK, Ireland, and continental Europe
NBN Plymbridge, Eastover Road, Plymouth PL6 7PY UK
Tel: 44 (0) 1752 202301   Fax: 44 (0) 1752 202331
Fax Order Line: 44 (0) 1752 202333
Customer Service: cservs@nbnplymbridge.com Orders: orders@nbnplymbridge.com

Australia and New Zealand
UNIREPS, University of New South Wales
Sydney, NSW, 2052
Tel: 61 2 9664 0999; Fax: 61 2 9664 5420
email: info.press@unsw.edu.au

Typesetting and assembly: True to Type Inc., Mississauga, Canada.

PRINTED IN CANADA

CONTENTS

CHAPTER 1: THE ARGUMENTS

CHAPTER 2: WOMEN IN THE CAMPAIGN TELL THEIR STORIES

ACKNOWLEDGEMENTS

I am grateful for the use of the archives and resources of the Fawcett Library, now the Women's Library, the British Library, and the British Library Newspaper Library, Colindale. I thank the staff of Wise Library, West Virginia University, for helping me locate and obtain material through inter-library loan. I am also grateful for funding provided by a Faculty Senate Research Grant from West Virginia University that helped to make my research possible.

I have made every reasonable effort to trace the copyright holders of the materials included in this book. I would be pleased to hear from any holders who have been omitted, and I will credit them in subsequent editions. I would like to acknowledge the following for permission to include copyrighted material: Gillon Aitken Associates for excerpts from Annie Kenney's *Memories of a Militant*; Faber and Faber Ltd for excerpts from Hannah Mitchell's *The Hard Way Up: The Autobiography of Hannah Mitchell*; Pearson Education Limited for excerpts from E. Sylvia Pankhurst's *The Suffragette Movement*; and Victor Gollancz Ltd for excerpts from Emmeline Pethick-Lawrence's *My Part in a Changing World*. I also thank the National Portrait Gallery, London, for the photographs of Emmeline Pankhurst, Dame Millicent Fawcett, and the Suffragettes Group, and for the permission to reproduce them.

PICTURES AND ILLUSTRATIONS

Mill's Logic; or Franchise for Females
From *Punch, or the London Charivari* (30 March 1867)

The Ladies' Advocate
From *Punch, or the London Charivari* (1 June 1867)

"The Angel in 'The House;'" or, The Result of Female Suffrage
From *Punch, or the London Charivari* (14 June 1884)

"Taxation without Representation"
From *Votes for Women* III (7 January 1910)

"The Government's Methods of Barbarism"
From *Votes for Women* III (28 January 1910)

Cover page of *Votes for Women* V (5 January 1912)

Dame Millicent Fawcett by Walery (Stanislas Julian Walery, Count Ostrorog)
circa 1889
By courtesy of the National Portrait Gallery, London

Emmeline Pankhurst by (Mary) Olive Edis (Mrs. Galsworthy)
1920s
By courtesy of the National Portrait Gallery, London

Suffragette march in Hyde Park by Mrs. Albert Broom
23 July 1910
By courtesy of the National Portrait Gallery, London

LIST OF FIGURES

INTRODUCTION

The years of the women's campaign for the vote in England are remembered as a time of great political conflict and debate. The participants in this campaign were interesting and colourful figures who left a voluminous literary record for us. We read this literature today in hindsight, knowing that women ultimately won the vote. Those historic women committed to the cause never doubted the final outcome; they believed that they would ultimately triumph because they had justice on their side. The image of the breaking dawn, with its implications of a new day for women when they had achieved their goal of political enfranchisement, appears repeatedly in suffrage literature, particularly in the songs. It represents the optimistic faith the supporters of suffrage carried thoughout the years of struggle and which can be found in the literature they produced. Their tireless effort to gain the vote, during a time when the forces of government opposed them, and many in the general public, including other women, failed to support them, is a remarkable story that is an important chapter in women's political, social, and literary history.

The campaign for votes for women took place over a long period of time. While there is no specific date on which the women's suffrage movement began, the first articles on the question and petitions asking for the vote began to appear in the middle of the nineteenth century. Women finally got the vote in two stages in the following century: in 1918 and 1928. During the intervening years, women actively involved in the suffrage cause, along with their partisans, used various devices to sway the minds of the public and of politicians, including street demonstrations, marches, rallies, speeches, and eventually violent actions. At the same time, many suffrage supporters made their appeal for votes for women through their writing, producing a tremendous amount of literature intended to challenge traditional thinking on the political position of women and their right to be considered voting citizens in a democratic state. Most of the suffrage organizations, and even anti-suffrage groups, published their own newspapers that appeared weekly for many years. Because the suffrage movement generated so much written material, a great deal of which has been preserved for us, today we have a comprehensive documented record of that campaign, including the participants' names, their activities and organizations, and their impressions of the movement in which they played a part.

This text brings together a representative variety of literary materials that were generated during the women's suffrage campaign in England, which was fought, at least partially, through the written word. It will introduce students of literature and history to documents that played an important role in the suffrage debate and that are now often difficult to locate because they have not been included in most traditional literary anthologies or reprinted since the campaign ended. The selections are representative of the genres of literature produced by the suffrage movement and the positions taken by various people and organizations on many of the suffrage debates. Most of the selections included were written by supporters of women's suffrage, but the anti-suffrage position is represented as well to acquaint readers with some of the opposing arguments. This book also includes arguments that became important *within* the suffrage movement, including debates concerning the value of militancy and violence as a tactic to achieve the vote. It contains autobiographical accounts of women involved in the movement, as well as the plays women staged, the poetry and songs they composed, and the fiction they wrote relating to the suffrage experience. This literature of the women's suffrage campaign provides a fascinating insight into a political and social movement that had profound implications for the lives of women as well as for men.

The earliest advocates for women's suffrage were forced to argue from a defensive position, to make a case for women's political rights at a time when women had few other rights. Women also had to argue from a politically powerless position, pleading with men who possessed political power to share that power and privilege with women. For years women worked quietly and peacefully to that end, believing that by behaving in a feminine way and working constitutionally they would eventually be rewarded with the vote. In the mid-nineteenth century, in the earliest years of the campaign, many women believed that other issues, such as women's lack of access to higher education and the professions, and the discriminatory laws relating to divorce and married women's property, were just as important to address as voting. However, by the latter part of the nineteenth century, the suffrage campaign became increasingly separated from other feminist issues; obtaining the vote for women became the primary focus of feminist activism.

This new focus occurred for several reasons. First, by the end of the nineteenth century women had already achieved some of their goals, such as increased access to higher education. Colleges for women, such as Girton and Newnham, were opened in 1869 and 1871, and in 1872 the London School of Medicine for Women opened. The Custody of Infants Act of 1873 gave women the right to seek custody of their children after divorce, and the Second Married Women's Property Act of 1882 protected married women's property as separate from their husbands' and let them keep some of their own earnings. Secondly, suffrage became the focus for activism because women believed that their enfranchisement would be the key to remediating many of the conditions of their lives. Rather than relying on men to represent their interests, they could better represent themselves. With the vote they would possess the political leverage necessary to change discriminatory laws against women. Finally, women believed that they had a *right* to the vote, and without it they would never have full citizenship. Years of quiet work had brought them no closer to their goal of enfranchisement, and women, such as Lydia Becker, who had spent their entire lives working for women's suffrage, still did not have the vote at the time of their deaths. In the twentieth century the debate over the vote intensified, with women in support of suffrage becoming much more active in the public arena. The political debate was no longer presented simply as formal argument; it became an integral part of the plays, autobiographies, poetry, and fiction written by partisans on various sides of the controversies relating to suffrage.

While it might seem self-evident today that women needed to be enfranchised as citizens, in the late nineteenth and early twentieth centuries many people believed that allowing women to vote in national elections represented a very fearful step into unknown territory. If it is true, as Virginia Woolf asserted, that "the history of men's opposition to women's emancipation is more interesting perhaps than the story of that emancipation itself" (*A Room of One's Own*), it is important to know at least a few of the countless arguments made against women's suffrage and to understand the basis for the hostility faced by women in pursuit of the vote. A few essays representing this opposition are included in this text, but many more arguments, made both publicly and privately, warned about the dangers of enfranchising women. Indeed, the very idea of votes for women was thought by many men, including some in Parliament, to be absurd and treated with laughter and mockery. Even some women opposed their own enfranchisement, arguing that men could adequately represent their interests at the national level.

One recurrent claim made by the Antis, as they were called, was that men and women occupied separate spheres due to their essential differences that were biologically determined. Since the sphere for women was the home, their leaving the domestic world for the public space of political activity threatened the clear social divisions that were supposedly natural and that many found comfortable. It was also feared that involvement in politics would have a corrupting effect on women who were believed to be more morally pure than men. The obvious paradox was that if the separate spheres claim was valid, and if women were essentially different from men—a claim most women at the time did not dispute—it followed that women needed the vote because their concerns and interests *were* essentially different from men's. Furthermore, women were already in the public arena, having involved themselves in political campaigns for many years by working for male candidates for office. And finally, making the claim that women should be excluded from political life because they were morally superior to men said a great deal about men's fears of legislation that would hold men to the same moral and legal standards as women. The claim was also made that Britain's empire depended on perceived military might and, because women did not participate in the military, they should not be making parliamentary decisions that had to be enforced by military backing. In response women pointed out that men who did not serve in the military were not automatically disenfranchised and that many men serving in the military did not have the vote.

Countless arguments were made against the enfranchisement of women, but a deep-seated fear about change, particularly sharing power with a group that were never seen as men's equals, was the basis of many of them. At a time when women did not have the same educational opportunities as men and could not enter most of the professions, it was difficult for many people to believe that women were just as capable as men of serious involvement in the political life of the nation and possessed the ability to make intelligent choices as voters. Women were still often stereotyped as emotional beings incapable of making rational decisions. Of course, when the nineteenth-century suffrage campaign for women began, many men did not have the vote either. Some of the arguments for and against women's suffrage are included in the first section of the book, called The Arguments. It begins with important early essays by Harriet Taylor, John Stuart Mill, and Lydia Becker.

Throughout the long suffrage campaign, various issues arose that caused divisions within the suffrage movement. The result was the formation of many suffrage organizations, all pursuing similar ends but with different leaders, philosophies, and strategies. For example, the National Union of Women's Suffrage Societies (NUWSS) was formed as a democratic organization and had an elected leader, Millicent Fawcett, while the Women's Social and Political Union (WSPU) was run on more autocratic lines, similar to a military organization, and was dominated by the personalities of Emmeline and Christabel Pankhurst. However, the women in the different organizations did not form completely separate and discrete groups. Some women participated in the activities of more than one organization while others, during the course of the campaign, changed their membership from one organization to another or belonged to several organizations at the same time. In their autobiographies and memoirs, writers explain what attracted them to the suffrage movement, what they experienced during the campaign, and why they joined specific suffrage organizations. They also provide first-hand perspectives on the leadership styles of the most prominent members of the organization.

Which categories of women should be enfranchised and what methods should be used to gain the vote became two of many divisive issues that separated the different suffrage organizations throughout the campaign. Some organizations wanted all women to be enfranchised at the same time, while others believed that working for the enfranchisement of a small group, such as unmarried women or property owners, was a plan that would lead to earlier success. Conservatives feared that enfranchising all women, including those of the working class, would give the Liberal or Labour Party a numerical advantage. Enfranchising only property owners would likely favour the Conservatives in elections. Working-class women objected to the requirement that women voters must be property owners. Because of the conditions of their lives and their lack of any social or economic power, working-class women felt that they had the most to gain by voting and that they should not be excluded from the franchise if it were given to other women. Some women believed that if all women could not be enfranchised together, unmarried women should be the first to get the vote. Unmarried women who were property owners paid taxes just as men did. However, excluding married women from the vote while enfranchising single women was not a compromise all women were willing to make. Also, a strange situation could arise if only unmarried women were enfranchised: during the course of their lives women would lose the vote if they married and gain it again if they became widowed, thus creating an ever-changing group of women voters.

The conflict over whether all or only certain groups of women should be enfranchised was partly related to class divisions within British society, and it had the potential of pitting working-class women against those who were more privileged. The list of signatories of the 1889 "Appeal Against Female Suffrage," who were mostly wealthy and titled women, clearly reveals these class divisions. Those women who opposed all votes for women usually led the most privileged lives and were able to exercise the power that derives from wealth and social standing. Virginia Woolf demonstrated the value of money as a means to gaining power when she claimed that she, or her fictional self, benefited more from the legacy she received from her aunt than she did from gaining the vote (*A Room of One's Own*). Queen Victoria, whose power and privilege elevated her above the lot of ordinary women, felt quite capable of ruling an empire and yet opposed women's suffrage. In a letter to Sir Theodore Martin, she stated: "The Queen is most anxious to enlist every one who can speak or write to join in checking this mad, wicked folly of 'Woman's Rights', with all its attendant horrors, on which her poor feeble sex is bent, forgetting every sense of womanly feeling and propriety ... Woman would become the most hateful, heathen, and disgusting of human beings were she allowed to unsex herself; and where would be the protection which man was intended to give the weaker sex" (quoted in Hardie 140). Women with economic power and social leverage failed to empathize with those women at the lower economic and social levels of society who suffered most from gender inequities in the legal system.

A type of compromise on the issue of which women to enfranchise was achieved when the vote was finally granted to women. It came in two stages. In 1918 the vote was given to those 30 and over if they were householders, the wives of householders, occupiers of property with an annual rent of £5, or university graduates. Middle-class housewives comprised the largest group to be enfranchised in 1918, a group likely to vote Conservative. That same year all men 21 and over received the vote. In 1928 all women 21 and over were given the vote. If all women 21 and over had been granted the vote in 1918, they would have far outnumbered male voters because of the huge loss of men during World War I. However, women still outnumbered men in 1928 when they represented 52.7 per cent of potential voters.

Another divisive issue within the movement concerned tactics. Millicent Fawcett and her organization, the NUWSS, believed that women should work constitutionally with existing political organizations. Members of her organization and other non-militants were called suffragists. While Fawcett understood the reason women turned to militancy and was somewhat sympathetic with militant tactics, she believed that the use of violence was ultimately counterproductive. In contrast, Emmeline Pankhurst and her suffrage organization, the WSPU, adopted militancy soon after their campaign began and increasingly resorted to violence to draw attention to their cause. The militants, or suffragettes as they were called, believed that years of peaceful campaigning had achieved nothing for women and that men would never share political power with women unless force and violence compelled them to do so. They also believed that, without the vote, no constitutional way existed for women to work within the existing political structure. The WSPU refused to work with any political party and restricted its membership to women only. During the suffrage campaign, many other suffrage organizations took a variety of positions on suffrage issues, particularly on the use and effectiveness of militancy.

The militants claimed that throughout history men had repeatedly used violence to achieve their political goals and that militancy was the only way that those in power would ever concede to women's demands. However, it became clear that when women resorted to violence it created a far greater anxiety in the public mind. Suffrage activists were not just stepping out of their traditional domestic roles by demonstrating on the streets and in public places, they were also engaging in behaviours that had always been associated with men. The charge made against militant women was that their actions were not "womanly." The often-violent response to the women's actions, even to their peaceful demonstrations, revealed male anxiety about women interjecting themselves into men's public space. Many women were also uncomfortable with militancy; the NUWSS, with its nonmilitant philosophy, attracted many more members than the WSPU. Extreme violence, such as the arson and window breaking employed during the latter part of the campaign, alienated people who believed that such actions achieved nothing and actually contributed to a loss of support for the suffragettes. Emmeline Pankhurst, who encouraged the violence, revealed her own ambivalence about abandoning womanly behaviour when she instructed her followers to dress like ladies when they took to the streets in demonstrations; she herself was always impeccably attired. Whether the constitutional or militant organizations were ultimately responsible for gaining the vote is still a matter of debate. Both groups no doubt contributed to the final victory. But other factors played a role, such as women's contributions to the nation during the war. Also, historical inevitability suggests that women in England would have been enfranchised after World War I. By 1918 women in other European countries already had the vote, including Norway, Finland, Denmark, and Iceland, as well as Australia, New Zealand, and 18 American states.

Because the issue of militancy played such an important role within the suffrage campaign, it is discussed in many of the women's memoirs and autobiographies. The short story and novel writers engage the issue as well through their fictional characters. Militant actions led to imprisonment, and hundreds of suffragettes were imprisoned during the years of the suffrage campaign. Imprisoned women began to use the hunger strike as a tactic to demand that they be treated as political prisoners and placed in the first division of prison where they would receive better treatment than that given regular criminals placed in the second and third divisions. Suffrage fiction dramatically portrays the suffering of women during hunger strikes and the attendant horrors of force-feeding, which the government decided was the solution to the problem presented by the hunger-striking women. Force-feeding became a potent weapon of the imprisoned suffragettes because it sparked public sympathy for women whose militancy was not necessarily favoured by the public at large. Essays relating to the debate over militancy are included in the first section of the book, called The Arguments: The Question of Militancy and the Hunger Strike, but the issue is discussed in many other works.

Those who participated in the suffrage campaign record in their memoirs and autobiographies the reasons they were drawn to the movement and the sacrifices they were willing to make to get the vote for women. Their accounts provide fascinating descriptions of the women who led the different suffrage organizations and the characteristics that enabled those leaders to inspire such devotion in their followers. Their poems, autobiographies, and fiction also describe the price they paid for their participation in militant events, including their prison experiences. They describe the bonds they formed with one another as well as with lower-class women working in the prison or serving time for quite different crimes. Women who had never been in contact with prisoners suddenly found themselves sharing prison life with women from quite different social worlds. They also tell of their hunger strikes and the horrors of forcible feeding.

The stereotype of suffragettes, as has been true of feminists generally, was that they were grim, humourless fanatics. The satiric poems they wrote and the comic plays they produced dispel that stereotype. The short one-act plays which the Actresses' Franchise League produced for the suffrage movement are mainly comic, and they dramatize the many absurdities of existing laws. They also reveal just how illogical were the arguments against enfranchising women who desired the leverage of political power to create a more just society. Far from dwelling on the grim realities of the lives of many poor women, the playwrights demonstrated the comic implications of a world where men, who may be illiterate or behave irresponsibly at best, are considered to be the head of the home and have complete authority over their children while intelligent women possess few rights and have no political leverage. They also illustrate the reality that if all laws regarding the sexes were actually enforced, the world would not be an ideal place for men or for women.

Suffrage fiction was written by people on both sides of the issue, and it was rarely nonpartisan. During the time of the campaign, suffrage supporters produced most of the fiction; thus, it provides highly sympathetic portrayals of suffragists and suffragettes, even of women who participated in violence. Fiction relating to suffrage is realistic, depicting events closely approximating actual events in which women were involved, such as their participation in violence, hunger strikes, and suffrage marches. While stories and novels might appear to be less polemical than the arguments and the plays that often contain actual debates between two people, they, too, function as political propaganda. Fiction draws readers into the suffrage experience, forcing them to consider their commitment to the cause and to decide what actions they would take to achieve the vote. The reader becomes a participant in the suffering endured in prison by the militant suffragettes and the exultation women experienced in the suffrage marches. Novels about suffrage women continue to be engaging narratives and certainly have literary value as realistic literature. Their heroines are fictional women who step outside the domestic sphere to act on a much larger public stage. These narratives of a historic political struggle were written, not by a writer imagining a historic past and recreating it, but by women who actually participated in the events which they describe in their fiction.

Suffrage literature engages the reader in a debate that is both historical and relevant today. The measures taken by the women of the suffrage movement to gain their political rights and achieve full citizenship still have implications for citizens in a democracy, regardless of gender. The decisions these women made to devote years of their lives to the pursuit of a political goal is impressive, particularly since the earliest suffrage writers did not live to see the day when women could vote. The suffrage movement raises a series of questions: What tactics are permissible to use to gain one's rights? Under what conditions is violence justified? Are the penalties of aggressive political action, such as ridicule, imprisonment, and force-feeding, worth enduring for a just cause? All these questions, and many more raised during the days of the suffrage movement, were debated on the street, on the printed page, and in the Houses of Parliament. It is important for us today to recognize the significant role that literature played in a great national debate that ultimately succeeded in gaining the vote for women.

Introductions are provided at the beginning of each chapter to contextualize the material and to provide a brief background discussion of the selections that follow. The names of most of the writers whose works are included in the book, as well as some names that are frequently mentioned in the selections, are included in the section called Biographical Notes. The most significant suffrage organizations, along with names of some of their members, are listed in the section called Suffrage Organizations. A chronology of significant events relating to women's emancipation and suffrage is also provided to enable the reader to put the events of the suffrage campaign in a larger, historical context and to understand the laws relating to women's lives during the nineteenth and twentieth centuries.

SIGNIFICANT DATES IN WOMEN'S STRUGGLE FOR EMANCIPATION AND SUFFRAGE

1666 Margaret Fell Fox, a Quaker, published "Women's Speaking Justified," a pamphlet defending the right of women to speak in the church and arguing for the equality of women in creation. The Society of Friends, known as the Quakers, was the most consistent proponent of women's equality during the seventeenth century.

1792 Mary Wollstonecraft published *A Vindication of the Rights of Woman*, an important document that protested against women's subjugation and argued for women's political, economic, and legal equality.

1825 William Thompson published "Appeal of One Half of the Human Race, Women, Against the Pretensions of the Other Half, Men, to Retain Them in Political, and Thence in Civil and Domestic Slavery." The essay argues for equal political rights for women, including the right to vote. According to Thompson, women need representation because their interests differ from those of men.

1832 *The Great Reform Act* gave the vote to men who owned or rented property worth £10 or more annually. Thus, in addition to landowners, about one-half of the middle class could vote, giving about one-fifth of all men the vote. The Act specifically excluded women. By substituting the term "male person" for the first time in English history, in lieu of the word "man" as in earlier acts, women were legally prevented from voting in parliamentary elections.

1839 The *Custody of Infants Act* gave a mother of "unblemished character" (meaning, not adulterous) the right of custody of her children until they were seven years old and access to those under 16. However, the father retained almost complete control of the children. (Before 1839, a woman who was divorced was not allowed to see her children unless she had an "unblemished" character. Fathers had absolute control over their children.)

1848 London University admitted female students.

1850 *Lord Brougham's Act* ruled that in the law of the United Kingdom "words importing the masculine gender shall be deemed to include females unless the contrary is expressly provided."

1857 The *Matrimonial Causes Act* established secular divorce, which no longer required an Act of Parliament. A husband could obtain a divorce from his wife on the simple grounds of adultery. However, a woman seeking to obtain a divorce had to prove adultery aggravated by desertion, cruelty, rape, sodomy, incest, or bigamy.

1861 John Stuart Mill wrote *The Subjection of Women.*

1864 First *Contagious Diseases Act* was passed. More *Contagious Diseases Acts* were passed in 1866 and 1869. These Acts allowed women thought to be prostitutes to be forcibly inspected for disease and detained for up to nine months for treatment.

1866 On June 7, John Stuart Mill and Henry Fawcett presented to the House of Commons a petition for extension of the franchise to all male and female householders. It was drafted and signed by 1,499 women, including many prominent women of the day such as Mary Somerville, Florence Nightingale, Harriet Martineau, Helen Taylor, Josephine Butler, Elizabeth Garrett (later Garrett Anderson), and Emily Davies.

1867 *The Second Reform Act* doubled the electorate by giving the vote to almost all working men. Mill attempted to include a franchise for women in the bill but his amendment was defeated by 196 to 73 votes.

The first women's suffrage societies were founded in Manchester, London, and Edinburgh. In Manchester Lydia Becker founded the Society for the Promotion of Women's Suffrage.

1868 The judges in the *Chorlton v. Lings* case ruled that, although the word "man" in an Act of Parliament must be held to include women, "this did not apply to the privileges granted by the State." Thus the same words in the Act of Parliament that applied only to men concerning the vote, for the purposes of taxation included women.

Women's suffrage societies were founded in Bristol and Birmingham.

1869 John Stuart Mill published *The Subjection of Women.*

Girton College, Cambridge, was established as the first residential college for women.

1870 Women were granted the Municipal Franchise enabling them to vote in local elections. Under the *Education Act*, women were given the right to vote for members of School Boards and also to be elected to the boards.

Passage of the first *Married Women's Property Act*, which allowed women to keep £200 of their own earnings and to inherit personal property and small amounts of money. (Before 1870, a woman's husband owned all her money, belongings, and clothes. She was not allowed to keep any of her earnings.)

Dr. Richard Pankhurst drafted the first Women's Suffrage Bill. Between 1879 and 1914, 28 unsuccessful suffrage bills were drafted.

1871 Newnham College, Cambridge, was founded. Women were not allowed the same degrees as men until 1949.

1872 The London School of Medicine for Women opened.

1873 *Custody of Infants Act*: all women after divorce or separation were allowed access to their children. Women could be awarded custody of children up to age 16.

1880 In the general election, Liberals were returned to power and William Gladstone became Prime Minister. Suffrage was extended to women in the Isle of Man.

1882 A second *Married Women's Property Act* was passed, protecting married women's separate property. Women could retain what they owned at the time of marriage, including ownership of property they received from a parent, and keep some of their earnings.

1883 The Primrose League, an organization of women who took an active political role in canvassing and speaking for Conservative candidates, was formed.

1884 The *Third Reform Act* entitled about 5 million men in all (nearly two-thirds of the male population) to vote. Those who could not vote were the poorest men, servants who lived in the homes of their employers, criminals, and patients in lunatic asylums. Gladstone, the Prime Minister, opposed the amendment to include women's suffrage in the Reform Bill, thus assuring its defeat.

1885 Criminal Law Amendment raised the age of consent from 13 to 16.

1886 The Women's Liberal Federation was formed, under the Presidency of Mrs. Gladstone, to work on behalf of Liberal male candidates. Within a few years the organization gave its support to women's suffrage; some members left over this issue.The *Contagious Diseases Acts* were repealed following a campaign led by Josephine Butler.

1889 Mrs. Humphry (Mary) Ward, Miss Beatrice Potter (later Mrs. Sidney Webb), and Mrs. Creighton led a group of women in opposition to women's suffrage. They signed and published "An Appeal Against Female Suffrage" in the *Nineteenth Century*. (Mrs. Creighton and Mrs. Webb later become suffragists.)

1893 The National Women's Liberal Association was formed by women who left the Women's Liberal Federation over its support of women's suffrage.
Independent Labour Party was formed. It was the first political party to give support to women's suffrage, although some members of the ILP still opposed votes for women.

1894 Married women were given the right to all local franchises and could be elected as Poor Law Guardians.

1897 The National Union of Women's Suffrage Societies (NUWSS) was formed by uniting various suffrage societies from around England under the leadership of Millicent Garrett Fawcett.

1903 The Women's Social and Political Union (WSPU) was formed by Emmeline Pankhurst and her family in Manchester. Its motto was

"Deeds Not Words." It attracted members from the Independent Labour Party.

1905 First militant incident: on October 13, Christabel Pankhurst and Annie Kenney were arrested for their protest at a Liberal meeting at the Free Trade Hall in Manchester. They chose imprisonment rather than pay a fine.

1906 The split widened between those loyal to Millicent Fawcett's National Union of Women's Suffrage Societies, who were law abiding, and the militant members of the Pankhursts' Women's Social and Political Union.
     WSPU moved its headquarters to Clement's Inn in London.

1907 Three senior members broke away from WSPU to form the Women's Freedom League (WFL), also militant, but democratic. Charlotte Despard was the President. In October, *Votes for Women*, the official publication of the WSPU, was begun with Frederick and Emmeline Pethick-Lawrence as joint editors.

1908 Anti-suffragist Herbert Henry Asquith became Prime Minister.
     Mary Leigh and Edith New became the first suffragette window breakers; they attacked the windows at No. 10 Downing Street.
     The Women Writers' Suffrage League (WWSL) and the Actresses' Franchise League (AFL) were formed. Both organizations agreed to be neutral in regard to suffrage tactics.

1909 WSPU campaign turned to arson. The sculptor Marion Wallace Dunlop started the first hunger strike on July 5 in protest of the treatment of the suffragettes in prison. Forcible feeding for hunger strikers began in September.

1910 King Edward VII died. A "Conciliation Bill" was introduced to give women a limited franchise. Mrs. Pankhurst declared a truce. On June 18 the WSPU organized a huge procession in support of the Bill with 617 women who had been imprisoned for the cause marching at the head. Prime Minister Asquith killed the Bill and the truce ended. On Black Friday (November 18) a WSPU deputation to Parliament was met with great police brutality; 120 women were arrested.
     In December the National League for Opposing Women's Suffrage was formed by combining a men's anti-suffrage organization formed by Lord Cromer and a women's anti-suffrage society formed in 1908 under the leadership of Mary [Mrs. Humphry] Ward.

1911 Second Conciliation Bill failed. On November 21, suffragettes smashed the windows of government and private offices and West End shops. More than 200 women were arrested. Window smashing was now WSPU policy.

1912 March: The police raided WSPU headquarters, arresting the Pethick-Lawrences. Christabel Pankhurst fled to Paris and stayed there until the war began.

The Pethick-Lawrences were expelled from the WSPU in October, taking with them *Votes for Women*. Christabel and Emmeline Pankhurst began the paper *The Suffragette*. WSPU offices moved to Lincoln's Inn, London.

1913   April: *Prisoner's Temporary Discharge for Ill Health Act* (known as the Cat and Mouse Act) was passed. Under the terms of the Act, hunger strikers could be released, then, after recovery, rearrested and returned to prison to complete their sentences.

June: Emily Wilding Davison rushed out onto the racecourse at the Derby horse race at Epson and grabbed the reins of the King's horse. She died on June 8 of head injuries. WSPU organized a spectacular funeral procession through the streets of London.

1914   Sylvia Pankhurst was expelled from the WSPU and formed the East London Federation of Suffragettes, which became an independent organization. Its paper, *The Women's Dreadnought*, campaigned for votes for women but also for improved conditions for poor women. In March, Mary Richardson attacked the *Rokeby Venus*, a painting by Velásquez at the National Gallery in London, and was sentenced to 18 months in prison. Many art galleries and museums were now closed to the public or open only to men.

August: With the outbreak of World War I, the WSPU ended its militancy, and on August 10 the government released all WSPU prisoners.

1918   *The Representation of the People Act* gave the vote to women 30 and over if they were householders, the wives of householders, occupiers of property with an annual rent of £5, or graduates of British universities. About 8½ million women were able to vote in the 1918 election. All men 21 and over were given the vote.

November: World War I ended.

1919   *Sex Disqualification Removal Act* opened all the professions (except the Church) to women. They could now become MPs, solicitors, barristers, and magistrates, as well as serve on juries. Lady Nancy Astor became the first woman MP (taking a seat left vacant by her husband when he became a member of the House of Lords) although Countess Markiewicz was the first woman to win a place in Parliament in her own right. (She was not allowed to take her seat because as a member of Sinn Fein she refused to take the oath of allegiance.)

1928   *Equal Franchisement Act* gave the vote to all women 21 and over. Emmeline Pankhurst died.

1929   Women constituted 52.7 per cent of the electorate in the General Election and there were 14 women Members of Parliament. Millicent Fawcett died.

1930   On March 6, a statue of Emmeline Pankhurst was unveiled outside the Houses of Parliament.

1958 Women admitted to the House of Lords for the first time.

1969 *Representation of the People Act* gave all men and women over 18 the vote.

Biographical Information

Below is a list of writers whose works are included in this text as well as some of the people who are referenced in the writings. It is not meant to be a comprehensive list of all those involved in the suffrage movement. Dates are omitted when they could not be established with certainty.

SUSAN B. ANTHONY (1820-1906)
Anthony, an American suffrage leader, was a Quaker, a religion that deeply affected her thinking about human rights and the equality between men and women. After teaching for several years, Anthony became involved in the temperance movement and then the abolitionist movement and the women's suffrage movement. Along with Elizabeth Cady Stanton, Anthony spent years campaigning for women's rights, particularly for the vote. Together they formed the National American Woman Suffrage Association in 1890. Neither woman lived to see the passage of the Nineteenth Amendment in 1920 that granted American women the right to vote.

HENRY ARNCLIFFE-SENNETT
Arncliffe-Sennett was married to the actress Maud Mary Arncliffe-Sennett, who was active in various suffrage organizations, including the AFL. He wrote the suffrage play *An Englishwoman's Home.*

HERBERT HENRY ASQUITH (1852-1928)
Asquith, a Liberal, served in the House of Commons from 1886 to 1918, and from 1920 to 1924. He was leader of the Liberal Party from 1908-26 and served as Prime Minister from 1908 to 1916 when David Lloyd George replaced him. Unlike many members of the Liberal Party, Asquith was a strong opponent of women's suffrage.

STANLEY BALDWIN (1867-1947)
Baldwin, a Conservative politician, was a member of the House of Commons from 1908-1937, leader of the Conservative Party from 1923-37, and Prime Minister from 1923-24, 1924-29, and 1935-37. He was the Prime Minister when all women 21 and over received the vote in 1928. Two years later he spoke at the ceremony when the statue of Emmeline Pankhurst was unveiled.

LYDIA BECKER (1827-90)

Becker, born in Manchester, was an important leader of the early British suf-frage movement. She gave many public speeches for suffrage, was the Secre-tary of Central Committee of the national Society for Women's Suffrage in 1880, and founded and edited the *Women's Suffrage Journal* (1870-90).

INEZ BENSUSAN

Bensusan was an Australian actress and playwright who immigrated to Eng-land. As a member of the AFL she headed the play department that arranged entertainment and provided propaganda play performances for the suffrage societies. She succeeded in getting numerous writers, men as well as women, to write monologues, duologues, and short plays that could be staged easily in a variety of locales. She wrote the one-act suffrage play *The Apple.*

TERESA BILLINGTON-GREIG (1877-1964)

Billington taught school in Manchester where she met Emmeline Pankhurst, through whose influence she became a member of the Independent Labour Party. In 1903 she joined the WSPU and, in 1907, went to London to become a full-time worker for the organization. For her participation in suffrage demonstrations in London, she was imprisoned in Holloway. In London she met and married Frederick Greig, a Scot, who shared his wife's interest in women's rights. In 1907, objecting to the Pankhursts' style of leadership, Billington-Greig left the WSPU, along with Charlotte Despard, to form the WFL. In 1911 she left the WFL and attacked the militant movement. Memoir: *The Militant Suffrage Movement* (1911).

MONA CAIRD (1854-1932)

Caird was one of the New Woman writers of the 1890s. Her fiction and polem-ical essays developed her progressive ideas about women and marriage, which she represented in her novel *The Daughters of Danaus* (1894). In 1891 she became a member of the Women's Emancipation Union and in 1909 joined the London Society for Women's Suffrage.

MARY CHOLMONDELEY (1859-1925)

Cholmondeley was a fiction writer whose widely read novel *Red Pottage* (1899) illustrated the economic and social forces that restricted the lives of women in the late nineteenth century. She was a New Woman writer and her fiction gave particular emphasis to the plight of the unmarried woman. She wrote the suffrage play *Votes for Men.*

GERTRUDE COLMORE (Mrs. Gertrude [Renton] Baillie-Weaver) (1855-1926)

Gertrude Baillie Weaver, who wrote under the name Gertrude Colmore, was born Gertrude Renton. A member of the WFL, Colmore spoke at WSPU meetings and later joined the United Suffragists. She wrote stories for *Votes for Women* and *The Suffragette* and the suffrage novel *Suffragette Sally* (1911), which was based in part on the experiences of actual women involved in the suffrage movement. She was also the author of *The Life of Emily Davison* (1913). During the war she was a pacifist. She was married twice, first to H.A. Colmore-Dunn and then to Harold Baillie-Weaver.

WILLIAM LEONARD COURTNEY (1850-1928)
Courtney was a playwright and poet as well as a writer of fiction. His play *Undine* was first produced at the Shakespeare Theatre, Liverpool, England, in 1903. His poem, "There Was a Maiden," was set to music by Herbert Howells. He wrote the short story "The Soul of a Suffragette."

EMILY WILDING DAVISON (1872-1913)
Davison was a teacher who was educated at London University. She gave up teaching in order to devote more time to the WSPU, which she had joined in 1906. Repeatedly imprisoned for her suffrage activities, including the breaking of windows, and released after going on hunger strikes, she was eventually sentenced to hard labour and sent to Strangeways Gaol in Manchester where she was force-fed. In prison, after she barricaded the door of her cell to prevent prison doctors from entering, a hose of cold water was turned on her from the window but she never gave in. Finally the door was broken down, and she was carried to the hospital. Davison continued her militancy, setting fire to pillar-boxes. In prison, she injured her spine by jumping over the railings. Finally, on 4 June 1913, she suffered a fractured skull after running out onto the racetrack at the Derby and trying to grab the King's horse. At the time she had two WSPU flags pinned inside her coat. On June 8 she died from her injuries. When her funeral was held at St. George's Church in London on June 14, women mourners marching through the streets to the church created a huge spectacle. Many women believed she had died a martyr's death.

CHARLOTTE DESPARD (1844-1939)
Charlotte French, the daughter of a naval commander from Ireland, was a novelist and social reformer. In 1870 she married Max Despard who shared her commitment to radical politics. After the death of her husband in 1890, Charlotte lived and worked with the poor in London, becoming a member of the Independent Labour Party. She joined the NUWSS but then in 1906 left that organization to join the WSPU. She was sent to prison on several occasions for her activities. In 1907, unhappy with the Pankhursts and their leadership, Despard, along with Teresa Billington-Greig and Edith How Martyn, formed the Women's Freedom League (WFL), a militant but less violent organization. During the war Despard was a pacifist. She also was involved in Irish politics and was a supporter of the Sinn Fein. She died in Ireland.

Because Despard often wore a black lace mantilla, she is represented in some suffrage literature, even in fiction, by this identifying mark.

(Mary Margaret) Maye Dilke (1857-1914)

Maye Dilke was active in several suffrage organizations, including the WFL, the Women's Emancipation Union, and the London Society for Women's Suffrage. In 1888 she travelled with Elizabeth Cady Stanton to the International Council of Women in Washington. In 1876 she married Ashton Dilke, a Member of Parliament; after his death, she married Russell Cooke in 1891.

Millicent Garrett Fawcett (1847-1929)

Fawcett, a lifelong suffrage advocate, made her first speech on women's suffrage in 1868. In 1867 she married Henry Fawcett, who was a friend of J.S. Mill as well as a reform member of Parliament; he was blind. After the death of her husband in 1884, Fawcett became more actively involved in politics. In 1888, along with Lydia Becker, she split from other suffrage groups, believing that suffrage organizations should not be affiliated with political parties. When the NUWSS was formed in 1897, bringing together 17 suffrage societies, Fawcett acted as its head and was elected as president in 1907. Fawcett and her organization differed with the WSPU and other militant suffrage organizations on the use of militancy; they believed women should work for the vote within the constitutional system. When World War I began, she supported the war effort, suspending her political activity for the duration of war. Books: *Women's Suffrage* (1911) and *What I Remember* (1924).

Mary Gawthorpe (1881-1973)

Gawthorpe, a socialist and a teacher, became a member of the Independent Labour Party. She joined the NUWSS, but after meeting Christabel Pankhurst she became a paid organizer for the WSPU. A popular suffrage speaker, she was imprisoned several times for her militant activities. She later moved to the United States where she worked in the suffrage movement and married John Sanders, an American. Memoir: *Uphill to Holloway* (1962).

William Gladstone (1809-98)

Gladstone was Liberal Prime Minister four times: 1868-74, 1880-85, 1886, and 1892-94. Emmeline Pankhurst, in *My Own Story*, called Gladstone "an implacable foe of woman suffrage" who "so arranged Parliamentary business that the bill [for suffrage] never even came up for discussion." He opposed any attempt to enfranchise women.

Evelyn Glover

Glover wrote suffrage plays, including *A Chat with Mrs. Chicky; a duologue,* and *Miss Appleyard's Awakening: a play in one act.*

CICELY HAMILTON (1872-1952)

Hamilton spent ten years of her early life as an actress in touring companies performing around the country. After giving up acting, Hamilton turned to writing stories and then plays. Her first successful play was *Diana of Dobson's*, produced in 1908. Hamilton became involved with the suffrage campaign in 1907, participating in a march organized by the NUWSS. She later joined the WSPU. Owing to her disagreement with Emmeline Pankhurst's leadership style, Hamilton soon left the WSPU to join the Women's Freedom League (WFL). She helped found the Actresses' Franchise League (AFL) and the Women Writers' Suffrage League (WWSL), both of which remained neutral on suffrage tactics. Hamilton wrote two suffrage plays with Christopher St. John, *How the Vote was Won* and *The Pot and the Kettle*. She also authored *A Pageant of Great Women*. All of these plays were first performed in 1909. Hamilton wrote the words for the suffrage song "March of the Women" for which Ethel Smyth composed the music. Her book *Marriage as a Trade* (1909) is an important feminist document that portrays the role that economics plays in middle-class marriage. Autobiography: *Life Errant* (1935).

JAMES KEIR HARDIE (1856-1915)

Hardie, born to a poor family in Scotland, began working at the age of 11 as a coal miner. He was a labour leader, socialist, and pacifist. He helped form the Independent Labour Party, served as its first chairman, and then became leader of the Labour Party in the House of Commons from 1906-08. Supportive of the WSPU, Hardie pleaded the case for women's suffrage in the House where he also condemned the treatment of suffrage prisoners. Hardie and Sylvia Pankhurst, as socialists, close friends, and colleagues, shared similar political beliefs and a commitment to working with the poor.

HEBER HART (1865-1948)

Hart was a member of the executive of the National League for Opposing Women's Suffrage.

BESSIE HATTON

Hatton, a playwright and journalist, wrote romantic novels. With Cicely Hamilton she helped found the Women Writers' Suffrage League and served as its secretary. She was also a member of the WSPU. Hatton wrote the suffrage play *Before Sunrise*.

ANNIE KENNEY (1879-1953)

Kenney was the only working-class woman to rise to the highest levels of leadership in the suffrage movement. She was born in Lancashire as one of 11 children and began working in a cotton mill at age 10. In 1905 she heard Christabel Pankhurst speak in Manchester. Shortly thereafter she joined the

WSPU and never wavered in her devotion to Christabel. On 13 October 1905, she and Christabel went to the Free Trade Hall in Manchester for a public political meeting. They were both evicted from the meeting after repeatedly asking the question of when the Liberal Government would give the vote to women. The confrontation by Kenney and Christabel with authorities and their supposed assault on the police heralded the beginning of the militant movement of the WSPU. They were arrested and sent to prison. Kenney was then sent by Emmeline Pankhurst to "rouse London." She opened a branch of the WSPU there and worked as a full-time organizer. Kenney remained loyal to the Pankhursts when the WSPU began to follow a policy of more extreme militancy that included the burning of private residences. She was repeatedly imprisoned, went on hunger and thirst strikes, and was force-fed on many occasions. When Christabel fled to Paris in 1912, Kenney travelled back and forth between London and Paris with messages and orders from Christabel. Along with the rest of the WSPU, Kenney ended her militancy when World War I broke out. In 1918 she married James Taylor and left political life. Autobiography: *Memories of a Militant* (1924).

DAVID LLOYD GEORGE (1863-1945)

Lloyd George was a Liberal member of the House of Commons from 1890-1945. He served as Prime Minister from 1916-22 and leader of the Liberal party from 1926-31. He was a member of the Liberal administration that initially opposed women's right to vote and that passed the "Cat and Mouse Act" which allowed for force-feeding of hunger strikers in prison. He later spoke in favour of woman suffrage but opposed the Conciliation Bill of 1910. However, he was Prime Minister when the bill that enfranchised women aged 30 and over finally passed.

CONSTANCE LYTTON (1869-1923)

Because her father, Earl of Lytton, was a diplomat, Lytton spent her childhood in a variety of countries. She lived for a time in India where her father was the Viceroy and in Paris where he was an ambassador. As an adult, Lytton continued living with her mother. She suffered from various physical ailments and never married. She became involved with the suffrage movement after a meeting with Annie Kenney and Emmeline Pethick-Lawrence in 1908, an event she relates in her memoir. In 1909 she joined the WSPU. Her militant acts resulted in her imprisonment in Holloway and Newcastle Prisons but she was not force-fed, even when she went on a hunger strike, because her social position was known to prison authorities. She decided to return to prison, this time in Liverpool, as "Jane Warton." Under that name she was forcibly fed many times before her identity was discovered. She subsequently suffered a stroke and a heart attack and was partially paralyzed as a result of her prison treatment. Memoir: *Prisons and Prisoners: The Stirring Testimony of a Suffragette* (1914).

CONSTANCE ELIZABETH MAUD (d. 1929)
Maud, the daughter of the rector of Sanderstead, was educated on the continent, later drawing on her experiences in France for such books as *An English Girl in Paris* (1920) and *A Daughter of France* (1908). She also wrote about music, including such works as *Wagner's Heroes* and *Wagner's Heroines*. She contributed articles to *Votes for Women*, the official organ of the WSPU, and wrote the suffrage novel *No Surrender*.

JOHN STUART MILL (1806-73)
Mill was a long time champion of the rights of women and of women's suffrage. In 1866, as a Liberal member of the House of Commons, Mill presented a petition organized by a group of women in favour of women's suffrage. He added an amendment to the 1867 Reform Act that would give women the same political rights as men. The amendment was defeated by 196 votes to 73. Mill collaborated with Harriet Taylor, who later became his wife, on "The Enfranchisement of Women," published in 1851 in the *Westminster Review.* They also collaborated on another important work, *The Subjection of Women* (1869), that was published after Taylor's death.

HANNAH MITCHELL (1871-1956)
Mitchell, the daughter of a farmer in Derbyshire, had almost no education; she taught herself to read. She married Gibbon Mitchell, a socialist, in 1895, and together they became involved in the trade union movement. In 1904 she joined the WSPU and became a full-time worker for the organization the following year. In 1907, under the influence of Charlotte Despard, she joined the Women's Freedom League, and served as a speaker and activist for the suffrage cause. As a pacifist she opposed war and joined the Women's Peace Council. After the war she served on the Manchester City Council. Autobiography: *The Hard Way Up* (1968).

GRAHAM MOFFAT (1866-1951)
Moffatt, a Scottish playwright, actor, producer, and landscape photographer, was the author of the suffrage play *The Maid and the Magistrate: a duologue in one act.*

MARGARET WYNNE NEVINSON (1860-1932)
Nevinson, born Margaret Jones to Reverend Timothy Jones, a classical scholar, was educated at home, where her father taught her Latin and Greek. She got a degree from St. Andrews and taught school. She married Henry Nevinson, a radical journalist, in 1884. In 1907 Nevinson left the WSPU, of which she was a member, along with many other women, including Charlotte Despard, to form the Women's Freedom League (WFL). As a member of the Women Writers' Suffrage League she wrote pamphlets and a play, *In the Work-*

house (1911), to advance the suffrage movement. Autobiographies: *Fragments of Life, Tales and Sketches* (1922) and *Life's Fitful Fever* (1926).

ADELA PANKHURST (1885-1961)
Adela, the youngest daughter of Emmeline and Richard Pankhurst, was active in the WSPU, serving prison time for her activities. In 1914 her mother banished her to Australia where she married Tom Walsh, a Socialist, in 1917 and had five children. She joined the Victorian Socialist Party in 1917 and then the Australian Communist Party in 1921. In the following years she became increasingly conservative in her politics. In 1929 she helped found the Australian Women's Guild of Empire which opposed Communism, and later she became a fascist supporter. She converted to Roman Catholicism shortly before her death.

CHRISTABEL PANKHURST (1880-1958)
Christabel was the oldest child of Richard and Emmeline Pankhurst; she was her mother's favourite child. Christabel was a born politician, a charismatic leader, and the strategist for the WSPU. The militant campaign began in 1905 when she and Annie Kenney disrupted a Liberal Party meeting in Manchester and were thrown out. Christabel studied law at Owens College, Manchester, but, after receiving her degree, and because as a woman she was limited in her ability to practice law, she moved with her mother to London where the two directed the activities of the WSPU. Their increasingly autocratic leadership style and advocacy of violent militancy provoked women to leave the organization to form other suffrage groups. In 1912, to avoid arrest after the WSPU's participation in activities such as the destruction of property, Christabel fled to Paris where she continued to direct the organization. After the split with the Pethick-Lawrences in 1912, Christabel began the paper *The Suffragette*, which she edited and which then became the official paper of the WSPU. During World War I, Christabel and her mother became extreme patriots, calling off all suffrage activities and supporting the war effort. They changed the name of *The Suffragette* to *Britannia*. In 1917 Christabel and her mother formed the Women's Party; in 1918 Christabel stood for Parliament as a member of the party but was defeated. She then turned her zeal toward religion, becoming a travelling evangelist in the United States; she died in Santa Monica, California. Memoir: *Unshackled* (1959).

E. SYLVIA PANKHURST (1882-1960)
Sylvia was the second child of Richard and Emmeline Pankhurst and a trained artist. She studied at the Manchester Municipal School of Art and the Royal College of Art in London. She participated in the militancy of the WSPU and was imprisoned many times where she was force-fed. However, as a socialist her sympathies lay primarily with the poor and working-class

women of the East End of London. Her independence, her socialist ideas, and her interest in working for social and economic change, particularly for poor women, led to a split with Christabel and Emmeline. In January 1914, Sylvia's organization, the East London Federation of the WSPU, was expelled from the WSPU and became the East London Federation of Suffragettes. Sylvia published a paper called *The Women's Dreadnought* (1914-17), which was later renamed *The Workers' Dreadnought* (1917-24). During the war, in contrast to her mother, Sylvia was a pacifist; she attended the Women's Peace Conference at the Hague. After the war she became a committed socialist and supported the Bolshevik revolution in Russia. In 1927 she had a son, Richard, fathered by the Italian socialist and anarchist Silvio Corio. She became estranged from her mother during the last years of Emmeline's life, and they never reconciled. Sylvia spent her later years in Ethiopia where she died. Autobiography: *The Suffragette Movement: An Intimate Account of Persons and Ideals* (1931).

EMMELINE PANKHURST (1858-1928)

Emmeline Goulden Pankhurst was born in Manchester to parents with radical political beliefs. Her mother was an early supporter of women's suffrage. In 1879 Emmeline married Dr. Richard Pankhurst, a radical Manchester lawyer, who was committed to women's suffrage. He had helped John Stuart Mill write the first women's suffrage bill and had drafted the bill giving married women their property. Both Emmeline and her husband were active in the Independent Labour Party. After her husband's death in 1898 and believing that the traditional methods used by the NUWSS and other organizations had made little progress in getting women the vote, Emmeline, along with her daughters Christabel and Sylvia, founded the WSPU in 1903. Emmeline and Christabel then severed ties with all political parties, including the Labour Party. In 1907 Emmeline moved with Christabel from Manchester to London to co-ordinate and direct the organization. Emmeline Pankhurst's charismatic leadership and effective speaking abilities led to a great expansion of the organization. She was repeatedly arrested for her militant activities, spent time in prison, and endured many hunger strikes which adversely affected her health. While Mrs. Pankhurst, as she was known during her lifetime, attracted many loyal and devoted followers, her autocratic style of leadership and her organization's increasing violence alienated some of its members. Pankhurst was a controversial figure in her lifetime and remains so today. After the outbreak of the war in 1914, she abandoned all suffrage activity and threw herself into the war effort. She formed the Women's Party in 1917 and in 1925 joined the Conservative Party. On her death in 1928, she was buried in Brompton Cemetery in London. A statue in her honour, erected in 1930, stands outside the Houses of Parliament. Autobiography: *My Own Story* (1914).

EMMELINE PETHICK-LAWRENCE (1867-1954)

Emmeline and her husband Frederick Pethick-Lawrence, a barrister, were for many years closely involved with Emmeline and Christabel Pankhurst in the leadership of the WSPU. They joined the organization in 1906, and Emmeline became its treasurer. The offices for the WSPU were located for a time in their London home, Clement's Inn, where Christabel Pankhurst lived with them for five years. In 1907 Emmeline and her husband began and edited the paper *Votes for Women*. As a militant, Emmeline was often arrested; she was imprisoned five times and force-fed on several occasions. In 1907, when the split in the WSPU led to the formation of another militant organization, the Women's Freedom League, the Pethick-Lawrences remained committed to the Pankhursts and the WSPU. However, in 1912, when the WSPU began to advocate more extreme militancy with attacks on public and private property, the Pethick-Lawrences expressed their disapproval. Emmeline and Christabel Pankhurst then expelled them from the organization. The Pethick-Lawrences took with them the paper *Votes for Women*; it ceased being an organ of the WSPU. In 1914 Emmeline and her husband became founding members of the United Suffragists. During the war she was a member of the Women's International League for Peace and Freedom. Autobiography: *My Part in a Changing World* (1938).

LADY RHONDDA (Margaret Haig Thomas) (1883-1958)

Lady Rhondda joined the WSPU in 1908, shortly after her marriage to Humphrey Mackworth. As part of the arson campaign of the WSPU, she tried to burn a post box. For this activity she was sent to prison where she went on a hunger strike. When she was returning from the United States with her father in 1915, a German submarine torpedoed her ship, the Lusitania; she was one of the survivors. Lady Rhondda inherited her title from her father, David Alfred Thomas, on his death in 1918. She then attempted to take her seat in the House of Lords as Viscountess Rhondda but was refused because she was a woman. Autobiography: *This Was My World* (1933).

ELIZABETH ROBINS (1862-1952)

Robins was an American who grew up in Ohio, attended Vassar, and then went on the stage in Boston. She married a fellow actor who committed suicide shortly after their marriage. In 1888 she went to London where she had a successful acting career, playing the role of several women in Henrik Ibsen's plays, including Hedda Gabler and Nora Helmer (in *A Doll's House*). Robins was first a member of the NUWSS and then joined the WSPU. She was also a member of the Actresses' Franchise League and president of the Women Writers' Suffrage League. She wrote novels under the name C.E. Raimond. Her three-act suffrage play, *Votes for Women!* (1907), was one of the earliest suffrage dramas; she subsequently turned the play into a novel, *The Convert*.

Although she was never imprisoned, Robins wrote speeches supporting militant suffrage and provided her home as a place for women to recover from their prison ordeals. She contributed articles to *Votes for Women*. In 1912 she left the WSPU over her differences with the Pankhursts and their tactics. She remained active in women's issues all her life. Autobiography: *Both Sides of the Curtain* (1940).

EVELYN SHARP (1869-1955)
Sharp, a journalist and novelist, first joined the NUWSS and then, in 1906, the WSPU after hearing a speech by Elizabeth Robins and recognizing the need for militancy. She was also a member of the Women Writers' Suffrage League. For her involvement in militant activities, Sharp served time in prison on several occasions. In 1912, when the Pethick-Lawrences were expelled from the WSPU, Sharp also left the organization. In 1914 she became a member of the United Suffragists. During the war Sharp, a pacifist, helped found the Women's International League for Peace and Freedom. After the war she continued her work as a journalist. She married Henry Nevinson in 1933, after the death of his first wife, Margaret Nevinson. Autobiography: *Unfinished Adventure* (1933).

ETHEL SMYTH (1858-1944)
Ethel Smyth was an accomplished musician and composer who had studied at the Leipzig Conservatory. Among her compositions are two operas, *Der Wald* and *The Wreckers*, as well as a *Mass in D* that premiered at Albert Hall. After meeting Emmeline Pankhurst and hearing her speak, Smyth decided to give two years of her life to the suffrage movement. She joined the WSPU and was imprisoned with Mrs. Pankhurst and other suffragettes for her militant activities. Smyth composed songs for the suffrage movement, most notably "The March of the Women." Autobiography: *Female Pipings in Eden* (1933).

CHRISTOPHER ST. JOHN (Christabel Marshall) (d. 1960)
Christopher St. John was the pseudonym assumed by Christabel Marshall. St. John wrote original plays and adapted plays for performance in England and America. She was a friend of the actress Ellen Terry and went with her to America in 1907. Through Terry, St. John met Edith Craig, Terry's daughter, who was also an actress, and the two formed a life-long friendship. Along with Clare Atwood, they lived together for many years, first in London and then at the Priest's House in Smallhythe, near the cottage of Ellen Terry. Both St. John and Craig were supporters of woman suffrage but neither was imprisoned for her activities. St. John edited the correspondence of Ellen Terry and George Bernard Shaw and helped Terry with the revision of her autobiography. Together St. John and Cecily Hamilton wrote the suffrage play *How the Vote Was Won*.

HARRIET TAYLOR (1807-58)

Taylor worked closely with John Stuart Mill, formulating the ideas that were eventually published as "The Enfranchisement of Women" (1851) and a much longer work, completed and published after her death, *The Subjection of Women* (1869). Taylor was a married woman with children when she met Mill. They worked together as colleagues and intellectual collaborators for many years and married after the death of her husband, John Taylor, in 1849. Harriet and John Taylor's daughter Helen (1831-1907) continued her association with Mill after her mother's death, working and speaking for the suffrage cause.

MARY AUGUSTA (MRS. HUMPHRY) ARNOLD WARD (1851-1920)

Ward was an outspoken opponent of women's suffrage. She was a signer of the June 1889 "An Appeal Against Female Suffrage," published in the *Nineteenth Century*. In 1908 she became a member of the executive committee of the Women's National Anti-Suffrage League. She also began the *Anti-Suffrage Review*. Ward, the niece of the poet and critic, Matthew Arnold, was also a well-known novelist. Her novels include *Robert Elsmere* (1888), which sold over a million copies, *Marcella* (1894), and *Helbeck of Bannisdale* (1898).

Suffrage Organizations

The following is a partial list of the many suffrage organizations, not all of which were supportive of women's suffrage.

AFL: The Actresses' Franchise League was formed in 1908 by a group of actresses who called on the government to enfranchise women immediately. The actresses supported all suffrage societies and took no position on tactics, although most of them were more sympathetic to the militancy of the WSPU. When actresses in the AFL toured the country, they spoke at meetings of local suffrage societies. They also had a repertoire of short one-act plays, written by a variety of people, which they performed in many locations around England. These dramas were intended to convert women to the suffrage cause. The first plays written for the AFL were staged in 1909 at the WSPU's Prince's Skating Rink Exhibition in Knightsbridge. The AFL's membership included Elizabeth Robins, Maud Mary Arncliffe-Sennett, Inez Bensusan, Cicely Hamilton, Edith Craig, and Ellen Terry.

ASL: The Artists' Suffrage League was founded in 1907 by the artist Mary Lowndes. In order to further the suffrage cause through the work of artists, it produced posters, post cards, illustrated leaflets, and banners for marches. It worked most closely with the NUWSS.

THE EAST LONDON FEDERATION OF THE WSPU: Founded in 1912 as a democratic organization to work among the poor and working classes in the East End of London, it was led by Sylvia Pankhurst. In 1914 Christabel and Emmeline Pankhurst expelled Sylvia and the Federation from the WSPU. The organization then became the East London Federation of the Suffragettes, then the Workers' Suffrage Federation (WFS), and finally the Workers' Socialist Federation. Its paper was *The Women's Dreadnought* from 1914-17, when it was renamed *The Workers' Dreadnought*. The organization was active in opposing the war. Its colours were purple, white, green, and red.

THE MEN'S LEAGUE FOR WOMEN'S SUFFRAGE: Formed in 1907, the Men's League for Women's Suffrage included clergymen, writers, academics, lawyers, and political leaders who supported women's suffrage. Members included Laurence Housman, Henry Nevinson, Frederick Pethick-Lawrence, Israel Zangwill, and George Landsbury. It favored a peaceful approach to gaining the vote, similar to that used by the NUWSS, and was not aligned with any political party. Its goal was to obtain the vote for women on the same terms as it was granted to men.

NLOWS: The National League for Opposing Women's Suffrage was formed in 1910 when the Women's National Anti-Suffrage League joined the Men's League for Opposing Women's Suffrage. Its membership included Lord Cromer, Lord Curzon, and Heber Hart. The League published a monthly *Anti-Suffrage Review.* Its colours were white, pink, and black.

NUWSS: The National Union of Women's Suffrage Societies, the largest suffrage organization in England, was formed in 1897 when women's suffrage groups from all over England joined together. The NUWSS was a democratic organization with Millicent Fawcett as its leader; she was elected as its president in 1907. The organization was nonmilitant in its approach, seeking to gain the vote by constitutional methods and on the same terms as it was granted to men. Its members were called suffragists. Its newspaper, *Common Cause,* began its publication in 1909. Its colours were red and white and, after 1909, green was added.

UNITED SUFFRAGISTS: The United Suffragists was founded in early 1914 and was open to men and women, militant and nonmilitant. Many of its leaders were former members of the WSPU who had left that organization. The Pethick-Lawrences gave the publication *Votes for Women* to the United Suffragists with Evelyn Sharp as the editor.

WFL: The Women's Freedom League was established in 1907 by WSPU members who broke away to form a more democratically run organization. Its leaders were Charlotte Despard, its first president, Teresa Billington-Greig, and Edith How Martyn. Although it was a militant organization, its members did not participate in the violence of the WSPU. It demanded rights and opportunities for women as well as the vote. Its paper, *The Vote,* began in 1909 and continued until 1933. Its colours were green, white, and gold.

WSPU: The Women's Social and Political Union was formed in 1903 in Manchester under the leadership of Emmeline Pankhurst and her daughter Christabel. At first it worked with the Independent Labour Party, but after the 1906 election it distanced itself from that party and gave support to no political party. Only women were allowed to be members of the WSPU. Under the Pankhursts the organization became increasingly autocratic, with the result that some women left to form more democratically run organizations. The WSPU was the militant wing of the suffrage movement, having as its motto "Deeds, Not Words." Its members were called suffragettes. Its official organ was *Votes for Women* until 1912; then, until 1915, it was *The Suffragette*, edited by Christabel Pankhurst. In November 1917, the WSPU was renamed the Women's Party. From 1915 to 1918 the official organ of these two organizations was *Britannia*. Its colours were purple, white, and green.

WWSL: The Women Writers' Suffrage League, founded in 1908 by Cicely Hamilton and Bessie Hatton, included in its membership many well-known writers, such as Sarah Grand, Cicely Hamilton, Evelyn Sharp, Charlotte Despard, Margaret Nevinson, Olive Schreiner, Violet Hunt, May Sinclair, and Elizabeth Robins, who was its first president. It was neutral in regard to suffrage tactics. Its members decided that they would use their writing to get the vote for women on the same terms as it was given to men. Its colours were black, white, and gold.

CHAPTER ONE

THE ARGUMENTS

THE CASE FOR AND AGAINST WOMEN'S SUFFRAGE

The first essays, pamphlets, and tracts presenting a case for the enfranchisement of women began to appear in England in the mid-nineteenth century. In 1869 John Stuart Mill published an important theoretical argument for the social and economic emancipation of women and for their political rights, *The Subjection of Women*, which had been written years before, in 1861. Even earlier, in 1851, Mill and Harriet Taylor had published an essay, "Enfranchisement of Women," which formulated many of the arguments that would later be developed more fully in *The Subjection of Women*. Another early argument for women's suffrage, "Female Suffrage," written by Lydia Becker, a nineteenth-century suffrage activist, appeared in the *Contemporary Review* in March 1867. Becker makes a rather conservative argument. She does not ask for the enfranchisement of all women or for the seating of women in the House of Commons, yet at the time her proposals were considered to be radical.

Both Mill and Taylor were interested in changing laws and customs that restricted women's choices in marriage, education, and the professions. Mill met Taylor, a married woman with two children, in 1831. She became an important influence on his thinking, and for many years they worked together collaboratively, finally marrying in 1851 after the death of Taylor's husband. Their essay, "Enfranchisement of Women," is one of the earliest published arguments in favour of women's suffrage and certainly the earliest made by well-known public figures. How many of the ideas found in the essay are Taylor's and how many are Mill's is not certain, but Mill gave all the credit to Taylor. In 1866, as a Member of Parliament, Mill introduced into the House of Commons the first suffrage petition, signed by 1,499 women; it sought to extend the franchise to all male and female householders. In 1867 he attempted to include a franchise for women in the Second Reform Act, which extended male suffrage, but his amendment was defeated.

The opposition to women's suffrage was well-organized. In 1908 the Women's National Anti-Suffrage League was formed, as was a separate organization for men, the Men's Committee for Opposing Female Suffrage. In 1910 the two groups merged as the National League for Opposing Women's Suffrage. The organization had its own publication, *The Anti-Suffrage Review*, and its membership included many titled aristocrats. In June 1889 Mary (Mrs. Humphry) Ward, a well-known novelist and a member of the National League for Opposing Women's Suffrage, along with many other prominent or well-connected women, published "An Appeal Against Female Suffrage" in the *Nineteenth Century*. First among the signatories of the "Appeal" was Lady Stanley of Alderley (1807-95). Married to Edward John Stanley, a Member of Parliament, Lady Stanley was active in the Liberal party and promoted the cause of women's education. Other signatories to the "Appeal," as they signed their names, were Lady Randolph Churchill, Mrs. Leslie Stephen (mother of Virginia Woolf), Mrs. Lynn Linton, Mrs. Alma-Tadema, Mrs. Matthew Arnold, and Mrs. Arnold Toynbee.

In the July 1889 issue of the *Nineteenth Century*, Millicent Garrett Fawcett and Mary Margaret Dilke responded to the "Appeal," each with a separate "Reply." Both Dilke and Fawcett had been actively involved in women's suffrage for a long time; Fawcett was one of the early leaders of the movement. In 1897 she became president of the National Union of Women's Suffrage Societies (NUWSS) which united all the earlier suffrage organizations and was the largest suffrage organization in England. The NUWSS supported the franchise for women on the same terms as men, although Fawcett's "Reply" did not take this position in 1889 when she distinguished between married and unmarried women. Another response to the June article, "An Appeal Against Female Suffrage," appeared in the *Fortnightly Review* in July 1889 entitled "Women's Suffrage: A Reply." Appended to it were the signatures of hundreds of women, including women in education, medicine, art, literature, music, and business, who were "in favour of the extension of the parliamentary franchise to women."

In the early twentieth century, individual writers, particularly men, also published numerous pamphlets and books in opposition to women's suffrage. Each writer tried to provide a convincing case for excluding women from political life, but they did not all speak with one voice, as is clear from the various excerpts represented below. Some feared that enfranchising women might encourage them to leave their domestic sphere for a more public political life. Men also realized that, because women outnumbered men, women with the vote could pass laws that gave them the same rights as men, for example in cases such as divorce or inheritance. Some writers even believed that the enfranchisement of women would lead to national and racial decline. The misogyny of many of these writers is clearly evident in their statements about women, particularly in their dismissal of women's intelligence and contributions to the nation.

Harriet Taylor and
John Stuart Mill

From "Enfranchisement of Women"

[*Westminster Review* 55 (July 1851): 289-311]

Most of our readers will probably learn from these pages for the first time, that there has arisen in the United States, and in the most civilized and enlightened portion of them, an organised agitation on a new question— new, not to thinkers, nor to any one by whom the principles of free and popular government are felt as well as acknowledged, but new, and even unheard of, as a subject for public meetings and practical political action. This question is, the enfranchisement of women; their admission, in law and in fact, to equality in all rights, political, civil, and social, with the male citizens of the community....

That women have as good a claim as men have, in point of personal right, to the suffrage, or to a place in the jury-box, it would be difficult for anyone to deny. It cannot certainly be denied by the United States of America, as a people or as a community. Their democratic institutions rest avowedly on the inherent right of everyone to a voice in the government. Their Declaration of Independence, framed by the men who are still their great constitutional authorities—that document which has been from the first, and is now, the acknowledged basis of their polity, commences with this express statement:—

"We hold these truths to be self-evident: that all men are created equal; that they are endowed by their Creator with certain inalienable rights; that among these are life, liberty, and the pursuit of happiness; that to secure these rights, governments are instituted among men, deriving their just powers from the consent of the governed."

We do not imagine that any American democrat will evade the force of these expressions by the dishonest or ignorant subterfuge, that "men," in this memorable document, does not stand for human beings, but for one sex only; that "life, liberty, and the pursuit of happiness" are "inalienable rights" of only one moiety of the human species; and that "the governed," whose consent is affirmed to be the only source of just power, are meant for that half of mankind only, who, in relation to the other, have hitherto assumed the character of *governors*. The contradiction between principle and practice cannot be explained away. A like dereliction of the fundamental maxims of their political creed has been committed by the Americans in the flagrant instance of the negroes; of this they are learning to recognise the turpitude. After a struggle which, by many of its incidents, deserves the name of heroic, the abolitionists are now so strong in numbers and in influence that they hold the balance of parties in the United States. It was fitting that the men whose names will remain associated with the extirpation, from the democratic soil of America, of the aristocracy of colour, should be among the originators, for America and for the rest of the world, of the first collective protest against the aristocracy of sex; a distinction as accidental as that of colour, and fully as irrelevant to all questions of government.

Not only to the democracy of America, the claim of women to civil and political equality makes an irresistible appeal, but also to those radicals and chartists[1] in the British islands, and democrats on the Continent, who claim what is called universal suffrage as an inherent right, unjustly and oppressively withheld from them. For with what truth or rationality could the suffrage be termed universal, while half the human species remain excluded from it? To declare that a voice in the government is the right of all, and demand it only for a part—the part, namely to which the claimant himself belongs—is to renounce even the appearance of principle. The chartist who denies the suffrage to women, is a chartist only because he is not a lord; he is one of those levellers[2] who would level only down to themselves.

Even those who do not look upon a voice in the government as a matter of personal right, nor profess principles which require that it should be extended to all, have usually traditional maxims of political justice with which it is impossible to reconcile the exclusion of all women from the common rights of citizenship. It is an axiom of English freedom that taxation and representation should be co-extensive. Even under the laws which give the wife's property to the husband, there are many unmarried women who pay taxes. It is one of the fundamental doctrines of the British constitution, that all persons should be tried by their peers: yet women, whenever tried, are tried by male judges and a male jury. To foreigners the law accords the privilege of claiming that half the jury should be composed of themselves; not so to women. Apart from maxims of detail, which represent local and national rather than universal ideas; it is an acknowledged dictate of justice to make no degrading distinctions without necessity. In all things the presumption ought to be on the side of equality. A reason must be given why anything should be permitted to one person and interdicted to another. But when that which is interdicted includes nearly everything which those to whom it is permitted most prize, and to be deprived of which they feel to be most insulting; when not only political liberty but personal freedom of action is the prerogative of a caste; when even in the exercise of industry, almost all employments which task the higher faculties in an important field, which lead to distinction, riches, or even pecuniary independence, are fenced round as the exclusive domain of the predominant section, scarcely any doors being left open to the dependent class, except such as all who can enter disdainfully pass by; the miserable expediencies which are advanced as excuses for so grossly partial a dispensation, would not be sufficient, even if they were real, to render it other than a flagrant injustice. While, far from being expedient, we are firmly convinced that the division of mankind into two castes, one born to rule over the other, is in this case, as in all cases, an unqualified mischief; a source of perversion and demoralization, both to the favoured class and to those at whose expense they are favoured; producing none of the good which it is the custom to ascribe to it, and forming a bar, almost insuperable while it lasts, to any really vital improvement, either in the character or in the social condition of the human race.

These propositions it is now our purpose to maintain. But before entering on them, we would endeavour to dispel the preliminary objections which, in the minds of persons to whom the subject is new, are apt to prevent a real and conscientious examination of it. The chief of these obstacles is that most formidable one, custom. Women never have had equal rights with men. The claim in their behalf, of the common rights of mankind, is looked upon as barred by universal practice. This strongest of prejudices, the prejudice against what is new and unknown, has, indeed, in an age of changes like the present, lost much of its force; if it had not, there would be little hope of prevailing against it. Over three-fourths of the habitable world, even at this day, the answer, "it has always been so," closes all discussion. But it is the boast of modern Europeans, and of their American kindred, that they know and do many things which their forefathers neither knew nor did; and it is perhaps the most unquestionable point of superiority in the present above former ages, that habit is not now the tyranny it formerly was over opinions and modes of action, and the worship of custom is a declining idolatry. An uncustomary thought, on a subject which touches the greater interests of life, still startles when first presented; but if it can be kept before the mind until the impression of strangeness wears off, it obtains a hearing, and as rational a consideration as the intellect of the hearer is accustomed to bestow on any other subject.

In the present case, the prejudice of custom is doubtless on the unjust side. Great thinkers, indeed, at different times, from Plato to Condorcet,[3] besides some of the most eminent names of the present age, have made emphatic protests in favour of the equality of women. And there have been voluntary societies, religious or secular, of which the Society of Friends is the most known, by whom that principle was recognized. But there has been no political community or nation in which, by law, and usage, women have not been in a state of political and civil inferiority. In the ancient world the same fact was alleged, with equal truth, in behalf of slavery. It might have been alleged in favour of the mitigated form of slavery, serfdom, all through the middle ages. It was urged against freedom of industry, freedom of conscience, freedom of the press; none of these liberties were thought compatible with a well-ordered state, until they had proved their possibility by actually existing as facts. That an institution or a practice is customary is no presumption of its goodness, when any other sufficient cause can be assigned for its existence. There is no difficulty in understanding why the subjection of women has been a custom. No other explanation is needed than physical force.

That those who were physically weaker should have been made legally inferior, is quite conformable to the mode in which the world has been governed. Until very lately the rule of physical strength was the general law of human affairs. Throughout history, the nations, races, classes, which found themselves the strongest, either in muscles, in riches, or in military discipline, have conquered and held in subjection the rest. If, even in the most improved nations, the law of the sword is at last discountenanced as unworthy, it is only since the calumniated eighteenth century. Wars of conquest have only ceased since democratic revolutions began. The world is very young, and has been just begun to cast off injustice. It is only now getting rid of negro slavery. It is only now getting rid of monarchical despotism. It is only now getting rid of hereditary feudal nobility. It is only now getting rid of disabilities on the ground of religion. It is only beginning to treat any *men* as citizens, except the rich and a favoured portion of the middle class. Can we wonder that it has not yet done as much for women? As society was constituted until the last few generations, inequality was its very basis; association grounded on equal rights scarcely existed; to be equals was to be enemies; two persons could hardly co-operate in anything, or meet in any amicable relation, without the law's appointing that one of them should be the superior of the other. Mankind have outgrown this state, and all things now tend to substitute, as the general principle of human relations, a just equality, instead of the dominion of the strongest. But of all relations, that between men and women being the nearest and most intimate, and connected with the greatest number of strong emotions, was sure to be the last to throw off the old rule and receive the new: for in proportion to the strength of a feeling, is the tenacity with which it clings to the forms and circumstances with which it has even accidentally become associated.

When a prejudice, which has any hold on the feeling, finds itself reduced to the unpleasant necessity of assigning reasons, it thinks it has done enough when it has re-asserted the very point in dispute, in phrases which appeal to the pre-existing feeling. Thus, many persons think they have sufficiently justified the restrictions on women's field of action, when they have said that the pursuits from which women are excluded are *unfeminine*, and that the *proper sphere* of women is not politics or publicity, but private and domestic life.

We deny the right of any portion of the species to decide for another portion, or any individual for another individual, what is and what is not their "proper sphere." The proper sphere for all human beings is the largest and highest which they are able to attain to. What this is, cannot be ascertained, without complete liberty of choice. The speakers at the Convention in America have therefore done wisely and right, in refusing to entertain the question of the peculiar aptitudes either of women or of men, or the limits within which this or that occupation may be supposed to be more adapted to the one or to the other. They justly maintain, that those questions can only be satisfactorily answered by perfect freedom. Let every occupation be open to all, without favour or discouragement to any, and employments will fall into the hands of those men or women who are found by experience to be most capable of worthily exercising them. There need be no fear that women will take out of the hands of men any occupation which men perform better than they. Each individual will prove his or her capacities, in the only way in which capacities can be proved—by trial; and the world will have the benefit of the best faculties of all its inhabitants. But to interfere beforehand by an arbitrary limit, and declare that whatever be the genius, talent, energy, or force of mind of an individual of a certain sex or class, those faculties shall not be exerted, or shall be exerted only in some few of the many modes in which others are permitted to use theirs, is not only an injustice to the individual, and a detriment to society, which loses what it can ill spare, but is also the most effectual mode of providing that, in the sex or class so fettered, the qualities which are not permitted to be exercised shall not exist.

We shall follow the very proper example of the Convention, in not entering into the question of the alleged differences in physical or mental qualities between the sexes; not because we have nothing to say, but because we have too much…. But if those who assert that the "proper sphere" for women is the domestic, mean by this that they have not shown themselves qualified for any other, the assertion evinces great ignorance of life and of history. Women have shown fitness for the highest social functions, exactly in proportion as they have been admitted to them. By a curious anomaly, though ineligible to even the lowest offices of state, they are in some countries admitted to the highest of all, the regal; and if there is any one function for which they have shown a decided vocation, it is that of reigning….

Concerning the fitness, then, of women for politics, there can be no question: but the dispute is more likely to turn upon the fitness of politics for women. When the reasons alleged for excluding women from active life in all its higher departments, are stripped of their garb of declamatory phrases, and reduced to the simple expression of a meaning, they seem to be mainly three: the incompatibility of active life with maternity, and with the cares of a household; secondly, its alleged hardening effect on the character; and thirdly, the inexpediency of making an addition to the already excessive pressure of competition in every kind of professional or lucrative employment.

The first, the maternity argument, is usually laid most stress upon: although (it needs hardly be said) this reason, if it be one, can apply only to mothers. It is neither necessary nor just to make imperative on women that they shall be either mothers or nothing; or that if they have been mothers once, they shall be nothing else during the whole remainder of their lives. Neither women nor men need any law to exclude them from an occupation, if they have undertaken another which is incompatible with it. No one proposes to exclude the male sex from Parliament because a man may be a soldier or sailor in active service, or a merchant whose business requires all his time and energies. Nine-tenths of the occupations of men exclude them *de facto* from public life, as effectually as if they were excluded by law; but that is no reason for making laws to exclude even the nine-tenths, much less the remaining tenth. The reason of the case is the same for women as for men. There is no need to make provision by law that a woman shall not carry on the active details of a household, or of the education of children, and at the same time practise a profession or be elected to parliament. Where incompatibility is real, it will take care of itself: but there is gross injustice in making the incompatibility a pretence for the exclusion of those in whose case it does not exist. And these, if they were free to choose, would be a very large proportion. The maternity argument deserts its supporters in the case of single women, a large and increasing class of the population; a fact which, it is not irrelevant to remark, by tending to diminish the excessive competition of numbers, is calculated to assist greatly the prosperity of all. There is no inherent reason or necessity that all women should voluntarily choose to devote their lives to one animal function and its consequences. Numbers of women are wives and mothers only because there is no other career open to them, no other occupation for their feelings or their activities. Every improvement in their education, and enlargement of their faculties—everything which renders them more qualified for any other mode of life, increases the number of those to whom it is an injury and an oppression to be denied the choice. To say that women must be excluded from active life because maternity disqualifies them for it, is in fact to say, that every other career should be forbidden them in order that maternity may be their only resource.

But secondly, it is urged, that to give the same freedom of occupation to women as to men, would be an injurious addition to the crowd of competitors, by whom the avenues to almost all kinds of employment are choked up, and its remuneration depressed. This argument, it is to be observed, does not reach the political question. It gives no excuse for withholding from women the rights of citizenship. The suffrage, the jury-box, admission to the legislature and to office, it does not touch. It bears only on the industrial branch of the subject. Allowing it, then, in an economical point of view, its full force; assuming that to lay open to women the employments now monopolized by men, would tend, like the breaking down of other monopolies, to lower the rate of remuneration in those employments; let us consider what is the amount of this evil consequence, and what the compensation for it. The worst ever asserted, much worse than is at all likely to be realized, is that if women competed with men, a man and a woman could not together earn more than is now earned by the man alone. Let us make this supposition, the most favourable supposition possible: the joint income of the two would be the same as before, while the woman would be raised from the position of a servant to that of a partner. Even if every woman, as matters now stand, had a claim on some man for support, how infinitely preferable is it that part of the income should be of the woman's earning, even if the aggregate sum were but little increased by it, rather than that she should be compelled to stand aside in order that men may be the sole earners, and the sole dispensers of what is earned. Even under the present laws respecting the property of women,[4] a woman who contributes materially to the support of the family, cannot be treated in the same contemptuously tyrannical manner as one who, however she may toil as a domestic drudge, is a dependent on the man for subsistence. As for the depression of wages by increase of competition, remedies will be found for it in time. Palliatives might be applied immediately; for instance, a more rigid exclusion of children from industrial employment, during the years in which they ought to be working only to strengthen their bodies and minds for after life. Children are necessarily dependent, and under the power of others; and their labour, being not for themselves but for the gain of their parents, is a proper subject for legislative regulation. With respect to the future, we neither believe that improvident multiplication, and the consequent excessive difficulty of gaining a subsistence, will always continue, nor that the division of mankind into capitalists and hired labourers, and the regulation of the reward of labourers mainly by demand and supply, will be for ever, or even much longer, the rule of the world. But so long as competition is the general law of human life, it is tyranny to shut out one half of the competitors. All who have attained the age of self-government, have an equal claim to be permitted to sell whatever kind of useful labour they are capable of, for the price which it will bring.

The third objection to the admission of women to political or professional life, its alleged hardening tendency, belongs to an age now past, and is scarcely to be comprehended by people of the present time. There are still, however, persons who say that the world and its avocations render men selfish and unfeeling; that the struggles, rivalries and collisions of business and of politics make them harsh and unamiable; that if half the species must unavoidably be given up to these things, it is the more necessary that the other half should be kept free from them; that to preserve women from the bad influences of the world, is the only chance of preventing men from being wholly given up to them.

There would have been plausibility in this argument when the world was still in the age of violence; when life was full of physical conflict, and every man had to redress his injuries or those of others, by the sword or by the strength of his arm. Women, like priests, by being exempted from such responsibilities, and from some part of the accompanying dangers, may have been enabled to exercise a beneficial influence. But in the present condition of human life, we do not know where those hardening influences are to be found, to which men are subject and from which women are at present exempt. Individuals now-a-days are seldom called upon to fight hand to hand, even with peaceful weapons; personal enmities and rivalries count for little in worldly transactions; the general pressure of circumstances, not the adverse will of individuals, is the obstacle men now have to make head against. That pressure, when excessive, breaks the spirit, and cramps and sours the feelings, but not less of women than of men, since they suffer certainly not less from its evils. There are still quarrels and dislikes, but the sources of them are changed. The feudal chief once found his bitterest enemy in his powerful neighbour, the minister or courtier in his rival for place: but opposition of interest in active life, as a cause of personal animosity, is out of date; the enmities of the present day arise not from great things but small, from what people say of one another, more than from what they do; and if there are hatred, malice, and all uncharitableness, they are to be found among women fully as much as among men. In the present state of civilization, the notion of guarding women from the hardening influences of the world, could only be realized by secluding them from society altogether. The common duties of common life, as at present constituted, are incompatible with any other softness in women than weakness. Surely weak minds in weak bodies must ere long cease to be even supposed to be either attractive or amiable.

But, in truth, none of these arguments and considerations touch the foundations of the subject. The real question is, whether it is right and expedient that one-half of the human race should pass through life in a state of forced subordination to the other half. If the best state of human society is that of being divided into two parts, one consisting of persons with a will and a substantive existence, the other of humble companions to these persons, attached, each of them to one, for the purpose of bringing up *his* children, and making *his* home pleasant to him; if this is the place assigned to women, it is but kindness to educate them for this; to make them believe that the greatest good fortune which can befal them, is to be chosen by some man for this purpose; and that every other career which the world deems happy or honourable, is closed to them by the law, not of social institutions, but of nature and destiny.

When, however, we ask why the existence of one-half the species should be merely ancillary to that of the other—why each woman should be a mere appendage to a man, allowed to have no interests of her own, that there may be nothing to compete in her mind with his interests and his pleasure; the only reason which can be given is, that men like it. It is agreeable to them that men should live for their own sake, women for the sake of men: and the qualities and conduct in subjects which are agreeable to rulers, they succeed for a long time in making the subjects themselves consider as their appropriate virtues. Helvetius[5] has met with much obloquy for asserting that persons usually mean by virtues the qualities which are useful or convenient to themselves. How truly this is said of mankind in general, and how wonderfully the ideas of virtue set afloat by the powerful, are caught and imbibed by those under their dominion, is exemplified by the manner in which the world were once persuaded that the supreme virtue of subjects was loyalty to kings, and are still persuaded that the paramount virtue of womanhood is loyalty to men. Under a nominal recognition of a moral code common to both, in practice self-will and self-assertion form the type of what are designated as manly virtues, while abnegation of self, patience, resignation, and submission to power, unless when resistance is commanded by other interests than their own, have been stamped by general consent as pre-eminently the duties and graces required of women. The meaning being merely, that power makes itself the centre of moral obligation, and that a man likes to have his own will, but does not like that his domestic companion should have a will different from his....

There is hardly any situation more unfavourable to the maintenance of elevation of character or force of intellect, than to live in the society, and seek by preference the sympathy, of inferiors in mental endowments. Why is it that we constantly see in life so much of intellectual and moral promise followed by such inadequate performance, but because the aspirant has compared himself only with those below himself, and has not sought improvement or stimulus from measuring himself with his equals or superiors. In the present state of social life, this is becoming the general condition of men. They care less and less for any sympathies, and are less and less under any personal influences, but those of the domestic roof. Not to be misunderstood, it is necessary that we should distinctly disclaim the belief, that women are even now inferior in intellect to men. There are women who are the equals in intellect of any men who ever lived: and comparing ordinary women with ordinary men, the varied though petty details which compose the occupation of most women, call forth probably as much of mental ability, as the uniform routine of the pursuits which are the habitual occupation of a large majority of men. It is from nothing in the faculties themselves, but from the petty subjects and interests on which alone they are exercised, that the companionship of women, such as their present circumstances make them, so often exercises a dissolvent influence on high faculties and aspirations in men. If one of the two has no knowledge and no care about the great ideas and purposes which dignify life, or about any of its practical concerns save personal interests and personal vanities, her conscious, and still more her unconscious influence, will, except in rare cases, reduce to a secondary place in his mind, if not entirely extinguish, those interests which she cannot or does not share.

Our argument here brings us into collision with what may be termed the moderate reformers of the education of women; a sort of persons who cross the path of improvement on all great questions; those who would maintain the old bad principles, mitigating their consequences. These say, that women should be, not slaves, nor servants, but companions; and educated for that office: (they do not say that men should be educated to be the companions of women). But since uncultivated women are not suitable companions for cultivated men, and a man who feels interest in things above and beyond the family circle wishes that his companion should sympathize with him in that interest; they therefore say, let women improve their understanding and taste, acquire general knowledge, cultivate poetry, art, even coquet with science, and some stretch their liberality so far as to say, inform themselves on politics; not as pursuits, but sufficiently to feel an interest in the subjects, and to be capable of holding a conversation on them with the husband, or at least of understanding and imbibing his wisdom. Very agreeable to him, no doubt, but unfortunately the reverse of improving. It is from having intellectual communion only with those to whom they can lay down the law, that so few men continue to advance in wisdom beyond the first stages. The most eminent men cease to improve, if they associate only with disciples. When they have overtopped those who immediately surround them, if they wish for further growth, they must seek for others of their own stature to consort with. The mental companionship which is improving, is communion between active minds, not mere contact between an active mind and a passive. This inestimable advantage is even now enjoyed, when a strong-minded man and a strong-minded woman are, by a rare chance, united: and would be had far oftener, if education took the same pains to form strong-minded women which it takes to prevent them from being formed. The modern, and what are regarded as the improved and enlightened modes of education of women, adjure, as far as words go, an education of mere show, and profess to aim at solid instruction, but mean by that expression, superficial information on solid subjects. Except accomplishments, which are now generally regarded as to be taught well if taught at all, nothing is taught to women thoroughly. Small portions only of what it is attempted to teach thoroughly to boys, are the whole of what it is intended or desired to teach to women. What makes intelligent beings is the power of thought: the stimuli which call forth that power are the interest and dignity of thought itself, and a field for its practical application. Both motives are cut off from those who are told from infancy that thought, and all its greater applications, are other people's business, while theirs is to make themselves agreeable to other people. High mental powers in women will be but an exceptional accident, until every career is open to them, and until they, as well as men, are educated for themselves and for the world—not one sex for the other.

In what we have said on the effect of the inferior position of women, combined with the present constitution of married life, we have thus far had in view only the most favourable cases, those in which there is some real approach to that union and blending of characters and of lives, which the theory of the relation contemplates as its ideal standard. But if we look to the majority of cases, the effect of women's legal inferiority on the character both of women and of men must be painted in far darker colours. We do not speak here of the grosser brutalities, nor of the man's power to seize on the woman's earnings, or compel her to live with him against her will. We do not address ourselves to any one who requires to have it proved that these things should be remedied. We suppose average cases, in which there is neither complete union nor complete disunion of feelings and of character; and we affirm that in such cases the influence of the dependence on the woman's side, is demoralizing to the character of both.

The common opinion is, that whatever may be the case with the intellectual, the moral influence of women over men is almost always salutary. It is, we are often told, the great counteractive of selfishness. However the case may be as to personal influence, the influence of the position tends eminently to promote selfishness. The most insignificant of men, the man who can obtain influence or consideration nowhere else, finds one place where he is chief and head. There is one person, often greatly his superior in understanding, who is obliged to consult him, and whom he is not obliged to consult. He is judge, magistrate, ruler, over their joint concerns; arbiter of all differences between them. The justice or conscience to which her appeal must be made, is his justice and conscience: it is his to hold the balance and adjust the scales between his own claims or wishes and those of another. His is now the only tribunal, in civilized life, in which the same person is judge and party. A generous mind, in such a situation, makes the balance incline against its own side, and gives the other not less, but more, than a fair equality; and thus the weaker side may be enabled to turn the very fact of dependence into an instrument of power, and in default of justice, take an ungenerous advantage of generosity; rendering the unjust power, to those who make an unselfish use of it, a torment and a burthen. But how is it when average men are invested with this power, without reciprocity and without responsibility? Give such a man the idea that he is first in law and in opinion—that to will is his part, and hers to submit; it is absurd to suppose that this idea merely glides over his mind, without sinking into it, or having any effect on his feelings and practice. The propensity to make himself the first object of consideration, and others at most the second, is not so rare as to be wanting where everything seems purposely arranged for permitting its indulgence. If there is any selfwill in the man, he becomes either the conscious or unconscious despot of his household. The wife, indeed, often succeeds in gaining her objects, but it is by some of the many various forms of indirectness and management.

Thus the position is corrupting equally to both; in the one it produces the vices of power, in the other those of artifice. Women, in their present physical and moral state, having stronger impulses, would naturally be franker and more direct than men; yet all the old saws and traditions represent them as artful and dissembling. Why? Because their only way to their objects is by indirect paths. In all countries where women have strong wishes and active minds, this consequence is inevitable; and if it is less conspicuous in England than in some other places, it is because Englishwomen, saving occasional exemptions, have ceased to have either strong wishes or active minds.

We are not now speaking of cases in which there is anything deserving the name of strong affection on both sides. That, where it exists, is too powerful a principle not to modify greatly the bad influences of the situation; it seldom, however, destroys them entirely. Much oftener the bad influences are too strong for the affection, and destroy it. The highest order of durable and happy attachments would be a hundred times more frequent than they are, if the affection which the two sexes sought from one another were that genuine friendship, which only exists between equals in privileges as in faculties. But with regard to what is commonly called affection in married life—the habitual and almost mechanical feeling of kindliness, and pleasure in each other's society, which generally grows up between persons who constantly live together, unless there is actual dislike—there is nothing in this to contradict or qualify the mischievous influence of the unequal relation. Such feelings often exist between a sultan and his favourites, between a master and his servants; they are merely examples of the pliability of human nature, which accommodates itself in some degree even to the worst circumstances, and the commonest natures always the most easily....

For the interest, therefore, not only of women but of men, and of human improvement in the widest sense, the emancipation of women, which the modern world often boasts of having effected, and for which credit is sometimes given to civilization, and sometimes to Christianity, cannot stop where it is. If it were either necessary or just that one portion of mankind should remain mentally and spiritually only half developed, the development of the other portion ought to have been made, as far as possible, independent of their influence. Instead of this, they have become the most intimate, and it may now be said, the only intimate associates of those to whom yet they are sedulously kept inferior; and have been raised just high enough to drag the others down to themselves.

We have left behind a host of vulgar objections, either as not worthy of an answer, or as answered by the general course of our remarks. A few words, however, must be said on one plea, which in England is made much use of for giving an unselfish air to the upholding of selfish privileges, and which, with unobserving, unreflecting people, passes for much more than it is worth. Women, it is said, do not desire—do not seek, what is called their emancipation. On the contrary, they generally disown such claims when made in their behalf, and fall with *acharnement*[6] upon any one of themselves who identifies herself with their common cause.

Supposing the fact to be true in the fullest extent ever asserted, if it proves that European women ought to remain as they are, it proves exactly the same with respect to Asiatic women; for they too, instead of murmuring at their seclusion, and at the restraint imposed upon them, pride themselves on it, and are astonished at the effrontery of women who receive visits from male acquaintances, and are seen in the streets unveiled. Habits of submission make men as well as women servile-minded. The vast population of Asia do not desire or value, probably would not accept, political liberty, nor the savages of the forest, civilization; which does not prove that either of those things is undesirable for them, or that they will not, at some future time, enjoy it. Custom hardens human beings to any kind of degradation, by deadening the part of their nature which would resist it. And the case of women is, in this respect, even a peculiar one, for no other inferior caste that we have heard of, have been taught to regard their degradation as their honour. The argument, however, implies a secret consciousness that the alleged preference of women for their dependent state is merely apparent, and arises from their being allowed no choice; for if the preferences be natural, there can be no necessity for enforcing it by law. To make laws compelling people to follow their inclination, has not hitherto been thought necessary by any legislator. The plea that women do not desire any change, is the same that has been urged, times out of mind, against the proposal of abolishing any social evil— "there is no complaint;" which is generally not true, and when true, only so because there is not that hope of success, without which complaint seldom makes itself audible to unwilling ears. How does the objector know that women do not desire equality and freedom? He never knew a woman who did not, or would not, desire it for herself individually. It would be very simple to suppose, that if they do desire it they will say so. Their position is like that of the tenants or labourers who vote against their own political interests to please their landlords or employers; with the unique addition, that submission is inculcated on them from childhood, as the peculiar attraction and grace of their character. They are taught to think, that to repel actively even an admitted injustice done to themselves, is somewhat unfeminine, and had better be left to some male friend or protector. To be accused of rebelling against anything which admits of being called an ordinance of society, they are taught to regard as an imputation of a serious offence, to say the least, against the proprieties of their sex. It requires unusual moral courage as well as disinterestedness in a woman, to express opinions favourable to women's enfranchisement, until, at least, there is some prospect of obtaining it. The comfort of her individual life, and her social consideration, usually depend on the good will of those who hold the undue power; and to possessors of power any complaint, however bitter, of the misuse of it, is a less flagrant act of insubordination than to protest against the power itself.... Successful literary women are just as unlikely to prefer the cause of women to their own social consideration. They depend on men's opinions for their literary as well as for their feminine successes; and such is their bad opinion of men, that they believe there is not more than one in ten thousand who does not dislike and fear strength, sincerity, or high spirit in a woman. They are therefore anxious to earn pardon and toleration for whatever of these qualities their writings may exhibit on other subjects, by a studied display of submission on this: that they may give no occasion for vulgar men to say (what nothing will prevent vulgar men from saying), that learning makes women unfeminine, and that literary ladies are likely to be bad wives.

But enough of this; especially as the fact which affords the occasion for this notice, makes it impossible any longer to assert the universal acquiescence of

PUNCH, OR THE LONDON CHARIVARI—March 30, 1867.

MILL'S LOGIC; OR, FRANCHISE FOR FEMALES.
"PRAY CLEAR THE WAY, THERE, FOR THESE—A—PERSONS."

Figure 1: Mill's Logic; or Franchise for Females
"Pray clear the way, there, for these—a—persons."
From *Punch, or the London Charivari* (30 March 1867)

John Stuart Mill, a Member of Parliament and advocate of women's suffrage, added an amendment to the 1867 Reform Act that would give women the same political rights as men. He made a motion that all references to "man" be changed to "person." His amendment was defeated.

women (saving individual exceptions) in their dependent condition. In the United States at least, there are women, seemingly numerous, and now organised for action on the public mind, who demand equality in the fullest acceptation of the word, and demand it by a straightforward appeal to men's sense of justice, not plead for it with a timid deprecation of their displeasure....

There are indications that the example of America will be followed on this side of the Atlantic; and the first step has been taken in that part of England where every serious movement in the direction of political progress has its commencement—the manufacturing districts of the North. On the 13th of February 1851, a petition of women, agreed to by a public meeting at Sheffield, and claiming the elective franchise, was presented to the House of Lords by the Earl of Carlisle.

Lydia E. Becker

From "Female Suffrage"

[*Contemporary Review* IV (March 1867): 307-16]

The action taken by Mr. J.S. Mill in the House of Commons on behalf of the freeholders and householders, the petition for whose enfranchisement he presented, raises a question of very great importance to women, and to the community of which they form the numerical majority.

It is probably the first occasion on which the claims of female persons to political rights have been seriously brought before the British Parliament, and as the attention of the nation is now being directed to the question of the expediency of making some re-distribution of political power, it seems an appropriate season for the grave consideration of all that can be urged in favour of this claim being allowed.

Hitherto the difficulty has been to get the question of the political rights of individuals of the female sex recognised as one open to discussion at all. The advocate has not been allowed to come into court. It has been assumed that the male sex, by a sort of divine right, has the exclusive privilege of directing the affairs of the community; and any serious claim made by the other half of the human race, to a share in controlling its destinies, has been met, not by argument showing the groundlessness or inexpediency of the demand, but by a refusal to entertain it, as if it were something intrinsically absurd.

But in this inquiring age, first principles of all sorts, whether in religion or politics, are being sharply scrutinised, and those who maintain them must be prepared to justify them at the bar of intelligence of the age. The principle of confining political privileges exclusively to one sex, though persons of both sexes are equally affected by the course pursued in deciding political questions, is now challenged, and the case must be fairly judged on its merits.

The sheer novelty of the proposal is the weakest part of the case for the petitioners; the opposition will find their most formidable stronghold in taking up the position that women never have voted in choosing members of Parliament, and therefore they ought not to do so now. They may also possibly make the assertion that women do not desire the franchise, it is therefore needless to inquire whether it ought to be given to them.

The best answer to this last proposition is, that many persons otherwise qualified, but at present excluded from the franchise on account of their sex, do petition that the privilege shall be extended to them; and that a number

Figure 2: The Ladies' Advocate

Mrs. Bull. "Lor, Mr Mill! What a lovely speech you *did* make. I do declare I hadn't the slightest notion we were such miserable creatures. No one can say it was *your* fault that the case broke down."

From *Punch, or the London Charivari* (1 June 1867)

Mrs. Bull, wife of John Bull, the personification of the Englishman, commiserates with John Stuart Mill, after the defeat of his attempt to enfranchise women in the 1867 Reform Bill.

of ladies, honourably distinguished among the people of England for their intellectual attainments, and therefore most worthy representatives of womankind, are very much in earnest in seeking to obtain a favourable hearing for the petition. This being the case, it is difficult to see on what principles of equity its continuous rejection can be justified.

It surely will not be denied that women have, and ought to have, opinions of their own on subjects of public interest, and on the events which arise as the world wends on its way. But if it be granted that women may, without offence, hold political opinions, on what ground can the right be withheld of giving the same expression or effect to their opinions as that enjoyed by their male neighbours? To individual men the law says, "All of you whose rental reaches the prescribed standard shall have your political existence recognised. You may not be clever nor learned, possibly you do not know how to read and write. Still you know your own wants and wishes better than others know them for you; you have a stake in the country, and your interests ought to be consulted; you contribute directly to the national revenue a certain proportion of your property or earnings, and you shall enjoy in return a small share of direct political power, for the exercise of which, according to the best light you possess, you shall be legally responsible to no one."

But to individual women the law says, "It is true that you are persons with opinions, wants, and wishes of your own, which you know better than any other can know for you; we allow that your stake and interest in the country are equal to that of your next-door neighbour, and that your intelligence is not inferior to that of great numbers of male voters; we will tax your property and earnings as we see fit, but in return for your personal contribution to the national revenue you shall not possess the minutest fraction of personal political power; we will not allow you to have the smallest share in the government of the country of which you are a denizen, nor any voice in the making of the laws which determine the legal and political status of persons of your sex."

Now can any man who feels that he would not like to be addressed in language of this sort, seriously believe that women do like it? Surely there is no such difference in the feelings of persons of opposite sexes as to make language which would sound mortifying and unjust to one set of persons, seem agreeable and equitable to another set. If we do not hear much of such discontent as may exist, it must be remembered that women are naturally shy at expressing any sentiments liable to draw upon them the disapprobation or ridicule of their male friends; and that these, instead of talking of the question quietly and calmly, as one to be settled by fair reasoning, are apt, in discussing it with ladies, to assume a bantering air, and in asking their female friends whether they want votes, to indicate by their tone and manner the kind of answer they expect, or, at any rate, would approve of. They put, as it were, leading questions, and often receive the reply they prepare for. Men do not ask women earnestly, whether they will have votes, but jestingly, whether they would like them; and it is not very wonderful if the answers they receive to questions put in this spirit are much to the effect that the grapes are sour.

It is admitted that cultivated and intelligent women at least, even if it be denied of others, have opinions of their own on political and kindred matters; and the tendency of public opinion, if it has not already reached this point, is in the direction that the formation of these opinions should be encouraged, and that it is desirable that women should take an interest in the general welfare. But if this is right, where is the consistency or propriety of saying to them, "Open your eyes to what is going on in the world, think for yourselves on the subjects that engage public attention, and when you have taken pains to inform yourselves on the topics of the day, and on the merits of the various questions that stir the mind of the nation, your opinions shall be treated as worthless, your voices counted as nothing, and not a point of independent standing-ground shall be given to one of you from which you may endeavour to give effect to the strongest desire or opinion that may influence you." Is not this style of dealing with the opinions women are encouraged to form, something after the manner of the famous recipe for treating a cucumber—Carefully prepare the fruit, adjust the proportions of the seasoning, and when all is done, and the dish dressed to perfection, open the window and fling it away!

The question should be fairly put, and honestly answered, Ought the wishes and opinions of women to be allowed any political influence at all, any weight whatever in the general councils of the nation? It is for those who answer this question in the affirmative to show cause why they should not be permitted to exercise whatever influence it is thought right they should possess, in a direct, straightforward manner.

But many who allow that women's voices ought to count for something in estimating public opinion, say that the proper manner for them to exercise power in the State is through the influence they possess over the minds of their male relatives—when they happen to have any—and that this indirect method of making their opinions known ought to satisfy them. This may sound plausible, but the legal measure of influence accorded under this arrangement to the opinions of women of independent position is found, on examination, to vanish to a nullity. By what process can the votes of men be made to represent the opinions of women? Is a man bound, before giving his vote, to consult the wishes of the woman or women on whose behalf, as well as his own account, he is supposed to be acting? Each individual voter can give but one voice—his own; that voice represents the sentiments of a single mind. It adds nothing to the weight of this voice in choosing a representative, that any number of his female neighbours coincide in the views of the elector; and if they do not so coincide, far from representing their wishes, he is thwarting them. If, then, the opinions and wishes of women ought to have any political influence whatever, a channel should be open to them for expressing them independent of the votes of men, for these may or may not represent their opinions truly.

Some persons will boldly maintain that women ought not to think on political questions at all, and these are at least consistent in denying them votes. But it cannot surely be deemed desirable, or even possible, that more than half of the adult population of the realm should remain wholly apart from, and uninterested in, the events that daily happen among them.... If women are found to take a genuine interest in public affairs, they are liable to be forbidden to follow the promptings of their natural tastes, to be reproached for intruding into matters "beyond the province of their sex," and to be told that as they are excluded by law from participation in political power, they have no right to concern themselves with public interests....

The admission of female freeholders and householders to the privilege of voting would enfranchise, not simply the individual voters, but the whole sex. Every woman in the land would have an immediate accession of personal dignity, for she would belong to a class no longer denied the logical right to hold political opinions. Though she might not happen to possess the requisite qualification for a vote, personal exclusion from political power would lose its sting, for it would cease to imply presumed mental incapacity for its exercise. English women would be relieved from the mortifying consciousness, that while feeling no moral nor intellectual inferiority to the generality of the men of their own families, or whom they meet in society, and unable to perceive any difference between men's and women's manner of judging, or sentiments on public affairs,—except such as may be attributed to individual differences of tastes and circumstances,—the opinions of their male acquaintances are respected, as forming a legitimate portion of the motive power of the State, while their own are rejected, as only women's, and therefore not to be taken into account. It is to this feeling, and not to any unworthy desire to interfere in party squabbles, that the movement of women for enfranchisement is to be attributed....

It has been objected that conferring the franchise on women, and thus holding out to them an inducement to occupy their attention with political affairs, would tend to withdraw their minds from domestic duties, and take up their time to the disadvantage of those pursuits which have a more special claim on their attention. This seems to imply that women are the only persons who have peculiar duties, and that the privilege of voting properly belongs to those who have nothing to do. The objection might be urged with equal force against conferring the franchise on men who do not possess independent property. It is true that the peculiar duty of woman is to mind the house, and attend to the comfort of the inmates; but it is equally true that it is man's special province to labour for the maintenance of the household, and in this division of family cares, the share of the man is at least as important and engrossing as that of the woman....

It is said that if we allow women the privilege of voting for members of Parliament, and thus concede to them the right to interest themselves in political subjects, we shall next be asked to admit them as eligible for seats in the House of Commons.... But it is a mistake to suppose the one privilege to follow necessarily from the other. It is a perfectly fair position to maintain, that a woman, by circumstances incidental to her sex, is disqualified for discharging the burdensome and responsible duties of a member of Parliament, and yet that she is quite capable of exercising with advantage the very simple functions of an elector. It may be admitted that the personal participation of woman in the active struggles of parliamentary life, would be as incongruous as would have been her appearances armed in the lists, where of old her fate was ofttimes decided, without therefore believing that it is necessary to the preservation of her womanly character, to deprive her judgment of all voice in the selection of the champion to whose efforts the interests of herself and those dear to her are confided....

Let it be remembered, in considering the plea for the admission of a small percentage of their number to political existence, that persons of the female sex form the numerical majority of the adult population of the country, and that measures specially affecting their legal status, and the disposal of their persons and property, are enacted without their consent being obtained, or even asked. As an instance, there is a law which gives to the husband of a woman who marries without a settlement, the power of spending any money she may possess, or even of leaving it away from her in his will. The wisdom and beneficence of these arrangements are not here impugned; the question is simply suggested, whether, in case of a proposal to assimilate the English law affecting the property of women who marry, to that which prevails in other civilised countries, the legislative assembly best qualified to arrive at a decision which should be beyond suspicion of being partial, would be one in the election of which no woman had a vote....

"Woman have nothing to do with politics," we are told, and this assertion is given as an answer to their request for enfranchisement. But on the right solution of political questions depends the progress of the nation in material prosperity and intellectual culture. Female persons, especially those occupying an independent position, have the same stake in the country as their male fellow-citizens, and it is of just as much importance to women as to men, that the national counsels should be directed to the end of promoting the comfort and happiness of the masses of the people....

"Women have nothing to do with politics" is a mere assertion, founded on sentimental, not on scientific grounds. It may be true, it may be false; it is a proposition fairly open to dispute. But though this proposition may be doubted, there is no doubt at all about its converse. It may be denied that women have anything to do with politics; it cannot be denied that politics have a great deal to do with women.

"An Appeal Against Female Suffrage"

[*Nineteenth Century* 25 (June 1889): 781-88]

We, the undersigned, wish to appeal to the common sense and the educated thought of the men and women of England against the proposed extension of the Parliamentary suffrage to women.

1. While desiring the fullest possible development of the powers, energies, and education of women, we believe that their work for the State, and their responsibilities towards it, must always differ essentially from those of men, and that therefore their share in the working of the State machinery should be different from that assigned to men. Certain large departments of the national life are of necessity worked exclusively by men. To men belong the struggle of debate and legislation in Parliament; the hard and exhausting labour implied in the administration of the national resources and powers; the conduct of England's relations towards the external world; the working of the army and navy; all the heavy, laborious, fundamental industries of the State, such as those of mines, metals, and railways; the lead and supervision of English commerce, the management of our vast English finance, the service of that merchant fleet on which our food supply depends. In all these spheres women's direct participation is made impossible either by the disabilities of sex, or by strong formations of custom and habit resting ultimately upon physical difference, against which it is useless to contend. They are affected indeed, in some degree, by all these national activities; therefore they ought in some degree to have an influence on them all. This influence they already have, and will have more and more as the education of women advances. But their direct interest in these matters can never equal that of men, whose whole energy of mind and body is daily and hourly risked in them. Therefore it is not just to give to women direct power of deciding questions of Parliamentary policy, of war, of foreign or colonial affairs, of commerce and finance equal to that possessed by men. We hold that they already possess an influence on political matters fully proportioned to the possible share of women in the political activities of England.

At the same time we are heartily in sympathy with all the recent efforts which have been made to give women a more important part in those affairs of the community where their interests and those of men are equally concerned; where it is possible for them not only to decide but to help in carrying out, and where, therefore, judgment is weighted by a true responsibility, and can be guided by experience and the practical information which comes from it. As voters for or members of School Boards, Boards of Guardians, and other important public bodies, women have now opportunities for public usefulness which must promote the growth of character, and at the same time strengthen among them the social sense and habit. All these changes of recent years, together with the great improvements in women's education which have accompanied them, we cordially welcome. But we believe that the emancipating process has now reached the limits fixed by the physical constitution of women, and by the fundamental difference which must always exist between their main occupations and those of men. The care of the sick and the insane; the treatment of the poor; the education of children: in all these matters, and others besides, they have made good their claim to larger and more extended powers. We rejoice in it. But when it comes to questions of foreign or colonial policy, or of grave constitutional change, then we maintain that the necessary and normal experience of women—speaking generally and in the mass—does not and can never provide them with such materials for sound judgment as are open to men.

To sum up: we would give them their full share in the State of social effort and social mechanism; we look for their increasing activity in that higher State which rests on thought, conscience, and moral influence; but we protest against their admission to direct power in that State which *does* rest upon force—the State in its administrative, military, and financial aspects—where the physical capacity, the accumulated experience and inherited training of men ought to prevail without the harassing interference of those who, though they may be partners with men in debate, can in these matters never be partners with them in action.

2. If we turn from the *right* of women to the suffrage—a right which on the grounds just given we deny—to the effect which the possession of the suffrage may be expected to have on their character and position and on family life, we find ourselves no less in doubt. It is urged that the influence of women in politics would tell upon the side of morality. We believe that it does so tell already, and will do so with greater force as women by improved education fit themselves to exert it more widely and efficiently. But it may be asked, On what does this moral influence depend? We believe that it depends largely on qualities which the natural position and functions of women as they are at present tend to develop, and which might be seriously impaired by their admission to the turmoil of active political life. These qualities are, above all, sympathy and disinterestedness. Any disposition of things which threatens to lessen the national reserve of such forces as these we hold to be a misfortune. It is notoriously difficult to maintain them in the presence of party necessities and in the heat of party struggle. Were women admitted to this struggle, their natural eagerness and quickness of temper would probably make them hotter partisans than men. As their political relations stand at present, they tend to check in them the disposition to partisanship, and to strengthen in them the qualities of sympathy and disinterestedness. We believe that their admission to the suffrage would precisely reverse this condition of things, and that the whole nation would suffer in consequence. For whatever may be the duty and privilege of the parliamentary vote for men, we hold that citizenship is not depen-

dent upon or identical with the possession of the suffrage. Citizenship lies in the participation of each individual in effort for the good of the community. And we believe that women will be more valuable citizens, will contribute more precious elements to the national life without the vote than with it. The quickness to feel, the willingness to lay aside prudential considerations in a right cause, which are amongst the peculiar excellencies of women, are in their right place when they are used to influence the more highly trained and developed judgment of men. But if this quickness of feeling could be imme- diately and directly translated into public action, in matters of vast and com- plicated political import, the risks of politics would be enormously increased, and what is now a national blessing might easily become a national calamity. On the one hand, then, we believe that to admit women to the ordinary machinery of political life would inflame the partisanship and increase the evils, already so conspicuous, of that life, would tend to blunt the special moral qualities of women, and so to lessen the national reserves of moral force; and, on the other hand, we dread the political and practical effects which, in our belief, would follow on such a transformation as is proposed, of an influence which is now beneficent largely because it is indirect and gradual.

3. Proposals for the extension of the suffrage to women are beset with grave practical difficulties. If votes be given to unmarried women on the same terms as they are given to men, large numbers of women leading immoral lives will be enfranchised on the one hand, while married women, who, as a rule, have passed through more of the practical experiences of life than the unmarried, will be excluded. To remedy part of this difficulty it is proposed by a large sec- tion of those who advocate the extension of the suffrage to women, to admit married women with the requisite property qualification. This proposal—an obviously just one if the suffrage is to be extended to women at all—introduces changes in family life, and in the English conception of the household, of enormous importance, which have never been adequately considered. We are practically invited to embark upon them because a few women of property possessing already all the influence which belongs to property, and a full share of that public protection and safety which is the fruit of taxation, feel them- selves aggrieved by the denial of the parliamentary vote. The grievance put for- ward seems to us wholly disproportionate to the claim based upon it.

4. A survey of the manner in which this proposal has won its way into prac- tical politics leads us to think that it is by no means ripe for legislative solu- tion. A social change of momentous gravity has been proposed; the mass of those immediately concerned in it are notoriously indifferent; there has been no serious and general demand for it, as is always the case if a grievance is real and reform necessary; the amount of information collected is quite inade- quate to the importance of the issue; and the public has gone through no suf- ficient discipline of discussion on the subject. Meanwhile pledges to support female suffrage have been hastily given in the hopes of strengthening exist- ing political parties by the female vote. No doubt there are many conscien-

'THE ANGEL IN 'THE HOUSE;'' OR, THE RESULT OF FEMALE SUFFRAGE.
(*A Troubled Dream of the Future.*)

Figure 3: "The Angel in 'The House;'" or, The Result of Female Suffrage
(A Troubled Dream of the Future.)
From *Punch, or the London Charivari* (14 June 1884)

*"The Angel in the House" is a reference to the very popular poem by Coventry Patmore, which cele-
brates a sentimentalized ideal woman. In this cartoon, the woman speaking is not in her house, but
the House of Commons, wearing mannish clothing and standing and gesturing in a masculine
manner. She has put aside her knitting of a "blue stocking," a derisive allusion to bluestockings, or
pedantic women. The man on the front bench, forced to listen to her, resembles the Prime Minister at
the time, William Gladstone.*

tious supporters of female suffrage amongst members of Parliament; but it is
hard to deny that the present prominence of the question is due to party considerations of a temporary nature. It is, we submit, altogether unworthy of the
intrinsic gravity of the question that it should be determined by reference to
the passing needs of party organisation. Meanwhile we remember that great

electoral changes have been carried out during recent years. Masses of new electors have been added to the constituency. These new elements have still to be assimilated; these new electors have still to be trained to take their part in the national work; and while such changes are still fresh, and their issues uncertain, we protest against any further alteration in our main political machinery, especially when it is an alteration which involves a new principle of extraordinary range and significance, closely connected with the complicated problems of sex and family life.

5. It is often urged that certain injustices of the law towards women would be easily and quickly remedied were the political power of the vote conceded to them; and that there are many wants, especially among working women, which are now neglected, but which the suffrage would enable them to press on public attention. We reply that during the past half century all the principal injustices of the law towards women have been amended by means of the existing constitutional machinery; and with regard to those that remain, we see no signs of any unwillingness on the part of Parliament to deal with them. On the contrary, we remark a growing sensitiveness to the claims of women, and the rise of a new spirit of justice and sympathy among men, answering to those advances made by women in education, and the best kind of social influence, which we have already noticed and welcomed. With regard to the business or trade interests of women,—here, again, we think it safer and wiser to trust to organisation and self-help on their own part, and to the growth of a better public opinion among the men workers, than to the exercise of a political right which may easily bring women into direct and hasty conflict with men.

In conclusion: nothing can be further from our minds than to seek to depreciate the position or importance of women. It is because we are keenly alive to the enormous value of their special contribution to the community, that we oppose what seems to us likely to endanger that contribution. We are convinced that the pursuit of a mere outward equality with men is for women not only vain but demoralising. It leads to a total misconception of woman's true dignity and special mission. It tends to personal struggle and rivalry, where the only effort of both the great divisions of the human family should be to contribute the characteristic labour and the best gifts of each to the common stock.

FEMALE SUFFRAGE: A WOMEN'S PROTEST.

The undersigned protest strongly against the proposed Extension of the Parliamentary Franchise to Women, which they believe would be a measure distasteful to the great majority of the women of the country—unnecessary—and mischievous both to themselves and to the State.

[The Appeal is signed by 104 women.]

MILLICENT GARRETT FAWCETT

FROM "THE APPEAL AGAINST FEMALE SUFFRAGE:
A REPLY. I"

[*Nineteenth Century* 26 (July 1889): 86-96]

…. The ladies who sign the *Nineteenth Century* Protest against the enfranchisement of women … do not wish it to be supposed that they are opposed to the recent improvements that have taken place in the education of women, or to their increased activity in various kinds of public work. "All these changes," they say, "together with the great improvements in women's education which have accompanied them, we cordially welcome. But we believe that the emancipating process has now reached the limits fixed by the physical constitution of women." In other passages they attribute the greatest value to the influence of women in politics, recognising it as a moral force, which is likely to grow stronger as the results of the improved education of women make themselves felt. In the concluding paragraph they, with some want of humour, I think, asseverate that nothing is further from their mind, "than to seek to depreciate the position and importance of women." To acknowledge the importance of women conveys a height and depth and breadth of condescension which is difficult to measure…. The hundred and four ladies have acknowledged in the handsomest way "the importance of women." Let us inquire a little in detail into the line of argument adopted, in the Protest, and also analyse somewhat the list of names by which the arguments are supported.

The Protest speaks in congratulatory words of all recent changes which have given extended opportunities of usefulness to women. Special reference is made to improvements in education, and among other subjects mentioned are "the care of the sick and the insane, the treatment of the poor, the education of children: in all these matters, and in others besides, they [women] have made good their claim to larger and more extended powers. We rejoice in it." But, on reading the names appended to the Protest, the most striking fact about them is that hardly any out of the hundred and four ladies who now rejoice in these changes have helped them while their issue was in any way doubtful. They hardly deserve even to be called the patrons of any effort to improve the social, legal, or educational position of women—unless, indeed, we adopt Dr. Johnson's[7] famous definition of the word "patron": "Is not a patron, my lord, one who looks with unconcern on a man struggling for life in the water, and, when he has reached the ground, encumbers him with help?" A good many of the hundred and four hardly preserved an attitude of neutrality whilst the changes they now rejoice in were "struggling for life in the water;" while success was still uncertain, many a backhander has been dealt at them by the same ladies who now announce themselves as rejoicing in their success. Very few are there, among the hundred and four, who moved purse, tongue, or pen in support of these changes before they became accomplished facts. This is the general character of the list of names. But let it be at once acknowledged that there are exceptions, chief of whom is the lady whose name heads the list—the Dowager Lady Stanley of Alderley. She has been a constant, a generous, and an outspoken friend of better education for women of all classes. There are other exceptions, but they are less striking, and I think they could easily be counted on the fingers of one hand. The women to whose initiative we owe the improvements which the hundred and four rejoice in, are not to be found in the *Nineteenth Century* list. Work for others is one of the most educating influences either man or woman can have. Professor Marshall recently said in his presidential address at the Co-operative Congress: "He who lived and worked only for himself, or even only for himself and his family, led an incomplete life. To complete it he needed to work with others for some broad and high aim." The women who have worked with others for the object of lifting the lives of women to a higher level educationally, socially, and industrially, are not in the *Nineteenth Century* list. The names of the women to whose unselfish and untiring labours we owe what has been done for women during the last twenty-five years in education, in social and philanthropic work, in proprietary rights, in some approach towards justice as regards the guardianship of children, in opening the means of medical education, are conspicuous by their absence, and for an excellent reason: they support the extension of the suffrage to duly qualified women....

A further consideration of the *Nineteenth Century* list of names shows that it contains a very large preponderance of ladies to whom the lines of life have fallen in pleasant places. There are very few among them of the women who have had to face the battle of life alone, to earn their living by daily hard work. Women of this class generally feel the injustice of their want of representation. The weight of taxation falls upon them just as if they were men, and they do not see why representation should not go with taxation in their case, simply because their physical strength is less than that of men. No one proposes to relieve them of fiscal burdens because of "the limits fixed by the physical constitution of women."....

A large part of the Protest is directed against women taking an active part in the turmoil of political life. This has nothing to do with voting or not voting. For instance, women vote in school board elections; but they can please themselves about taking part in the turmoil of a school board contest. Thousands of women vote who keep completely clear of meetings, canvassing, committees, and all the rest of the electioneering machinery. On the other hand, women do not vote in Parliamentary elections, but they are invited and pressed by all parties to take an active part in the turmoil of political life. Among other inconsistencies of the protesting ladies, it should not be forgotten that many of them, as presidents and vice-presidents of women's political associations, encourage the admission of women to the ordinary machinery of political life, although they say in this Protest that this admission would be dangerous to the best interests of society. If women are fit to advise, convince, and persuade voters how to vote, they are surely also fit to vote themselves. On the other hand, if it is true, as the *Nineteenth Century* ladies state, that women on the whole "are without the materials for forming a sound judgment" on matters of constitutional change, why are we invited by those same ladies to form our unsound judgments, and do all in our power to induce others to share them? If we have no materials, or insufficient materials, for forming a sound judgment in politics, we should not be invited to enrol ourselves in Primrose Leagues, or in the Women's Liberal Federation, or in the Women's Liberal Unionist Association.[8] To say simultaneously to women, "The materials for forming a sound judgment are not open to you," and "We beg you to influence electors to whom is entrusted the fate of the empire," is to run with the hare and hunt with the hounds. One position or the other must be abandoned, unless these ladies have cultivated with unusual skill the art of believing two contradictory things at the same time....

The "party, nothing but party" politician in England, as well as in America, looks with distrust on women's suffrage. Women would be an unknown quantity, less amenable to party discipline, less expectant of party loaves and fishes, and consequently less obedient to the party whip than the present electorate. They might take the bit in their mouth and insist on voting in a way inconvenient to their party on temperance, and on matters of religion and morals. These fears tell against us very heavily, and we cannot allay them; because the fear that women will be independent and will dare to vote for what they think is right, whether the professional politician likes it or not, is, in our minds, not a fear but a hope, and a hope which is at the root of all we are working for. If women's suffrage should tend to strengthen the group, which exists in every constituency, of the voters whose political views are not dictated to them from a central office in Parliament Street or Victoria Street, but are the result of independent thought, study of facts, and conscientious obedience to moral considerations, it is a matter of very small importance which party will gain or lose by the female vote; all parties will be the better for it....

It was natural that the subscribers to the Protest should make the most of a subject on which the supporters of women's suffrage are not at one: viz.[9] the admission or the exclusion of married women. The party in favour of an extension of the suffrage is seldom in absolute harmony upon the extent of the change which they demand. Some of the supporters of the Reform Bills of 1832, 1867, and 1884[10] would have liked, far better than these gradual extensions, to have leapt at once to universal suffrage. But our national habit in these things is to go slowly, one step at a time, and be sure of a firm foothold in one place before we go on to another. Both the Bills for women's suffrage that were introduced this session were drawn in this spirit: they would have enfranchised those women who have already received the municipal, county council, and school board suffrages; *i.e.* single women and widows who are householders, property owners, and otherwise fulfil the conditions by law on male electors.

The *Nineteenth Century* ladies think that these Bills would "enfranchise large numbers of women leading immoral lives," and on the other hand, by excluding wives, would shut out those women "who, as a rule, have passed through more of the practical experiences of life than the unmarried." Both these statements invite comment. By the words "large numbers of women leading immoral lives," it may be presumed that the ladies refer to some women who might become qualified to vote under the lodger franchise. Among "the materials for forming a sound judgment" in this matter are the following facts, which are not beyond the grasp of the female intellect. Two consecutive years' residence in the same apartments, and also personal application to be placed upon the Parliamentary register are required of any one claiming the lodger franchise. These conditions have, as regards the male sex, made this franchise almost a dead letter: for example, in the borough of Blackburn, with 13,000 electors, only fifteen men vote under the lodger franchise. In most constituencies the lodgers are an absolutely insignificant fraction of the whole body of electors. The conditions which prevent men lodgers from becoming electors would be even more effective in preventing women lodgers, of the unhappy class referred to, from getting upon the register. On the other hand, the large class of most respectable and worthy women who live in lodgings, such as teachers and others engaged in education, would have no difficulty in fulfilling the conditions demanded, and would form a valuable addition to the electorate.

Foreigners often talk of English hypocrisy; and this bugbear about women's suffrage rendering it possible for an immoral woman to vote for a member of Parliament, appears an excellent example of it. How long has a stainless moral character been one of the conditions for exercising the Parliamentary suffrage? When it is remembered that no moral iniquity disqualifies a man from voting, that men of known bad character not only vote but are voted for, it is hardly possible to accept as genuine the objection to women's suffrage based on the possibility of an immoral woman voting. In times gone by women of this character had more political power than any other women. The mistresses of kings and of their ministers have often been centres of political power. But the modern democratic movement of society has modified this state of things; there is a transfer of political power from the Perrerses and the Du Barrys[11] to the humbler but more self-respecting women who worthily represent the true womanhood of the country. Who can say, if women's suffrage were carried, that the new electors would not be of a character calculated to raise, rather than depress, the moral level of the constituencies to which they belong?

The next objection of the hundred and four is that, if wives are excluded, those who would be shut out are women "who have, as a rule, passed through more of the practical experiences of life than the unmarried;" whilst if they are included, "changes of enormous importance, which have never been adequately considered, would be introduced into home life." The editor echoes, and in echoing magnifies, the fear here implied, for he "submits" that ladies should "for once" come forward and signify publicly their "condemnation of the scheme now threatened," "in order to save the quiet of home life from total disappearance." He must be very unhappy if he feels that the quiet of home life depends for its existence on an Act of Parliament. The quiet of home life, for those who are blessed with what deserves to be called a home, is one of those things that "looks on tempests and is never shaken."[12] Love is said to laugh at locksmiths. I think he will survive women's suffrage. The ladies, however, have stated their case with more moderation: they mention the undoubted fact that married women must either be included or excluded in any women's suffrage Bill: if they are excluded, many of the best women will be shut out; if they are included, changes will be introduced into home life which have not been adequately considered. For my own part, it has always seemed for many reasons right to recognise this, and therefore to support the measures which would enfranchise single women and widows, and not wives during the lifetime of their husbands. The case for the enfranchisement of women who are standing alone and bearing the burden of citizenship as ratepayers and taxpayers, seems unanswerable. If we have household suffrage, let the head of the house vote, whether that head be a man or a woman. The enfranchisement of wives is an altogether different question. The enfranchisement of single women and widows gives electoral power to a class who are in a position of social and financial independence. To give these women votes would be a change in their political condition, bringing it into harmony with their social, industrial, and pecuniary position. This would not be the case with wives. If they were enfranchised, the effect, in ninety-nine cases out of a hundred, would be to give two votes to the husband. Wives are bound by law to obey their husbands. No other class in the community is in this position, and it seems inexpedient to allow political independence (which would only be nominal) to precede actual independence. The legal position of a married woman has changed considerably in the direction of independence, but the change is, after all, only partial (it is not argued here whether or not it is desirable to make it complete); and, in my opinion, a change in political status should always be attendant on a corresponding and preceding change in the social and legal status. The limitation of female suffrage to those women not under coverture[13] would no doubt exclude from representation many women of high character and capacity. A similar objection can be made to every limitation of the suffrage. It must also be remembered that if the Bill lately before Parliament were carried, no set of women would be definitely and permanently excluded, as at present all women are. Marriage is to nearly all women a state either of experience or of expectation. There would be a constant passing to and fro, from the ranks of the represented and the unrepresented, and consequently the closest identity of interest would exist between them. In this way the direct representation of some women would become the indirect representation of all women. Many valued friends of the Women's Suffrage movement take a different view, and urge that we should seek to remove the disability of coverture simultaneously with the disability of sex; and that to exclude married women is to place a slight upon marriage. Others, with whom I sympathise, believe this to be a mistaken view; as regards the alleged slight on marriage, married women never discovered that they were insulted when their single or widowed sisters were entrusted with the school board, municipal, and county council suffrages. It is on the lines laid down by our previous experiences of women's suffrage that it will probably be found best to proceed in the future.

In conclusion, the ladies of the *Nineteenth Century* Protest may be reminded that the friends of women's suffrage value the womanliness of women as much as themselves. True womanliness grows and thrives on whatever strengthens the spontaneity and independence of the character of women. Women, for instance, are more womanly in England, where Florence Nightingale and Mary Carpenter[14] have taught them how women's work ought to be done, than they are in Spain, where they accept the masculine standard in matters of amusement and go in crowds to see a bull-fight. The most unfeminine of English women are to be found in those classes which are either so high or so low in the social scale as to have been comparatively little influenced by the emancipating process of the last fifty years. They set their ideas of pleasure and amusement by the masculine, not by the feminine standard. At the top of the social scale, these women (who are bad imitations of men) go on the turf, practice various kinds of sport, or if they do not kill with their own hands, stand by and see others kill pheasants in a battue, or pigeons at Hurlingham. At the other end of the social scale there are women whose feminine instincts are so little developed that betting and drinking are their chief enjoyments. These are the really unfeminine women. We do not want women to be bad imitations of men; we neither deny nor minimise the differences between men and women. The claim of women to representation depends to

Figure 4: Dame Millicent Fawcett by Walery
(Stanislas Julian Walery, Count Ostrorog)
circa 1889
By courtesy of the National Portrait Gallery, London

a large extent on those differences. Women bring something to the service of the state different from that which can be brought by men. Let this fact be frankly recognised and let due weight be given to it in the representative system of the country.

MARY MARGARET DILKE

"THE APPEAL AGAINST FEMALE SUFFRAGE: A REPLY. II"

[*Nineteenth Century* 26 (July 1889): 97-103]

It has been no secret to the supporters of woman suffrage that a section of prominent women in London society have remained unconvinced by the arguments for the enfranchisement of women; but their opposition long remained of so indefinite and nebulous a character, that it was obviously difficult to grapple with it. Now that they have written an appeal and stated their objections in clear, straightforward language, and signed their names to the number of a hundred and more; now that they have entered the lists to fight, not for, but against the extension of political rights to their own sex, it is possible to gauge their strength, to test their reasoning powers, to place, indeed, once more before the public the reasons *pro* and *con* the most absorbing and important movement of the century. Those who have spoken and written repeatedly on this subject for the last dozen years have a feeling of hesitation and shyness at being obliged to use the same arguments again and again, and to bring but little fresh fuel to feed the furnace of public opinion; but it is only necessary to read through the appeal with care to find that the opponents of further progress have simply burnished up the old weapons and sharpened the time-worn steel. No new artillery of novel design makes necessary the reconstruction of fortress or line of defence; the only real difference, and it is of importance in politics as in war, is that the sharpshooters and freelances who for long carried on a war of chance encounters and night surprises now find themselves in possession of an important fortress, and instead of devising a telling attack, they have to maintain their hard-won position and repulse an apparently formidable assault.

We have to thank these ladies for their approval of the reforms that have been already carried, to be grateful to them for their acceptance of accomplished facts. And yet with the honourable exception of Lady Stanley of Alderley, whose name, with a consciousness of its exceptional weight, they have placed at the head of the list, it is not in this list that we find the names of the women who have given time and energy and money to carry these reforms. It is notorious that those women who have the best right to speak for their sex, as they have already made many and great sacrifices for it, have again and again signed memorials and petitions in favour of woman suffrage, pleading that their just work was made difficult, and even in the end was but inefficiently accomplished, because they had no vote to legalise their proceedings and facilitate its accomplishment. These ladies take upon themselves to say the time has come to arrest all further progress; ignoring the fact that as the old bonds and fetters fall away from women's limbs new requirements arise, new possibilities open out before them, and careers that but a short quarter of a century ago would have seemed far out of their reach now open before them and seem to call able and well-educated women to fill posts for which their training has fitted them.

While men have been considering the danger to society of allowing women to take the first step that is said to cost so much, that step and many others have been quietly taken, and women have already half climbed the ladder. But can any position be more useless and illogical than that of a person who having half climbed a ladder is told to pause, to remain 'twixt heaven and earth, and to forego the object with which the climb was undertaken? Ladies of intellect and social standing can always make their voices heard, can always write to the papers and magazines, can command the sympathy and attention of public men whenever they feel they receive less than justice. But the supporters of woman suffrage aspire to help those other women whose lives are spent in humble toil, whose work is ill paid, whose education has been defective or entirely neglected. They wish to see women's power and influence more evenly divided, more fairly distributed. They wish women to vote because they are different from men, and because no alteration of laws, or customs, or social habits will make them the same as men.

The supporters of woman suffrage do not believe in indirect representation under any circumstances, but least of all when the influx of women into the labour market brings them, whether they will it or no, into competition with those whose interests and capacities are different; it is not the Woman Suffrage Societies that have brought about this great social change. A man is no longer expected, even in well-to-do middle-class society, to support his adult sisters and daughters as well as his wife and infant children. The societies, accepting the new state of things, wish to protect the earning of these women, to teach them self-reliance, to help them in the only way human beings can be efficiently helped—shown how to help themselves.

It is strange that the vote should have come to be looked on as necessarily a masculine adjunct. It was certainly originally intended to give effect to the opinions of the quiet, orderly citizen, instead of leaving power in the hands of the strong and warlike. The citizen may be ill or crippled, immoral or sentimental, illiterate or drunken, without risking his right to vote; and women will always resent having their claim to vote denied because individuals among them may suffer from any or all of these disadvantages. No reliable substitute for a vote has ever been invented, or is likely to be discovered in the future. A vote is not an end in itself, it is only a means to an end. It is as useful as a lever to lift a weight, or as a key to open a door, but has in itself no intrinsic value. Women do not imagine that the Millennium will have been attained when some or indeed all of them have votes; but as long as they have no votes they risk the loss of all those improvements in the position of their sex for which they have toiled so unremittingly. People without votes who deliberately say they do not want them are like a crowd standing outside a concert-hall, eager to hear every note of the music, refusing to take the key and unlock the door so that they may enter, and yet triumphantly pointing out to those who advise the use of that simple implement that, the windows being partly open, faint echoes of the melody reach them now and again if they listen with sufficient attention.

We are told again and again that society rests ultimately on force, and women, in the willing tribute they pay to brave, strong, and courageous men, are the first to acknowledge it; but more than half the men of every European country, even in these days of compulsory military service, have to stand aside and relegate the actual defence of their country to those who can most efficiently perform it. Women will always have to stand aside, and while battle wages give, like every other citizen, money to supply the sinews of war; and for their own special contribution, that care of the sick and wounded that has become so much more efficient and valuable since science and hospital experience and technical training of the best kind have developed their finest faculties. If the men had not some special sphere—that of war—in which nature has intended that they shall specially excel, they would not be the equals but the inferiors of women, who have other spheres equally necessary, for which they and they alone are indispensable.

But there are other great facts of life besides force which are of equally paramount importance. One of these great facts is, that every mother who brings a child into the world risks her life in that most necessary beginning of all existence; and surely, if men take so much credit for endangering their lives in war, this should not be forgotten or ignored in calculating the services the two sexes severally give to society. Again, while we say that society rests ultimately on force, we also say with equal truth and cogency that society rests on work. The problems connected with the labour question are most urgent and pressing, and it is impossible to attempt to solve them without taking woman into account. Women's home work has always been unpaid, whether well or ill-performed, but, taken as a whole, has in the past times been quite as often well done, and been quite as fundamental a part of civilised life, as the paid labour of men. But every census shows that more women enter the paid labour market year by year.

The main causes are, the preponderance of female compared to male population owing to emigration, the invention of labour-saving household implements that lighten indoor work, the co-operative tendencies of city life that cause baking, washing, dressmaking, and upholstering to be done outside;

and more especially the increased orderliness and propriety of English life that enables women to go and come in the streets and public conveyances without fear of insult or assault. The rapidly increasing wealth of the middle classes has deprived thousands of women of the necessity for household toil; but education and increased opportunities for intellectual and public work draw these same women, if not in the first, then in the second generation, into busy useful lives, giving satisfaction to themselves and benefit to the community at large. If, then, society rests on labour, and women contribute more and more to that labour, it becomes absolutely necessary for them to have a voice in all labour laws and regulations, and in all social questions.

It is quite possible that the most crying injustices from which women suffer may be removed by a Parliament of men, elected only by men; but women have had to complain in the past more of the ignorance and prejudice of men in regard to labour legislation than of their unfairness or injustice. They have repeatedly attempted by legislation to prevent women from working in the most difficult and exhausting fields of labour. The result has been merely to reduce their wages and increase their hours of work in the unrestricted employments; whereas, had men invited the co-operation of women in trades unions as well as in legislation, it is probable their efforts would have been better directed, and have borne good fruit for men and women alike. Moreover, all trade legislation undertaken by men alone is open to the accusation, often, unfortunately, too well founded, of restricting women's labour, not in the most irksome, but in the best-paid posts.

Were men of their own free will to remove all the unjust laws of which women complain, they would find they had removed all the barriers to feminine emancipation invented in the past to shut women out from wage-earning and public life. They would find women placed immediately in such a position of social and economic equality with men, that to withhold merely the vote would be illogical and inconvenient. We have one great proof in England that legislation in this direction has not gone faster than public wants and opinions. When the law allowed women to become guardians of the poor, excellent women of character were ready at once to occupy the posts. When the law allowed women to become members of School Boards, no difficulty was found in securing suitable candidates. When women can vote, they do vote, in ever-increasing numbers. They have never yet shirked the responsibility once it has been imposed, and, though Mr. Labouchere[15] may say not one women in a thousand wants a vote, we have only to turn to well-ascertained facts to point to a very different conclusion.

One of the grave disadvantages about substituting feminine influence for feminine votes is the extremely demoralising effect it has always had on men's characters to find the female part of the community entirely dependent on them for their rights and privileges. Men are but human, and while they never fail to taunt lady canvassers with working most heartily for the best-looking candidate, they must be aware that the personal charms of the women who ask them for help and protection have much more to do with securing their attention and devotion than such an abstract consideration as justice.

We are anxious to relieve men of this responsibility, and provide members of Parliament, through the ballot-box, with a means of impartially carrying out the ascertained wishes of their feminine constituents, whether old or young, ill-favoured or fair to look upon.

It is really an interesting study to notice how every argument used to delay the enfranchisement of working men and farm labourers reappears to do duty against women. How often has the question been asked, "What does Hodge know about finance and foreign policy, colonial affairs and commercial interests?"

The fact is, we have made up our minds in England that to insure every class obtaining justice every class must be directly represented; and that, while we pay large salaries to specialists to look after these great questions, we cannot have too wide an opinion from the people as a whole on the main principles that are to guide our life as a nation. Woman may never be intellectually fitted for the position of minister of the Crown or ambassador, though with her present rate of progress he would be a rash man who would attempt to predict exactly how far she will go; but that does not affect one way or the other her right to vote, or the right of the nation to have her recorded opinion on every question with which she is familiar. Why should she sit on a School Board, and in that capacity make recommendations to the Government on the Education Code, and yet when that same Code is before Parliament have no power to support its provisions or secure its rejection? Why should she sit on boards of guardians, and after visiting pauper schools, and planning perhaps some new scheme that will turn our most hopeless and wretched population into valuable bread-winners, yet have no influence with Parliament to get that scheme carried into effect?

We cannot afford as a nation to allow such a potent moral influence as that of women to lie fallow. It is very well to call it a reserve force, but a reserve force that is never to be put into action is of small practical value. We think the time has come when that moral influence must be both organised and put in action. In old times, when population was scattered and manners were patriarchal, individual charity and personal influence could work wonders. With our vast cities and ever-increasing complication of interests and industries, combination of influence and co-operation in good works have become absolutely necessary, unless the feminine element is to be entirely eliminated. Men are going forward so fast, that the rift between the sexes will become wider if women are to continue working on the old lines and never take a step in advance. The choice is not between going on and standing still, it is between advancing and retreating.

The practical difficulties that beset the question of dividing women into

VOL. III. (New Series), No. 96.   FRIDAY, JANUARY 7, 1910.   Price 1d. Weekly. (Post Free.)

TAXATION WITHOUT REPRESENTATION.

POLITICAL CANDIDATE: "As your husband is dead, madam, and women do not vote, it is no use my staying."
TAX COLLECTOR: "As your husband is dead, madam, and women have to pay taxes, you will have to pay the tax instead of him."

Figure 5: Taxation without Representation
Political Candidate: "As your husband is dead, madam,
and women do not vote, it is no use my staying."
Tax Collector: "As your husband is dead, madam, and women
have to pay taxes, you will have to pay the tax instead of him."
From *Votes for Women* III (7 January 1910)

electors and non-electors are precisely similar to the same division among men. It is equally objectionable to base the suffrage on marriage or no marriage, as it is on property or no property. But this molehill that seems such a mountain can easily be swept aside by practical persons. The nation, we believe, would like to make an experiment in woman suffrage by enfranchising a limited number and then judging of the result before going further. We believe the experiment will be successful, and will prove a precedent for future legislation whatever the section of women selected in the first instance; and that there should be a difference of opinion among women themselves on this point only proves how keen they are to take a responsible part in the national life, and directly contradicts the supposed apathy that is said to exist.

The appeal is superior to the ordinary male attack on woman suffrage, in so far that it does not condescend to discuss which political party will momentarily benefit by the passing of a Suffrage Bill into law. For this we are duly thankful. These ladies seem to consider that the question has not been sufficiently discussed, and they take the best possible means for remedying the want by raising afresh this controversy, in a way that has called forth an echo in almost every periodical in the United Kingdom.

It is not controversy that we fear. We passed successfully through the storm of ridicule and contempt, and we have languished through years of indifference and neglect; and, just when we thought the public tired with our innumerable meetings and bored with signing our petitions—when we were beginning to think that every one had made up his mind, and that the kindest and most judicious course for us to pursue would be to take every opportunity in Parliament of getting the matter settled once and for all—we are refreshed and invigorated by being told that more information is wanted, and that the public has gone through no sufficient discipline of discussion on the subject. We should be the last to shrink from this test. We have always found that every discussion, every large audience, every newspaper controversy, has added to our numbers and increased our organisations. Converts among our opponents have not been rare of late years, but undoubtedly our greatest victories have been won in the past (and are possibly awaiting us in the near future) among those men and women who have never thought about the subject at all.

"WOMEN'S SUFFRAGE: A REPLY"

[*Fortnightly Review* 52 (1 July 1889): 123-31]

One hundred and four ladies have appealed in the June number of *The Nineteenth Century* to "the common-sense and educated thought of the men and women of England against the proposed extension of the Parliamentary suffrage to women."

For more than twenty years the supporters of women's suffrage have been appealing to "the common-sense and educated thought" of the men and women of their country, to show cause why those women who fulfil the qualifications demanded by law of male electors and have been admitted with good results and with no appreciable harm whatever, to various other franchises, should still be denied the exercise of the parliamentary vote. "Common-sense" may take fright at an entirely new experiment. It was not unnatural that persons of a cautious disposition should view with apprehension any change in the status of women which it was feared might endanger the quiet of home life, and introduce an element of discord between men and women. This apprehension was even felt at one time in regard to the admission of ladies to hear debates in the House of Commons. But experience and a more cultivated common-sense have removed these fears. Women have been admitted to many kinds of electoral privileges and to much public work involving grave responsibility, and none of the apprehended evils have followed....

The ladies who sign the protest avow their belief that the influence of women in politics tells on the side of morality. "Common-sense" appears to indicate that any force which tells on the side of morality in politics would be of benefit to the State if it were given a legitimate and constitutional form of expression through admission to the franchise. The protesting ladies, however, fear that the beneficial moral influence now exerted by women on politics would be "seriously impaired by their admission to the turmoil of active political life." It should not be forgotten that whether women vote or not, all parties in the State are now inviting them to take part in the turmoil of active political life. Within a few days of the appearance of the protest, Lord Salisbury was addressing the ladies of the Primrose League and Mr. Gladstone was addressing the ladies of the Liberal Federation,[16] and each party leader was calling on women to enter into the fight to help his own side. As a matter of fact, no contested election now passes without each party availing itself of the help of women. It is not intended here to argue whether this is desirable or undesirable in itself; but it must be obvious that it is a state of things which puts the quiet, retiring woman, to whom the publicity and rowdyism of elections are distasteful, at a disadvantage. It would be easy for such a woman to walk to the polling booth and give a vote; but so long as women may make speeches and canvass electors but not vote, the quiet, typically domestic woman is precluded from the only expression of her political views which would not be repugnant or impossible to her.

It is certainly strange to hear ladies who are foremost in inviting women to organize themselves on this side or that of the greatest constitutional struggle which has taken place during the last two hundred years, gravely asserting, as they do in this protest, that it would be a misfortune to admit women to a share in the ordinary machinery of political life. Women form a part of "the machinery" already; and the very same ladies, or some of them, who depre-cate, in *The Nineteenth Century*, the introduction of women into political con-troversy, are, as presidents and vice-presidents of political associations, urging upon their fellow-countrywomen the duty of mastering difficult and compli-cated political problems, and describing to them how they should organize themselves, and what work they should undertake, with the view of influenc-ing the verdict of the country at the next general election. It would be almost incredible, if it were not true, that some of the very ladies who are working most actively in this way and urging other women to work, assert in this protest that the necessary and normal experience of women "does not and can never provide them with such materials for forming a sound judgment," in questions of grave constitutional change, "as are open to men." The com-parison with men cannot but remind us that, in Lord Tennyson's words, we have for good or ill taken "the suffrage of the plough." The woman house-holder and property-owner, whom it is proposed to enfranchise, need not fear comparison in education, in knowledge, in variety of experience, and generally speaking, in materials for forming a sound judgment in questions involving grave constitutional change, with the vast mass of the newly enfran-chised electors. If personal fitness for the intelligent exercise of the franchise be the main consideration, the women who would be enfranchised cannot be held to be less fit to vote than the chimney-sweeps and labourers who vote already. Not here and there one, but in thousands of cases all over the coun-try, women, as employers of labour, enable a number of men to possess votes, while they, whose education and means of forming a judgment on political questions may be presumed to be superior to that of the men they employ, are precluded from voting. One of the things that recommends women's suf-frage to many minds is the undoubted fact that it would tend to raise the aver-age of intelligence and education among the electorate.

The ladies' protest gives prominence to the fact that women's work for the State is different from that of men, and that many minor differences follow as a natural consequence from the fundamental differences of sex. This dif-ference is one of the strongest claims which women have to representation. If men and women were exactly alike, and thought and felt alike on all sub-jects, if their work in the world were exactly the same, women would not suf-fer, and the State would not suffer, from the non-representation of one part of the homogeneous mass. But being different, that wherein they differ remains unrepresented. It is a loss to the State that women's knowledge of home and domestic life, their experience on such subjects as the care of children and the service of the poor, should not have its weight in influencing the representation of the country and the course of legislation. It is not urged that these things, of which women have a special knowledge, should have a preponderating influence; but if Parliament is to be the mirror of the nation, they should have their place in the representative system. More than one instance could be adduced in which blunders have been made in Parliament because, while the naval, military, banking, agricultural, and other interests were fully and zealously represented, the interests of the home and domestic life were too much forgotten. If every member of Parliament had ten or twelve per cent of women among his constituents he would be much more apt than he is at present to think, when any new bill is placed in his hands, "How will this affect home-life? what will the women in my constituency think of this?"

Equally gratuitous with the assumption that "common-sense" supports the exclusion of a valuable moral force from representation, is the assertion that the demand for women's suffrage proceeds merely from a few women of property who feel themselves aggrieved by the denial of the parliamentary vote. It may be noted in passing that the names of women who live by their work are very scantily represented in *The Nineteenth Century* protest; whilst those who are in ordinary parlance spoken of as working women are conspicuously absent. On the other hand, hundreds of thousands of women, chiefly of the working class, have for years been petitioning Parliament for the suffrage. The largest halls in all the largest towns of the country have been filled to overflowing by women of all classes making the same demand. In working women's clubs the subject of women's suffrage is not much discussed because, to quote one of the members, "you can't discuss when you're all agreed." Large numbers of the poorer classes of professional women, those who maintain themselves by teaching and writing, are warmly in favour of an extension of the suffrage of their own sex. It is desired to speak with all personal respect of the ladies who signed *The Nineteenth Century* protest; they have as great a right to express their opinions as those who disagree with them (that is, if all women are not out of court, because of their alleged "lack of material for forming a sound judgment on questions of grave constitutional change"). But the obvious criticism of the list of names in *The Nineteenth Century* is that they are those of ladies who "have but fed on the roses and lain in the lilies of life."[17] They have been surrounded by every comfort, unpurchased by effort on their part. The names of very many are chiefly known through those of the distinguished men who have fought the battle of life for them. Hardly one has stood alone in the world to "journey her stage and earn her wage" with no one but herself to look to for help. May it not be hoped that these ladies will see that "the materials for forming a sound judgment on this question of grave constitutional change" are more likely to be possessed by those to whom fortune has decreed a less sheltered nook from the storms of life?...

The position of women of the industrial classes is one where the protection of representation would be of special use. Their industrial position is constantly liable to be threatened by hostile legislation. Trades unions are exceedingly and naturally jealous of the competition of women's labour. They are powerfully represented in Parliament, and hardly a session passes without some attempt being made to protect by law the trade interests of men, and to hamper and restrict the industrial employment of women.... If the women were represented as well as the men, attempts to deprive women by law of an honest and healthy way of earning a living would never be made, and, consequently, much friction and mutual anger, always so much to be deprecated between the sexes, would be avoided.

The ladies in *The Nineteenth Century* support their case by stating that "all the principal injustices of the law towards women have been amended by means of the existing constitutional machinery." They may not know that the law still recognises in a mother no legal rights over her children during the lifetime of her husband. A husband may remove his children entirely from their mother, not allowing her even to see them or correspond with them, and this for no moral fault on her part, but just because he chooses to have it so. The inequality of the divorce law is another well-known instance of the cases in which the existing constitutional machinery has remained placidly content with a state of things unjust to women. The inequalities of the law of intestacy, as regards men and women, are so flagrant as to be almost ludicrous. Existing constitutional machinery has arranged that in almost every case of intestacy the male relatives got the lion's share. Thus, if a woman die intestate, all she has, to the exclusion of her children and nearest relatives, goes to her husband. But if a husband die intestate, in no case does his wife inherit all he has. If there are a child or children, two-thirds go to the child or children, and one-third to the wife. If there are no children, but the intestate leaves a wife and a father, they receive half each. If, there are a wife and distant relatives, the wife receives half, and the other half is divided amongst the next-of-kin. If there is a wife and absolutely no other relative whatever, the wife still receives only half, and the other half goes to the Crown.

A similar kind of inequality is maintained as regards probate. A widow has to pay duty on every piece of furniture and every article of plate and jewellery in her house. Every item of her and her husband's common property is assumed by the law to be the property of the husband only, and on passing into possession of it the widow has to pay duty to the uttermost farthing. She is thus frequently called upon to pay duty on articles which she may have bought with her own earnings, or which have been given her by her own relatives. If she is so unwary as to have had a common banking account with her husband standing in his name, she has to pay probate on her own money as well as on his. It is unnecessary to point out that to the whole professional class this necessity of paying probate on what in many cases is the widow's own property, comes at a time when she is impoverished by the death of the chief bread-winner of the family. No such harassing and exacting demands are made upon a man who loses his wife. The assumption of the law is that all their joint property is his only, and he pays no probate on plate, furniture, &c., which they may have worked for and bought together.

It is not, however, denied that some of the most gross of the injustices of the law to women have been remedied during the last ten or twelve years. This has been due in great part to the untiring exertions of the same men and women who are now urging the justice and the expediency of extending the parliamentary suffrage to women. Neither the removal of injustices nor the progress that has been made in the social status of women owe much to the ladies who sign *The Nineteenth Century* protest; but they are kind enough to say that they rejoice in every improvement that has already taken place in the position of women, and they appear to acquiesce in the removal of injustices which have been already removed. But they seem to think improvement may be carried too far.... "The emancipating process has now," they declare, "reached the limits fixed by the physical constitution of women." It is not plain why the recording of a vote for a member of Parliament should be beyond the limits fixed by the physical constitution of women. If women may "nurse the sick and take care of the insane," if they may sit on school boards and on boards of guardians, it is not easy to see why their physical constitution stands in the way of their putting a piece of paper in the ballot box at a parliamentary election. Miss Florence Nightingale, when she went out to the Crimea, had, for several months, ten thousand sick and wounded men under her care. She has been known, in the discharge of her duties, to stand for twenty hours at a stretch. Here was work of which it might, with much plausibility, have been said that it was outside "the limits fixed by the physical constitution of women." And yet it was found that her work was truly womanly, and has had a lasting influence for good on an important department of women's work for all time.

If the extension of the suffrage to duly qualified women is granted, no more will be required of each woman elector in the way of physical or mental effort than is now required of each male elector. In the first place, she will be free to vote or not vote as she chooses. Talk about having the suffrage forced upon her is nonsense. She will not be required to have a complete mastery of finance, or to take the lead and supervision of commerce, or to direct the discipline of the army and navy, or to have mastered the whole of the recent history of British policy in Egypt, South Africa and India. If no men were allowed to vote unless they obtained a pass in all these subjects, the number of electors would be considerably reduced....

Again the ladies say: "We look for the increasing activity of women in that higher state which rests on thought, conscience, and moral influence; but we protest against their admission to direct power in that State which does rest on force—the State in its administrative, military, and financial aspects—where the physical capacity, the accumulated experience and inherited training of men ought to prevail without the harassing interference of those who, though they may be partners with men in debate, can in these matters never be partners with them in action." In the first place it may be pointed out that the distinction sought to be drawn between the State which rests on force, and the State which does not rest on force, is illusory. The ultimate basis of all law is a combination of moral and physical forces. This is as true of the law administered by a school board or a board of guardians as it is of the highest departments of the State. Municipal government, in connection with which women have votes, rests on the police force, and ultimately on the power of demanding military support. Women occupy towards the physical force on which all government rests, exactly the same relation as the great majority of men, that is they help to pay for it. If no man were allowed to vote unless he provided in his own person part of the physical force in which governments, whether municipal or imperial, rest, we should go back to the crudest form of Cæsarism, or government by an armed force. Every man whose age or physical infirmity unfitted him to bear arms would be disfranchised, and of course deprived of all administrative authority. Two-thirds of the statesmen who, at present, on both sides of politics, direct the policy of the country, nearly all the journalists who influence the ultimate decision of the nation as to the peace and war and other great questions of state, would, if the rule laid down by the ladies were made absolute, be excluded from all interference with politics, because their age, physical infirmities, or physical incapacity precluded them from providing in their own persons the physical force by which the decrees of governments are carried out....

There are many assumptions entirely unsupported by facts and experience in *The Nineteenth Century* protest. One is that women, if they vote, must say farewell to that "womanly influence" which is supposed to be such a powerful factor in politics at the present time. Every woman's influence is just so much, making allowance for the factitious influence of rank, as her character entitles her to. If she is courageous, modest, truthful, diligent, sympathetic, and regardful of the rights and interests of others, she will be a power for good in whatever entourage she finds herself. Influence comes from character. Having a vote or not having a vote will not affect "influence," except in so far as it affects character. *The Nineteenth Century* ladies no doubt think that voting in parliamentary elections will lower the character of women, but they by no means prove that this belief is well founded. All experience, as far as it has gone, points in the opposite direction. In those countries in which the course of civilisation has developed and encouraged the independence and emancipation of women, the character of women, and consequently the whole national character, is far higher than in those countries where women have been subjected to more complete political and social subservience. Those who support women's suffrage do so, not in any spirit of vulgar antagonism or rivalry with men; they recognise frankly and fully the differences between men and women; they do not at all wish to see those differences disregarded, least of all do they wish women to cease to be womanly; they do not base the claims of women to representation mainly on the acknowledged injustice of the existing laws to women; but they support it because the experience of other enfranchising acts has shown that the responsibility which goes with the right of voting has a good influence on character; because the exclusion of otherwise qualified citizens from the right of voting on the ground of sex alone, encourages the view that women are not called upon to act or think about the concerns of their country; and because the admission of women to representation is an adjustment of their political status, bringing it into harmony with changes which have already taken place in their social, educational, and industrial status.

[Hundreds of women's names are signed to this petition.]

T. Dundas Pillans

From *Plain Truths About Woman Suffrage*

[London: Watts and Co., 1909]

... The demand of a certain small section of the female population of England for active participation in the government brings us face to face with an entirely novel issue. For the last thirty or forty years it has been hovering in the background, furnishing in the main a ready theme for ridicule, and commonly dismissed with amused contempt. Recently, however, its more extreme advocates have forced upon public attention, if not the consideration of the demand on its merits, at least the extraordinary methods adopted by them to give their cause and themselves notoriety. If in these days the old practical common sense of the British race still prevailed, the antics of the people known as "suffragettes" would be the ruin of their cause. Unhappily, emotion and political hysteria seem in large measure to have taken the place of that ancient virtue. Theatrical demonstrations gain what is denied to reason and justice; and there is therefore a danger that this tremendous innovation may be conceded for the sake of peace and quiet, without any regard to its desirability, or an appreciation of its far-reaching consequences.

The present position of woman in society is not, as is sometimes maintained, due to the despotism of man. It is the inevitable consequence of the natural differences between the sexes. For all practical purposes woman is now what she has been from the remotest antiquity, the receptive sex, as compared with man, the originator. She has exercised an enormous influence in the history of the world, but not as the active partner. It is undoubtedly the fact that men would not have done the great things they have accomplished without the love, the encouragement, the sympathy of women. It is also certain that nothing great would ever have been achieved by the initiative of the female sex. History, indeed, is a record of the actions of men and the influence of women....

Woman possesses some attributes which man lacks, but they are precisely those that disqualify her for government. Woman is emotional, impulsive, impressionable, swayed by personal love—and hate; essentially an advocate rather than a judge, apt to jump at conclusions, deficient in long-sightedness and a capacity for taking broad views on great questions....

The admission of absolute equality between the sexes involves consequences ... far beyond the right to drop a marked paper into a ballot-box. It means the complete readjustment of the relations between men and women.

At present woman occupies a privileged position, on the underlying assumption that she is not the equal of man, but a being whose weakness and frailty demand from him his love, protection, and care....

To be the guardians and instructors of children during their most impressionable years, and thus to be responsible for the formation of the character of future citizens; to be the solace and comfort of men in their strenuous journey through life; to sustain by their love and sympathy the fathers, brothers, and husbands who think it their noblest and highest duty to repay these inestimable services with respect, honour, and protection— surely this is a far higher mission for women than to spout from waggons under the Reformers' Tree and emulate the rowdyism of the hooligan.

As I stated at the outset, history affords us no guidance as to the effects likely to be produced by this unexampled innovation. All we can say is that no great imperial race has ever admitted woman to a direct participation in its government. The State has always been organised, managed, and controlled by men. At the present time no other nation even tolerates the idea of such a revolution. Neither republican America nor monarchical Europe would endure it for a moment.

Is it to be reserved for the British people, that once virile race, to concede a claim based upon a delusion, repugnant to nature, supported by violence, and fatal to the true interests of society?

H.B. SAMUELS

FROM *WOMAN SUFFRAGE: ITS DANGERS AND DELUSIONS*

[London: Published by the author, (1910)]

The Woman Suffrage movement, from having been only a curiosity, has now become a danger. The vast sums of money subscribed by wealthy ladies whose outlook on life is blurred by a false sense of superiority, added to by donations from others whose ambition it is to prove to an uninterested world how essential they are to the world's well-being, have resulted in attracting large numbers of sensitive and impressionable females to the "Cause." Many of them, having no desire or capacity to do anything useful, imagine themselves equal in value and intelligence to the average man. The average man, however, is not impressed, and estimating them at their real value passes by on the other side. These females, fortified by the indisputable fact that sex-inequalities exist everywhere, foolishly assert that a Parliamentary vote would prove a magic wand with which to dispel all the "irksome and irritating" conditions that laws, customs and Nature itself have imposed on womankind....

Anything...that tends to divert and distract the minds of women from their own peculiar and proper work must be detrimental to the best interests of the community. Domestic and household duties, the rearing of children, the care and comfort of the home, the larger tasks of teaching, nursing and training, and many accomplishments which make the sex so companionable, lovable and stimulating—all this makes woman's sphere different to man's, and although these different spheres often overlap they are none the less quite distinct, and should be kept so in the interest of women themselves. The claims put forward by the Woman Suffragists, for equal electoral rights, equal political power—are all based upon a fallacy, the fallacy of supposing that women can govern a State, a Nation and an Empire just as well as men. There could hardly be a greater delusion. Nowhere in the world, at any time, has such an idea, such a claim, been accepted. And England, with all her vast territories, responsibilities, dangers and duties—National and Imperial—should be the last even to dream of admitting to the circle of political power the element of femininity, frailty and faddism....

Women are unfit for political and public work (with few exceptions) through the fact that they are ignorant of and uninterested in National and Imperial questions, and to a great extent ignorant even of municipal affairs and local matters. The contention that, given the vote, women would begin to take an interest in National problems and public affairs is an idle one.

Woman's nature, instincts, desires and natural ambitions, based as they are on physiological sex traits, including the maternal influences, debar her from participating in the work of governing and guarding the State. If women were to study public questions, educate themselves in political matters, engage in agitation and controversy, exercise their minds on problems of National and Imperial importance, offering and exchanging opinions on all sorts of questions of a public nature, all the time and energy involved would be taken from their real work, the work that Nature intended and which all human societies have encouraged—domestic work and the duties of wifehood and motherhood. To argue—as some Suffragists do—that woman is not simply a domestic animal, that to "condemn her to a life of house-work" is degrading, etc., begs the whole question: While homes have to be made and kept and beautified and enlivened, house-work is a necessity, and someone must do it. Clearly, then, the duty devolves upon the wife or daughter or female, as the case may be, whose time would most naturally be taken up in these duties and responsibilities, which are as essential to the well-being of the home and the welfare of the community as work performed by man.

FROM CHAPTER V, "SUPERFLUOUS WOMAN," AND CHAPTER X, "SEX AND POLITICS"

[*Woman Adrift: A Statement of the Case Against Suffragism*. New York: E.P. Dutton and Company, (1912). (Published in England as *Woman Adrift: The Menace of Suffragism*. London: S. Paul, 1912.)]

In the previous chapter it was parenthetically stated that the function of bringing children into the world was the only function which made woman *essential* to the State.

That may seem a very surprising statement to those who have not thought the matter out beyond the "logical" or "democratic" basis of women's claim to vote. But it is strictly true. A modified form of that statement would be, however, of wider truth, and if we say that woman is not essential to the state except in so far as she is essential to the Home we have said all that can be said for woman's essentially necessary place in the social organism.

If we first consider the State as a centralised government, and examine woman's relation to it; and if we then consider the State as limited not only to a centralised executive government, but including also those material and moral activities which make up a modern community of human beings, not touching the family life, we shall see that it is equally true, whether the first limited or the second wider view is taken of what constitutes the State, that woman is wholly superfluous to the State except as a bearer of children and a nursing mother.

It is obvious that the State, considered merely as a government, has no need of woman at all, and that *is* the State into which she wishes to penetrate by the legal key of a vote that will afterwards unlock all other doors. The State does not need woman, first, as soldiers or as sailors, that is for its defence. I need not linger on that proposition, as it expresses a self-evident fact. Nor does the State, considered as government, need women as statesmen, ambassadors, civil servants or police. That statement also is self-evident, for it is the statement of existing fact. And the whole machinery of government could still go on working if the direct calamity that ever could afflict man fell upon him, and woman ceased to be. To give no opportunity for a debating point—or rather to close it right away—I admit it is clear to the lowest intelligence that the State, in such a case, would not need to provide for any remote contingencies, but that is because the function reserved to woman, making her by that alone indispensable to the State, is that she should bear children (although, as we shall later see, maternity serves the family rather than the State just as paternity does). But for the time being, and for the purposes of its current existence, woman could be dispensed with entirely, so far as the State is concerned. That proposition also requires no proof. For as things actually are—save for a few women officials in the central administration— the whole machinery of the State into which some women wish that all women may enter, at the present moment goes on absolutely unimpeded and unassisted by women. There are also women outside the central administration—in the Post Office, for instance, and as workhouse and infirmary officials, and as school teachers. But they are there not because they are *sexually* necessary, and they could be replaced by men to-morrow (with those few exceptions where women are preferable because of the domestic nature of their occupations) without materially affecting the efficient working of the machinery of government—central, subordinate, and local. So that almost at the outset of considering this whole question, we are confronted by the fact that the sphere into which woman wishes to enter is a sphere that has no need of her whatever....

But let us imagine a Parliament returned by the votes of women as well as men; let us further imagine, or realise, that the votes of women would be in a majority. Then let us consider the almost certain contingency that some highly controversial measure (and Heaven knows what acute controversies our national politics might not develop with a female electorate) were passed solely because the votes of women, allied with those of a few men, turned the scale. Can one imagine that laws so passed, forced upon men to their repugnance by women; scrambling through Parliament only by virtue of the female franchise, would command the respect that it is desirable even obnoxious laws should command? To ask the question is to answer it, and there would be no stability in a State in which the distribution of parliamentary power did not correspond with the distribution of that final and effective power in earthly matters, the wills and strength of men.

HEBER L. HART

FROM *WOMAN SUFFRAGE: A NATIONAL DANGER*

[London: P.S. King and Son, 1912 (First published 1909)]

There is undoubtedly something very fascinating in the modern ideal of complete equality between the sexes and the close assimilation of their education, pursuits and habits....

But if the nearer we approach to the realization of the ideal—to the dazzling goal of perfect equality between the sexes—the fewer our numbers become: if the luxury of the complete emancipation of women from the narrow life of the family and the home, can only be attained at the cost of the decline of the race, it must be admitted that there is another side to the question. For it would at least seem matter for regret that the British race should fail before a better is ready to sustain the moral hegemony of the nations.

We ought therefore carefully to consider whether there is in fact good reason for believing that woman suffrage would conduce to a degree of assimilation between the sexes dangerous to the race itself.

At first sight it may appear reasonable to suppose that the enjoyment by a woman of the right of going once in every few years to a polling-booth would have no appreciable effect upon her domestic or social position. The act of voting is transient, and its effect upon the voter impalpable. The possession of the franchise would, however, involve a change in the attitude of women to public life. That many women would desire political offices, and that countless numbers of them would tend more and more to become interested in political affairs, is almost certainly true. The extension of the franchise would, therefore, set up a constant stream of tendency away from family interests and in the direction of a larger public life. The suffrage would be the outward and visible sign that, for the interest of women, the State had become a competitor with the home—that the character of wife, mother, sister, or daughter, was being gradually submerged by that of the citizen.

THE QUESTION OF MILITANCY AND THE HUNGER STRIKE

The advocacy of militant action and its accompanying violence became one of the most controversial issues for women who supported the suffrage cause. Questions were raised within the suffrage movement and by the public at large concerning the justification for and effectiveness of militancy. The Pankhursts' organization, the Women's Social and Political Union (WSPU), used increasingly violent tactics to draw attention to their demands and to further their goal. They believed that years of peaceful effort had achieved nothing, and, because women were excluded from the political process, they really had no constitutional means by which to effect change. Militant women set fires to houses, smashed windows, burned golf greens with acid, blew up fuse boxes, attacked letter boxes, and slashed paintings at art galleries. Women participating in these actions believed that the great anger aroused in the public by their violence against property was proof that the government and the nation had more concern for property than for the rights of women. In contrast to the acts of violence to which men had resorted for centuries to gain their rights, no lives were lost from any of these actions by women.

Over a thousand women involved in protests of various kinds were arrested and sent to prison; many went to Holloway Prison in London. To protest against their arrest and imprisonment as common criminals who were placed in the second or third divisions of prison, rather than getting the better treatment accorded to political prisoners in the first prison division, increasing numbers of women in prison went on hunger strikes. A policy of force-feeding was then enacted in which the hunger strikers were physically restrained and then fed through nasal or stomach tubes. The effect of these feedings was devastating to the health of the women undergoing them, and many suffered life-long physical problems resulting from their prison treatment. To mitigate public criticism for its policy of force-feeding, in 1913 the government passed the Prisoner's Temporary Discharge for Ill-Health Act, popularly known as the Cat and Mouse Act, that allowed hunger strikers to be released from prison until they recovered their health and then to be rearrested and returned to prison to serve the rest of their sentence.

In contrast to the increased militancy of the WSPU, the NUWSS, headed by Millicent Fawcett, remained non-militant in its approach. The NUWSS doubted the efficacy of violence, believing that it created a backlash, turning the public against the women's cause. Fawcett and her organization also believed that women would eventually achieve the vote through peaceful means by working with politicians who were supportive of their goals and by convincing the public at large of the wisdom of enfranchisement. However, despite the decision of the NUWSS not to participate in violence, Fawcett understood the reasons the militants felt justified in using militancy when they had no constitutional means at their disposal to change laws, and she acknowledged the courage of the imprisoned suffragettes.

Figure 6: Cover page of *Votes for Women* V (5 January 1912)

Joan of Arc was an important image for the women's suffrage campaign; Christabel Pankhurst called her the patron saint of Suffragettes.

Teresa Billington-Greig, Emmeline Pethick-Lawrence, and Mona Caird all supported militancy, arguing that earlier, more peaceful methods, such as petitions and speeches, had not been successful. After all the years of trying to work with politicians, the women still did not have the vote. Billington-Greig and Pethick-Lawrence participated in acts of protest for which they were imprisoned. Caird never went to jail, but she was supportive of women's militant actions. In her essays, Elizabeth Robins discusses the use of militancy and the hunger strike and the effect their prison experiences had on women. They were changed in many ways by these experiences. Women emerging from prison realized the indignities and torments to which their government was willing to subject them rather than accord them their basic rights as citizens.

FROM CHAPTER VI: "THE MILITANT SOCIETIES"

[*Women's Suffrage: A Short History of a Great Movement.*
London: T.C. and E.C. Jack, (1912) 58-68]

At the end of 1905 the general public first became aware of a new element in the suffrage movement. The Women's Social and Political Union had been formed by Mrs. and Miss [Christabel] Pankhurst in 1903, but the "militant movement," with which its name will always be associated, had not attracted any public notice till the end of 1905. Its manifestations and multifarious activities have been set forth in detail by Miss Sylvia Pankhurst in a book, and are also so well known from other sources that it is unnecessary to dwell upon them here.[18] It is enough to say that by adopting novel and startling methods not at the outset associated with physical violence or attempts at violence, they succeeded in drawing a far larger amount of public attention to the claims of women to representation than ever had been given to the subject before. These methods were regarded by many suffragists with strong aversion, while others watched them with sympathy and admiration for the courage and self-sacrifice which these new methods involved. It is notorious that differences of method separate people from one another even more acutely than differences of aim. This has been seen in the history of religion as well as in politics:—

"Christians have burnt each other, quite persuaded
That the apostles would have done as they did."

It was a most anxious time for many months when there seemed a danger that the suffrage cause might degenerate into futile quarrelling among suffragists about the respective merits of their different methods, rather than develop into a larger, broader, and more widespread movement. This danger has been happily averted, partly by the good sense of the suffragists of all parties, who held firmly to the sheet anchor of the fact that they were all working for precisely the same thing, the removal of the sex disability in Parliamentary elections, and, therefore, that what united them was more important than that which separated them. The formation of the anti-suffrage societies was also from this point of view most opportune, giving us all an immediate objective. It was obvious to all suffragists that they should turn their artillery on their opponents rather than on each other. Therefore, while recognising fully all the acute differences which must exist between the advocates of revolutionary and constitutional methods, each group went on its own way; and the total result has undoubtedly been an extraordinary growth in the vigour and force of the suffrage movement all over the country. The most satisfactory feature of the situation was that however acute were the differences between the heads of the different societies, the general mass of suffragists throughout the country were loyal to the cause by whomsoever it was represented....

The National Union of Women's Suffrage Societies endeavoured to steer an even keel. They never weakened in their conviction that constitutional agitation was not only right in itself, but would prove far more effective in the long run than any display of physical violence, as a means of converting the electorate, the general public, and, consequently, Parliament and the Government, to a belief in women's suffrage. But the difficulties for a long time were very great. A few of our own members attacked us because we were not militant; others resigned because they disapproved of the militantism which we had repudiated....

Personally it was to myself the most difficult time of my forty years of suffrage work.... I am far from claiming that we actually accomplished the difficult feat of doing what was right, but I believe we tried to. But the brutal severity with which some of the militant suffragists were treated gave suffragists of all parties another subject on which they were in agreement....

The militant societies split into two in 1907, when the Freedom League was formed under the Presidency of Mrs. [Charlotte] Despard. Shortly after this both the militant groups abandoned the plan upon which for the first few years they had worked—that of suffering violence, but using none. Stone-throwing of a not very formidable kind was indulged in, and personal attacks upon Ministers of the Crown were attempted.[19] These new developments necessitated, in the opinion of the National Union of Women's Suffrage Societies, the publication of protests expressing their grave and strong objection to the use of personal violence as a means of political propaganda. These protests were published in November 1908 and October 1909. The second, and shortest, was as follows:—

"That the Council of the National Union of Women's Suffrage Societies strongly condemns the use of violence in political propaganda, and being convinced that the true way of advocating the cause of Women's Suffrage is by energetic, law-abiding propaganda, reaffirms its adherence to constitutional principles, and instructs the Executive Committee and the Societies to communicate this resolution to the Press."

To this was added:—

"That while condemning methods of violence the Council of The N.U.W.S.S. also protests most earnestly against the manner in which the whole Suffrage agitation has been handled by the responsible Government."....

We wanted to show that we could make the grand advance in human freedom, at which we aimed without the display of any kind of violence. We have been disappointed in that ambition, but we may still lay the flattering unction to our souls that the violence offered has not been formidable, and that the fiercest of the suffragettes have been far more ready to suffer pain than to inflict it. What those endured who underwent the hunger strike and the anguish of forcible feeding can hardly be overestimated. Their courage made a very deep impression on the public and touched the imagination of the whole country.

Of course a very different measure is applied to men and women in these matters. Women are expected to be able to bear every kind of injustice without even "a choleric word"; if men riot when they do not get what they want they are leniently judged, and excesses of which they may be guilty are excused in the House of Commons, in the press, and on the bench on the plea of political excitement. Compare the line of the press on the strike riots in Wales and elsewhere with the tone of the same papers on the comparatively infinitesimal degree of violence shown by the militant suffragists. No one has been more severe in his condemnation of militantism than Mr. Churchill,[20] but speaking in the House of Commons in August 8, 1911, about the violent riots in connection with Parliamentary Reform in 1832, he is reported to have said: "It is true there was rioting in 1832, *but the people had no votes then, and had very little choice as to the alternatives they should adopt.*" If this is a good argument, why not extend its application to the militant suffragists?

TERESA BILLINGTON-GREIG

FROM *SUFFRAGIST TACTICS: PAST AND PRESENT* [A PAMPHLET]

[London: Women's Freedom League, (1913).]

When the spirit of revolt among women manifested itself in the political world, it was met by almost universal condemnation. The public, the Press, and the politician united with the older school of Suffragists in indignant and scandalised protest. The little group of rebel women responsible for the new tactics was condemned as a body of hooligans, fanatics, and disreputable notoriety-hunters. Caricature and lampoon greeted their every effort. The attitude of the Press varied from stately and unsparing protest in publications of consequence, through ridicule, misrepresentation and contemptuous familiarity, to gutter abuse. The officials of the orthodox Suffrage Societies hastened to repudiate the rebels anew after every act of rebellion. Sympathetic members of the House of Commons withdrew their support from the principle at stake, such support being based evidently not on conviction, but on an assumed universal pledge of women to behave as good girls. According to the agonised predictions of conventional Suffragists and the jubilant announcements of their foes, the methods of rebellion succeeded in putting back the Suffrage movement at least a couple of hundred years in the space of a few months....

When in 1867 the first organised Women's Suffrage Societies came into existence, they set for themselves the task of securing a parliamentary majority in the House of Commons. By every available method of constitutional agitation they sought to break down prejudice and bring conviction to the individual. The pioneer Suffragists assumed that argument and reason would finally triumph, and strong in this belief, devoted their powers to the presentment of an irrefutable case. During the twenty years in which they were building up the desired majority, they evolved a theory which has done much to prevent the attainment of their end. It might be aptly called the theory of good conduct, for it limited the Suffrage propaganda to the mildest persuasion, the politest and most dignified advocacy, and condemned all warmth, all vigour, all attack as unworthy of the woman's cause....

The policy of pleading for privilege continued for twenty years after events had called for change. The insulted Suffragists clung tenaciously to their doctrine of decorum. At any cost women must preserve their external dignity, and a policy of protest and attack was supposed to be incompatible with it.... As insult after insult was heaped upon them, as year after year they suffered betrayal, the prospects of the statutory recognition of women as citizens surely receded. An agitation without spirit is dead: the public neither knows or cares about it; the politician, measuring it by its capacity to help or punish— by its emotional and voting strength, contemptuously ignores it; prejudice and indifference combine to close against it the great avenues of the Press. A movement that does not resent and punish betrayal is doomed....

But it is not alone by the inadequacy and failure of peaceable methods in the past, and by the demonstrated certainty of their greater failure in the future, that the tactics of rebellion are justified. They are justified also by the history of human liberty as recorded in the chronicles of nations. Every agitation for liberty has won success by revolt and sacrifice. Our own history, from the days of unlimited monarchy until to-day, is a record of rebellions from which liberties have been reaped. The liberty of the subject, liberty of speech, and religious liberty are all harvested from the same field of human labour—the field of revolt. Existing authority has never hastened to extend freedom, and every franchise reform has been preceded by a greater or less degree of organised disorder. The seeker after liberty must suffer for it. We recognise this in reference to the past. Our highest worship is given to those who made the history of the past glorious and became law-breakers for the freedom of the people. That the women who are rebels and law-breakers to-day are carrying on the same fight and suffering for the same human liberty is not recognised. Yet it is folly to condemn in them what is extolled in their prototypes.

EMMELINE PETHICK-LAWRENCE

FROM *THE NEW CRUSADE* [A PAMPHLET]

[London: The National Women's Social and Political Union, (1907)]

[A speech delivered by Mrs. Pethick-Lawrence at Exeter Hall on 30 May 1907.]

The other day I heard of a Boys' School which met to debate the aims and methods of the Women's Social and Political Union; they passed a resolution approving heartily of the methods, but not of the aims of the Society. This verdict pleased us greatly, for it had the charm of novelty.

"Oh yes, I approve of your aims, of course; I have always believed in the justice of the claim that taxation and representation should go together. But I don't approve of your methods, you know: they are unpleasant, they are unladylike; they do more harm than good."

We get a little tired of this sort of thing, we hear it so often. When men say this, we smile. Sometimes they are Members of Parliament, who we know by experience would have preferred to be left alone to forget all about us. But even other men pretend to be shocked sometimes.

They know perfectly well in their own hearts that it is all nonsense, they know that women have at last adopted the only political methods that will win a political victory for those who possess no foothold in the political constitution. You may depend upon it that men's enthusiasm for women's enfranchisement is a very frail and tender growth, if it is chilled by our militant methods. In fact now that we are succeeding so well, the doubters of yesterday begin to affirm that they always knew that women would get the vote if they made a sufficiently loud and determined demand.

We accept the objection of women to our methods much more seriously. We do not expect that women will understand and approve all at once the straight and direct method of winning a concession from an opponent. The direct method is so completely new to them. In the past they have been so hampered and bound by legal and conventional restrictions that, finding direct resistance to opposition useless, they, like any other people in a similar position, have been forced to adopt indirect methods in order to attain their end. Women have been not only individually helpless, but they have been in the past isolated in their respective homes, economically dependent on their respective owners. They have been forced, in the absence of any standing ground of equality as human beings, to fall back upon the only power which they could bring to bear upon men, the power of sex attraction. The use of this power has been developed into an art, with all sorts of refinements and delicate differentiation. Women have learnt to gain their end by flattery and cajolery, by pleading persuasion, by smiles and frowns, by sweet and pleasant manners, by display of personal attractions, by assumption of helplessness and admission of inferiority.

They are now beginning to learn that though the practice of these arts may be potent to win favour from those individuals who come under the spell of their personal fascination, they are of no account whatever in the sphere of political or industrial competition. The game of practical politics is played by another set of rules altogether. Women of spirit and pride welcome the direct methods of striving for their human rights. But the timid say that it does not do for women to use unpleasant and unladylike methods: they are sure to lose by it.

Lose what? Lose the approval of men, the smile and favour of the social world?

Yes, we know that we lose that. Women who work for women politically, lose socially; women who work for men politically do not lose socially. We lose more than that, for we recognise the law of life which decrees that no new extension of life can be purchased for the human race except by those who are content to lay down their personal life to gain it. It may be that some of these women who are not prepared to join us or to help us, though they want the end for which we are striving, have come into this hall tonight. If there is one such here, I would say "My dear madam, are you not like the little boy who, when asked what he would wish to be when he was a man, replied 'A missionary—at least, I mean, a *returned* missionary;' certain pictures of cannibal feasts had put him off the methods of a missionary's career, without destroying his ultimate ambition. Like many older people, he preferred the verb *achieve* to have one tense only, and that the perfect tense."

You would like to have the vote. You would like, as a woman, to have the dignity and honour that only free citizenship in the State can give, but you are not prepared to pay one jot of the price! But you who approve of our aims and not of our methods do not see that in politics, as in every department of life, people who want to succeed and to win have to "play the game." We have not invented the game. We have to take it as we find it. We have to understand its rules and play as other people play. Practical politics is a game. We women do not make it, we take it as we find it. The rules of the game are that those who want any reform carried must make as much noise as they can, must hit as hard as they can, and must bring as much pressure as they can to bear on the Government which is in power, for the Government is a machine which can only act under pressure. The worst Government is that which does not respond to any pressure until it becomes a danger and a menace.

I want to ask the fathers and mothers here a question. "If you had two babies and they both awoke together in the night at the hour when they are accustomed to receive refreshment, and one of them lay smiling and contentedly sucking its thumb, and the other began to scream loud enough to wake up the whole house, which of these babies would you attend to first?" (laughter). I see there is no hesitation in your minds about the answer. You would go to the one that was making the most noise.

But what about your theories of patience and good temper that should be rewarded, and all that sort of thing? Well, they are forgotten at the moment in the desire to stop that child's mouth; so you see that even human fathers and mothers are to a certain extent machines that act under pressure. Is it any wonder, then, that a Government is a machine that acts under pressure? Then the Government is in a much worse position than you could be as parents of two children simultaneously demanding your attention, for the Government has more than two children; it has any number, and they are all crying for its attention, and all these babies except one are screaming through a megaphone, for you know the ballot box is a megaphone which lends volume and significance to quite a small cry, whereas we women have no megaphone. We cannot cry through a ballot box, therefore we have to make it up by exercising our own lungs to the fullest possible extent. That is our only hope of getting any attention at all. It would be of no use for us to wait patiently until all the others were attended to, for long before then the poor old paternal Government will have tumbled back into bed and have gone to sleep, quite worn out with its exertions....

I have been talking about playing a game, but I also have something to say to-night about fighting the fight. You know the two things are very closely connected. A battle is a game, and most games are mimic battles. The soldier, at the moment when he is under fire, thinks of little beside the game, and how best to play it, but, behind the confusion of the battlefield, where, for the moment, everything seems given over to violence and strife and death, there are great causes and great ideals, and the dearest faiths of a nation.

So it is with the women's movement, and in the din and strife of strenuous political warfare we women realise the greatness of the cause for which we are fighting. There are great forces behind this movement—forces of nature, forces of destiny, forces of divine and human will. There are great ideals—the old ideal of human and civic freedom which has fashioned the modern world, freedom which is as dear to women as it has been to men in the past, freedom for which, if men now wish it, women can die as men themselves have died in the past, with women to console them and women to mourn for them. There is a great faith behind it, faith in the future, faith in the possibilities of race evolution, when women have won the right to their own bodies and souls, when they no longer have to sell themselves for bread, either in the city streets or in the economic-marriage market, when, as citizens, economically, politically and intellectually free, they can join together with men in building up a more perfect human race, and can help to make and mould the human world in which their children have to go out and live.

There are forces behind this movement of which the politician has no conception, which he has never for one moment taken into account; forces which are bound to sweep away all resistance. You cannot stop the awakening of the soul of women. I have called our movement a great fight; I go further and call it a great crusade. "But," you say, "the crusaders wore as their sign and symbol a cross. Do you claim that you are soldiers of the cross?" We do.

Evolution means conflict. When a great new ideal is born into the world, it runs counter to the whole conception of life which has been accepted by the world. The new ideal crosses the old conception. And this is the Cross upon which the regenerators of Humanity are crucified. They are sustained by the vision of the Future, for they know that by their pain and shame they pay down the price of a new redemption of Mankind.

The new conception of life which has been given to us is that of the woman, possessor of her own body and soul, free from degrading servitude, and also from ignoble exemptions from honourable service, free to develop within herself the thought and purpose of her Maker, unsubservient to the will or desire of man, responsible for the conditions of the human world in which she lives, and responsible for the future generation. This new ideal is not only the cross, it is also the sword. "I came not to bring peace on earth, but a sword."[21] This word, spoken by the Prince of Peace, is one of the great paradoxes of which life is full.

I call upon the men and women here to-night, those who have vision, to take up the cross, to grasp the sword of this new conception, and with it to wage holy warfare against prejudice and custom, and the instinct of dominance, which enforce bondage and hold the woman's body and soul in subjection, and thus crush out the possibilities of race evolution. Come and join our crusade. You do not know, if you have never tried, the wonderful worth and dignity which participation in such a movement as this will lend to your personal life.

I appeal to the men and women here. I appeal first to the men, you who love the freedom which your fathers won for you; pay your debt to your forebears by winning freedom for your daughters. I have spoken of warfare, but this crusade is no sex war. The best men are on our side, and every woman who joins us brings one man at least to take his stand beside her. I am not going to tell the men here how they are to help us. Men, by their work and vote, have freed the slaves in the past, have emancipated the working-man, have saved the little children from commercial servitude, and they can free the women of this country if they will, and they will know the best way to set about the business.

I appeal especially to the women here. I can tell them just what they ought to do. Every woman, loyal and self-respecting, and worthy of her womanhood, must be with us out and out. I appeal to you to join our Union. Can you speak? Can you organize? Are you inventive and resourceful? Come, then, and help us. Come and teach us. The work is so great and so growing, we are desperately in need of more good speakers, good organisers, inventive and resourceful initiators. Do you say, "I have no gifts, I cannot organize, I cannot speak, I cannot do anything!" Come and join us; we will teach you. We will organise your work, and develop in you some gift. We need you badly. At the present moment we can organise the services of hundreds of women just like you. Send your name to-night or to-morrow to the Honorary Secretary, Women's Social and Political Union, 4 Clement's Inn. You will soon see how much help you can give us. If you have an influential position, socially or professionally, we want you. If you have much to lose by joining our movement, you should be happy, for that means that you have much to give. If you are a working woman, burdened with incessant labours and manifold cares, we want you. We want you specially; it is your sympathy we crave most of all, for it is your battle essentially that is now being fought. If you are a woman we want you, and want what you have to give—time, service, heart, everything.

I also appeal to all men and women who are with us to generously support this movement with money. I am never afraid to ask for money. I know both how much and how little money can do, of how much and of how little value it can be. I know that where the spirit is, there it will draw to itself the material. I know that money will come. Money that represents enthusiasm, self-sacrifice and devotion. That is the money we want. When I came into this movement a year ago, there was no money at all. There was not a penny to hand over to me as treasurer. There was love, devotion and self-sacrifice. Bills were paid out of the personal savings of half a dozen women dependent upon their own work for their livelihood. Since then money has come in and money has been spent to the sum of nearly £3,000, as you may see in the first year's Report of the Union.

The movement will still go on, with or without money. A year ago I found the leaders of this Union coining their very flesh and blood. They are still prepared to do it, I know. There are more ways than one of laying down one's life. But I say to you men and women that we dare not allow it. We cannot afford it. We shall want our leaders more than ever when the vote is won, for then the real work of this Union will begin. You must do your part. Money must be forthcoming to do the work of money and human flesh, and blood and spirit will do the work that no other power can accomplish.

To win this great reform, there must be a great national agitation, as great as any national campaign that has ever been fought in the past. Hundreds of thousands of pounds were raised as a campaign fund by the men who brought about the repeal of the Corn Laws.[22] Great sacrifices were made by men and women who took their political and moral faith seriously. The emancipation of the slaves in our own Colonies cost several millions of pounds. The emancipation of the women of our own race and country is worth more than can be expressed in terms of finance.

We must go into every town and village in the land if possible, and preach to the women there the word of freedom, and bid them rise up now and work out their own salvation.

Railway fares are amongst those things that cannot be paid for in flesh and blood, or spirit, but must be paid for in hard cash. Halls must be taken for public meetings. At every bye-election, the women's cause must be kept to the front. The electorate must be educated by letters and circulars sent through the post. This national propaganda work must be supported by a National Fund. You may depend upon it that in this Union not a penny is wasted. Women know how to economize. They know how to make a pound do the work of twenty shillings, and a little more.

Our greatest asset is the inspiration, the love, the courage and devotion of the women who are in the forefront of this movement. Is there anyone who says: "I care very much for this question and I wish I could help, but I am really not in a position to give anything towards its support." Well, then I say: "Sir or Madam, you never cared for anybody or anything in this world, otherwise you would know that love must give, love cannot help giving; it is the very law of its being. If you care, you must give."

It is because we count upon the true heart of the people of this country that we boldly and confidently ask for the sum of £20,000 for this great national campaign. We ask for 10,000 names of men and women who will give a pound a year until women are enfranchised, and we ask those who can give larger sums to raise the remaining £10,000 between them. Help us to fight this great crusade. We go forward into the future with glad heart, regardless of opposition, violence, imprisonment. Victory is assured, for ultimately Truth prevails.

Mona Caird

"Militant Tactics and Woman's Suffrage"

[*Westminster Review* 170 (November 1908): 525-30]

We are assured on all hands that the actions of the militant suffragists have betrayed to an outraged world, the inherent and Heaven-inflicted unsuitability of women for the franchise, a privilege (it may be remarked in passing) not denied to duly qualified men, though in the earlier stages of intoxication.

The test of "suitability" seems to differ largely for the two sexes.

The Militants, we are told, have damaged their own cause past redemption.

Well, that is a matter of opinion.

A few years ago the claims of women were so loftily let alone that few people bestowed on them more than a languid smile or hoary jest. Now the subject is on every lip; and while smiles and witticisms have remarkably quickened in pace and frequency, if not in quality, we now have angry invective and insult, and finally organized opposition— as evidenced by the Anti-Suffrage League—to show that the question is no longer merely "speculative," but is practical enough to stir up all the sediment of prehistoric prejudice, or (not to beg the question) has roused opponents to a sense of impending national danger—as they deem it. And the national danger is that the right to a voice in the representation of the country may no longer be refused to women who have to obey the laws, to endure punishment if they break them, and—as a neat finish to the irony of the situation—to help to pay for the infliction of that very punishment on themselves, be it what it may!

Looking back, in the light of history, to the quiet old days of wit and smiles, does it really seem that militant suffragism has very seriously set back the hands of the clock?

It is not necessary to see eye to eye with the Militants in all their forms of warfare in order to recognise that their tactics have brought the question out of the intermediate (and necessary) intellectual stage to that of "practical politics," with which, of course, intellect has little to do!

It is surely largely a consequence of the nature of "practical politics" that in this later stage of the movement (as in all movements as far as we have yet gone) the methods required to bring the matter home to the general public are crude and disagreeable, irritating to the authorities, shocking to our susceptibilities (when women are the agitators), and painful—to put it mildly— to those who have to use them!

"If only women would stick to constitutional methods!" Well, in the good old times, about two years ago, women did most energetically stick to constitutional methods, but nobody then assured them that because of that dutiful conduct they would be listened to. On the contrary they were told that there was no evidence that their sex wanted the vote. "Those that ask shan't have, and those that don't ask, don't want," is the principle on which the matter has been hitherto treated.

The older established suffrage societies, it must be remembered do still stick to constitutional methods, holding to their faith (after forty or fifty years of steady agitation) that men *will* eventually listen to reason and justice without having anything political to gain by consent or to lose by refusal.

It is an attitude of mind which appeals to the sympathies and represents the methods by which one would like to see, and always hoped to see, the woman's cause victorious.

Such a point of view and such a hope ought to be powerfully represented by large societies. But it is idle to deny (be one's opinion of militancy what it may) that these later methods have brought the subject into the realm of immediate politics. *After* that has been achieved, the chance of successfully pressing the claim by the old constitutional means, is, of course, greatly increased, and the highly constitutional society represented by Mrs. Fawcett and Lady Frances Balfour[23] is leaving no stone unturned to do this.

Yet Mr. Asquith[24] refuses to receive *their* deputations with the same quiet persistence with which he refuses to receive their militant sisters—those much decried "suffragettes" who have done such unspeakable things that their male rulers have had to break their own august laws and to institute new legal precedents in order adequately to punish them!

If any one doubts the importance, nay, the dire necessity of the franchise as a mere safeguard of the most elementary rights, surely the astounding spectacle of a Liberal Government acquiescing in if not directly ordaining the treatment of political offenders as common criminals, is enough to convince the slowest of minds and the deadest of consciences.

Not only must women obey and suffer under laws which they have no voice in making, but they are not even secure in the enjoyment of such small benefits as those laws accord them! Legislators, if irritated, do not hesitate, it would appear, to set aside their own edicts in order to punish feminine offenders with illegal severity!

The temper which actuates many of these arbiters of our destiny is not exactly judicial! When the women in the recent arrests—braving a cruel ordeal in devotion to a principle—were sentenced to suffer as if they were common street-brawlers, I heard a Justice of the Peace exclaim gleefully, "Well, I hope *that*'ll bring 'em to their senses!"

What has become of the boasted liberty and security of the British subject? Even the liberties of men are threatened, for such precedents are never without progeny. What becomes of our famous "Constitution" which indeed now seems to exist mainly for purposes of moral coercion to be directed against those who plead for their rights?

Are these things to go on in England without let or hindrance because the victims belong to the politically helpless half of the community?

There would be nothing inconsistent in the most bitter enemy of the Suffrage denouncing such an outrage against the letter and the spirit of English institutions. Surely one need not share the views of the victims of an outrage before protesting against it.

Are English institutions to be set at naught in order to subject a few offending women to bitter punishment and indignity? It seems a strange way of showing a "divine right" to exclusive political power.

Yet many people are still sure that women do not "need the vote." Do those persons know that if it had not been for the desperate efforts and life-long work of such women as Mrs. Wolstenholm Elmy[25] and other much-decried champions of their sex, a man would still have the right to leave the guardianship of his children away from their mother (no matter how admirable the mother) and to place it in the hands of some one entirely distasteful and repugnant to her? Even now, though the mother, through the woman's movement, has acquired the right to appoint a guardian to act with the father after her death, "the Court (to quote Miss Christabel Pankhurst's history of the movement) will not confirm this unless the father be shown to be unfit to have the sole care of his children." Moreover, "the father, during his lifetime, has still the sole right to decide as to the children's education, religion and place of residence. A mother has no right to the custody of her children. Her husband can separate them from her altogether, and the law will only help her to rejoin them if it can be proved that they have suffered severe physical or mental injury from the father's treatment or if his conduct has been such as to entitle her to a separation."

Such concessions as we are now enjoying were admitted into the Statute Book only after weary years of struggle on the part of many of our best and ablest women, and it is them we have to thank for the fact that in the Custody of Infants Act, "some regard" is directed to be paid to "the wishes of the mother, as well as of the father." That idea was brand-new to our legislators, and produced fiery controversies, many regarding it as a most subversive and dangerous innovation. Yet the Anti-Suffrage League unhesitatingly proclaims that it is for men to legislate and for women to obey.

Hampered politically, socially, as they are, this luckless sex is further enjoined to eschew all but strictly constitutional means in their agitation, lest perchance their example might incite others to similar—or rather, to really violent measures.

Not only are they handcuffed by their voteless position, but they must not try to free themselves from the handcuffs by moving so much as a little finger "unconstitutionally"—bound over to this inaction by an appeal to their natural reluctance to start a dangerous precedent. Surely this is carrying the time-honoured system of combined legal and moral coercion a little too far! It is for the State which refuses legitimate means of expression to consider the possible consequences of such a policy.

When women possess full human and civic rights, they may justly be called upon (in common with other possessors of such rights) to confine themselves to constitutional measures, but since quiet appeals of forty or fifty years' duration failed to obtain a hearing, it can hardly be said that constitutional measures of any efficacy are really open to them. If men think otherwise it is for them to prove it. Certainly it would be pleasanter for women to adopt more feminine tactics. They do not voluntarily expose themselves to insult and incur punishments such as are now meted out to them—solitary confinement, for instance, which is known to break down the stoutest nerves, and if prolonged, to destroy the reason—merely for fun.

There are indeed few roads in the realms open to women that lead to Rome, and if they want to get there they cannot very fastidiciously [*sic*] pick and choose their route. They are, as it were, running round the circumference of a "vicious circle." Not having the vote (and the position it implies) they cannot get the vote; and they may not ask for it in a manner to command a hearing, because that is unconstitutional. What are they to do?

I do not venture to assert absolutely that there may not be some long and weary way of avoiding both horns of the dilemma—but such an alternative is very hard to find, especially in view of the recent behaviour of a Liberal Government, and it is preposterously unfair to condemn these women, who, not being able to find it, and not believing in its existence, are taking what they deem to be the one and only means of righting a great wrong, a means involving extremely painful sacrifices for themselves.

It is sad to find the English sense of fair play so little awake to the truly ridiculous injustice of such condemnation.

How would a man, convinced as these women are convinced, act in such a dilemma? Let reasonable and just men (and women) ask themselves that question. It sounds very fine and substantial to talk about constitutional means. But in this case it is very much like telling a prisoner to escape from his dungeon without breaking the prison rules.

Or—to take another figure—it is analogous to insisting on a man's presenting his case in a language which he is forcibly prevented from acquiring, all other languages being objected to on the ground of illegality.

A State which refuses the ordinary constitutional means of expression and self-defence to half its members must not be surprised if sooner or later they resort to unauthorized ones. History teems with instances of this fact.

As for the accusations of interfering with freedom of debate and the lack of a sense of fair play evinced by militant suffragists, surely there is a curious mental confusion here!

Without necessarily approving of all the militant tactics employed or even in the case of entirely disapproving of them, we might none the less clearly see the illogical unfairness of their opponents' criticism. For women are, politically speaking, out-laws, not perhaps in the ordinary sense of that word, but in the sense of being denied the full privileges of their state and era. Therefore it is impossible justly to judge their actions on the same lines as we should be justified in judging those of the enfranchised who employed similar tactics. The cases do not run on all fours.

In the games of Englishmen which are quoted as a reproachful example to suffragists, the players, be it noted, are *equally subject to the rules of the game, and share equally in its rights and privileges.* But what if one half of the players be hopelessly handicapped, manacled and tethered; denied bat and ball and other necessaries of the contest; bound by a set of severe restrictions *applying only to them,* while the other players need not observe the rules, except amongst themselves, breaking them at will should they happen to feel annoyed and the rules to offer some protection to the manacled group?

Suppose now that this group makes a struggle for freedom, in spite of all the desperate odds against them, and that one or two manage to cause some trouble and inconvenience to their masters? An indignant yell from these astonished masters of "Play the game, play fair" would be apt to rouse a shout of laughter were it not that they and their subordinates are so accustomed to the relationship that neither group—not even the subordinates—realize how supremely ridiculous the whole situation is! It would take the cynical keenness of a La Fontaine or an Æsop[26] to fully enjoy its savour!

A call for "play fair" from those who have denied to women the elementary rights of citizenship in a representative state—a call by men from the loftiest heights of masculine superiority, addressed in all solemnity to their immemorial victims in the Game of Life—! truly that is a spectacle to rouse the inextinguishable laughter of the Gods.

But alas! When all that it implies, in its full and cruel significance, all the suffering and injustice and indignity of which it is the outward and visible sign, for so many centuries, is even faintly realised, it is also a spectacle to move the least pitiful of mortals to inextinguishable tears!

Elizabeth Robins

From Chapter IX, "The Hunger Strike"

[*Way Stations*. London, New York, and Toronto: Hodder and Stoughton, 1913. First published as a letter in the *Westminster Gazette* (21 July 1909).]

Sir,

Without going into the question of the lawfulness or the unlawfulness of the actions of the militant Suffragettes (about which even the Doctors of the Law appear to disagree), I would like, as dispassionately as possible, to draw attention to a factor in the case not yet touched upon, not even recognised.

I would first of all remind you that, for several years, women have endured for their political opinion's sake such treatment as is meted out to drunkards and to thieves. Suffragettes have endured this for a cause which has been before the country for forty years, a cause to which 420 members of the present Parliament have given their adhesion, a cause of which a majority of the present Cabinet are in favour. Now, if the traditional avenue through which voteless citizens can carry a grievance (the orderly petitioning of the King's representative)—if that be barred, what are voteless citizens to do?

If they are men, their practice has been either to make the general public suffer for its apathy (by burning down buildings and by indiscriminate bloodshed), or else they have made their opponents suffer in prison.

The women's way has all along been to take the brunt of the suffering upon themselves.

It is this difference which has blinded many men to the force that lies behind the woman's movement. It has led responsible officials to jeer at a "policy of pinpricks," and to speak with pride of the way in which men forced the door "at which the ladies are scratching."....

I find that no one thing so divides the world as the opinion as to how much may be expected from self-interest. To discover that certain people are ready to lay down what most regard as of paramount importance, that is perplexing enough. Though the story of human fortitude is older than any history that is written in any book, the fortitude that will go any length still wears to the average mortal an air so strange that it runs the risk of not being recognised. Now, Sir, my point is that these women know that. They undertake their "hunger strike" realising that it will be supposed they will not go so far with it as to do themselves mortal injury. They know the supposition will be that they are trying merely to frighten authority, and that they will prudently stop this side of a course that will bring them a release for which neither the Home Secretary's order, nor that of the King, will be needed.

There are, without doubt, persons so angered against the Suffragettes as to say, "Very well; let them expiate their foolishness with their lives."

But that will not be the public view of the matter. Nor will it be the (intended) policy of the Government. It therefore seems necessary to say that in dealing with these women it will not do to count upon the usual canons of self-interest. There are those (whether among the Suffragettes now in Holloway or the thousands outside)—there are those prepared to pay any price that may be exacted for protesting against more women being made to suffer the indignities of the Second or Third Division—for what? For following to its logical conclusion an opinion they share with the majority of the legislators of this country. The prisoners know quite well how it may end for any one of them. The people who are not fully informed are those whom the country will hold responsible for the issue. And that seems to me not fair. There should be no avoidable misunderstanding as to the spirit (however reprehensible) in which the "Hunger Strike" is undertaken. The women are laying hands upon a very terrible weapon, but there is no ground for hoping that, if they let it fall, others will not take the weapon up. That this should be so may be fanaticism. But it is also hard fact. Calling it names, good or bad, will not alter it.

I know it is said that if the authorities do not deal stringently with these cases general disorder will ensue in England; and everyone hereafter who has a grievance will think he has only to break a few windows and gather a crowd in Westminster to get his will. But that is childishness. "Anyone" with a grievance hereafter who can get thousands of reputable people to espouse his cause, hundreds to go to prison for it, and the general public to give him fifty thousand pounds a year to spend on it, will have reason to be listened to. No cause is fed so fat on air.

But my aim, Sir, in addressing you, is to prevent anyone's having a right, when one of these women succumbs in Holloway Gaol, to call the occurrence "death by misadventure." It will be no accident. But for the Government it would be a misadventure which even their opponents would gladly see them spared, if one of these women (with the memory of the smiling Members of Parliament out for "fun," to see how women meet the nerveshattering horror of a contest with mounted police)—if, with that memory to nerve her, one of these prisoners forces the gates of Holloway and sets out upon the Great Adventure which even heroes evade as long as they may with honour.

I am, Sir, yours truly,

Elizabeth Robins.

Henfield, Sussex, July 21, 1909.

ELIZABETH ROBINS

"IN CONCLUSION"

[*Way Stations*. London, New York, and Toronto: Hodder and Stoughton, 1913. First printed in *McClure's Magazine* (March 1913) under the title "Woman's War."]

The later history of the Women's Movement will be more readily recalled than the circumstances I have set down, circumstances which furnish the key to more recent happenings.

Unprejudiced minds will have noted how women passed from stage to stage, trying all peaceful measures, trying them over and over with a persistence and a hopefulness that in the retrospect moves us to marvel not that some women sometimes showed impatience, but that so many for so long repressed impatience.[27]

And what, finally, has been the effect alike of patience and impatience?

The vote is not yet won. It is irrevocably coming, as its opponents know and frequently admit. In despair at relinquishing their hope to do more than delay Woman Suffrage for a space, the Antis are filling the void with Cassandra-prophecies of the evils that Suffrage will bring. They point to manifestations which Militancy has made common among women as heralds of the bitter days to be.

We do not deny that women are changed. They are more changed than their critics know.

Let us consider some of the more obvious changes wrought by Militancy, first upon the individual, and second upon the generality.

Take the effect upon individual women. These years of conflict—of severance from friends, of brutalities suffered in the streets and at public meetings, of torture undergone in prison—have for their immediate effect upon the individual the strengthening of many a soul and the shattering of a good many bodies. In addition to this, some observers think they see the marks of the long strain upon the public policy of individual women in the movement and in the private relationships between certain of the workers.

To have escaped some such result of a struggle so protracted and kept at so high pitch, women must needs have ceased being human. Admittedly, the opponents of Woman Suffrage have never been able so to hamper our advance as have other Suffragists—whether by leading a section of the forces off the main route, or by standing neutral at some crisis when not to be for was to be against. This is not an experience peculiar to women's parties. Nor

VOL. III. (New Series), No. 99.   FRIDAY, JANUARY 28, 1910.   Price 1d. Weekly. (Post Free 1½d.)

THE GOVERNMENT'S METHODS OF BARBARISM.

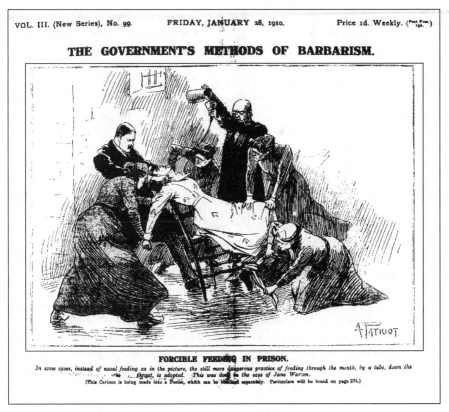

FORCIBLE FEEDING IN PRISON.

In some cases, instead of nasal feeding, as in the picture, the still more dangerous practice of feeding through the mouth, by a tube, down the throat, is adopted. This was done in the case of Jane Warton.

(This Cartoon is being made into a Poster, which can be obtained separately. Particulars will be found on page 274.)

Figure 7: The Government's Methods of Barbarism
Forcible Feeding in Prison.
From *Votes for Women* III (28 January 1910)

In some cases, instead of nasal feeding, as in the picture, the still more dangerous practice of feeding through the mouth, by a tube, down the throat, is adopted. This was done in the case of Jane Warton.

for the first time in the history of political movements have these errors been encouraged or instigated by the enemy. For an ally to take the wrong road in all good faith, or for conscientious Doubt to call a halt (Doubt full as honest as the Conviction that cried "on")—incidents such as these could, at their worst, only complicate and momentarily hamper the campaign. The *morale* of the Woman's Movement could be affected only by the setting in opposition forces which had been fighting for the same end. To do this has always been a highly effectual tactic on the part of a common enemy—the more effectual, perhaps, when employed by men against the subtler forces of women in revolt than in conflicts between men.

When the present First Lord of the Admiralty was Home Secretary[28] he unfolded to a soldier-friend his difficulty in dealing with the Militants, and told of precautions he was taking for the future—extra police protection and severities of sorts. The soldier shook his head. "You will never make a success," he said, "of setting men to fight women." This theory was turned into visible practice when it was so ably supported by the strategist of the Cabinet, the "Suffragist" Minister[29] who drove the wedge of discord into the compact body of Suffragist support to the Conciliation Bill of 1910.

But if what has befallen men's parties, time after time, befalls women's also—what then?

What if that close union within the Union is dissolved? We would rather the dissolution had never come, or had come after the vote was won. Yet who shall feel sure that the purpose for which the association was formed had not already been accomplished? Its true mission was the Awakening of Women. Not solely to get them votes, but to make them realise the power resident in the vote; and the woman's need (man's need as well) that women should exercise that power. Touched by the pathetic fear of the Anti that Woman Suffrage spells chaos and old England's Doom, instead of her Regeneration, Suffragists of the "soothing" sort have been known to point to places where giving the vote to women has "made no perceptible difference." If such comfort is not illusory, it is a shame to any land of which it could be justly said. It is a shame to the women of that land—a proof that they are unfaithful stewards of their trust, or that even more needful than we knew was the fuller enlightenment the Militants have won.

Had the Powers That Be as much foresight as they have inflexibility, they would have granted a meagre instalment of Woman Suffrage as soon as the demand became earnest. Deprived of the main ground of complaint (since the principle would have conceded), the majority even of enfranchised women would have looked upon the vote with so little realisation of its power, that the weapon might have lain in their hands, little used, perhaps for a generation.

The longer all the women in the country are denied a vote, the wider must be the door which ultimately admits them, and the greater the changes which their entrance on the scene will effect. Meanwhile, they have learned from the repressive measures of those who would keep them out, more than ever the Suffrage leaders could teach them.

As I have admitted, those who cry, that Militancy has left its mark on women, are right. So far as concerns the active Militants themselves, we have seen that women who were so concerned to know that Government offices were empty before they sent stones through the windows in June, were less concerned in November for the bodily safety of those within. Why was that? Not solely because women *en bloc* are very much like men *en bloc*, nor merely because all women will not turn the other cheek any more than will all men.

The consideration that urged on the Militants in November, was that the officials nominally behind Government windows were found to be in no danger so great as the danger of remaining indifferent to, or ignorant of, their non-performance of public duty. No public servant, however unfaithful, had suffered, or was likely to suffer, as scores of women had been made to suffer. We do not deny that the earlier concern for the bodily safety of officials became secondary to a concern for Suffragists, after seeing them come out of prison sick and broken from the disgusting struggle with prison authority armed with hose-pipes and unclean nasal-tubes.

Each individual woman who went through the horror of such experience became a centre of enlightenment for all whom she might thereafter reach. Never again for her, or for her friends, any cobweb left of that old illusion as to the chivalry of the average official. This and this "they did to me rather than admit my purpose honest, rather than treat me as decently as they treat men convicted of the baser crimes."

Is it rational to expect these experiences to leave a woman unchanged? If she were to remain unchanged, would she not prove herself more insensate than the brutes?

People who would insist that such things shall leave a woman unmoved are not merely those who would deny her right to the ballot. They would deny her right to the feelings of a human being.

A great deal of water will flow under Westminster Bridge before women forget what men were willing to see them suffer rather than see them voters; before they forget the forbearance shown to malcontents in Ulster and at Tonypandy, as contrasted with the brutality shown malcontents at Wrexham and Llanistumdwy. Much as we desire to see understanding and goodwill between the sexes—do we *want* women to forget these lessons?

Let us be frank about this.

Let us recognise that many a woman who took no part in it owes to the public struggle her first knowledge of those struggles, carried on for ages, out of the public eye. This dear-bought knowledge has changed the intellectual outlook on the world for many a woman who has no fault to find with her own individual lot, nor with the attitude towards herself of the men she has known best. The first shrinking realisation of what kind of a world this is to tens of thousands of women has brought many a happy and peace-loving soul to wonder whether the fiery ordeal in the open, and the lonely battle in the gaols, may not have been needed to set free the spirit of a sex limited for ages to those small garden plots of life—to stray outside which was to fall upon dishonour.

The most ardent pacifist will hesitate to deny the truth of that militant saying: "Few of us believe in peace at any price." Who, seeing a little child attacked or in need of protection from violence, who of us would withhold help, even if help (to effect its end) involved our using physical force? Tolstoy told a private friend that even in such a case he would refrain. Few other men, I think, and few women.

Those who thought it permissible only in men to defy tyranny, had said that nothing but evil could come of women's expressing moral indignation with all their might, and as variously as men have done, at every crisis in history. Only evil could come of it? One of the best things in civilisation has come of it. Proof of moral and physical courage in women not as a rare exception, here or there, at call of motherhood, or of any personal devotion, but as a basis in character, to be looked for, counted on.

The militant campaign has not yet won votes? No. But the Militants have campaigned to such purpose that there are to-day more free women in England than anywhere in the world—free with a freedom of which the ballot will be a symbol, but which the ballot cannot in itself endue with the essence of liberty, or charge with effective authority.

Those who have watched the chains fall off from one after another during these last half-dozen years will understand. Persons from whom these moral and spiritual experiences have been hidden may allow me, in a page or two, to illustrate what has been happening.

One object-lesson came at a time of such need that, if it can be passed on faithfully enough, it may hearten others.

At perhaps the most crucial hour in the history of women's struggle for the vote, certain politicians from whom better things were expected had made a grave mistake—through lack of information, as some women believed. How to bring that information home was the concern of those who (in face of some evidence to the contrary) held to their faith in men's fundamental fairness. Those who spend their lives in the House of Commons could not get this information there. And, at the time I speak of, they could not get such information from the Press, since, owing to the tension, that often open door was closed. Word was brought of letters to the more influential papers being refused, or held back till they were useless.

To a woman lying ill came an appeal that she should set down a statement of how the matter looked to a suffragist. The first impulse to call such an undertaking impossible was repressed. An article, destined for an editor wideminded, chivalrous, was written—at what cost need not be insisted on. Time was the great factor. The editor had telegraphed he would reserve space. The article was finished; but it might be thought too long, or in some detail need revision. The writer left her bed and took the article to London.

She found the editor genial and serene, even a little jocular on the score of "the eternal theme." He read the first paragraph, and under the eyes of his old contributor became a stranger—a man she had not only never seen before, but never guessed at. What he said was less illuminating than what he looked.

What! to want to talk about the motive behind deeds that called for nothing but wholesale condemnation? "And this ... this stone-throwing! *You* justify...!"

"I explain it," she answered.

"Isn't it possible for you to understand? An article like this would bring down a charge of conspiracy on anyone who signed it." The contributor's readiness to take the risk was fuel on the flame. Any editor who published such opinions would be indictable! He stood up with that changed face, repeating, "Stones!–and people like you," etc., pelting the contributor again, and yet again, with "Stones!"

Only for unadulterated blame and execration of Militancy was any admittance there, or anywhere else—according to the most open-minded of editors.

The initial "Conspiracy," then (that of the authorities to deny fair hearing to their women opponents), was, as we had been told, matched by conspiracy in the Press. The public was to be shut out from so much as a chance of hearing the other side.

NOTES

1 Political reformers who were prominent between 1837 and the European revolutions of 1848. They represented the interest of labourers and the underprivileged and called for universal (male) suffrage.

2 During the English Revolution, the Levellers were a pressure group (1645-49) who sought the extension of the electoral franchise to include "freeborn Englishmen," but who excluded servants, wage labourers, paupers, women, and children.

3 Plato (about 428-347 BCE), an Athenian philosopher, in the *Republic* argued that women who possess the appropriate natural gifts could be eligible for selection by the Guardians for training to become Rulers in the ideal republic. Marie Jean Antoine Nicolas Caritat, Marquis de Condorcet (1743-94), a French philosopher, argued for the perfectibility of mankind and saw the history of the human race as a gradual progress from barbarism to civilization. He foresaw progress toward equality between nations, classes, and genders.

4 The truly horrible effects of the present state of the law among the lowest of the working population, is exhibited in those cases of hideous maltreatment of their wives by working men, with which every newspaper, every police report, teems. Wretches unfit to have the smallest authority over any living thing, have a helpless woman for their household slave. These excesses could not exist if women both earned, and had the right to possess, a part of the income of the family. [Author's note.]

5 Claude Adrien Helvetius (1715-71), a French philosopher, was a moral idealist and utilitarian.

6 Ferocity, relentlessness, determination (French).

7 Dr. Samuel Johnson (1709-84) was a poet, essayist, and compiler of the first standard English dictionary.

8 Women in these organizations worked for the election of male party candidates within their respective parties: the Primrose League for Conservative candidates and the Women's Liberal Federation for Liberal candidates.

9 Namely (Latin).

10 The Reform Bills of 1832, 1867, and 1884 gradually expanded the male electorate. In 1832, the vote was extended to the lower middle classes. In 1867 it was extended to householders and male lodgers paying £10 for rooms and who lived in boroughs. In 1884 men in the counties got the same voting rights as those living in boroughs.

11 Alice Perrers (d. 1400) was the mistress of Edward III of England. She had great influence over him and was later banished from the royal household by Parliament. However, she returned to the court of Richard II in 1377. Madame Marie Jeanne Du Barry (1743-93) was the mistress of Louis XV of France.

12 Shakespeare, in Sonnet 116, speaks of love: "O no, it is an ever fixèd mark/That looks on tempests and is never shaken."

13 Coverture was the legal status of a woman after she married: her legal existence as an individual was suspended and she was under the authority and protection of her husband. A married woman could not own property, make a contract or a will, or sue or be sued.

14 Florence Nightingale (1820-1910) is considered the founder of the modern nursing profession. Mary Carpenter (1807-77) was a philanthropist, social reformer, and founder of free schools for poor children, the "ragged schools."

15 Henry Labouchere (1831-1912), a Liberal member of the House of Commons from 1880-1906, was a supporter of William Gladstone and an opponent of women's suffrage.

16 Robert Cecil, Lord Salisbury (1830-1903), was leader of the Conservative Party and became Prime Minister in 1885. William Gladstone was Liberal Prime Minister four times. See Note 8 above on the Primrose League and the Liberal Federation.

17 The speaker in *Maud* (1855), by Alfred, Lord Tennyson (1809-92), speaking of the woman he loves, who is of a higher social class, says, "You have but fed on the roses and lain in the lilies of life" (Part I, IV, 10, l. 162).

18 See *The Suffragette*, by Miss E. Sylvia Pankhurst (Gay and Hancock, 1911). [Author's note.]

19 I am requested by the Women's Freedom League to state that they have never resorted to stone-throwing or to personal assaults. [Author's note.]

20 Winston Churchill (1874-1965) was elected to the House of Commons in 1900. He became Home Secretary in 1910 and left that post in 1911 to become First Lord of the Admiralty. He served as Prime Minister from 1940 to 1945 and from 1951 to 1955.

21 In Matthew 10:34, Jesus said, "Think not that I am come to send peace on earth:
I came not to send peace, but a sword" (King James Version).

22 The Corn Laws were tariffs placed on imported grains that allowed landowners
to keep their prices high. They were repealed in 1846.

23 Millicent Fawcett (1847-1929) was the president of the NUWSS. Frances Balfour
(1858-1930) joined the Liberal Women's Suffrage Society in 1887. She was a
non-violent suffragist and sister-in-law to Constance Lytton.

24 Herbert Henry Asquith (1852-1928) was Liberal Prime Minister from 1908 to
1916.

25 Elizabeth Wolstenholm Elmy (1834-1913), a member of the WSPU, worked to
open schools for girls, campaigned against the Contagious Diseases Acts, and
supported women's suffrage.

26 Jean de La Fontaine (1621-95), a Frenchman, and Aesop (late sixth century
BCE), a Greek, wrote fables.

27 Since writing this, the same view has been publicly expressed by a member of
the Government, Mr. F[rancis] D[yke] Acland, Under Secretary for Foreign
Affairs. [Author's note.]

28 A reference to Winston Churchill who was Home Secretary in 1910 and in 1911
became First Lord of the Admiralty.

29 A reference to Herbert Henry Asquith who, as Prime Minister in 1910, helped
kill the Conciliation Bill which suffrage supporters had believed would be passed
because it was supported by a majority in the House of Commons.

CHAPTER TWO

WOMEN IN THE CAMPAIGN
TELL THEIR STORIES

Many of the women actively involved in the suffrage campaign recorded their impressions of the events in which they participated and the people whom they encountered during those years of struggle. Some women, such as Constance Lytton and Annie Kenney, published entire narrative accounts of their suffrage experiences. Other writers, such as Hannah Mitchell and Cicely Hamilton, included a chapter or chapters in their autobiographies recounting their years campaigning for women's suffrage. These accounts are valuable as historical documents, but they are also engaging personal narratives through which we gain an understanding of one individual's role in a great political movement. We learn as well what converted women to the cause of suffrage, why some turned to violence, how they experienced prison and force-feeding, and what their impressions were of the women who led them. Some of these narratives were published before the vote was granted to women; other accounts were written later, the writer looking back at actions in which she participated and placing them in the context of subsequent events. As time passed some women changed their perspective on a number of things, such as the need for militancy, the role it played in gaining the vote, and the personalities and motives of the movement's leaders.

Figure 8: Emmeline Pankhurst
by (Mary) Olive Edis (Mrs. Galsworthy)
1920s
By courtesy of the National Portrait Gallery, London

EMMELINE PANKHURST

FROM *MY OWN STORY*

[New York: Hearst's International Library Co., 1914]

FOREWORD

The closing paragraphs of this book were written in the late summer of 1914, when the armies of every great power in Europe were being mobilised for savage, unsparing, barbarous warfare—against one another, against small and unaggressive nations, against helpless women and children, against civilisation itself. How mild, by comparison with the despatches in the daily newspapers, will seem this chronicle of women's militant struggle against political and social injustice in one small corner of Europe. Yet let it stand as it was written, with peace—so-called, and civilisation, and orderly government as the background for heroism such as the world has seldom witnessed. The militancy of men, through all the centuries, has drenched the world with blood, and for these deeds of horror and destruction men have been rewarded with monuments, with great songs and epics. The militancy of women has harmed no human life save the lives of those who fought the battle of righteousness. Time alone will reveal what reward will be allotted to the women.

This we know, that in the black hour that has just struck in Europe, the men are turning to their women and calling on them to take up the work of keeping civilisation alive. Through all the harvest fields, in orchards and vineyards, women are garnering food for the men who fight, as well as for the children left fatherless by war. In the cities the women are keeping open the shops, they are driving trucks and trams, and are altogether attending to a multitude of business.

When the remnants of the armies return, when the commerce of Europe is resumed by men, will they forget the part the women so nobly played? Will they forget in England how women in all ranks of life put aside their own interests and organised, not only to nurse the wounded, care for the destitute, comfort the sick and lonely, but actually to maintain the existence of the nation? Thus far, it must be admitted, there are few indications that the English Government are mindful of the unselfish devotion manifested by the women. Thus far all Government schemes for overcoming unemployment have been directed towards the unemployment of men. The work of women, making garments, etc., has in some cases been taken away.

At the first alarm of war the militants proclaimed a truce, which was answered half-heartedly by the announcement that the Government would release all suffrage prisoners who would give an undertaking "not to commit further crimes or outrages." Since the truce had already been proclaimed, no suffrage prisoner deigned to reply to the Home Secretary's provision. A few days later, no doubt influenced by representations made to the Government by men and women of every political faith—many of them never having been supporters of revolutionary tactics—Mr. McKenna[1] announced in the House of Commons that it was the intention of Government, within a few days, to release unconditionally, all suffrage prisoners. So ends, for the present, the war of women against men. As of old, the women become the nurturing mothers of men, their sisters and uncomplaining helpmates. The future lies far ahead, but let this preface and this volume close with the assurance that the struggle for the full enfranchisement of women has not been abandoned; it has simply, for the moment, been placed in abeyance. When the clash of arms ceases, when normal, peaceful, rational society resumes its functions, the demand will again be made. If it is not quickly granted, then once more the women will take up the arms they to-day generously lay down. There can be no real peace in the world until woman, the mother half of the human family, is given liberty in the councils of the world.

FROM CHAPTER 1

Those men and women are fortunate who are born at a time when a great struggle for human freedom is in progress. It is an added good fortune to have parents who take a personal part in the great movements of their time. I am glad and thankful that this was my case.

One of my earliest recollections is of a great bazaar which was held in my native city of Manchester, the object of the bazaar being to raise money to relieve the poverty of the newly emancipated negro slaves in the United States. My mother took an active part in this effort, and I, as a small child, was entrusted with a lucky bag by means of which I helped to collect money.

Young as I was—I could not have been older than five years—I knew perfectly well the meaning of the words slavery and emancipation. From infancy I had been accustomed to hear pro and con discussions of slavery and the American Civil War. Although the British government finally decided not to recognise the Confederacy, public opinion in England was sharply divided on the questions both of slavery and of secession. Broadly speaking the propertied classes were pro-slavery, but there were many exceptions to the rule. Most of those who formed the circle of our family friends were opposed to slavery and my father, Robert Goulden, was always a most ardent abolitionist. He was prominent enough in the movement to be appointed on a committee to meet and welcome Henry Ward Beecher when he arrived in England for a lecture tour. Mrs. Harriet Beecher Stowe's novel, "Uncle Tom's Cabin,"[2] was so great a favourite with my mother that she used it continually as a source of bedtime stories for our fascinated ears. Those stories, told almost fifty years ago, are as fresh in my mind to-day as events detailed in the morning's papers. Indeed they are more vivid, because they made a much deeper impression on my consciousness. I can still definitely recall the thrill I experienced every time my mother related the tale of Eliza's race for freedom over the broken ice of the Ohio River, the agonizing pursuit, and the final rescue at the hands of the determined old Quaker. Another thrilling tale was the story of a negro boy's flight from the plantation of his cruel master. The boy had never seen a railroad train, and when, staggering along the unfamiliar railroad track, he heard the roar of an approaching train, the clattering car-wheels seemed to his strained imagination to be repeating over and over again the awful words, "Catch a nigger—catch a nigger—catch a nigger—" This was a terrible story, and throughout my childhood, whenever I rode in a train, I thought of that poor runaway slave escaping from the pursuing monster.

These stories, with the bazaars and the relief funds and subscriptions of which I heard so much talk, I am sure made a permanent impression on my brain and my character. They awakened in me the two sets of sensations to which all my life I have most readily responded: first, admiration for that spirit of fighting and heroic sacrifice by which alone the soul of civilisation is saved; and next after that, appreciation of the gentler spirit which is moved to mend and repair the ravages of war.

I do not remember a time when I could not read, nor any time when reading was not a joy and a solace. As far back as my memory runs I loved tales, especially those of a romantic and idealistic character. "Pilgrim's Progress" was an early favourite, as well as another of Bunyan's visionary romances, which does not seem to be as well known, his "Holy War." At nine I discovered the Odyssey and very soon after that another classic which has remained all my life a source of inspiration. This was Carlyle's "French Revolution," and I received it with much the same emotion that Keats experienced when he read Chapman's translation of Homer—"...like some watcher of the skies, When a new planet swims into his ken."[3]

I never lost that first impression, and it strongly affected my attitude toward events which were occurring around my childhood. Manchester is a city which has witnessed a great many stirring episodes, especially of a political character. Generally speaking, its citizens have been liberal in their sentiments, defenders of free speech and liberty of opinion. In the late sixties there occurred in Manchester one of those dreadful events that prove an exception to the rule. This was in connection with the Fenian Revolt in Ireland.[4] There was a Fenian riot, and the police arrested the leaders. These men were being taken to the jail in a prison van. On the way the van was stopped and an attempt was made to rescue the prisoners. A man fired a pistol, endeavouring to break the lock of the van door. A policemen fell, mortally wounded, and several men were arrested and were charged with murder. I distinctly remember the riot, which I did not witness, but which I heard vividly described by my older brother. I had been spending the afternoon with a young playmate, and my brother had come after tea to escort me home. As we walked through the deepening November twilight he talked excitedly of the riot, the fatal pistol shot, and the slain policeman. I could almost see the man bleeding on the ground, while the crowd swayed and groaned around him.

The rest of the story reveals one of those ghastly blunders which justice not infrequently makes. Although the shooting was done without any intent to kill, the men were tried for murder and three of them were found guilty and hanged. Their execution, which greatly excited the citizens of Manchester, was almost the last, if not the last, public execution permitted to take place in the city. At the time I was a boarding-pupil in the school near Manchester, and I spent my week-ends at home. A certain Saturday afternoon stands out in my memory, as on my way home from school I passed the prison where I knew the men had been confined. I saw that a part of the prison wall had been torn away, and in the great gap that remained were evidences of a gallows recently removed. I was transfixed with horror, and over me there swept the sudden conviction that that hanging was a mistake—worse, a crime. It was my awakening to one of the most terrible facts of life—that justice and judgment lie often a world apart.

I relate this incident of my formative years to illustrate the fact that the impressions of childhood often have more to do with character and future conduct than heredity or education. I tell it also to show that my development into an advocate of militancy was largely a sympathetic process. I have not personally suffered from the deprivations, the bitterness and sorrow which bring so many men and women to a realisation of social injustice. My childhood was protected by love and a comfortable home. Yet, while still a very young child, I began instinctively to feel that there was something lacking, even in my own home, some false conception of family relations, some incomplete ideal.

This vague feeling of mine began to shape itself into conviction about the time my brothers and I were sent to school. The education of the English boy, then as now, was considered a much more serious matter than the education of the English boy's sister. My parents, especially my father, discussed the question of my brothers' education as a matter of real importance. My education and that of my sister were scarcely discussed at all. Of course we went to a carefully selected girls' school, but beyond the facts that the head mistress was a gentlewoman and that all the pupils were girls of my own class, nobody seemed concerned. A girl's education at that time seemed to have for its prime object the art of "making home attractive"—presumably to migratory male relatives. It used to puzzle me to understand why I was under such a particular obligation to make home attractive to my brothers. We were on excellent terms of friendship, but it was never suggested to them as a duty that they make home attractive to me. Why not? Nobody seemed to know.

The answer to these puzzling questions came to me unexpectedly one night when I lay in my little bed waiting for sleep to overtake me. It was a custom of my father and mother to make the round of our bedrooms every night before going themselves to bed. When they entered my room that night I was still awake, but for some reason I chose to feign slumber. My father bent over me, shielding the candle flame with his big hand. I cannot know exactly what thought was in his mind as he gazed down at me, but I heard him say, somewhat sadly, "What a pity she wasn't born a lad."

My first hot impulse was to sit up in bed and protest that I didn't want to be a boy, but I lay still and heard my parents' footsteps pass on toward the next child's bed. I thought about my father's remark for many days afterward, but I think I never decided that I regretted my sex. However, it was made quite clear that men considered themselves superior to women, and that women apparently acquiesced in that belief.

I found this view of things difficult to reconcile with the fact that both my father and mother were advocates of equal suffrage. I was very young when the Reform Act of 1866 was passed, but I very well remember the agitation caused by certain circumstances attending it. This Reform Act, known as the Household Franchise Bill, marked the first popular extension of the ballot in England since 1832. Under its terms, householders paying a minimum of ten pounds a year rental were given the Parliamentary vote. While it was still under discussion in the House of Commons, John Stuart Mill moved an amendment to the bill to include women householders as well as men. The amendment was defeated, but in the act as passed the word "man," instead of the usual "male person," was used. Now, under another act of Parliament it had been decided that the word "man" always included "woman" unless otherwise specifically stated. For example, in certain acts containing rate-paying clauses, the masculine noun and pronoun are used throughout, but the provisions apply to women rate-payers as well as to men. So when the Reform Bill with the word "man" in it became law, many women believed that the right of suffrage had actually been bestowed upon them. A tremendous amount of discussion ensued, and the matter was finally tested by a large number of women seeking to have their names placed upon the register as voters. In my city of Manchester 3,924 women, out of a total of 4,215 possible women voters, claimed their votes, and their claim was defended in the law courts by eminent lawyers, including my future husband, Dr. Pankhurst. Of course the women's claim was settled adversely in the courts, but the agitation resulted in a strengthening of the woman-suffrage agitation all over the country....

I was fourteen years old when I went to my first suffrage meeting. Returning from school one day, I met my mother just setting out for the meeting, and I begged her to let me go along. She consented, and without stopping to lay my books down I scampered away in my mother's wake. The speeches interested and excited me, especially the address of the great Miss Lydia Becker, who was the Susan B. Anthony of the English movement, a splendid character and a truly eloquent speaker. She was the secretary of the Manchester committee, and I had learned to admire her as the editor of the *Women's Suffrage Journal*, which came to my mother every week. I left the meeting a conscious and confirmed suffragist.

I suppose I had always been an unconscious suffragist. With my temperament and my surroundings I could scarcely have been otherwise. The movement was very much alive in the early seventies, nowhere more so than in Manchester, where it was organised by a group of extraordinary men and women....

When I was fifteen years old I went to Paris, where I was entered as a pupil in one of the pioneer institutions in Europe for the higher education of girls....

I was between eighteen and nineteen when I finally returned from school in Paris and took my place in my father's home as a finished young lady. I sympathised with and worked for the woman-suffrage movement, and came to know Dr. Pankhurst, whose work for woman suffrage had never ceased. It was Dr. Pankhurst who drafted the first enfranchisement bill, known as the Women's Disabilities Removal Bill, and introduced into the House of Commons in 1870 by Jacob Bright. The bill advanced to its second reading by a majority vote of thirty-three, but it was killed in committee by Mr. Gladstone's peremptory orders. Dr. Pankhurst, as I have already said, with another distinguished barrister, Lord Coleridge,[5] acted as counsel for the Manchester women, who tried in 1868 to be placed on the register as voters. He also drafted the bill giving married women absolute control over their property and earnings, a bill which became law in 1882.

My marriage with Dr. Pankhurst took place in 1879.

I think we cannot be too grateful to the group of men and women who, like Dr. Pankhurst, in those early days lent the weight of their honoured names to the suffrage movement in the trials of its struggling youth. These men did not wait until the movement became popular, nor did they hesitate until it was plain that women were roused to the point of revolt. They worked all their lives with those who were organising, educating, and preparing for the revolt which was one day to come. Unquestionably those pioneer men suffered in popularity for their feminist views. Some of them suffered financially, some politically. Yet they never wavered.

My married life lasted through nineteen happy years. Often I have heard the taunt that suffragists are women who have failed to find any normal outlet for their emotions, and are therefore soured and disappointed beings. This is probably not true of any suffragist, and it is most certainly not true of me. My home life and relations have been as nearly ideal as possible in this imperfect world. About a year after my marriage my daughter Christabel was born, and in another eighteen months my second daughter Sylvia came. Two other children followed, and for some years I was rather deeply immersed in my domestic affairs....

Gladstone was an implacable foe of woman suffrage. He believed that women's work and politics lay in service to men's parties. One of the shrewdest acts of Mr. Gladstone's career was his disruption of the suffrage organisation in England. He accomplished this by substituting "something just as good," that something being Women's Liberal Associations. Beginning in 1881 in Bristol, these associations spread rapidly through the country and, in 1887, became a National Women's Liberal Federation. The promise of the Federation was that by allying themselves with men in party politics, women would soon earn the right to vote. The avidity with which the women swallowed this promise, left off working for themselves, and threw themselves into the men's work was amazing.

The Women's Liberal Federation is an organisation of women who believe in the principles of the Liberal Party. (The somewhat older Primrose League is a similar organisation of women who adhere to Conservative party principles.) Neither of these organisations have woman suffrage for their object. They came into existence to uphold party ideas and to work for the election of party candidates.

I am told that women in America have recently allied themselves with political parties, believing, just as we did, that such action would break down opposition to suffrage by showing the men that women possess political ability, and that politics is work for women as well as men. Let them not be deceived. I can assure the American women that our long alliance with the great parties, our devotion to party programmes, our faithful work at elections, never advanced the suffrage cause one step. The men accepted the services of the women, but they never offered any kind of payment....

Well, the suffragists, when they were admitted into the Women's Liberal Federation must have felt that they had passed their resolution. They settled down to work for the party and to prove that they were as capable of voting as the recently enfranchised farm labourers. Of course a few women remained loyal to suffrage. They began again on the old educational lines to work for the cause. Not one woman took counsel with herself as to how and why the agricultural labourers had won their franchise. They had won it, as a matter of fact, by burning hay-ricks, rioting, and otherwise demonstrating their strength in the only way that English politicians can understand. The threat to march a hundred thousand men to the House of Commons unless the bill was passed played its part also in securing the agricultural labourer his political freedom. But no woman suffragist noticed that. As for myself, I was too young politically to learn the lesson then. I had to go through years of public work before I acquired the experience and the wisdom to know how to wring concessions from the English Government. I had to hold public office. I had to go behind the scenes in the government schools, in the work-houses and other charitable institutions; I had to get a close-hand view of the misery and unhappiness of a man-made world, before I reached the point where I could successfully revolt against it. It was almost immediately after the collapse of the woman suffrage movement in 1884 that I entered upon this new phase of my career.

FROM CHAPTERS II AND III

All these years my daughters had been growing up. All their lives they had been interested in women's suffrage. Christabel and Sylvia, as little girls, had cried to be taken to meetings. They had helped in our drawing-room meetings in every way that children can help. As they grew older we used to talk together about the suffrage, and I was sometimes rather frightened by their youthful confidence in the prospect, which they considered certain, of the success of the movement. One day Christabel startled me with the remark: "How long you women have been trying for the vote. For my part, I mean to get it."

Was there, I reflected, any difference between trying for the vote and getting it? There is an old French proverb, "If youth could know; if age could do." It occurred to me that if the older suffrage workers could in some way join hands with the young, unwearied and resourceful suffragists, the movement might wake up to new life and new possibilities. After that I and my daughters together sought a way to bring about that union of young and old which would find new methods, blaze new trails. At length we thought we had found a way.

In the summer of 1902—I think it was 1902—Susan B. Anthony paid a visit to Manchester, and that visit was one of the contributory causes that led to the founding of our militant suffrage organisation, the Women's Social and Political Union. During Miss Anthony's visit my daughter Christabel, who was very deeply impressed, wrote an article for the Manchester papers on the life and works of the venerable reformer. After her departure Christabel spoke often of her, and always with sorrow and indignation that such a splendid worker for humanity was destined to die without seeing the hopes of her lifetime realised. "It is unendurable," declared my daughter, "to think of another generation of women wasting their lives begging for the vote. We must not lose any more time. We must act."

By this time the Labour Party, of which I was still a member, had returned Mr. Keir Hardie to Parliament, and we decided that the first step in a campaign of action was to make the Labour Party responsible for a new suffrage bill. At a recent annual conference of the party I had moved a resolution calling upon the members to instruct their own member of Parliament to introduce a bill for the enfranchisement of women. The resolution was passed, and we determined to organise a society of women to demand immediate enfranchisement, not by means of any outworn missionary methods, but through political action.

It was in October, 1903, that I invited a number of women to my house in Nelson street, Manchester, for purposes of organization. We voted to call our new society the Women's Social and Political Union, partly to emphasise its democracy, and partly to define its object as political rather than propagandist. We resolved to limit our membership exclusively to women, to keep ourselves absolutely free from any party affiliation, and to be satisfied with nothing but action on our question. Deeds, not words, was to be our permanent motto.

FROM CHAPTER IV

To account for the phenomenal growth of the Women's Social and Political Union after it was established in London, to explain why it made such an instant appeal to women hitherto indifferent, I shall have to point out exactly wherein our society differs from all other suffrage associations. In the first place, our members are absolutely single minded; they concentrate all their forces on one object, political equality with men. No member of the WSPU divides her attention between suffrage and other social reforms. We hold that both reason and justice dictate that women shall have a share in reforming the evils that afflict society, especially those evils bearing directly on women themselves. Therefore, we demand, before any other legislation whatever, the elementary justice of votes for women.

There is not the slightest doubt that the women of Great Britain would have been enfranchised years ago had all the suffragists adopted this simple principle. They never did, and even to-day many English women refuse to adopt it. They are party members first and suffragists afterward; or they are suffragists part of the time and social theorists the rest of the time. We further differ from other suffrage associations, or from others existing in 1906, in that we clearly perceived the political situation that solidly interposed between us and our enfranchisement.

For seven years we had had a majority in the House of Commons pledged to vote favourably on a suffrage bill. The year before, they had voted favourably on one, yet that bill did not become law. Why? Because even an overwhelming majority of private members are powerless to enact law in the face of a hostile Government of eleven cabinet ministers. The private member of Parliament was once possessed of individual power and responsibility, but Parliamentary usage and a changed conception of statesmanship have gradually lessened the functions of members. At the present time their powers, for all practical purposes, are limited to helping to enact such measures as the Government introduces or, in rare instances, private measures approved by the Government. It is true that the House can revolt, can, by voting a lack of confidence in the Government, force them to resign. But that almost never happens, and it is less likely now than formerly to happen. Figureheads don't revolt.

This, then, was our situation: the Government all-powerful and consistently hostile; the rank and file of legislators impotent; the country apathetic; the women divided in their interests. The Women's Social and Political Union was established to meet this situation, and to overcome it. Moreover we had a policy which, if persisted in long enough, could not possibly fail to overcome it. Do you wonder that we gained new members at every meeting we held?

There was little formality about joining the Union. Any woman could become a member by paying a shilling, but at the same time she was required to sign a declaration of loyal adherence to our policy and a pledge not to work for any political party until the women's vote was won. This is still our inflexible custom. Moreover, if at any time a member, or a group of members, loses faith in our policy; if any one begins to suggest that some other policy ought to be substituted, or if she tries to confuse the issue by adding other policies, she ceases at once to be a member. Autocratic? Quite so. But, you may object, a suffrage organisation ought to democratic. Well the members of the WSPU do not agree with you. We do not believe in the effectiveness of the ordinary suffrage organisation. The WSPU is not hampered by a complexity of rules. We have no constitution and by-laws; nothing to be amended or tinkered with or quarreled over at an annual meeting. In fact, we have no annual meeting, no business sessions, no elections of officers. The WSPU is simply a suffrage army, and no one is obliged to remain in it. Indeed we don't want anybody to remain in it who does not ardently believe in the policy of the army.

The foundation of our policy is opposition to a Government who refuse votes to women. To support by word or deed a Government hostile to woman suffrage is simply to invite them to go on being hostile. We oppose the Liberal party because it is in power. We would oppose a Unionist government if it were in power and were opposed to woman suffrage. We say to women that as long as they remain in the ranks of the Liberal party they give their tacit approval to the Government's anti-suffrage policy. We say to members of Parliament that as long as they support any of the Government's policies they give their tacit approval to the anti-suffrage policy. We call upon all sincere suffragists to leave the Liberal party until women are given votes on equal terms with men. We call upon all voters to vote against Liberal candidates until the Liberal Government does justice to women....

The contention of the old-fashioned suffragists, and of the politicians as well, has always been that an educated public opinion will ultimately give votes to women without any great force being exerted in behalf of the reform. We agree that public opinion must be educated, but we contend that even an educated public opinion is useless unless it is vigorously utilised. The keenest weapon is powerless unless it is courageously wielded. In the year 1906 there was an immensely large public opinion in favour of woman suffrage. But what good did that do the cause? We called upon the public for a great deal more than sympathy. We called upon it to demand of the Government to yield to public opinion and give women votes. And we declared that we would wage war, not only on all anti-suffrage forces, but on all neutral and non-active forces. Every man with a vote was considered a foe to woman suffrage unless he was prepared to be actively a friend.

Not that we believed that the campaign of education ought to be given up. On the contrary, we knew that education must go on, and in much more vigorous fashion than ever before. The first thing we did was to enter upon a sensational campaign to arouse the public to the importance of woman suffrage, and to interest it in our plans for forcing the Government's hands. I think we can claim that our success in this regard was instant, and that it has proved permanent. From the very first, in those early London days, when we were few in numbers and very poor in purse, we made the public aware of the woman suffrage movement as it had never been before. We adopted Salvation Army methods and went out into the highways and the byways after converts. We threw away all our conventional notions of what was "ladylike" and "good form," and we applied to our methods the one test question, Will it help? Just as the Booths and their followers[6] took religion to the street crowds in such fashion that the church people were horrified, so we took suffrage to the general public in a manner that amazed and scandalised the other suffragists.

E. Sylvia Pankhurst

From *The Suffragette Movement: An Intimate Account of Persons and Ideals*

[London: Virago, 1977. First published in 1931.]

from Part II, Book VI, Chapter V

An outcry was raised against the new Suffragette policy of stone throwing and damage to private property, which had appeared in such sensational guise. The *Daily News* appealed to Mrs. Pankhurst to check these "disgraceful developments." She replied that to turn back now would be "folly, weakness and wickedness"; to ask her followers to desist would be betrayal of her "sacred trust." Christabel, in a letter to *The Times*, avowed and defended the new tactics. Mrs. Lawrence upheld them in *Votes for Women*. She explained, as was the fact, that the difficulty of keeping up the heckling of Cabinet Ministers by ordinary means was daily becoming greater. The women were kept out of the halls, and if they attempted to hold a protest meeting in the street they were taken into custody and held at the police station until the Minister and his following had departed for the night. Therefore, they had been faced, she declared, by the "inevitable choice, either to admit the game was up and give in," or discover a new method.

After this lapse of time when all is won, and all is over, I must frankly say that I did not think the old methods had yet been exploited to their full capacity. I believed, then and always, that the movement required, not more serious militancy by the few, but a stronger appeal to the great masses to join the struggle. Yet it was not in me to criticize or expostulate. I would rather have died at the stake than say one word against the actions of those who were in the throes of the fight. I knew but too surely, that the militant women would be made to suffer renewed hardships for each act of more serious damage. Yet in the spate of that impetuous movement, they would rush enthusiastic to their martyrdom, and bless, as their truest saviours, the leaders who summoned them to each new ordeal. I realized how supremely difficult is the holding of calm thought and the sense of perspective at such a time, how readily one daring enthusiast influences another, and in the gathering momentum of numbers all are swept along. Posterity, I knew, would see the heroism of the militants and forget their damage, but in the present they would pay severely. There never was any doubt of the responsibility of the militant leaders for the doings of their followers; they accepted that always, without flinching, making themselves an open target for Government attack. Christabel, especially, when not actually the instigator, was, as a rule, aware of every intended militant act, down to its smallest detail; for the W.S.P.U. was conducted with the rigid discipline of an army. When the roof tactics were first discussed, Jennie Baines asked for hatchets. "What would you do with them?" Christabel asked. "Well, we could be hacking and chopping, couldn't we?" replied the fiery-spirited one; and so the idea developed.

The Government was not slow to take advantage of the new tactics to inflict harsher punishment upon their instruments. These women should not be permitted to terminate their imprisonment by the hunger strike, as thirty-seven women had already done, four of them twice in succession. The Birmingham prisoners commenced their fast on September 18th [1909]. The Home Secretary ordered the medical officer of the prison to feed them forcibly by means of a rubber tube passed through the mouth or nose into the stomach. The fact appeared in the Press on September 24th. It was received with horrified consternation by everyone connected with the militant movement; by no one more than by Keir Hardie, in whom emotional distress now invariably caused the reaction of physical illness. He immediately tabled a Parliamentary question. Masterman, replying for the Home Secretary, described the forcible feeding as "hospital treatment." Hardie, white with wrath, retorted: "A horrible, beastly outrage." Philip Snowden cried: "Russian barbarism!"[7] The supporters of the Government shouted with laughter.

FROM PART II, BOOK VIII, CHAPTER V

Then, swift as a shaft of light from a thundrous sky, followed a tragic happening. Emily Wilding Davison rushed out on to the Derby race-course, and was fatally injured in stopping the King's horse. She had long believed that the deliberate giving of a woman's life would create the atmosphere necessary to win the victory, and bring all the suffering of the militants to an end. That had been her intention when, in prison a year before, she had flung herself over the corridor railings. A statement she then wrote revealed that she had made three successive attempts to kill herself, twice being caught by the wire netting forty feet below, and finally throwing herself on to the iron staircase. Already in that fall she had received injuries from which she had never entirely recovered. Her statement, sent at the time to the *Suffragette*, was not published until after her death, for there had been a general desire at Lincoln's Inn House[8] to discourage her in such tendencies; some of her colleagues even suggested her attempt had been a sensational pretence. She was condemned and ostracized as a self-willed person who persisted in acting upon her own initiative without waiting for official instructions. All such criticism was now for ever silenced; she had risen to the supreme test of her faith. There remained only the memory of her brave gallantry and gay comradeship, her tall, slight, awkward figure and the green, elusive eyes in the small, jauntily poised head.

On the eve of the Derby she went with two friends to a WSPU bazaar in the Empress Rooms, Kensington, where, amid the trivial artificiality of a bazaar-fitter's ornamental garden, and the chatter of buying and selling at the stalls, she had joined in laying a wreath on the plaster statue of Joan of Arc, whom Christabel had called "the patron saint of Suffragettes." With a fellow militant in whose flat she lived, she had concerted a Derby protest without tragedy— a mere waving of the purple-white-and-green at Tattenham Corner, which, by its suddenness, it was hoped would stop the race. Whether from the first her purpose was more serious, or whether a final impulse altered her resolve, I know not. Her friend declares she would not thus have died without writing a farewell message to her mother. Yet she had sewed the WSPU colours inside her coat as though to ensure that no mistake could be made as to her motive when her dead body should be examined. So she set forth alone, the hope of a great achievement surging through her mind. With sure resolve she ran out on to the course and deliberately flung herself upon the King's horse, Anmer, that her deed might be the more pointed.[9] Her skull was fractured. Incurably injured, she was removed to the Epsom Cottage Hospital, and there died on June 8th without regaining consciousness. As life lingered in her for two days, Mansell Moullin performed an operation, which, in surgeon's parlance, "gave great temporary relief," but the injured brain did not mend.

A solemn funeral procession was organized to do her honour. To the militants who had prepared so many processions, this was the natural manifestation. The call to women to come garbed in black carrying purple irises, in purple with crimson peonies, in white bearing laurel wreaths, received a response from thousands who gathered from all parts of the country. Graduates and clergy marched in their robes, suffrage societies, trade unionists from the East End, unattached people. The streets were densely lined by silent, respectful crowds. The great public responded to the appeal of a life deliberately given for an impersonal end. The police had issued a notice which was virtually a prohibition of the procession, but at the same time constables were enjoined to reverent conduct....

I marched with the hunger strikers to the burial service at St. George's, Hart Street, the church of C. Baumgarten, a good friend of suffrage, and afterwards to King's Cross, where the last of what was Emily Wilding Davison steamed away to be buried at her mother's home in Morpeth. Her tall shape flitted across my eyes; I could see her in imagination as she ran out unflinching across the course. The thought of her great courage and of that terrible agony which had ended her held my mind as in a vice. The ordinary round of duties and interests had lost, for the time, their meaning. I went with

Norah Smyth to her brother's cottage at Ugly Green, amid the quiet of broad fields and towering elms. There, in the effort to realize and convey that heroism and its portent, I wrote some brief sentences, which someone returning to London thrust for me into the letter-box of the *Daily Mail*, chosen as the typical organ of the unheeding world.

"O DEED MAJESTIC! O TRIUMPHANT DEATH!

"The crowded, trivial race-course and the glaring sun.

"The swift rush out into that horror of horses' hoofs; a frantic, clinging impact.

"Then, unseen, the column of flame that rises up to Heaven as the great heart bursts—the ascending spirit is set free.

"O deed of infinite majesty! Great heart that none could ever know!

"Mean, sordid things they write of her in printed sheets whose objects fill our minds with petty things.

"Parliament sits—a House of Mockery! It proses on without a word of that great act, or the great Cause for which she gave her life.

"The world goes on as though it could not heed.

"They carry the poor broken body through the streets, women in white with lilies, clergy in their robes, poor people who have gone without some needed thing even to come thus far to follow her.

"All those four miles the roads are thronged with crowds who wait, silent and with bared heads, to see her pass.

"One should be there—another woman[10] whom they dragged back from following her, back to the gaol where with starvation and weakness she fights strong powers that be.

"O dullard minds in power that cannot see great Freedom's history making; great tragic acts under their very eyes!

"Parliament sat to govern us the while, and not a man arose to speak of it.

* * * * *

"In the wide stillness of the night, in the grey fields, under the quiet moon, that deed goes on. The beating of the horses' hoofs, the rushing of the horses—she and they.

"Upward the spreading column pours in the soul's ecstasy of light.

"All through Eternity that deed goes on; in the quiet fields, as in the hurrying world, and on the trivial race-course in the glaring sun.

"O deed majestic! O triumphant death!"

EMMELINE PETHICK-LAWRENCE

FROM *MY PART IN A CHANGING WORLD*

[London: Victor Gollancz, 1938]

FROM CHAPTER IX

I must go back to the days of my youth and make it clear, if I have not already done so, that my early enthusiasms were aroused not by ideas of political democracy but by dreams of economic and social deliverance of the toiling masses of the people. This was true not only of myself but of all those of my own generation with whom I was in association....

Political interests were subordinate to our fervent desire to bring about an amelioration of the social conditions of the workers. Nothing less than this absorbing interest could have made me indifferent to the question of woman's franchise. I was convinced that all injustice and wrong would come to an end if a system of socialism could supplant the old capitalist regime.

I had yet to be awakened to the fact that a system of socialism, planned by the male half only of humanity, would not touch some of the worst evils that were engendered by a politically and socially suppressed womanhood. Although I had never met the Pankhursts or the Kenneys or any of the other members of the little group in Manchester, I found later that they had passed through the same transition as myself, and had been occupied with the same ideas, which had come to some of them through somewhat different channels, through the *Clarion*, for example, the weekly paper edited by Robert Blatchford, author of *Merrie England*,[11] and through their association with the Independent Labour Party, in which Mrs. Pankhurst had played for some considerable time a prominent part. It was as an outcome of their socialistic fervour and of their concern for the welfare of the working woman in the North that a new demand for women's enfranchisement arose and latent feeling blazed up in the stormy scene of the Free Trade Hall which launched the revival of the old cause under the new cry: Votes for Woman! The demand in 1905 was the same as that of 1867, that the word "man" and "person" used in the Franchise Acts should include both sexes, so that the vote should be granted to women on the same terms as it was, or would be, granted to men. On this demand every section of the suffrage movement, old or young, was united.

Mrs. Pankhurst called on me in February 1906, because Keir Hardie had told her that in me she would find a practical and useful colleague who could

develop in London the new society which she had founded in Manchester—
The Women's Social and Political Union. She went back to Sylvia disappointed. "She will not help," she said, "she has so many interests." Then Annie Kenney was sent to me by Keir Hardie. She burst in upon me one day in her
rather breathless way and threw all my barriers down. I might have been a life-
long friend by the complete trust in me that she showed and by the conviction that she expressed that the only thing needed to bring the movement to
complete and speedy success in London was my co-operation.

There was something about Annie that touched my heart. She was very
simple and she seemed to have a whole-hearted faith in the goodness of
everybody that she met. She told me her version of what had happened at Sir
Edward Grey's meeting in the Free Trade Hall, for it was she, with Christabel
Pankhurst, who had made the scene which had shocked and horrified the
conventional world. She went on to tell me that because Christabel could do
nothing further for the suffrage movement until she had obtained the LL.B.
degree, Annie herself felt that she must leave Manchester and come to rouse
London, as she herself expressed it. The education authorities of Owen College had threatened to expel Christabel after her prison experience and had
finally made it an absolute condition that she should take no further part in
political action until after she had completed her period of studentship. So
the Pankhursts and a few working women in their little group had amassed
the sum of £2 and had given it to Annie for the purpose of her campaign. I
was amused at Annie's ignorance of what the task of rousing London would
involve, and yet thrilled by her courage. "How do you want me to help you,
Annie?" I asked. "Mr. Keir Hardie told me to ask you to be our national treasurer," said Annie, speaking as if by rote. "Your treasurer!" I exclaimed. "What
funds have you?" "That is just the trouble," said Annie, simply. "I have spent
the money already and I have had to go into debt. I do not understand
money, it worries me; that is why I have come to you for your help. You need
not decide at once," she went on hastily, no doubt seeing my lack of enthusiasm for the job. "We have a committee at Park Walk to-morrow, and you will
meet Sylvia Pankhurst, the honorary secretary, and the others, and will hear
a lot more about it then. You will come, won't you?" I gave my promise
because I could not repulse her wistful eagerness.

After she left me I did not feel quite happy about my promise to attend the
committee. To tell the truth, I had no fancy to be drawn into a small group
of brave and reckless and quite helpless people who were prepared to dash
themselves against the oldest tradition of human civilization as well as one of
the strongest Governments of modern times. I asked my lifelong friend and
colleague, Mary Neal, to go with me, as I wanted to have the reinforcement
of her extremely shrewd judgment and common sense.

We went together to Park Walk and found the small house where Sylvia
Pankhurst lodged. Gathered round the table were six people; Sylvia

Pankhurst, Mrs. Rose, her landlady, Mrs. Clarke, her aunt, Annie Kenney, Miss Fenwick Miller, and Mrs. Martel, an Australian woman.

How it happened, I hardly know, but that evening with Mary Neal and myself, we formed ourselves into a Central London Committee of the Women's Social and Political Union, and I was formally requested to become the honorary treasurer. I consented to accept this office on condition that my old friend, Alfred G. Sayers, a chartered accountant, would accept the position of honorary auditor. He inaugurated the system on which the books were kept, a system which won the tribute of the prosecuting Counsel when all our books, with our banking account, were seized by the Government for the purpose of the Conspiracy Trial in 1912. He was my unfailing good adviser in all the circumstances that attended my office as treasurer.

It was by a very extraordinary sequence of incidents that I, who am not of a revolutionary temperament, was drawn into a revolutionary movement like the Women's Social and Political Movement. The first thing that drew me to it was the story of the imprisonment of the two girls who had raised the suffrage issue at the memorable meeting in Manchester. Then I was touched by the appeal of Annie Kenney and made the promise to go to this pathetic little committee that talked so bravely of their plan to rouse London but seemed so helpless.

In reply to my question I found that there was no office, no organization, no money—no postage stamps even. The honorary secretary looked over-burdened and distraught, as well she might be, for, as she has told us in her own story *The Suffragette Movement,* her financial position just then was desperate. It was not without some dismay that it was borne in upon me that somebody had to come to the help of this brave little group, and that the finger of fate pointed at me.

I found Sylvia Pankhurst, whom I met for the first time at the inauguration of the Central London Committee, a baffling personality. She was the impersonation of what I had imagined those young Russian students to be who, in the last decades of the nineteenth century, had given up career and status to go amongst the masses of the people in order to instruct them, and so to prepare the ground for the revolution which they believed would some day take place. There was a certain infantile look about her, because her face had the roundness and smoothness of a child. In contrast to her childlike face was the outer hardness of her character, the hardness of finely tempered steel; she had a strong will, trained to endure.

This impression of her character was as far as I was able to get at the first interview. It has taken me more than thirty years of close association to penetrate to other layers of her complex character. I know now that under that outer coat of mail there hides the sensitive and tender child that corresponds to her appearance, still youthful in spite of the many tragic experiences that she has gone through. Quiet and shy in those days, she had surprised her friends by one brilliant success after another. She did it first when in 1901 she obtained the Lady Whitworth Scholarship awarded to the best woman student of the year at the Manchester School of Art, although she had only put in part-time attendance, devoting half her day to taking her "share in the disagreeable work" of the small business run by Mrs. Pankhurst. She did it again in 1912 when she won the National Silver Medal, the Primrose Medal, and the highest prize open to students of both sexes at the Manchester School— the Proctor Travelling Studentship—a vacation scholarship entitling the holder to study abroad. The expression of Sylvia's real self was to be found in her creative art and in the depth of her emotional attachment to a very few persons.

I did not meet Christabel until some months after I had been working with Sylvia and Annie. Christabel, in her self-confidence, struck the major note. She was the embodiment of "Youth knocking at the Door." She was cut out for public life. Her chosen career, that of Barrister-at-law, had been checked by the refusal of the Benchers at Lincoln's Inn to admit a woman as a student, so that the career of a political pioneer offered to her the finest kind of self-expression. She possessed the gifts necessary to success. Like all the Pankhursts she had great courage. She had a cool, logical mind, and a quick, ready wit. She was young and attractive, graceful on the platform, with a singularly clear and musical voice. She had none of Sylvia's passion of pity—on the contrary, she detested weakness, which was discouraged in her presence.

Although to all the Pankhursts the cause of woman suffrage was a religion that demanded from them everything that they had to give, the approach of each one was different. As to Sylvia, her passion for beauty, great as it was, had to yield in the end to her passion of imaginative pity. She entered into the humiliations and sufferings of the great company of over-worked and poverty-stricken people, especially of overworked mothers. She has never wavered in her loyalty to the victimized and the oppressed in every part of the world. Although, in comparison with many who took the lead in the suffrage movement, she was not considered as conspicuously popular or conspicuously effective, yet she, with her devoted following in the East End, was the first (in 1914) to break Mr. Asquith's resistance and to win from him the admission that the vote must be granted to working women like those she had sent to him as a deputation. (That story belongs to a later chapter.) To her, the Vote meant the amelioration of the lot of the workers.

Christabel was inspired not by pity but by a deep, secret shame—shame that any woman should tamely accept the position accorded to her as something less than an adult human being—a position half way between the child and the citizen. Christabel cared less for the political vote itself than for the dignity of her sex, and she denounced the false dignity earned by submission and extolled the true dignity accorded by revolt. She never made any secret of the fact that to her the means were even more important than the end. Militancy to her meant the putting off of the slave *spirit.*

To Mrs. Pankhurst the appeal was different again. She was, as she instinctively knew, cast for a great rôle. She had a temperament akin to genius. She could have been a queen on the Stage or in the Salon. Circumstances had baulked her in the fulfilment of her destiny. Married as young girl to an older husband whom she adored, left a widow with a family to educate in straitened circumstances, the fire in her had been damped down. But the smouldering spark leapt into flame when her daughter Christabel initiated militancy. It was fed by a passion for her first-born. Once years later her habitual reserve broke down when, on a future occasion, she and I were walking round the exercise yard in Holloway Prison. She dwelt upon the name of her daughter "Christabel the Anointed One," the young deliverer who was to emancipate the new generation of women. Mrs. Pankhurst was driven on by her "daemon" to fulfil her destiny and to provide herself, as she said, with a "niche in history."

Annie Kenney made the family party four-square. Her strength lay in complete surrender of mind, soul and body to a single idea and to the incarnation of that idea in a single person. She was Christabel's devotee in a sense that was mystical; I mean she neither gave nor looked to receive any expression of personal tenderness: her devotion took the form of unquestioning faith and absolute obedience. St. Paul says that the truest freedom is to be the slave of Christ. I understand that to mean that in absolute obedience there is no division of will and therefore no sense of external discipline. Just as no ordinary Christian can find that perfect freedom in complete surrender, so no ordinary individual could have given what Annie gave—the surrender of her whole personality to Christabel. That surrender endowed her with fearlessness and power that was not self limited and was therefore incalculable. She was lit up with a spiritual flame. The visible Annie was rather a moving person, at any rate to me, but it was the invisible Annie that possessed world-moving power; I felt it the first time I met her. I did not understand the secret of it then. It has taken me many years to come to a satisfactory understanding of these four gifted people who influenced my fate.

Though they each possessed extraordinary qualities, they did not understand organization, and they had absolutely no idea of finance. Theirs was the guerrilla method of political warfare. It became my business to give their genius a solid foundation. A room in our residential apartment at Clement's Inn which had been hitherto used by my secretary as her office became the first office of the W.S.P.U., and my secretary typed the business letters. This arrangement did not last for very long, but before premises could be rented funds had to be raised.

My husband gave the first donation, and Keir Hardie sent £100 that he had collected from friends. This enabled us to clear off outstanding debts and to meet initial expenses. Annie Kenney became the first London organizer.

Although my idea had been that by raising funds and undertaking the other duties of an Honorary Treasurer, I should be fulfiling all that had been asked of me, I soon found out that this was far from being the case.

Mrs. Pankhurst and Christabel were in Manchester, Sylvia had her career as an artist to make, Annie Kenney was a complete stranger to London. "The many interests" to which Mrs. Pankhurst referred had to be set aside, for I had been sucked into the whirlpool of the W.S.P.U. and from thence-forward for many years was wholly absorbed in it. Little by little my husband became absorbed in it also. Our life since we had met had been a comradeship of ideals and of work: and such it was to remain. I needed his help at every turn, and in the course of this story it will appear that his business enterprise and knowledge of finance built up in a few years an organization that was the wonder of the political world. The revolutionary side of the militant agitation was created and developed by the Pankhursts, the organic growth of the national organization was fostered and directed by our union with them. It is one of the intriguing facts about the W.S.P.U. that minds and temperaments so fundamentally dissimilar could have remained for so many years in practical working harmony under the inspiration of a great ideal.

FROM CHAPTER XI

The Women's Social and Political Union when it was first formed had adopted a constitution framed on the lines of that of the Labour Party, to which the Pankhursts and all the original members in Manchester belonged.

After the headquarters of the movement had been moved from Manchester to London, and after many new branches had been formed throughout the country, it was taken for granted that the movement, having become national in character, would, like the Labour Party, be controlled by an annual national conference composed of delegates from the branches and that these delegates would elect by their votes the personnel of the national executive committee for the ensuing year and would determine by its resolutions the development of the Union's policy.

The first national conference of delegates was due to take place in September 1907, but some months before this date differences of thought and opinion had begun to manifest themselves amongst some of the members. The Union had grown very rapidly since the foundation of the London headquarters in 1906, and to cope with its demands organizer after organizer had been added to the staff. They were appointed because of their great courage and eloquence, and their ability to control and dominate crowds. It will be remembered that it was some time before Christabel Pankhurst was able to take her LL.B. degree in Manchester, after which she was free to come to London, and some of these organizers had taken the brunt of action and had suffered arrest and imprisonment before she appeared on the scene. They had won individually the devotion of a personal following, so that when Christabel later was appointed as chief organizer in London there was not the same unquestioning acceptance of her sole leadership as there had been amongst the small circle of members in her native city.

As September approached, it became evident that some influential people who had been attracted by the movement wished to frame a constitution that would substitute the principle of democratic control for that of individual leadership. It seemed to them reasonable and right that, following the practice of other organizations, the WSPU branches should be accorded the power to criticize and, if they could secure a majority, to amend the policies and the programme of the movement.

But there was another aspect of this question, an aspect acutely realized at Headquarters. New-comers were pouring into the Union. Many of them were quite ill-informed as far as the realities of the political situation were concerned. Christabel, who possessed in a high degree a flair for the intricacies of a complex political situation, had conceived the militant campaign as a whole. In her mind it drew its justifications from the frustrations of fifty years. These frustrations, she maintained, were not due to natural causes, but were directly due to the extremely adroit tactics of successive Governments that had enabled them to avoid dealing with the question. If the suffrage movement was ever to rise from the grave where politicians had laid it, tactics equally adroit needed to be employed. She never doubted that the tactics she had evolved would succeed in winning a cause which, as far as argument or reason were concerned, was intellectually won already. She dreaded all the old plausible evasions and she feared the ingrained inferiority complex in the majority of women. Thus she could not trust her mental offspring to the mercies of politically untrained minds. Moreover, the very fact that militant action involved individual sacrifice imposed heavy responsibilities upon the leaders of the campaign. Individuals who were ready to make the sacrifice that militancy entailed had to be sustained by the assurance of complete unity within the ranks. I agreed with this view of the situation, although I felt that it would be a difficult one to sustain in the conference. The issue to be raised was that of "democracy." It was an irony that this question of principle should come up in a political union which was to win votes for women. It became evident that, young as the militant movement was, it had to meet a crisis the solution of which would influence its future history.

While these clouds had been slowly gathering at headquarters Mrs. Pankhurst was conducting a campaign of meetings in the North. She knew nothing of the difficulties of the position until she returned to London on the eve of the conference. I shall never forget the gesture with which she swept from the board all the "pros and the cons" which had caused us sleepless nights. "I shall tear up the constitution," she declared. This intrepid woman when apparently hemmed in by difficulties always cut her way through them.

The next day at the conference she asserted her position as founder of the Union, declared that she and her daughter had counted the cost of militancy, and were prepared to take the whole responsibility for it, and that they refused to be interfered with by any kind of constitution. She called upon those who had faith in her leadership to follow her, and to devote themselves to the sole end of winning the Vote. This announcement was met with a dignified protest from Mrs. Despard. These two notable women presented a great contrast, the one aflame with a single idea that had taken complete possession of her, the other upheld by a principle that had actuated a long life spent in the service of people.

Mrs. Despard calmly affirmed her belief in democratic equality and was convinced that it must be maintained at all costs. Mrs. Pankhurst claimed that there was only one meaning to "democracy," and that was equal citizenship in a State, which could only be attained by inspired leadership. She challenged all who did not accept the leadership of herself and daughter to resign from the Union that she had founded, and to form an organization of their own.

Thereupon Mrs. Despard, Mrs. How Martyn and Miss Billington (now Mrs. Billington Greig) and their followers formed a separate organisation, the Women's Freedom League. The severance was always referred to as "The Split."

In the years that were to come both these societies played an important part in the great struggle to obtain the Vote. The Women's Freedom League developed many interesting new forms of militancy approved of in conference by all its members; it stood four-square in all vicissitudes, carried on even during the years of the Great War, and is still pursuing its undeviating purpose to win not only political equality but complete social and economic equality for women. The WSPU, under unified leadership, henceforward gathered immense momentum. It became ultimately so strong that it left its mark on the history of the country. Finally the forces within it burst their framework. In 1914 the organization was scattered to the winds, but before its dissolution it had made women's enfranchisement such a vital question that its passage after the war was assured.

FROM CHAPTER XII

After the severance a complete reorganization of the basis of the WSPU was effected. Every member of the Union before being accepted had to sign the following pledge: "I endorse the objects and methods of the Women's Social and Political Union and hereby undertake not to support the candidate of any political party at Parliamentary elections until women have obtained the Parliamentary vote."....

In October 1907 my husband and I launched our paper, *Votes for Women*, and became its co-editors. Its first standing paragraph was as follows:

> "To the brave women who to-day are fighting for freedom: to the noble women who all down the ages kept the flag flying and looked forward to this day without seeing it: to all women all over the world of whatever race or creed or calling, whether they be with us or against us in this fight, we dedicate this paper."

On its cover was a picture of a woman in a seated attitude, head leaning on one hand, brooding over the House of Commons....

During April, May and early June [1908], the energies of the Union were concentrated upon the mass demonstration in Hyde Park which was to break all records and be a phenomenal event in English history.

At this demonstration we set before ourselves the task of bringing a quarter of a million people together. My husband, who was the honorary organizer-in-chief, took charge of the arrangements. Preparations were made on a gigantic scale. A quarter of a square mile of Hyde Park was set aside for the demonstration. Sixty-four trains were chartered to bring supporters from the provinces. In London an elaborate organization was built up. Every group taking part in the procession which marched to Hyde Park had its captain acting under a marshal and all the officers of every rank were under the final command of Mrs. Flora Drummond[12] who was given the title of "General," by which she has since been widely known. The result of this elaborate organization was that on June 21, the day of the demonstration, everything went like clockwork. Every hope and expectation was surpassed; great crowds accompanied the seven processions which, starting from north, south, east and west, passed through the London streets under seven hundred floating banners accompanied by forty bands. These processions were seen from the conning-tower erected in Hyde Park to enter simultaneously the seven entrances to Hyde Park, each took up its allotted position round the platforms. The standard that we had set as to the size of the audience was reached and passed. The correspondent of *The Times* wrote:

> "The organizers of the demonstration had counted on two hundred and fifty thousand; that expectation was certainly fulfilled—probably it was doubled; and it would be difficult to contradict anyone who asserted confidently that it was trebled."

It is no exaggeration to say that never before in the history of the world had such numbers of people been gathered on one spot.

FROM CHAPTER XIV

No political issue within memory of living persons had ever aroused so much support or enlisted so great an enthusiasm. But though the movement meant much to the public life of the country, to us who were personally involved in it it was fraught with deeper issues. It meant to women the discovery of their own identity, that source within of purpose, power and will, the *real* person that often remains throughout a life-time hidden under the mask of appearances. It meant also to women the discovery of the wealth of spiritual sympathy, loyalty and affection that could be formed in intercourse, friendship and companionship with one another. Gone was the age-old sense of inferiority, gone the intolerable weight of helplessness in face of material oppression, gone the necessity of conforming to conventional standards of behaviour, gone all fear of Mrs. Grundy.[13] And taking the place of the old inhibitions was the release of powers that we had never dreamed of. While working for the idea of political liberty, we were individually achieving liberty of a far more real and vital nature. And for the first time in women's lives, they realized on a great scale the power of the team spirit.

It has been well said—so well said that I wish I had originated the saying[14]—"the Suffrage Campaign was our Eton and Oxford, our regiment, our ship, our cricket match." It was our education in that living identification of the self with the corporate whole, which means an intensification and expansion of consciousness. "For thirty years," writes Rachael Ferguson, "I made jokes about the feminine ballot to please the men, and one fine day, I found myself at the head of a section surrounded by banners bearing many a strange device, marching down Whitehall and revelling in every moment of it. By my side marched a dowager duchess and a laundry maid."

Together with the quickening of the intelligence and wit, and with the development of the power of rapid action, there was in the *personnel* of the movement a quickening of the whole emotional life which went out in ardent admiration and sympathy to those who were in prison and to those who performed exceptional deeds of fortitude and daring; a new meaning was given to personal friendship, and in many a face that had borne traces of emotional starvation I saw the awakening of renewed youth and zest. Amongst the elderly, the shadow of loneliness passed away, for the light of love shone into the heart—love that was emulation was sometimes akin to worship. But it was from the young that came the overwhelmingly great response to the call of the hour. They laughed at danger, they laughed at arrest and imprisonment, and found cause for mirth in all their unusual experiences. Christabel had once said on a public platform: "We young people find a world run on ideas entirely contrary to our own. We mean to mould a new world to our will!" And youth rose to the challenge.

FROM CHAPTER XVIII AND XXII

The twenty-five years that have elapsed since then have put all these events in perspective. In order to understand fully Mrs. Pankhurst's determination to separate from us, one has to realize the background of her mind. She was always more interested in militancy than she was in the constitutional side of the movement. She had had nothing at first hand to do with the national organization. She had always regarded Christabel, and to a lesser extent her-self, as the main, if not the sole, inspiration of the movement. She had been distressed by the way in which Christabel consulted us about everything and was influenced by our opinion…. Where I think she was fundamentally wrong (and it seems to me that after-events confirmed this) is in supposing that a more revolutionary form of militancy, with attacks directed more and more on the property of individuals, would strengthen the movement and bring it to more speedy victory. So long as we attacked the Government, and even when we attacked Government property, we won wider and wider public sup-port. The stone-throwing raid, was a departure that to some extent lost us public sympathy at first. On the other hand the publicity accorded to the con-spiracy trial, and Christabel's sensational escape, reversed this disadvantage. At a later stage public interest was so great at one point that it gave immense opportunity for world-wide propaganda, could we have taken advantage of it. The further attacks on private property that developed in the course of the following two years roused a great deal of hostility which was only partly counter-balanced by the admiration felt for the heroism of Mrs. Pankhurst herself and other members of the fraternity. This, however, was not Mrs. Pankhurst's view, and probably is not the view to-day of any of her followers.

There was something quite ruthless about Mrs. Pankhurst and Christabel where human relationship was concerned. This ruthlessness was shown not only to us but to many others, notably to Sylvia, who had given up her career and, without any material compensation whatever, had sacrificed her life to the cause. Men and women of destiny are like that. They are like some irre-sistible force in nature—a tidal wave, or a river in full flood. Looking back on these events that happened so long ago, it seems to me a miracle that for six years there could have existed a fourfold partnership like ours in which each member played a unique and important part.

Thus, in October, 1912, my direct participation in the militant movement came to an end. The cleavage was final and complete. From that time forward I never saw or heard from Mrs. Pankhurst again, and Christabel, who had shared our family life, became a complete stranger. The Pankhursts did noth-ing by halves!…

I never pass that graceful bronze figure in Parliament Gardens, so charac-teristic of the dignified and yet appealing attitude of Mrs. Pankhurst, without a thrill of mingled emotion. There have been many pioneers of the movement that brought about women's political emancipation. One reputation cannot destroy another. All those pioneer women—Mrs. Millicent Fawcett and Dr. Garrett Anderson[15] were two with whom I came into personal contact—brought outstanding gifts of intellect and all possessed great courage and persistence of action. Mrs. Pankhurst brought to the movement in its later stages an essentially feminine temperament touched with genius, and a spice of dare devilry that revelled in scenes of dramatic excitement. I sometimes think that she will live in memory not so much as a great reformer (as, of course, she was) but rather as a great *woman*— worker of magic—creator and destroyer—the Woman whom men all down the ages have dreaded and loved.

ANNIE KENNEY

FROM *MEMORIES OF A MILITANT*

[London: Edward Arnold and Co, 1924. Copyright by Annie Kenney.]

FROM THE FOREWORD

Believing it necessary, as I have done for a long time, that a clear description should be given, however brief, of certain but important parts of the Militant Movement for Women's Suffrage, I have had to decide in what form I can present such a narrative to the public. I have come to the conclusion that the best way will be to write my life.

As I was one of the leading actors in the first play, so I was one of the leading actors in the last....

Mine being one of the active, impulsive, intuitive temperaments of the world, I naturally was drawn to a personality like that of Christabel Pankhurst. If I have faith in a person, no arguments, no persuasion, nothing outside can shake my faith. I had faith in Christabel. It was exactly the faith of a child—it knows but it cannot explain. What path of life my feet would have trod had it not been for Robert Blatchford and Christabel, who knows? The political parties as constituted to-day would never have appealed to me—they are too petty, too contentious. Few of their leaders have the grand passions of life that sweep all before them and abandon themselves to a big idea. Storms, surging floods, wind-swept moors, lightning and terrific thunder, in fact the militancy of nature, rouse within me emotions that in themselves are enough to sweep me away in their surging streams, and yet, as though to save me, deep down there is always the great stillness. A passionate and a big personality alone appealed to me. A Militant Movement alone could satisfy such a tempestuous nature as mine. That is why I can say with real honesty that I alone know what Christabel Pankhurst and the Militant Movement did for me. Whatever phase of life I have touched I have felt I knew it. I have always said that there is just one little secret spring somewhere hidden in my being. Once that spring snaps I shall behold the splendour of heaven and also understand the terrific suffering of the underworld.

The Women's Movement appealed to the best and the highest within me. I met some of the finest characters of the world while engaged in it. The experience gained, the sacrifices made, the labours done, all for a big ideal, were the finest school for the building up of those qualities which I needed to strengthen and evolve me as a human soul upon Life's path. Just as the coral reef is the work of millions of polypi, so the structure of our Movement was the work of thousands of women, who laboured silently, alone, and unacknowledged. I had the honour, the joy, of working with them at brief periods, of suffering with them at others.

No companionship can ever surpass the companionship of the Militants during the childhood and youth of the Suffrage fight. In humility of spirit, fully conscious of the debt I owe them, I dedicate my book to "The Unknown Warriors of the Women's Bloodless Revolution."

A.K.

July, 1924

FROM CHAPTERS IV AND V

What was to be done about Votes for Women? Who was to do it? The Militant Policy was then decided upon. It was not really "militant," except in so far as the methods of dealing with the question were changed, and a change in policy always has the appearance of rebellion.

The great difference between the old method and the new lay in the changing of a word. The old school said, "Are you in *favour* of women having the vote?" the new school said, "Will you *give* us the vote?"

Aspiring politicians could answer the old school; none would answer the new school. The wisest among them saw the cleverness of the change, but pretended otherwise. They knew that it was the only way to win the vote; they must have known!

Christabel Pankhurst decided that she and I would go to the Free Trade Hall meeting, wait until question time (quite a legitimate way of getting answers to problems perplexing voters), then rise and put this question to Mr. Churchill: "If you are elected, will you do your best to make Woman Suffrage a Government Measure?" Instinctively she knew that the question would never be answered, for two reasons: had he said Yes, the Cabinet would have practically been committed to carry it out; had he said No, the Liberal women would have pricked up their ears. Cabinet Ministers knew this; that was what made all the trouble. For the first time one single word from them was the only thing asked for—"Yes" or "No." Again the very simplicity of the case made it frightfully difficult for the average politician, the average voter, and the average party woman, to understand.

We made a banner, and inscribed on it the new war cry, "Votes for Women," and we decided if we were not answered, to stand up and unfurl the banner, so that all could see that the question that had been put was one on Votes for Women. We went to the meeting, listened very attentively to the speeches, and at the end questions were asked, some Labour men putting questions about the unemployed.

They were answered. Then I rose and put mine. No reply. The chairman asked for other questions. I rose again, and was pulled down by two enthusi-astic Liberals behind me.

We then unfurled the flag. That was enough. The little speck of cloud gath-ered, which afterwards covered the whole political horizon, only to be dis-persed by a greater, blacker, denser cloud taking its place—the war-cloud of 1914.

There was no answer to our question, and the strong arms of Liberal stew-ards dragged us from the meeting and literally flung us out of doors. This cre-ated a sensation. A great part of the audience followed. I addressed them. At least I made an effort to do so, but before I had explained what had hap-pened I found myself in custody and being marched off between two police-men. The strange thing was that I had not the least fear. I did not feel ashamed at the crowds seeing me marched off. I had indeed started a new life. My admiration for Christabel and my belief in what I was doing kept me calm and determined.

On the following day, October 14th, 1905, we put in an appearance at the court, and were found guilty of obstruction. The court procedure did not impress me in the least, though I had a little strange quivering sensation when I heard the magistrate sentencing me to three days' imprisonment, with the option of a fine of 5 s[hillings] with costs. It was no doubt thought by the authorities that the fine would be paid and all would be over and soon for-gotten.

But Christabel Pankhurst's mind did not work on those lines. One thing she did not wish, and that was that the episode should be forgotten. The bait had been strong enough; the Press had bitten; the night's catch was rich in the extreme. The very extremity of abuse, criticism, and condemnation hurled at us by the morning Press for such an inoffensive protest as that which we had made the previous night at the Free Trade Hall meeting, was in itself a sign that astute parliamentarians realized that we knew what we were about. As the question was not a party question we were treated with hostility by the Press of both political parties—the party Press invariably joins forces against non-party measures.

The court was crowded. Manchester was excited. The name of Pankhurst being well known in the city, the case was interesting to the people. Not only Manchester was roused, but the whole country read about the episode in the morning papers.

And so the fight began. Christabel Pankhurst had declared war....

None of my family had the faintest idea I was in prison until they read the news in the papers. Two of my sisters paid me a visit, and asked if they might pay the fine and give me my release—it was thoughtful of them not to pay it before asking me. I said No, our policy being "Prison, or Votes for Women," and at the moment I felt I might be in prison all my life.

The day of my release was a happy and exciting day for me. Members of the choir were waiting to welcome me, two of my girl friends from the factory, two sisters, and many strangers. A telegram had come from the overlooker at the factory during my absence, demanding my immediate return, but I of course had been in prison when it arrived.

Mrs. Pankhurst greeted me by saying, "Annie, as long as I have a home you must look upon it as yours. You will never have to return to factory life." The news did not surprise me, as I had been told by a still small voice in prison that this would happen to me on my release. As I had been living with them for weeks I accepted the offer as though I had been asked to stay to lunch, and what they thought of the calm way I took the news I do not know.

I was excited when I heard of a big rally to be held in the Free Trade Hall. It was to be a protest against our arrest and imprisonment. It is amazing the crowds that will assemble if they can protest against something or some one!

It was just a week from our being boo'd out of the same hall. It was packed, and hundreds were turned away. Bouquets and flowers were given to us, songs of liberty were sung in our favour. Labour was in great prominence, vowing support, and cheering us to the echo.

Christabel made a most eloquent speech, full of passion and fire. I delivered my speech, and I trembled as I made it. I felt nervous when I saw the great hall full of earnest, excited faces. I knew the change had come into my life. The old life had gone, a new life had come. Had I found on my return that I had taken on a new body, I should not have been in the least surprised. I felt absolutely changed. The past seemed blotted out. I had started on a new cycle. I was intelligently conscious that the change meant added responsibility. Truth is always illuminating, and Christabel Pankhurst's speech was truth to me. She it was who lit the fire which consumed the past. It was but a sign of growth that the eternal "I" within me had gained all the experience it could from the old life, and had taken unto itself a more complicated and varied life, to acquire, learn, and gain greater experience for the development of the undying spirit which is deathless, ever on an eternal journey.

FROM CHAPTER XXII

We did risk human life when we burnt houses, in spite of the care we took to see that all buildings were untenanted, but Providence protected us. No life was lost except on the Militants' side. Many Militants are in fact to-day lying on sick-beds suffering from the after-effects of imprisonments and forcible feeding. What a reward for a brave fight on behalf of a great Movement!

Wars and revolutions have their tragic side, and our Revolution was no exception to the rule. There were those who worked unceasingly and in the end were forgotten, lost sight of amidst the toil and strife. Extreme Militancy brought with it tragedy and suffering, heartache and loneliness. It was too severe to carry with it the lightheartedness of other days.

Was it worth the trouble, the sacrifices made, the suffering endured? To me it was worth it all, as I believed extreme Militancy necessary. Whether it could have been run in a different way it is difficult to say. Wars and revolutions are made up of surprises, hasty retreats, quick marches. This naturally destroys order for the time being, and yet there is at the head one who sees order where those in the midst of the fight see but confusion. Was extreme Militancy right, even though it was apparently justified? That is a question again which raises deep unsolved problems of Ethics. Each person can only answer the question as he sees or understands it. The day will come when War and Revolution will not only be thought wrong, but will not be necessary. But that time is not now, and during the Militant fight we were living in years preceding a greater Revolution which has done wonders for the evolution of thought,—thought which is now being acknowledged and recognized by Science as one of the greatest forces in the world.

FROM CHAPTER XXX: CONCLUSION

No Suffrage book would be complete without the name of Mrs. Fawcett, the leader of the Constitutional Movement.

Mrs. Fawcett's life has been one of devotion and service on behalf of women. Without the patient, persistent, plodding labour of the old Suffrage Society, the Militants would not have had an argument on which to base their claim that "other methods had failed." For over forty years the Constitutional Suffragists pleaded, they entreated, they persuaded, and then were told to wait until the time was ripe when there was a sign that women really wanted the Vote.

Mrs. Fawcett's name is world renowned as one of the pioneers and leaders in the Women's Movement.

Why were women Militant? What was the attraction which swept the cultured and highly educated women into the ranks of the fighting section? What was the secret of the success of the Militant Party when the party was at the height of its power? What inspired women to suffer imprisonment, to lose friends, and to be exiled from family and home? What impulse was it that made women leave a life of ease and luxury and take up one which had nothing to offer but hard, unpopular, and apparently unprofitable labour? What made the school-teacher, the nurse, the factory-girl, the shop-assistant, the clerk, the doctor, the scientist, the novelist, the housewife give all their spare time and hard-earned money to a cause that was creating unrest in the land? These are questions that will be asked by future students of past movements.

Coming generations will naturally be anxious to know why women were militant. The police courts, the prisons, Parliament, the British Museum, contain records in which all future generations may read, mark, and learn what the Militants did, and many most exciting things that they did not do!

The first question the inquiring student of the future will ask is: Why did Christabel Pankhurst choose militant methods to win a constitutional reform? The records of the Women's Constitutional Movement partly answer the question. Because all other methods had failed. But what gave her the idea, or how did the idea come to her? The germ of rebellion against the apathy and hostility of politicians was lying dormant. The germ became a living thought. Christabel's thoughts had wings. Once the idea was conceived, the battle was won in her mind. She was fearless and confident.

The success of the Movement lay primarily in the highly individualized and magnetic personality of Christabel Pankhurst, secondly in the sensitive, temperamental, cultured and gifted personality of Mrs. Pankhurst. These two women were the guiding spirits who influenced every action, every thought, of their followers. Devotion such as theirs wins devotion; love such as theirs attracts and draws towards the givers a veritable cordon of protection and love that only a few characters in the history of ages can claim....

Movements are built up by silent followers, and few realize the sacrifices they make, the secret suffering they endure, in their effort to be true to a great principle which has stirred their hearts. For the first few years the Militant Movement was more like a religious revival than a political movement. It stirred the emotions, it aroused passions, it awakened the human chord which responds to the battle-call of Freedom. It was a genuine reform for emancipation, led by earnest, unselfish, self-sacrificing women. A cause that works for emancipation must always draw to itself those who feel the need of freedom, and those who consciously feel their position rouse in others the same desire for liberty. The call was universal. All women were appealed to. Class barriers were broken down; political distinctions swept away; religious differences forgotten. All women were as one. The fight was "Women *versus* Parliament." The one thing demanded was loyalty to policy and unselfish devotion to the Cause.

The Movement represented the pent-up indignation and tightly suppressed anger or grief of highly individualized women, capable, clever, and learned. Their hearts in many cases had been scarred at the constant barriers that faced them in their walk in life. The life of Queen Elizabeth had been proof to them that women could understand the science of Government. The works and life of the first pioneer of women's economic independence, Mary Wollstonecraft, had been studied and re-studied by those advanced souls who could find no outlet for their desires and capabilities.

There was a woman, young in years, charming in appearance, cultured in manner, brilliant in learning, masterly in political strategy, fearless in action, courageous in danger, unflinching before opponents, speaking women's thoughts, expressing their ideas, but expressing them with passion, fervour, and determination. She was the idol, the loved and honoured one, who gained their hearts as well as their heads in a big fight. All petty ideals and feelings were forgotten with the arrival of a big person with big ideas who had faith in them and implicit trust in the wisdom, the courage, of those who followed her.

Harmony vibrated through Christabel's whole body. The one thing she dreamt about was women's immortal birthright. We were conscious that she was the woman of the age, and that she alone could lead us to the land of political freedom. Followers have rarely such a leader, but few leaders in the history of humanity have had such unselfish, unquestioning followers as those who followed the one who had come forth to "plough the rock until it bore."[16]...

The Militant Movement as an organization was a great success. It was one of the most highly organized movements we shall ever see. The success lay in the concentration, not only of the creative leader, but also of thousands of other women on one object. The whole Movement became so highly vitalized that we seemed to speak the word, and lo! the thing was done.

No small body of people ever had more obstacles to overcome than had the militant section when they first entered the political field on behalf of women. There had been the concentrated thought of generations ever revolving round the fixed point: "Woman's place is the home." Therefore concentration had to break through concentration and dissolve until the opposition of ages gradually crumbled away through sheer inability to overcome a great mental and moral force.

CICELY HAMILTON

FROM *LIFE ERRANT*

[London: J.M. Dent and Sons, 1935]

CHAPTER VI: WOMEN ON THE WARPATH

Like most women of the time who earned their living at "middle-class" call-ings, I was drawn into the Woman Suffrage agitation, and for several years I did a good deal of writing and speaking for the Cause. Not always, I fear, to the satisfaction of my fellow-workers; there were, as I had reason to know, a good many ardent workers in "the Movement" who regarded me and my views with considerable suspicion; chiefly, I suppose, because I never attempt-ed to disguise the fact that I wasn't wildly interested in votes for anyone, and that if I worked for women's enfranchisement (and I did work quite hard) it wasn't because I hoped great things from counting female noses at general elections, but because the agitation for women's enfranchisement must inevitably shake and weaken the tradition of the "normal woman." The "nor-mal woman" with her "destiny" of marriage and motherhood and house-keeping, and no interest outside her home—and especially no interest in the man's preserve of politics! My personal revolt was feminist rather than suf-fragist; what I rebelled at chiefly was the dependence implied in the idea of "destined" marriage, "destined" motherhood—the identification of success with marriage, of failure with spinsterhood, the artificial concentration of the hopes of girlhood on sexual attraction and maternity....

My militant activities were of the slightest; I was not of those who wore hon-ourable badges in token of a Holloway martyrdom. I did, more than once, interrupt at political meetings; but to my credit be it said, I never persuaded myself, on these occasions, that I was doing anything to further the cause of Free Speech; on the contrary, I knew I was preventing Free Speech, on the part of opponents, and behaving as I did in order to make myself objection-able. Actually, I think (though I never joined their association) I had more sympathy with the "constitutional" suffragists than with the "militants" who so heartily despised them; the more I thought of it, the more it seemed to me there was a lack of logic in the militant belief in violence. The acceptance of violence as the best means of obtaining political ends implied a secondary importance for the vote itself. For a few months I was a member of the Women's Social and Political Union; then, for somewhat longer, of the Women's Freedom League; but I was happier working with less political bodies, such as the Women Writers' Suffrage League, of which I was one of the founders.

Those who took active part in the militant suffrage movement will usually tell you that it was to Mrs. Pankhurst and her soldiers of the purple, white, and green that the ultimate granting of the vote was due. Many a time and oft I have been assured of this, but, even so, I am not quite convinced. The granting of enfranchisement to the women of Great Britain, in 1918, does not stand alone; in non-Latin races, about that epoch, there was a widespread willingness to admit women to citizenship. Republican Germany, for instance, admitted her women with a rush; and it hardly seems likely that, after four years of carnage—and in a country that had suffered, during most of those years, from food shortage—the thought of Mrs. Pankhurst and her hunger-striking militants would have been any real inspiration. Far be it from me to offer any definite opinion on the matter; but at the back of my mind there has always been the uneasy suspicion that enfranchisement was granted us in 1918, not as trophy won by the Women's Social and Political Union; not even, as was sometimes asserted, as reward for the services we rendered during the war; but chiefly—almost entirely—because of its supreme unimportance at that juncture of our national life. What use was the vote as a weapon against German guns, submarines, and Gothas?[17] The problem at the moment was to keep ourselves alive, and when a people is engaged in a life-and-death struggle, it is apt to lose interest in matters which yesterday were of sufficient importance to rouse it to a fury of dispute.... I remember—how well I remember—receiving the official intimation that my name had been placed on the register of the Chelsea electorate! I was in Abbeville at the time and as the post arrived, a battery of Archies, somewhere on the hill, began to thud; an enemy airplane was over, taking photographs. I remember thinking, as I read the notice, of all that the suffrage had meant for us, a year or two before! How we had marched for the suffrage and held meetings and been shouted at; and how friends of mine, filled with the spirit of the martyr, had hurled themselves at policemen—and broken windows—and starved themselves in prison: and that now, at this moment of achieved enfranchisement, what really interested me was not the thought of voting at the next election, but the puffs of smoke that the Archies sent after the escaping plane. Truth to tell, at that moment I didn't care a button for my vote; and rightly or wrongly, I have always imagined that the Government gave it me in much the same mood as I received it.

* * * * *

It was an interesting phenomenon, the militant suffrage agitation; even more interesting than I realized at the time. For it was the beginning—the first indication—of the dictatorship movements which are by way of thrusting democracy out of the European continent. Not the Fascists but the militants of the Women's Social and Political Union first used the word "Leader" as a reverential title; and the *Führerprinzip*, the principle of leadership, was carried to something like idolatry by the wearers of the purple, white, and green. Emmeline Pankhurst, in this respect, and on a smaller scale, was forerunner of Lenin, Hitler, Mussolini—the Leader whose fiat must not be questioned, the Leader who could do no wrong!

Until I was drawn into the suffrage agitation my interest in political movements and tendencies had been chiefly theoretical; derived from the reading of books and newspapers, and occasional lectures, mostly of a Socialist type. With the suffrage agitation I exchanged theory for practice—practice that was sometimes exciting, exhilarating; and under the influence of the new exhilaration one did all sorts of astonishing things—indulged in strange activities of which one had never imagined oneself capable. I remember, for instance, how, all unawares, I stumbled into public speech-making; at a suffrage meeting, when questions were asked for, I, being puzzled by some allusion the speaker had made, rose from my chair and requested further enlightenment; and the difficulty requiring a certain amount of explanation, I was on my feet for a minute or two. In consequence, the moment the meeting was over, I was seized on by one of its organizers; she was short of a speaker for an open-air meeting next day, and I must come along and help her out. I thought she mistook me for someone else, and began to explain that I couldn't possibly—I had never made a speech in my life, and I shouldn't know how.... "Nonsense!" she retorted; "you can speak quite well if you like— what were you doing just now?" And to my terror, next day I found myself standing on a chair in Battersea Park, addressing an audience which—much to my relief— was neither very large nor greatly interested. It listened in amiable stolidity to my nervous remarks, and I managed to get through my allotted ten minutes without breakdown.

That was the beginning of my career as a suffrage speaker, if career it can be called. "The Movement" was an epoch of many meetings, organizers were often hard put to it and, in spite of the fact that I could not always be counted on for an orthodox presentment of the case for enfranchisement, I was in fairly frequent demand—largely, no doubt, because my play, *Diana of Dobson's*, was produced about that time and my name, to a certain extent, became known to the public. I have never considered that platform oratory was my strong suit, but all the same, though I say it as shouldn't, I was popular as a suffrage speaker. A journalist, writing a character-sketch of me, summed me up as a speaker by remarking that my platform manner was atrocious, but I usually had something to say; and I suppose it was the matter, the something to say, that got over the atrocious manner. Not a job I had any liking for; it was bad enough to make a speech myself—always on the same subject, trying hard to think of something new to say; but even worse was the necessity of listening to all the old arguments as put forth by our fellow-orators. Never shall I forget the experience of a speaking-tour that I once let myself in for; a week or so of meetings, one every night, and sometimes an afternoon thrown in! The team consisted of myself and three companions, hardened suffrage speakers, who had ceased to care how many times they made or heard the same speech; and before the week was over my original kindly feelings towards them were shot through with murderous loathing. One of them, I remember, told night after night the same would-be humorous story of a Liberal statesman—in exactly the same words, with exactly the same emphasis—while every night, as I sat on the platform in view of the audience, I tried to register surprised appreciation in a smile that grew more and more wooden. The tour, I suppose, was a success, because there was a suggestion of prolonging it by two or three more meetings, but when I was approached on the subject I was adamant. It was me for London—and no more of that nightly wooden smile!

Of all the meetings of the suffrage epoch that I remember most clearly is the great gathering at the Albert Hall, organized by the Women's Liberal Federation, at which Lloyd George, then a Liberal Minister, was announced to speak in favour of enfranchisement. The fact that he was to advocate Votes for Women could not save him from the wrath of the Women's Social and Political Union, whose slogan of the moment was "Deeds not Words!" and which had given out that it would break up all meetings addressed by Cabinet Ministers until its demands were complied with. I was told at the time, and by one who should have known, that the promoters of the meeting had at first issued orders that the stewards were not to eject the inevitable interrupters; they were to let them shout and take no notice. It was pointed out to them, however, that if the stewards did not deal with determined interruption, the audience would; and if fighting started among all those massed thousands in the Albert Hall, the chances were that some of the interrupters would be killed, instead of being merely ejected. On this warning, the prohibition to the stewards was withdrawn; very wisely, I should say, judging by the spectacle the meeting presented before it was half-way through. For the interrupters were many and vigorous, and as they bobbed up and shouted all over the building, one could actually see the temper of the audience growing nastier. Looking down on the amphitheatre from a first-tier box, one saw orderly rows of decent human beings break up into struggling knots and groups whereof the centre was a woman, up on a chair and shouting something inaudible at the platform till her neighbours dragged her down. Into these groups the stewards ploughed their way—the difficulties of penetration being increased by the fact that the promoters of riot had usually established themselves well in the centre of a row—extracted their prisoner, and conveyed her to the nearest exit. The process was not always a pleasant one to behold; I have a memory of a woman who was carried out by two or three stewards, struggling and shouting—her war-cry no doubt—while more than one of the infuriated audience tried to hit her as she was dragged past them. And as the audience grew more violent, so, inevitably, did the protesters; where they had first got up and spoken, they now got up and screamed. By no means all of these protesters were women; there were several male sympathizers, belonging, I suppose, to the Men's League for Women's Suffrage. One of them, who had been sitting in a ground-tier box just below us, in a momentary lull, when Lloyd George was trying to speak, suddenly shot up, like a Jack-in-the-box, shook both his fists at the world in general, and roared out something indistinguishable. In an instant a dozen hands went up to seize him, someone in the box fell on him from the rear, and he was pushed, head foremost, into the arena, breaking a chair in the process, and being finally frog-marched to the exit. Judging from the sounds that proceeded from above, the same sort of tumult that was going on in the amphitheatre was also going on in the galleries, and it looked as if the meeting were hopeless, and would have to be abandoned—when suddenly humour took command! Over the tumult and the shouting and the hatred there floated from the organ a melody familiar and amiable:

> *Oh, dear, what can the matter be?*
> *Oh, dear, what can the matter be?*

I don't know who was the Albert Hall organist on that occasion, but I have always thought of him, affectionately, as the embodiment of humorous good sense. His musical comment was so apt and so ridiculous that mirth swept the meeting like a gust. Even the deadly earnestness of the suffragette (and oh, how deadly earnest the suffragette could be!) broke down before the laughter on the organ. Broke down for good; there were no more cries of "Deeds not Words!" Mr. Lloyd George picked up his argument, carried on in peace, and in due time wound up to applause.

Barring "Deeds not Words!" I don't think I remember a word that was said at that meeting, but all the same it was one of the incidents that have counted in my life. It was not the first time I had been at an angry meeting, though never, I think, at one quite so angry; but always before I had been in it, one of the crowd, and therefore had only a partial view of its excitement. In my box at the Albert Hall, on the other hand, I had been a spectator, sitting apart and looking down on the excitement, watching the effects of political passion on a crowd. And frankly I was horrified, amazed and horrified. The brawling men and women, the mobs that surged around them—I knew that if you could get them away from their causes, away from their crowds, they would be perfectly decent individuals. Yet, gathered together in the Albert Hall, they were violent, they were brutal, they were crazed.... And the reason for their violence, their lack of control, was crowd-life, overpowering sense of membership; for the time being they had resigned their responsible individuality, and were conscious only of their herd-, their community-life.

I don't suppose for a moment that the Lloyd George meeting at the Albert Hall was the first occasion on which it had struck me that the standard of man, as member of an organization, is infinitely lower than the standard of man, the decent individual; but from the day forth it was more than an idea—a conviction which years and experience have not weakened, a conviction to be acted on and lived by. No man, I suppose, can be strongly a member of any organization, however high its aims, without losing something of his honourable scruple and his charity; for the dangerous attraction of membership, comradeship, is that it gives free rein to passions and vices which, as individuals, we are bound to hold in check. We may hate, as members of a party or a nation, as we dare not hate for ourselves; as members of a class, evil-thinking—distortion of motive—may seem like a duty and a merit. That weed of our civilization which we call propaganda (and should call lying) is the natural product of close organization; and Mazzini[18] summed up the moral danger of community-life when he said that if he had done for himself what he did for Italy, he should be accounted a scoundrel. And the nation, in this respect, does not stand alone; organized man, all the world over, has the same tendency to scoundrelism. Internationalism organized has shown itself to the full as unscrupulous and merciless as nationalism; once we are closely united in membership, we can hate and malign in the name of a class, a religion, of freedom itself, just as effectively as we can in the name of a race. I suppose the organization—the collective being—is a creature of low morality because it exists merely for the furtherance of its own ends; whereas man, the individual, unless he be a creature utterly degraded, has other aims and hopes in life.

Is there any form of the life collective that is capable of love for its fellow—for another community? Is there any church that will stand aside that another church may be advantaged?... You and I are civilized, as man and man; but collectively we are part of a life whose only standard and motive is self-interest, its own advantage. A beast-life, morally, which demands from us sacrifices, makes none itself.... That's as far as we have got in the mass.

I wrote that years after the Albert Hall meeting, when war and revolution and post-war hatreds had emphasized the evils of the life collective, of binding us together in membership; but it was in contact with the politics of pre-war days that I first began to realize its ugly moral possibilities.

* * * * *

A curious characteristic of the militant suffrage movement was the importance it attached to dress and appearance, and its insistence on the feminine note. There was no costume-code amongst non-militant suffragists, but in the Women's Social and Political Union the coat-and-skirt effect was not favoured; all suggestion of the masculine was carefully avoided, and the outfit of a militant setting forth to smash windows would probably include a picture-hat. This taboo of the severer forms of garment was due, in part, to dislike of the legendary idea of the suffragette, as masculine in manner and appearance—many of the militants were extraordinarily touchy on that point. And there may have been some connection between this "dressiness" and the combative impulse, since soldiers, all the world over, are inclined to be fussy about their personal appearance. Be that as it may, I have heard Mrs. Pankhurst advise very strongly against what she considered eccentricity in the matter of dress; her reason being that it would shock male prejudice and make the vote harder to obtain. After the vote was won, she said, we could do as we liked in the matter of garments—but till then....

This preference, real or politic, for the conventional-feminine in dress is no doubt one of the reasons why her followers have woven around Mrs. Pankhurst a legend of womanly gentleness and charm—a legend that hardly does her justice. By that I must not be interpreted to mean that she was not, in her personal surroundings, a woman of gentleness and charm; but it was not by those drawing-room, domestic qualities that she attracted her following of adoring militants, exacted unquestioning obedience to her leadership and made her name a challenge from end to end of the country. She achieved what she did because she was a magnificent demagogue; and a demagogue, a ruler of the crowd-mind, must, on occasion, be capable of actions which are anything but gentle and charming. Nevertheless, the "sweet-womanly" legend is popular with those who once served her; as I discovered when the statue now placed in the Embankment Garden was commissioned from Arthur Walker, A.R.A., who at that time was a neighbour of mine. He showed me the model from which he intended to work, and asked if I thought it was like her—he, I think, had never seen, or at least, never known, the original. The only doubt I ventured to express was whether he had quite got Mrs. Pankhurst's forcefulness, her combative energy, and to this his rejoinder was: "But she was so feminine!" That, he said, had been insisted on by those who described her for his benefit; a woman essentially feminine.... I thought of Mrs. Pankhurst's back as I had once seen it while she preached defiance to her followers; the stubborn set of her shoulders and the determined set of her head—and the voice, the even more determined voice, with its queer pronunciation of the all-important word "Women"! Whatever Emmeline Pankhurst may have been in private life, her characteristic on the platform was a forcefulness, a driving energy that is not usually associated with women one describes as "so feminine"! And it was on the platform she counted, urging her women to defiance of the law—on the platform and not in private life!

FROM CHAPTER XX: SINGLE BLESSEDNESS

Like nearly all girls of my generation I was bred in the idea that my duty and advantage was to conform to the masculine ideal of womanhood; this or that habit or exercise was forbidden because it clashed with the ideal, and would therefore lessen our value in masculine eyes. I do not mean that this principle was a matter of bald statement; but as a tradition—unspoken or half-spoken—it was a constant influence on our thoughts and a constant director of our energies. If we were not to be failures, we must be attractive to the opposite sex; we must attain to charm—which was predecessor of sex appeal. Even when we had few qualifications for success, and our natural impulses were all the other way—even so we must strive to attain it!

I can look back, alas! on many wasted months and years of life, but none of them appear so completely wasted as the months and years when—obedient to tradition—I strove to cultivate the art and craft of the charmer. It was always an uncongenial job; all my real desires and impulses had another direction; but the influence of tradition was strong, and for several years of adolescence and young womanhood I did conscientiously strive to make myself attractive to the male. Not, I am afraid, with overmuch success; as already remarked, most of my offers of marriage came from men who had never set eyes on me. Still, for some time I struggled—quite gamely—with my natural disadvantages and natural distaste for the job.

I can't remember the exact age at which I went on strike against tradition; but to my credit be it said that I was still quite marriageable—it was some years before I reached thirty. Nor can I remember what particular event or incident decided the actual moment of the strike; but this I do remember, that I sat down and pondered, dispassionately, the whole business of feminine charm; and without much difficulty came to the decision that, for those not naturally gifted, its returns were small, as compared with the energy invested. Having come to that decision, I decided there and then to cut the whole thing out—a decision I have never regretted. It wasn't only that I ceased to waste my energies in small amiabilities and efforts to please; I felt friendlier towards my male fellow-creatures once I had realized I didn't care a button as to whether or no I resembled their ideal of womanhood. If they liked me, they liked me for myself and my own values—not because I had strained my natural thoughts and manners to a pattern they considered attractive.

HANNAH MITCHELL

FROM *THE HARD WAY UP: THE AUTOBIOGRAPHY OF HANNAH MITCHELL, SUFFRAGETTE AND REBEL*

[Ed. Geoffrey Mitchell, London: Faber and Faber Ltd., 1979. First published in 1968.]

FROM CHAPTER 12, "THE GREAT EXPERIENCE"

It seems to me now, looking back, that all my previous life had been a preparation for this great experience. While indirectly it caused me much sorrow, it brought me many contacts which have immeasurably enriched my life. Through the suffrage movement I came to know many notable women who honoured me by their friendship and encouragement. Chief among these was that fine and gracious woman, Charlotte Despard, who, I am proud to remember, to the end of her long life, always called me her "dear friend," Marian Coates-Hanson of Middlesbrough, to whom I owe much, Mrs. Pethick Lawrence, Mrs. Cobden Sanderson, Edith How Martyn, Elizabeth Robins the novelist, and many others.

From every part of Britain, women began to respond, everywhere we went women of all classes rallied to the militant banner. Indeed the struggle of women seemed like the quest of the Holy Grail....

In the early summer [1906], a great Liberal Rally was held at Belle Vue, with John Burns[19] and Winston Churchill as the star speakers. Elaborate precautions were taken to keep out the militants, most of whom were well known by now. I think my one and only brown costume would have been recognized anywhere in the North of England. So to grace the Liberal Rally, my friend Mary H. lent me a smart little costume of greenish tweed, and a stylish hat trimmed with green velvet. So, looking very different from the dingy brown sparrow the Manchester Liberals knew so well, I was shown to my 5 shillings seat by an obsequious steward, and soon recognized in the 10 shillings seats Adela Pankhurst in her mother's best hat and silk coat. The hat was trimmed with roses and didn't suit Adela at all, but it had a wide brim which hid her face, and the high collar of her coat helped the disguise. With her was a tall, scholarly-looking man. I never knew who he was. From his appearance he might have been a Professor from the University, but he was probably one of the local Socialists, who had come prepared if need be to keep the ring.

We had a definite plan, which no hysterical women—as the press called us—could have carried out. We rose, one at a time, as our appointed man was getting well under way with his speech, displayed our banners and called out the question:

"Will the Liberal Government give the vote to women?" holding up the meeting until we were put out, more or less violently. Then, when all had settled down again, and the next speaker was well away, another woman rose and repeated the procedure, and in turn was bundled out. This repeated ten times was enough to try the temper of the mildest steward, and the treatment grew worse with each interruption. I was thankful to be second out. Adela was the first to be ejected. John Burns was my man, and it gave me some satisfaction to interrupt him. We were indignant at his accepting office under the Liberals. As I was pushed past the platform, I called out "Burns, the traitor!"

I found Adela outside and we waited for the others. Soon a terrific uproar heralded another ejection, this time a man and woman, the man being handled in a brutal manner. As he seemed unable to stand when the police let go, we went to his assistance. He was Councillor Morrissey of Liverpool, whose wife was the third interrupter. Seeing her roughly handled by the stewards he tried to protect her, whereupon the angry men had vented their rage upon him. As he already had an injured leg, a savage kick on it caused him to faint. He sat on a stone outside Belle Vue, and we stayed until he was able to walk. When we moved to cross the road, the police closed in and arrested us all.

When I asked my escort what I was to be charged with, he replied gruffly, "Come on, yer one on 'em."

"Very well," I said, "take your hands off me. I'll come with you."

He at once released me, and I followed Adela who was in the grip of a big burly officer, who kept telling her she ought to be smacked and set to work at the wash tubs. She grew so angry that she slapped his hand, which was as big as a ham. For this she was charged with assaulting the police, as well as obstruction, with which we were all charged. At the police station, the sergeant in charge told us to send for someone to bail us out. This we refused to do, saying we would stay in custody until Monday....

Although our case was tried by the stipendiary magistrate, Mr. Brierley, the lay magistrates, *all men*, sat on the Bench to stare at us as if we had escaped from the zoo. I don't know if the police of that day suffered from delusions, but when I heard my own particular constable say, "The defendant Mitchell, when told to go away, refused to do so, saying she should stay as long as she liked," I wondered why he thought I had said it. If he had ordered me to go away, I should have gone at once, to a safe distance, and returned as soon as his attention was diverted.

Remembering that trial, now a magistrate myself, I do not always believe that a policeman cannot be mistaken. They are only human like the rest of us, and I fear at times their sex prejudice over-rode their sense of justice. We were troublesome women to them; often we outwitted them, and then they became angry.

We were fortunate in being tried by the stipendiary, who did not seem to have either illiberal or anti-feminist views. My own impression was that he was somewhat amused. He listened gravely to the recital of our misdeeds, and apparently decided that something less than boiling oil would meet the case. He imposed on each a nominal fine: mine was half-a-crown. Adela, who was supposed to have assaulted her giant captor, was fined ten shillings, but the magistrate's quizzical glance from the slight, girlish figure to the burly constable, seemed to me to speak volumes. I would have given much to know what he really thought. We all refused to pay the fine, except Mr. Morrissey, who was persuaded to pay his, and go home on account of his work. The three women were brought back into court, and given three days, that is Mrs. Morrissey and myself. Adela was awarded seven days' imprisonment, she having assaulted the "law."

We were then taken below to await the arrival of the prison van. Someone brought us a jug of tea, and told us that six women had been sent to prison that day in London for ringing the Prime Minister's door bell, and refusing to leave Downing Street.

FROM CHAPTER 13, "PRISON FOR A NIGHT"

The basement of the Manchester Police Court was then, and still is, a horrible place to wait in, like a cattle stall with bars in front. One other woman went with us in the van to Strangeways. She was being sent to prison for fighting with her neighbours.

"I only called her a cow," she told us, "and so she is."

She gave us her opinion of the police in language which coincided with my own thoughts on the subject. We all felt that we had not had even half-a-crown's worth of defiance out of the affair, as we had no intention of clashing with the police at Belle Vue, but we mentally vowed that next time the law should have something to complain of.

At Strangeways, we were not badly treated, being excused the bath which our fellow prisoner was compelled to take. We heard her loudly complaining that the water was cold and dirty and there was no soap. The wardress kindly allowed us to change in her own room, giving us a sheet to use as a screen. The prison dress was horrible, coarse and unshapely. It consisted of a wide skirt, thickly gathered at the waist, a sort of short jacket or bed gown, such as was worn a hundred years ago, in a horrible drab stuff stamped with a black arrow,[20] one flannel singlet, a coarse calico chemise, no knickers or corsets, short thick stockings without garters and heavy shoes which would have fitted a navvy; mine were different sizes. There was a blue check apron with a sort of check duster for a handkerchief. Even our hairpins were taken away, and we were compelled to push our hair into the prison cap. This cap was the only decent thing given to us. Adela whispered to me that I looked like a queen in mine. I did not feel very queenly; ugly dress makes one feel ugly. Besides, it was very uncomfortable. It was all too big, and the absence of garters and knickers made one feel almost naked.

We all had a sort of numbered badge; mine was H.10, the number of my cell. The cell itself was not too unpleasant, and quite clean. There were two blankets and a straw mattress which would have been comfortable enough, but it was too short, being only long enough for a child's cot. However, I was so tired that I slept fairly well until the bell rang at 6 a.m., when the door was unlocked, and we were ordered out to the lavatories where we washed and emptied our slops. We were then taken out for exercise, so called, which meant just walking round and round in a circle, without being allowed to speak to each other. I found this very hard, as my shoes kept slipping off, and the stockings, also much too big, fell down over my ankles. When I returned to the cell, I remedied this by tearing up the rags given me to polish my "tins" with, and using them for garters. I think I was then expected to "make my bed" by rolling up the bedding and stacking it along with the bed against the wall. Instead I just sat on the bed, not caring very much what happened next. I was feeling very ill, having had no food since lunch on the previous day. A tin mug of gruel and a small brown loaf were handed in. The gruel was not too bad, but the bread was quite uneatable. If it had been of sawdust flavoured with road sweepings it could not have tasted worse. My head ached terribly, and I would have given anything for a cup of tea.

But when the door was opened by the Deputy Governor, a woman, and I was told to get ready to go out, as my fine had been paid, I was very angry, and refused to go. She urged me to go, saying kindly that prison was no place for women like us. When I agreed, and my clothes were given to me, I found my one decent suit rolled up in a bundle as if it were the rags of some drunken tramp.

I was not pleased to find my husband outside. He knew that we did not wish our fines to be paid, and was quite in sympathy with the militant campaign, but men are not so singleminded as women are; they are too much given to *talking* about their ideals, rather than *working* for them. Even as Socialists they seldom translate their faith into works, being still conservatives at heart, especially where women are concerned. Most of us who were married found that "Votes for Women" were of less interest to our husbands than their own dinners. They simply could not understand why we made such a fuss about it.

FROM CHAPTER 16, "DICKENS IN PETTICOATS"

When the women began to destroy letter-boxes and set fire to churches, I could not bring myself to blame them. Those who do so, should remember the long years of peaceful propaganda, the insolence of politicians, the brutality of stewards, the indifference of the police, the prison sentences, "forcible feeding" with all its horrors, The Cat and Mouse Act which repeatedly sent women back to prison, and caused many to flee from this country to some freer state.

Personally, I did not like the destruction of an ancient church, or the burning of letters which may have contained poor people's money. One broadminded cleric whose church had been set on fire, luckily with little damage, said he hoped we wouldn't blame him for the failure: he was sure his sermons were dry enough. And then there did seem something to laugh at in the idea of the plus-foured M.P. toddling along to his favourite golf links, to find, cut in the sacred sward, the terrible slogan "Votes for Women." One could smile at the smugness of the male elector, whose forebears had won the vote for him by similar methods, denouncing the Suffragettes, and declaring they ought to be horse-whipped.

"If you were my wife I'd give you poison," said one of these heroes, to the speaker, at one of our meetings.

"If I were your wife I'd drink it," she answered quickly.

After all I don't think I was a very good militant; I didn't mind badgering politicians at their meetings, or ringing their doorbells, but I think my most lawless act was fly-posting on church doors and letter boxes. This involved going out about midnight, carrying your posters, a tin of paste and a brush, and needed a quick-eyed confederate to watch out for the police. Some of our young male friends rather enjoyed this part of the adventure. The poster was a facsimile of a royal proclamation, beginning "*Whereas....*" in bold lettering; it set **forth** the fact that:

> "*voteless women, driven by the stupidity and cruelty of the government, use this method to draw attention to our grievance, and pray the King to use his Royal power to help us....*"

We only did this occasionally, but it was effective. A whole district would wake one morning to find one of these posters on every church door and PO letter box. These would be removed by scandalized caretakers, or postmen, and the police kept a sharp look out the following night, expecting that we should try to replace them. But we were not so foolish. We lay low for a time; then we covered another district in the same way and were never caught. Then the WSPU adopted the policy of attacking the leaders of all political parties. I did not agree with this. I felt it was wrong to attack men like Keir Hardie and George Lansbury. Neither of these great souls ever wavered in their support for our cause. We should have made splendid exceptions of our friends in any party. They were few enough, God knows, in any party, even in the Labour movement. Perhaps we owed most gratitude to the ILP, for even when they strongly disapproved of militancy, they would lend us their platforms and stand by to protect us from the hooligans.

CONSTANCE LYTTON

FROM *PRISONS AND PRISONERS:*
THE STIRRING TESTIMONY OF A SUFFRAGETTE

[London: Virago Press, 1988.
First published in London by William Heinemann, 1914.]

FROM CHAPTER II, "MY CONVERSION"

It was in August—September, 1908, at "The Green Lady Hostel," Littlehampton, the holiday house of the Esperance Girls' Club, that I met Mrs. Pethick Lawrence and Miss Annie Kenney. I was two or three days in the house with them without discovering that they were Suffragettes or that there was anything unusual about their lives. But I realised at once that I was face to face with women of strong personality, and I felt, though at first vaguely, that they represented something more than themselves, a force greater than their own seemed behind them. Their remarkable individual powers seems illumined and enhanced by a light that was apart from them as are the colours and patterns of a stained-glass window by the sun shining through it. I had never before come across this kind of spirituality. I have since found it a characteristic of all the leaders in the militant section of the women's movement, and of many of the rank and file. I was much attracted by Mrs. Lawrence, and became intimate with her at once on the strength of our mutual friendship for Olive Schreiner.[21] We had, besides, many other interests and sympathies in common. The first Sunday that we were together, the girls of the club were asked to come in early that evening, so that Jessie Kenney, Annie Kenney's sister, who had only recently been released from Holloway, might tell them of her prison experiences. I then realised that I was amongst Suffragettes. I immediately confessed to them that although I shared their wish for the enfranchisement of women, I did not at all sympathise with the measures they adopted for bringing about that reform. I had, however, always been interested in prisons and recognised from the first that, incidentally, the fact of many educated women being sent to gaol for a question of conscience must do a great deal for prison reform, and I was delighted at this opportunity of hearing first-hand something about the inner life of a prison. I listened eagerly and was horrified at some of the facts recorded. Amongst these I remember specially that the tins in which the drinking water stood were cleaned with soap and brick dust and not washed out, the tins being filled only once or at most twice in twenty-four hours; the want of air in the cells; the conduct of prison officials towards the prisoners.

Having betrayed my disapproval of the Suffragette "tactics," which seemed to me unjustified, unreasonable, without a sense of political responsibility, and as setting a bad example in connection with a reform movement of such prominence, there was naturally something of coolness and reserve in my further intercourse with Mrs. Pethick Lawrence and the Kenneys. But before their brief stay at the club came to an end, I achieved a talk with each of the leaders.

One evening, after incessant rain, Annie Kenney and I marched arm-in-arm round the garden, under dripping trees. I explained that though I had always been for the extension of the suffrage to women, it did not seem to me a question of prime urgency, that many other matters of social reform seemed more important, and I thought class prejudice and barriers more injurious to national welfare than sex barriers. I was deeply impressed with her reply. She said, in a tone of utmost conviction: "Well, I can only tell you that I, who am a working-class woman, have never known class distinction and class prejudice stand in the way of my advancement, whereas the sex barrier meets me at every turn." Of course, she is a woman of great character, courage and ability, which gives her exceptional facilities for overcoming these drawbacks, but her contention that such powers availed her nothing in the face of sex prejudices and disabilities, and the examples she gave me to bear out her argument, began to lift the scales of ignorance from my eyes. She was careful to point out that the members of her own family had been remarkably free from sex prejudice, and her illustrations had no taint of personal resentment. She explained how the lot of women being not understood of men, and they being the only legislators, the woman's part had always got laid on one side, made of less importance, sometimes forgotten altogether. She told how amongst these offices of women was the glorious act of motherhood and the tending of little children. Was there anything in a man's career that could be so honourable as this? Yet how often is the woman who bears humanity neglected at such times, so that life goes from her, or she is given no money to support her child. I felt that through Annie Kenney's whole being throbbed the passion of her soul for other women, to lift from them the heavy burden, to give them life, strength, freedom, joy, and the dignity of human beings, that in all things they might be treated fairly with men. I was struck by her expression and argument, it was straightforward in its simplicity, yet there was inspiration about her. All that she said was obvious, but in it there was a call from far off, something inevitable as the voice of fate. She never sounded a note of sex-antipathy; it was an unalloyed claim for justice and equity of development, for women as for men.

Then Mrs. Pethick Lawrence and I, during a day's motoring expedition, achieved a rare talk out. She met all my arguments, all my prejudices and false deductions with counter-arguments, and above all with facts of which I had till then no conception. I trusted her because of what I had learnt of her personality, her character, mind, wide education and experience, and was to a certain extent at once impressed; still I only half believed many of the things she reported, the real purport of her statements did not yet sink into my soul as they were soon to do, fact upon fact, result upon result, as I found out their truth for myself.

During my stay at Littlehampton I witnessed a scene which produced a great impression upon my conscience. One morning, while wandering through the little town, I came on a crowd. All kinds of people were forming a ring round a sheep which had escaped as it was being taken to the slaughterhouse. It looked old and misshapen. A vision suddenly rose in my mind of what it should have been on its native mountain-side with all its forces rightly developed, vigorous and independent. There was a hideous contrast between that vision and the thing in the crowd. With growing fear and distress the sheep ran about more clumsily and became a source of amusement to the onlookers, who laughed and jeered at it. At last it was caught by its two gaolers, and as they carried it away one of them, resenting its struggles, gave it a great cuff in the face. At that I felt exasperated. I went up to the man and said, "Don't you know your own business? You have this creature absolutely in your power. If you were holding it properly it would be still. You are taking it to be killed, you are doing your job badly to hurt and insult it besides." The men seemed ashamed, they adjusted their hold more efficiently and the crowd slunk away. From my babyhood I have felt a burning indignation against unkindness to animals, and in their defence I have sometimes acted with a courage not natural to me. But on seeing this sheep it seemed to reveal to me for the first time the position of women throughout the world. I realised how often women are held in contempt as beings outside the pale of human dignity, excluded or confined, laughed at and insulted because of conditions in themselves for which they are not responsible, but which are due to fundamental injustices with regard to them, and to the mistakes of a civilisation in the shaping of which they have had no free share. I was ashamed to remember that although my sympathy had been spontaneous with regard to the wrongs of animals, of children, of men and women who belonged to down-trodden races or classes of society, yet that hitherto I had been blind to the sufferings peculiar to women as such, which are endured by women of every class, every race, every nationality, and that although nearly all the great thinkers and teachers of humanity have preached sex-equality, women have no champions among the various accepted political or moral laws which serve to mould public opinion of the present day.

Nothing could have exceeded the patience, the considerate sympathy even, with which both Annie Kenney and Mrs. Lawrence endured my arguments, arguments, as I now realise them to have been, without any genuine element, stereotyped and shallow. Before we parted, Mrs. Lawrence said to me, and it was the only one of her remarks which savoured in the least of the contempt which my attitude at that time so richly deserved, "You are sufficiently interested in our policy to criticise it, will you be sufficiently interested to study its cause and read up our case?"

For two months I "read up" the subject as I had never read in my life before; I took in the weekly paper *Votes for Women*, the only publication which gave events as they happened, not as they were supposed to happen. I attended as many meetings as I could, and the breakfasts of released suffrage prisoners, whereat the spirit behind this movement, its driving force, seemed best exemplified. Above all, I watched current politics from a different point of view. I still held back from being converted, I criticised and argued at every turn, over every fresh demonstration of the W.S.P.U., but I began to realise of what stuff the workers in the movement were made; what price they paid for their services so gladly given; how far removed they were from any taint of self-glorification, and how amazingly they played the game of incessantly advertising the Cause without ever developing the curse of self-advertisement. I have never been amongst people of any sort who were so entirely free from self-consciousness, self-seeking and self-vaunting.

FROM CHAPTER XIII,
"WALTON GAOL, LIVERPOOL: MY THIRD IMPRISONMENT"

Tuesday, January 18, [1910,] I was visited again by the Senior Medical Officer, who asked me how long I had been without food. I said I had eaten a buttered scone and a banana sent in by friends to the police station on Friday at about midnight. He said, "Oh, then, this is the fourth day; that is too long, I shall have to feed you, I must feed you at once," but he went out and nothing happened till about 6 o'clock in the evening, when he returned with, I think, five wardresses and the feeding apparatus. He urged me to take food voluntarily. I told him that was absolutely out of the question, that when our legislators ceased to resist enfranchising women then I should cease to resist taking food in prison. He did not examine my heart nor feel my pulse; he did not ask to do so, nor did I say anything which could possibly induce him to think I would refuse to be examined. I offered no resistance to being placed in position, but lay down voluntarily on the plank bed. Two of the wardresses took hold of my arms, one held my head and one my feet. One wardress helped to pour the food. The doctor leant on my knees as he stooped over my chest to get at my mouth. I shut my mouth and clenched my teeth. I had looked forward to this moment with so much anxiety lest my identity should be discovered beforehand, that I felt positively glad when the time had come. The sense of being overpowered by more force than I could possibly resist was complete, but I resisted nothing except with my mouth. The doctor offered me the choice of a wooden or steel gag; he explained elaborately, as he did on most subsequent occasions, that the steel gag would hurt and the wooden one not, and he urged me not to force him to use the steel gag. But I did not speak nor open my mouth, so that after playing about for a moment or two with the wooden one he finally had recourse to the steel. He seemed annoyed at my resistance and he broke into a temper as he plied my teeth with the steel implement. He found that on either side at the back I had false teeth mounted on a bridge which did not take out. The superintending wardress asked if I had any false teeth, if so, that they must be taken out; I made no answer and the process went on. He dug his instrument down on to the sham tooth, it pressed fearfully on the gum. He said if I resisted so much with my teeth, he would have to feed me through the nose. The pain of it was intense and at last I must have given way for he got the gag between my teeth, when he proceeded to turn it much more than necessary until my jaws were fastened wide apart, far more than they could go naturally. Then he put down my throat a tube which seemed to me much too wide and was something like four feet in length. The irritation of the tube was excessive. I choked the moment it touched my throat until it had got down. Then the food was poured in quickly; it made me sick a few seconds after it was down and the action of the sickness made my body and legs double up, but the wardresses instantly pressed back my head and the doctor leant on my knees. The horror of it was more than I can describe. I was sick over the doctor and wardresses, and it seemed a long time before they took the tube out. As the doctor left he gave me a slap on the cheek, not violently, but, as it were, to express his contemptuous disapproval, and he seemed to take for granted that my distress was assumed. At first it seemed such an utterly contemptible thing to have done that I could only laugh in my mind. Then suddenly I saw Jane Warton lying before me, and it seemed as if I were outside of her. She was the most despised, ignorant and helpless prisoner that I had seen. When she had served her time and was out of the prison, no one would believe anything she said, and the doctor when he had fed her by force and tortured her body, struck her on the cheek to show how he despised her! That was Jane Warton, and I had come to help her.

When the doctor had gone out of the cell, I lay quite helpless. The wardresses were kind and knelt round to comfort me, but there was nothing to be done, I could not move, and remained there in what, under different conditions, would have been an intolerable mess. I had been sick over my hair, which, though short, hung on either side of my face, all over the wall near my bed, and my clothes seemed saturated with it, but the wardresses told me they could not get me a change that night as it was too late, the office was shut. I lay quite motionless, it seemed paradise to be without the suffocating tube, without the liquid food going in and out of my body and without the gag between my teeth. Presently the wardresses all left me, they had orders to go, which were carried out with the usual promptness. Before long I heard the sounds of the forced feeding in the next cell to mine. It was almost more than I could bear, it was Elsie Howey, I was sure. When the ghastly process was over and all quiet, I tapped on the wall and called out at the top of my voice, which wasn't much just then, "No surrender," and there came the answer past any doubt in Elsie's voice, "No surrender." After this I fell back and lay as I fell. It was not very long before the wardress came and announced that I was to go back upstairs as, because of the feeding, my time in the punishment cell was over. I was taken into the same cell which I had before; the long hours till morning were a nightmare of agonised dread for a repetition of the process....

When it was evening the light was lit and the doctor and wardresses came again to feed me. I asked if I could not sit up in a chair and the doctor said "Yes." I told him that I was a small eater, that the capacity of my body was very limited and if only he would give less quantities the result might be better. I also begged that he would not press the tube so far into my body. He treated the request with contempt, saying that anyhow my stomach must be longer than his, since I was taller than he was. This third time, though I was continually sick, the doctor pressed the tube down firmly into my body and continued to pour food in. At last this produced a short of shivering fit and my teeth chattered when the gag was removed; I suppose that every vestige of colour must have left my face, for the doctor seemed surprised and alarmed. He removed the tube and told the wardresses to lay me on the floor-bed and lower my head. He then came and lay over my chest and seemed very sorry for what he had done. I told him I should not faint, that I was not liable to this or any form of collapse; I did not mention the slight chronic debility of heart from which I suffered. He called in the junior medical officer, who happened to be passing at the time, to test my heart. The junior doctor, who was in a jovial mood, stooped down and listened to my heart through the stethoscope for barely the space of a second—he could not have heard two beats—and exclaimed, "Oh, ripping, splendid heart! You can go on with her"; with that he left the cell. But the senior doctor seemed not to be reassured and he was kind to me for the first time. He tried to feed me with a spoon, but I was still able to clench my teeth and no food got down. He then pleaded with me, saying in a beseeching voice, "I do beg of you—I appeal to you, not as a prison doctor but as a man—to give over. You are a delicate woman, you are not fit for this sort of thing." I answered, "Is anybody fit for it? And I beg of you—I appeal to you, not as a prisoner but as a woman—to give over and refuse to continue this inhuman treatment." After I had lain quiet for some time I managed to clean the cell myself. I took out two pails to the sink, but had only strength to carry them a few yards. As I was journeying like this, getting on very slowly, a wardress told me to take only one at a time; her sympathy was moved to this extent, but no further. I took one pail back to my cell, went on with the other, and then came back for the first. When I had finished this business of washing up—which I was glad to do myself, even if it took half the day, that it might not be given to another prisoner, and also for the better cleaning of the hideous mess—I fell on my bed and lay there till evening; they now left me both bed and bedding, which was a tremendous blessing.

I lay facing the window, which was high up, and very little light seemed to come from it. As the sun went down I saw the shadow of the wooden mould-ings fall across the glass,—three crosses, and they were the shape of the three familiar crosses at the scene of Calvary, one in the centre and one on either side. It looked different from any of the pictures I had seen. The cross of Christ, the cross of the repentant thief, and the cross of the sinner who had not repented—that cross looked blacker than the others, and behind it was an immense crowd. The light from the other two crosses seemed to shine on this one, and the Christ was crucified that He might undo all the harm that was done. I saw amongst the crowd the poor little doctor and the Governor, and all that helped to torture these women in prison, but they were nothing compared to the men in the Cabinet who wielded their force over them. There were the upholders of vice and the men who support the thousand injustices to women, some knowingly and some unconscious of the harm and cruelty entailed. Then the room grew dark and I fell asleep.

MEMORIAL STATUE OF MRS. PANKHURST:
MR. BALDWIN'S TRIBUTE

[London *Times* (7 March 1930)]

[After Emmeline Pankhurst's death in 1928, three women, Kitty Marshall, Rosamund Massy, and Lady Rhondda, former members of the WSPU, began to raise money to pay for a headstone for her grave in Brompton Cemetery, to purchase for the National Portrait Gallery her portrait painted by Georgina Brackenbury, and to erect a statue in her honour in Victoria Tower Gardens beside the House of Commons. On 6 March 1930, the statue was unveiled outside the very Houses of Parliament that Pankhurst was so often barred from entering. The Conservative Prime Minister, Stanley Baldwin, who acknowledged that he "for many years was opposed to the work that Mrs. Pankhurst was doing," gave the tribute to her at its dedication. For the occasion Ethel Smyth conducted the band of the metropolitan police, the same police force that had arrested Pankhurst on numerous occasions. They played "The March of the Women," the song for which Smyth had composed the music and which she had dedicated to the WSPU. Flora Drummond, called the General for her role in organizing and leading so many suffrage marches, presided over the ceremony. Among those present were Frederick Pethick-Lawrence, now a Member of Parliament; Lady Rhondda, a member of the WSPU and a hunger striker; Lady Astor, the first woman Member of Parliament; and Sylvia Pankhurst. The following account of that event provides a portion of the text of Baldwin's tribute as it was recorded in the London *Times* (7 March 1930).]

Mr. Baldwin said:—There is something peculiarly consonant with the English character and English tradition in a ceremony of this nature—a ceremony taking place in the presence of men and women of all parties to commemorate a woman much of whose life was spent in very bitter political controversy. We are united to-day to dedicate this monument under the very shadow of our Houses of Parliament, and it has fallen to my lot to take part in the ceremony—one who for many years was opposed to the work that Mrs. Pankhurst was doing, but to whose lot it fell in time to put the coping-stone upon her labours. (Cheers.) We are too near to that campaign, in which so many of you took part, to judge either of its conduct or of its leaders in the true perspective; posterity will do that for us. But I say with no fear of contradiction that, whatever view posterity may take, Mrs. Pankhurst has won for herself a niche in the Temple of Fame which will last for all time. (Cheers.)

The great forces in human thought, in their birth and in their action, are not dependent on you and me, or on any individual. No individual is omnipotent, and no individual is indispensable. There would have been a Reformation without Luther, there would have been a Renaissance without Erasmus, there would have been a French Revolution without Rousseau, and Mrs. Pankhurst did not make, nor did she claim to make or to have been the creator of, the Women's Movement. It was too big a thing for that, and many may have claimed to have played their part in it…. But if Mrs. Pankhurst did not make the movement, it was she who set the heather on fire. (Cheers.) And, as is the way of all conflagrations, good and evil were consumed in it. That is part of the eternal human tragedy; the wheat and tares grow together until the harvest. Revolutionaries are made out of the clash of ideals, and ideals vary in quality as everything human does.

Dwelling on the life of Mrs. Pankhurst, Mr. Baldwin said she was brought up in a circle quick to sympathize with social suffering and with political injustice. She was a woman of exquisite sensibility, and that exquisite sensibility was one of the marks of genius, and it was a quality which sometimes appeared to the prosaic and the Philistine as a species of insanity. She saw (he continued) what could be caused by the brutalities of a certain type of callous man, and these things filled her soul with rage. It was a divine rage. It was fermented in her, and it drove her ultimately not into a class war, but into a sex war. Her fierce nature would not rest. She could not rest because of what she saw and thought, and, the fire burning within her, she was compelled to speak with her mouth. She sought one political party after another, and, failing with each in turn, she was impelled to enter on her crusade herself. And so it was that 27 years ago the Women's Social and Political Union was born.

It is impossible for us to-day to realize the disabilities under which women suffered a century ago, or even half a century ago, when women, as women, had no power to make a will, to enter into a contract, or to commence an action…. Looking back, it is even more remarkable that those disabilities existed to so late a date, and that when they were pointed out, and action was begun to be taken in an attempt to remove them, this action excited so much passion and fury. I think we must remember that those feelings did not arise only from a blind and prejudiced opposition. They were shared by men of culture and men with broad minds—men of the type of Professor Dicey and others, who firmly and truly thought what was called the liberation of women would be a bad thing for the country. It took a generation before those prejudices could be fought and overcome. What Professor Dicey and those who thought with him forgot was this: that you cannot share knowledge and refuse to share power and responsibility. (Cheers.)…. The demand for power and responsibility was bound to follow the accomplishment of education.

The hour struck, and the demand was made, and the demand, like the shot fired at Lexington, rang round the world. In Mrs. Pankhurst there stood forth a leader of power and magnetism, a woman who was an orator, a prophet and a despot. The World War came. In the twinkling of an eye, at the sound of the trumpet, the revolutionary died, and the patriot was born, and the militant suffragettes laid aside their banners. They put on their overalls and went into the factory and into the field; they were nursing, they made munitions, and they endured sacrifices with the men, and the effective opposition to the movement melted in the furnace of the War, and the walls of Jericho fell before the trumpet was sounded. What if there had been no War? That is a useless line to consider. Mrs. Pankhurst lived to see her work crowned with ultimate success. She had done more in those later days, perhaps, than any individual to secure for women an established right of way. It now rests with women to tread worthily in the way opened to them. Their rights have been vindicated, but the harder part of life is before them, and that is to perform and to discharge their duties. And in the attempt to discharge those duties no woman in the years to come can fail to draw inspiration from the example and the courage of that heroic woman whose statue we to-day unveil and whose memory we are here to honour. (Cheers.)

Mr. Baldwin having unveiled the statue, prayers were said by Canon Woodward, and the hymn, "Now thank we all our God," was sung.

After short addresses by Mr. Pethick-Lawrence, M.P., and Lady Rhondda there was a procession to the statue, and wreaths were laid at the monument. The statue, which is in bronze, is the work of Mr. A.G. Walker, A.R.A., and the base of Portland stone is by Sir Herbert Baker, A.R.A.[22]

NOTES

1   Reginald McKenna was Home Secretary from 1911-1915.

2   Harriet Beecher Stowe's best-selling American novel *Uncle Tom's Cabin* (1852) galvanized the anti-slavery cause. Henry Ward Beecher, Stowe's brother, was a clergyman and reformer.

3   John Bunyan (1628-88) wrote *Pilgrim's Progress* (1678) and *Holy War* (1682); the Greek poet Homer is credited with writing the epic poem the *Odyssey*; Thomas Carlyle (1795-1881) wrote the *French Revolution* (1837); and John Keats (1795-1821) wrote "On First Looking into Chapman's Homer" (1816), a poem about his delight on reading a new translation of Homer.

4   The Fenian Uprising of 1865-67 in Ireland derived from the bitterness brought on by the Great Hunger resulting from the potato famine in which one million people died of starvation and disease. The revolt was defeated.

5   John Duke, Lord Coleridge (1821-94), a barrister and judge, served in the House of Commons from 1865-73 as a member of the Liberal party.

6   William Booth (1829-1912) in 1865 founded the Salvation Army, a Protestant evangelical church and charitable organization. Taking its ministry to the streets, it held meetings, distributed literature, and played music to win converts.

7   Charles Masterman (1873-1927) was elected as a Member of Parliament for the Liberal party in 1906. In 1908 he was appointed by Herbert Asquith as Parlia-

mentary Secretary of the Local Government Board; from 1909-12 he was Under-Secretary of State of the Home Office; and in 1912-14 he was Financial Secretary of the Treasury. Philip Snowdon (1864-1937) joined the Independent Labour Party for which he was an effective speaker. After his marriage to Ethel Annakin, a member of the NUWSS, he joined the Men's League for Women's Suffrage and in 1906 was elected as Labour Member of Parliament.

8 The headquarters of the WSPU at that time.

9 At the previous opening of Parliament the WSPU had sent five women to present a petition to the King. They were now in prison. [Author's note.]

10 Detectives seized Mrs. Pankhurst, who had been released from prison on license, when she left her flat intending to attend Davison's funeral. She was returned to prison for 48 hours.

11 Robert Blatchford (1851-1943), a socialist, was the founder of the Manchester Fabian Society. He began and edited the socialist newspaper the *Clarion*. In 1893 he published *Merrie England*, a collection of his articles about socialism. He opposed the policies of the NUWSS and the WSPU and moved to the right in later years, becoming a nationalist and joining the Conservative party.

12 Flora Drummond (1879-1949) was an early member of the WSPU who remained loyal to the Pankhursts. She was called the General for her organization and command of the suffrage marches.

13 Mrs. Grundy is a neighbour repeatedly referred to (but never appearing) in Tom Morton's play *Speed the Plow* (1798). She represents conventional social disapproval, prudishness, and narrow-mindedness.

14 Rachael Ferguson in *Victoria Bouquet*. [Author's note.] The reference is to Rachel Ferguson, *Victorian Bouquet*, London: E. Benn, 1931.

15 Elizabeth Garrett Anderson (1836-1917), sister of Millicent Garrett Fawcett, was England's first female medical doctor. In 1872 she opened a hospital in London for women staffed entirely by women. She joined the WSPU but left in 1911, objecting to the arson campaign.

16 Perhaps a reference to Amos 6:12: "Shall horses run upon the rock? will *one* plow *there* with oxen?" (King James Version).

17 Large German airplanes that were used for long-distance bombing. Archies, mentioned below, are anti-aircraft guns. The term was originally applied to those used by the Germans in World War I.

18 Giuseppe Mazzini (1805?-72), an Italian patriot who helped unify Italy.

19 John Burns (1858-1943), a member of the House of Commons from 1892-1918, was a socialist aligned with the Liberal party.

20 The black arrow was stamped on all prison clothing, indicating it was government property but also to indicate that the wearer was a prisoner. It thus served as a form of humiliation.

21 Olive Schreiner (1855-1920), a South African novelist and political writer, participated in various suffrage groups. Her best-known work is *The Story of an African Farm* (1883).

22 Herbert Baker (1862-1946), an English architect, also designed the memorial for his friend Cecil Rhodes, located in Cape Town, South Africa. Arthur George Walker (1861-1936) also designed the bronze statue of Florence Nightingale that is part of the Crimean War Memorial. It is in Lower Regent Street and Pall Mall, London. The initials A.R.A. stand for Associate of the Royal Academy of Art.

CHAPTER THREE

SUFFRAGE POETRY AND SONGS

The suffrage campaign produced some interesting and memorable poetry written by women who were not accomplished poets. The tone and subject matter of this poetry was quite varied, ranging from the satirical and topical to the more emotional and personal. Some poems mocked politicians and official dogma about the dangers of granting votes to women while others were more serious, depicting the women's suffrage experiences, particularly their days in prison. Poems by imprisoned women provide an insight into the events they experienced, the people they encountered, and the friendships they formed while living under harsh and unpleasant circumstances. Surprisingly, almost all suffrage poetry expresses great optimism: the dawn will come, and women will be enfranchised.

Poetry can be found in the publications of various suffrage organizations, such as *Votes for Women*; in periodicals devoted to women's issues, such as *Shafts*; or in collections, such as *Holloway Jingles*. The satirical poem "A Jingle of the Franchise," one of the earliest suffrage poems, appeared in *Shafts*, a short-lived periodical that contained articles for women and the working classes. "Gladstone, leader of the nation" is William Gladstone who was Prime Minister of England four different times and an opponent of woman suffrage. "Cautionary Tales in Verse" satirizes the claim often made by anti-suffragists that giving votes to women would cause people in the British colonies to lose all respect for the nation by which they were governed.

A collection of poems written by imprisoned women in Holloway Prison in London during March and April 1912 was published by the Glasgow Branch of the WSPU as *Holloway Jingles*. Many of the women writing poems for this collection had been imprisoned for window breaking. The introduction by Teresa Gough recalls some memorable women who were their fellow prisoners. In the midst of the drab and depressing surroundings, the prisoners still saw the beauty of nature and experienced a love for one another. For the suffrage women, the prison experience was transforming; it bound them together as sisters and comrades, all enduring the same harsh conditions. The final poem of *Holloway Jingles*, "L'Envoi," is by Emily Wilding Davison, who died a year later when she ran onto the racetrack at the Derby to stop the King's horse.

Songs were also written for the suffrage campaign, one of the best known being "March of the Women," with words by Cicely Hamilton and music by Ethel Smyth, written specifically for the WSPU. Some suffrage songs were intended for marches; others were sung at suffrage meetings and rallies. Familiar tunes were frequently adopted for these songs.

Many suffrage poems and songs are unsigned while others have only initials attached to them, making identification of the writers difficult.

POETRY

"A JINGLE OF THE FRANCHISE"

[*Shafts* 1 (31 December 1892)]

Gladstone, leader of the nation,
  Says he deems it wise to pause
Ere sanctioning emancipation
  Of the women, lest it cause
Them to trespass, all unwitting,
On those gentle charms befitting
Woman's nature, thus committing
  Violence 'gainst nature's laws.

Chorus of Advocates:—For a difference he can see,
    Though not quite plain to you and me,
    'Twixt tweedledum and tweedledee.

"So, to grant this woman suffrage
  I am greatly disinclined;
For I fear 'twould sadly outrage"
  [Says the man of LIBERAL mind]
"Woman's pure and lofty nature,
As described by poet, preacher,
Politician, sage and teacher,
  And by Providence designed."

Chorus:—There's a difference that we,
    Lacking logic, cannot see,
    'Twixt tweedledum and tweedledee.

Feminine participation,
  When 'tis benefiting them,
In the "Liberal Federation,"[1]
Truly he does not condemn;
For this sort of influence is
Not opposed to Providence's
Great and wise decrees, and hence is
  Quite permissible.—Ahem!

Chorus:—For 'tis different, says he.
    It's just the difference, don't you see,
    'Twixt tweedledum and tweedledee?

By consensus of opinion,
    Women may participate,
Thus throughout the Queen's dominion,
    Working for male candidate,
Canvassing, electioneering,
In such cases is appearing
(Truly is the subject clearing!)
    Perfectly legitimate.

Chorus:—For 'tis different, don't you see?
    What wide distinction there must be
    'Twixt tweedledum and tweedledee!

Why direct participation
    Gladstone's moral sense so shocks;
Wherefore this slight innovation—
    Placing papers in a box—
Should result in our unsexing,
Is a question most perplexing,
Which our souls is greatly vexing,
    And our keenest wisdom mocks.

Chorus:—For this difference we can't see,
    So illogical are we,
    'Twixt tweedledum and tweedledee.

O wise parliamentary leader
    Of a nation great and free,
It is clear to every reader
    Of this singular decree,
That the jewel that your name is
Symbol of, sure, not the same is
As the one of old whose fame is,—
    That bright gem, Consistency!

Chorus:—None are so blind as who won't see
    That no distinction there can be
    'Twixt tweedledum and tweedledee.
                S.S.

"CAUTIONARY TALES IN VERSE"

[*Votes for Women* V (6 October 1911)]

How Wilful Annabel, refusing to listen to her Superiors, involved her country
in a Catastrophe of Considerable Dimensions.

When Annabel, a Suffragist,
Was put upon the Voters' List
(By whose mistake I need not quote)
She signified her wish to vote,
Because she had (and has them still)
Opinions on the Children Bill.
Her Truest Friends implored of her
To leave the Voting Register.
They told her what was Woman's Sphere,
And what the country has to Fear,
And how It all depends on Might,
And since a woman cannot fight,
Affairs of children under Ten
Should only be controlled by Men.
But Annabel, abandoned soul,
Was bent on going to the Poll,
And when these Dreadful Things occurred
Which justified their Every Word,
She had not left her home a minute
Before 'twas Lost with all things in it,
While, left to their deserted Sire,
Her children Fell into the Fire,
And as she touched the Ballot Box
The British Realm Succumbed to Shocks,
We lost our old prestige abroad,
We almost lost the House of Lords,
While Dusky Races far away
With one accord Renounced our Sway.
"Since women now have learnt to vote
"We're governed by a pettycoat.
"Such Dreadful Things were never seen
"When good Victoria was Queen.
"We will not do as we are bid,
"Let's all Revolt," and so they did,
And thus the British realm was wrecked,

And England Lost her Self-Respect,
And British Men were forced to be
In Bondage under Germany,
While Annabel (Whom none can praise)
Was Quite Unsexed for Several Days.

                    Moral
The Moral is, that Men should Vote
And Women wear a Petticoat.

FROM *HOLLOWAY JINGLES*

[WSPU, Glasgow Branch, 19??]

[These songs were written in Holloway Prison during March and April 1912. They were later collected and edited by N.A. John.]

FOREWORD

Comrades, it is the eve of our parting. Those of us who have had the longest sentences to serve have seen many a farewell waved up towards our cell windows from the great prison gate as time after time it opened for release. The jail yard, too, where we exercise, now seems spacious, though at first it was thronged with our fellow-prisoners. Yet not one of them has really left us. Whenever in thought we re-enter that yard, within its high, grim walls we see each as we knew her there: our revered Leader, Mrs. Pankhurst, courageous, serene, smiling; Dr. Ethel Smyth, joyous and terrific, whirling through a game of rounders with as much intentness as if she were conducting a symphony; Dr. L. Garrett Anderson, in whose eyes gaiety and gravity are never far apart— but we cannot name them all, for there are scores whose brave faces made that yard a pleasant place.

The passing of the weeks was punctuated by the flowers that blossomed in those grim surroundings; sturdy crocuses, then daffodils and tulips, and now the lilacs are in bloom. Always, too, we had the sunshine, for the skies were kind.

And within the walls? Ah! there, too, the love that shines through the sun and the skies and can illumine even the prison cell, was round us, and worked through us and miracles were wrought. We have each been witness of some wonder worked by that omniscient love which is the very basis of our movement.

At these words other faces will rise up before the mind's eye, bruised, perhaps degraded, crushed, sullen, sorrowful, sometime beautiful, but always endeared to us by the thought that it is for their sakes we get the strength to carry on this struggle.

In service to you, O sad sisters, in your hideous prison garb, we gain the supremacy of our souls. And "we need not fear that we can lose anything by the progress of the soul."

Theresa Gough (Karmie M.T. Kranich.)
Holloway Jail, 28th April, 1912.

THE WOMEN IN PRISON

Oh, Holloway, grim Holloway,
With grey, forbidding towers!
Stern are thy walls, but sterner still
Is woman's free, unconquered will.
And though to-day and yesterday
Brought long and lonely hours,
Those hours spent in captivity
Are stepping-stones to liberty.

—Kathleen Emerson

[OH! WHO ARE THESE IN SCANT ARRAY]

Oh! who are these in scant array
Whom we behold at break of day;
Strange their attire! oh, who are they?
   The Suffragettes in Holloway.

And who are these when chapel's done
Stream out beneath an April sun,
To laugh and jump or shout and run?
   The Suffragettes in Holloway.

Who is it say in tones which freeze,
"Pass on this way, convicted, please;
Don't dare to think or breathe or sneeze?"
   The Wardresses in Holloway.

And who is he, tho' grand his air,
Doffs not his hat to ladies fair?
Is it because he has no hair?
   The Governor in Holloway.

Then whilst we eat our frugal food,
Who breaks upon our solitude,
And says, "You're all so beastly rude"?
   Why "Mother's own" in Holloway.

And who, with sanctimonious drone,
Tells tales of highly moral tone,
Whilst gazing upwards at the dome?
   The Chaplain, sure, in Holloway.

Hark! who is this with stealthy tread,
Comes round each day to count his dead,
And scalps his victims, so 'tis said?
  The Doctor, in grim Holloway.

But who is this now comes in view,
His smiling face cheers others too?
Father M'Carroll, "here's to you,"
  The only *Man* in Holloway.

But there is one we'll ne'er forget,
She says she's not—and yet and yet
We feel she *is* a Suffragette?
  The Matron dear, of Holloway.

—Kathleen Emerson

TO A FELLOW PRISONER (MISS JANIE ALLAN)

[Janie Allan was a militant suffragette from Scotland who was imprisoned in
Holloway for window smashing.]

Upon thy pure and stedfast brow there lies
A tender sorrow—and in thine eyes
(Serene and passionless as dawn's deep grey,
E'er yet the golden sandalled day
Trips joyously o'er hill and wood,)
A melancholy, calm and sweet, doth brood.

No darkling shadow of the prison cell
Dare cast o'er thee its grim, benumbing spell.
Floats then some music, sad and soft to thee,
By angels borne to thine attunéd ears?
Dull echoes of the moaning, human sea
Whose waves are blood and tears,
Faint sob and murmur of despairing strife,
Low cry of yearning agonizing life?

Or is thy sorrow's food
Vision of outraged womanhood?
Throbs thy heart with stinging pain.
To the misery and the shame
Of these thy sisters—cast away
Like frail, sweet flowers of one brief day?

Or like the butterfly that dies
In dust from which it cannot rise;
Or wounded bird, beating with bleeding wings
The cold, hard earth—while rings
The merry laughter of its murderer's song?
How long shall these things be, oh God, how long?

"For these things our eyes are dim."—Lamentations V. 17.

—M. M'P. [Margaret McPhun?]

[THERE WAS A SMALL WOMAN CALLED G]

There was a small woman called G,
Who smashed two big windows at B—
They sent her to jail, her fate to bewail,
For Votes must be kept, must be kept for the male.

They asked that small woman called G,
Why she smashed those big windows at B—
She made a long speech, then made her defence,
But it wasn't no use, their heads were so dense;
They just hummed the refrain, altho' it is stale—
Votes must be kept, must be kept for the male.

They sent her to H for six months and a day,
In the coach Black Maria[2] she went sadly away;
But she sang in this strain, as it jolted and rumbled,
We will have the Vote, we will not be humbled.
We must have the vote by hill and by dale,
Votes shall not alone be kept for the male.

[No author listed]

[THERE'S A STRANGE SORT OF COLLEGE]

There's a strange sort of college,
And the scholars are unique,
Yet the lessons are important which they learn;
They fit them for the fight,
For all that's true and right,
And for liberty and justice make them burn.

There the scholars are the teachers,
    And the staff they are the taught,
Though they sometimes try to get the upper hand;
    But their rules they are too grim,
    So they find they must give in
To that gallant, honour-loving little band.

It is there you grow quite knowing,
    If you ever have been dull,
For the things you see and hear they make you wise;
    There we take our F.H.G.,
    A very high degree,
And the hand-grip of true friendship—that's the prize.

There the terms they often vary,
    Some are long and some are short,
But the rules they never alter in the least;
    They go on from day to day,
    In the same old prosy way,
And the food you get there isn't quite a feast.

Just watch those scholars' faces,
    It's truth on them you'll find,
Hear their laughter ringing out so clear and bright;
    "Unto others you must do
    As you'd have them do to you,"
Is their motto, and you know that they are right.

When you're singing "Rule, Britannia,"
    Britons never shall be slaves,
Remember it's not words which tell but deeds;
    'Tis actions brave and strong
    Which always right the wrong,
For justice unto freedom always leads.

Hark to the trumpet calling!
    Come out and take your place
'Neath the standard of the purple, white, and green;[3]
    True courage must prevail,
    For the tyrants we assail,
It's the grandest fight the world has ever seen.

The students and the college
Are known throughout the world,
Of God's truth the light upon them never sets;
   'Tis the prison, cold and grey,
   Of noted Holloway,
And the scholars are my colleague Suffragettes.

        —Edith Aubrey Wingrove
       Written during the hunger strike.

[BEFORE I CAME TO HOLLOWAY]

Before I came to Holloway,
   It was not cold nor illness,
Nor harshness that I feared, oh stay!
   It was the deathly stillness.

Inside, it's bang with supper, or
   It's dinner or "your apple;"
Or "pass out, please, to exercise,"
   Or "pass along to chapel."

'Tis "close your door there," "pass out, please,"
   It's clattering with the rations,
"Baths," turning locks, and clinking keys,
   And "any applications?"

All day it's "have you got those?" Oh,
   Bells, banging, people larking;
"You cleaners there," "Miss So-and-so,"
   Or "are you there, Miss Sharky?"

And if you think you're safely in,
   They must have done their caperin',
Then "governor," "visiting magistrates,"
   "The chaplain," "doctor," "matron."

At night, quite late, at nearly six,
   "Haven't they finished speaking?"
Your mattress like the whole D x^4
   Is simmering and creaking.

You hear them chopping, stoking too,
  And really all their clamour
Breaks up the peace far more than you
  Or I, with stone and hammer.

Before I came to Holloway
  It was not cold nor illness,
Nor harshness that I feared, oh stay!
  It was the deathly stillness.

            —M.C.R. [Madeleine Caron Rock]

FULL TIDE

The tide has turned—Oh rising tide, flow in!
  As snow upon the far horizon blue
I see the crested waves in long outline,
And soon the silver glitter of sunshine,
  Shall shimmer on the surfaces near to.
The tide has turned—Oh rising tide, flow in!

The tide has turned—Oh rising tide, flow in!
  The edges of the gently lifting levels
Make lengthened arcs along the gold sands pouring.
Hark, boatman! higher up thy craft needs mooring,
  An thou wouldst save it from encroaching revels.
The tide has turned—Oh rising tide, flow in!

Oh full tide flowing high—roll in, roll in!
  No need to meet it, o'er the hills 'tis rimming
Higher and higher yet, its waters welling,
All obstacles are swept into its swelling,
  And out to sea upon its bosom brimming
The eager boats have gone—Oh flowing tide roll on!

            —A.A. Wilson

WHO?

Who burst upon me in my cell,
With neither knock nor ring of bell?
(And I was dining very well, on bread and cheese and chicken wings,
And a few other naughty things.)

"Pray now," said he, "d'you like your food,
And don't you think it very good?"
"Indeed, kind sir, I cannot tell,
For I have 'stolen fruit' as well."

"Come, come," said he, "don't tell me that,
Upon my food you shall grow fat;
I mean you suffragettes to be
A credit to my diet'ry."

—Kate W. Evans

Who?

"They heed me not," he vainly cried—
And hung his head, and loudly sighed—
"It seems to me, in every mood,
The suffragette is very rude.

"When I into their cells do walk,
To have a little serious talk,
They almost mock me to my face,
It is, indeed, a sad disgrace.

"They come to chapel just to see
Their friends in F and B and D;
The air they say is awful bad,
And that my sermons make them mad.

"Alas! alas! what can I do,
Hard suffragettes, your hearts to woo?"
"To the best in yourself, kind sir, be true,
And join at once the M.P.U."[5]

—Kate W. Evans

The Cleaners of Holloway

For ever toiling up and down,
In various shades of dusty brown,
    You see the cleaners.

Struggling along in tired pairs,
With milk and food, up narrow stairs,
   Go the cleaners.

And if you wish they'd clean your cell,
And polish your pannikins as well,
   Obliging cleaners.

For they're a cheerful set, and kind,
And to your wants are never blind,
   Willing cleaners.

Bravely working from day to day,
So the long weeks pass away,
   Plucky cleaners.

At last there comes the longed-for day,
When "Going to leave you, Miss," they say,
   "Good-luck, cleaners."

               —Kate W. Evans

To D.R., In Holloway

Beyond the bars I see her move,
   A mystery of blue and green,
As though across the prison yard
   The spirit of the spring had been.
And as she lifts her hands to press
   The happy sunshine of her hair,
From the grey ground the pigeons rise,
   And rustle upwards in the air,
As though her two hands held a key
   To set imprisoned spirits free.

               —Laura Grey

Holloway, 8th March

They sat in church behind a screen,
   Those members of the band
Whose conduct "so unwomanly"
   Had just distressed the land.

From homes both far and near they came,
    Those women old and young;
Women of varying ways of thought,
    Who yet to one cause clung.

They stood, and sang of One who knew,
    Knew best what suffering meant;
Sang words to which the time and place
    A new, deep meaning lent.

And in the garden, secretly,
    And on the Cross on high,
He taught His brethren and inspired,
    "To suffer and to die."

So sang the women, who had come
    From homes most fair and sweet,
From treading paths of helpfulness,
    With swift, untiring feet.

And some from homes where friends belov'd
    No sympathy had shown,
But scorned and mocked, so that they trod
    The wine-press all alone.

And still, as in the days of old,
    Goes up the pleading cry;
"Oh help us women, and inspire,
    To suffer and to die."

—A. Martin

[THE BEECH WOOD SAUNTERS IDLY TO THE SEA]

The beech wood saunters idly to the sea,
Its trunks moss-green and grey, stand clear and bold
From out the blue and dreamy density
Of distance. Chequered here with gold,
And there with primrose stars, the leafy mould
Beneath. Above, the sky's profundity.
In this fair spot that breathes of liberty,
I checked the price at which my own was sold,
The grim walls stand as though they edged away

From the drear yard, but with a dull surprise
Through their barred windows sight the prospect grey,
Reflected from the yearning, human eyes.
"Has God, then, need of prisons?" they would say,
Yet here my soul met freedom in the way,
And saw the heavenly vision in the skies.
If, though we stand alone, in the dark place,
We stay the ladder on its lowest stair;
Then, the dear future daughters of our race
Shall mount, with laughter, to the sun and air.
Great God of Freedom, grant to us this grace!
This guerdon of our passion and our prayer!

—Katherine M. Richmond
March 6th, 1912

AN END

My heart is too much like the surging sea,
Thinking of self it hollows with distress;
Its climbing hills mount up in huge excess,
If then of life's bright hopes I think—and thee.

And yet I dread this tide monotony;
A birth, a growth, a death, of life I ask,
Whatever pangs, however hard the task,
A strife, a consummation let me see.

—A.A. Wilson

L'ENVOI

Stepping onwards, oh my comrades!
Marching fearless through the darkness,
Marching fearless through the prisons,
With the torch of freedom guiding!

See the face of each is glowing,
Gleaming with the love of freedom;
Gleaming with a selfless triumph,
In the cause of human progress!

Like the pilgrim in the valley,
Enemies may oft assail us,
Enemies may close around us,
Tyrants, hunger, horror, brute-force.

But the glorious dawn is breaking,
Freedom's beauty sheds her radiance;
Freedom's clarion call is sounding,
Rousing all the world to wisdom.

—Emily Wilding Davison
April 28th, 1912

SONGS

"THE WOMEN'S MARSEILLAISE"

Words: F.E.M. Macaulay
Music: Rouget Delisle

Arise, ye daughters of a land
  That vaunts its liberty!
Make restless rulers understand
  That women must be free,
  That women *will* be free.
Hark! Hark! The trumpet's calling!
  Who'd be a laggard in the fight?
  With victory even now in sight,
And stubborn foemen backward falling.

Chorus: To Freedom's cause till death
    We swear our fealty.
  March on! March on!
  Face to the dawn,
    The dawn of liberty.

Arise! Though pain or loss betide,
  Grudge naught of freedom's toll.
For what they loved the martyrs died;
  Are we of meaner soul?
  Are we of meaner soul?
Our comrades, greatly daring,
  Through prison bars have led the way:
  Who would not follow to the fray,
Their glorious struggle proudly sharing?

Chorus: To Freedom's cause till death
    We swear our fealty.
  March on! March on!
  Face to the dawn,
    The dawn of liberty.

Figure 9: Suffragette March in Hyde Park
(from left: Emmeline Pethick-Lawrence, Christabel Pankhurst, Sylvia Pankhurst,
Emily Wilding Davison) by Mrs. Albert Broom, 23 July 1910
By courtesy of the National Portrait Gallery, London

"The March of the Women"

Words: Cicely Hamilton
Music: Ethel Smyth

[London: J. Curwen and Sons Ltd., 1911]

Dedicated to the Women's Social and Political Union

Shout, shout, up with your song!
Cry with the winds, for the dawn is breaking;
March, march, swing you along,
Wide blows our banner and hope is waking.
Song with its story, dreams with their glory,
Lo! they call, and glad is their word!
Forward! hark how it swells,
Thunder of freedom, the voice of the Lord!

Long, long, we in the past
Cowered in dread from the light of heaven,
Strong, strong, stand we at last,
Fearless in faith and with sight new-given.
Strength with its beauty, Life with its duty,
(Hear the voice, oh hear and obey!)
These, these, beckon us on,
Open your eyes to the blaze of day.

Comrades, ye who have dared
First in the battle to strive and sorrow,
Scorned, spurned, nought have ye cared,
Raising your eyes to a wider morrow.
Ways that are weary, days that are dreary
Toil and pain by faith ye have borne;
Hail, hail, victors ye stand,
Wearing the wreath that the brave have worn!

Life, strife, these two are one,
Naught can ye win but by faith and daring;
On, on, that ye have done
But for the work of today preparing.
Firm in reliance, laugh a defiance,
(Laugh in hope, for sure is the end.)
March, march, many as one,
Shoulder to shoulder and friend to friend.

"Woman's Song of Freedom"

Words: Lilian Sauter
Music: Annette Hullah

[London: London Society for Women's Suffrage, (1911)]

Raise the song of liberation!
Rouse the fire in every heart!
For the weal of all the nation
Women claim their equal part!
Call the lowland and the valleys,
Wake the wide and windswept hills,
Voice the slums and crowded alleys,
In the workroom and the mills,
Raise the song of freedom!

Chorus at end of each verse:

On to longer duty, flinging   .
Wide the mother heart for all!
Till the nations hear our singing,
Till they answer freedom's call,
Raise the song of freedom!

Lift the heart to high endeavour!
Fire the thought and nerve the will!
Though the bonds be hard to sever,
Clasp your faith in justice still!
Like a wide and flowing river
Rolling onward to the sea,
Woman's life shall deepen ever,
O thou river wide and free,
Bear us on to freedom!

["When Good Queen Bess was on the Throne"]

Words: H. Crawford
Tune: "Vicar of Bray"

[London: London Society for Women's Suffrage, (?)]

[Sung at Albert Hall, Suffrage Saturday, June 13, 1908]

When Good Queen Bess was on the Throne
   Three hundred years ago, Sir,
For forty years she reigned alone
   As everyone must know, Sir.
She laboured for her country's sake,
   And no one questioned then, Sir,
The right of England's Queen to make
   The laws of England's men, Sir.

   But this is true, they will maintain,
      As true as holy writ, Sir—
   That whatsoever woman may do
      To vote she is not fit, Sir.

But still to-day the tale goes on
   Just as in days gone by, Sir:
Although three hundred years are gone
   You still may hear the cry, Sir,
That though to work in every sphere
   With hand and brain and heart, Sir,
Is woman's place, in Government
   She may not take a part, Sir.

   But this is true, they will maintain,
      As true as holy writ, Sir—
   That whatsoever woman may do
      To vote she is not fit, Sir.

For though with years that slowly pass
   Has liberty grown wider:
Woman imprisoned yet remains,
   Her freedom still denied her.
But surely those who everywhere

Can aid their country's cause, Sir,
Are able, too, to take a part
  In framing England's law, Sir.

That this is true we dare to say,
  And may the day come soon, Sir,
When those who shall the piper pay
  Shall also call the tune, Sir.

"CHRISTABEL"

Words by F.A.B. [Florence Antoinette Barry?]
Air: "Tramp! Tramp! Tramp!"

[Wimbledon: Wimbledon Women's Social and Political Union, 1908]

In the prison where I sit,
Thinking, sisters dear, of you,
Hark! a note of triumph rises far away.
For the gloom of night may fall,
But I hear our army call
That our victory is dawning with the day.
   Work! work! work! the vote is coming!
   Cheer up, girls! the day's at hand
   When, for all their chaff and knocks,
   We shall get the Ballot-box
   And a vote for the leaders of our land.

Men may drag us through the mire
By the ruthless hands they hire;
They may cage our bodies here behind the walls,
But our hearts are there outside,
For the spirit ranges wide,
And it pierces where the voice of freedom calls.
   Fight! fight! fight! the vote is coming!
   Cheer up, girls! the day's at hand
   When, for all their chaff and knocks,
   We shall get the Ballot-box
   And a vote for the leaders of our land.

Do they hear us from our House
With police ten thousand strong?
They will hide their head and stop their ears in vain:
Thro' the land there swells a crowd,
Like a storm-wind, roaring loud—
"Let the women take their olden right again."
   Shout! shout! shout! the vote is coming!
   Cheer up, girls! the day's at hand
   When, for all their chaff and knocks,
   We shall get the Ballot-box
   And a vote for the leaders of our land.

"RISE UP WOMEN"

Words: Theodora Mills
Tune: "John Brown"

[London: National Women's Social and Political Union, (?)]

Rise up women! for the fight is hard and long;
Rise in thousands, singing loud in battle song.
Right is might, and in its strength we shall be strong,
   And the Cause goes marching on.
     Glory, glory, hallelujah
     Glory, glory, hallelujah!
     Glory, glory, hallelujah!
     But the cause goes marching on.

We stormed the House of Commons with our little band so true,
And we frightened all the statesmen till they trembled through and through.
They clapped us into prison and we gladly went for you,
   And the Cause goes marching on.
     Glory, glory, etc.

Come, have courage, we shall win our liberty;
Day will dawn at last, and stout of heart are we;
Reinforcements make turn and flee,
   And the Cause goes marching on.
     Glory, glory, etc.

We would die for you if that would break the chain,
We will live to battle o'er and o'er again,
We will never yield until the wrong is slain,
   And the Cause goes marching on.
     Glory, glory, etc.

"Our Hard Case"

Words: S.J. Tanner
Tune: "Comin' thro' the Rye"

[*Women's Suffrage Songs*. London: Kenny & Co, (?)]

If a body pays the taxes,
  Surely you'll agree
That a body earns the franchise,
  Whether he or she.
Ev'ry man may be a voter,
  Ne'er a vote have we,
So it's hard we pay the taxes,
  Surely you'll agree.

Round there comes the tax collector,
  Asking us to pay;
But how they mean to spend our money,
  None of us can say.
Every man may be a voter,
  Ne'er a vote have we:
So it's hard to pay the taxes,
  Surely you'll agree.

Many bodies at elections,
  Who would members be,
Promise votes to every body,
  Whether he or she.
If those bodies in the Commons
  Do their pledge deny,
Then they must at next election
  Tell the reason why.

Notes

1 Women worked for the election of male candidates in such organizations as the Liberal Federation, which supported candidates of the Liberal party.
2 The name given to the vehicle that conveyed people to prison. There is no consensus on the derivation of the term.
3 The colours of the Women's Social and Political Union (WSPU).
4 D x refers to the block in Holloway prison where suffragettes were often placed.
5 M.P.U. refers to the Men's Political Union for Women's Enfranchisement, an organization that supported women's suffrage.

CHAPTER FOUR
SUFFRAGE DRAMA

Many of the activities of the suffrage campaign could be considered a form of street theatre in that they were spectacles performed in public places to attract audiences. Marches, parades, and demonstrations, with their theatricality and pageantry, were dramatic events staged for political purposes. Enormous parades were organized by various suffrage organizations and included thousands of women. The sheer number of participants in these events was meant to indicate to the public that thousands of women from all social classes supported votes for women. The marchers often dressed in white or in clothes indicative of their work; some held wands to represent their prison experience or banners to identify their organizations. A woman riding a horse and dressed as Joan of Arc, the nominal patron saint of the suffrage movement, was present in almost every suffrage parade. Suffrage speakers, who attracted huge crowds, often faced hostile audiences who interacted with them, creating dramatic situations through their shouting and heckling. Militant actions, such as the attempts by suffragettes to enter Parliament, disrupt campaign speakers, or break store windows, were also a type of street theatre.

Some women committed to suffrage turned to writing plays that could be staged in theatres or city halls and that would rally their audiences to join the movement. Elizabeth Robins, an American-born actress who moved to England at age 26, was the first to write and produce a play explicitly about suffrage. Robins, a well-known stage actress, had played an important role in bringing the plays of Henrik Ibsen to England. Playing the role of Hedda herself, she staged the first production of *Hedda Gabler* in London in 1891. In 1906 she joined the WSPU, making her first suffrage speech that same year. She then turned her talents to writing a play specifically about women's suffrage, embedding in it stories about the conditions of women's lives that necessitated their enfranchisement. In 1907 her three-act suffrage play, *Votes for Women!*, was performed at the Court Theatre in London. Vida Levering, the heroine of the play, uses the leverage of a past sexual relationship with a man, who is now a Member of Parliament, to blackmail him into supporting a bill for women's suffrage in Parliament. She also converts the man's fiancée to the suffrage cause. The play's second act, which dramatizes a suffrage rally in Trafalgar Square and includes the speeches of several suffrage speakers, very realistically recreates the dynamics of a suffrage rally with the heckling crowds shouting at the speakers and the speakers responding.

Robins's play used many of the devices of the well-made play of her time, such as the woman whose secret past is gradually revealed, the initials on a tell-tale handkerchief giving away a relationship, and a recognition scene in which the fiancée realizes her suitor has had a previous affair. But in her characterization of Vida Levering, Robins created a new type of heroine. The woman with the supposedly immoral past uses her experience to transform herself into a powerful speaker who can change other women's lives. She is not personally defeated by the events of her past but uses them to gain an understanding of the plight of other women and the need to change laws to remedy their situation. Instead of being the victim of blackmail, she blackmails a man to force him into supporting women's suffrage.

The plays that were produced as propaganda for the suffrage cause in the years following *Votes for Women!* were quite different from Robins's drama and did not rely on the forms of the traditional play of the time. These new plays, with only one act, were popular from 1908, the year the Actresses' Franchise League (AFL) was founded by women in the theatrical profession, until the beginning of World War I. Because of the demands on their time necessitated by their stage careers, few actresses participated in militant suffrage activities; they could not afford to spend time in prison. Instead they used their speaking abilities to address large crowds at suffrage meetings, often addressing gatherings in towns where they were appearing while on tour. For these occasions they also developed dramatic monologues, duologues, and one-act plays.

The AFL, under the direction of the actress Inez Bensusan, set up a department devoted to writing suffrage plays, encouraging anyone able to write plays to do so. Men as well as women contributed to the repertoire of suffrage plays that were then presented in a variety of venues around England. Because the plays usually had few speaking roles, required minimal stage sets, and contained only one act, they could be staged in homes or public halls, as well as in theatres. The first such plays were performed at a WSPU exhibition in 1909 at the Prince's Skating Rink in Knightsbridge, London. The AFL published some of its plays and provided available scripts to local suffrage societies for performances, but local groups also began to write and perform their own suffrage plays. In 1914, with the beginning of World War I, the AFL, as other suffrage organizations did, turned its attention to the war effort and away from writing and performing propaganda plays for the suffrage movement. Thus ended a period during which women played an important role as writers, producers, and actors of political plays written specifically for the suffrage campaign.

Suffrage drama employed a variety of tactics to argue for women's enfranchisement. Because they were intended to appeal to all classes of women, the plays often depicted working-class women in situations that implicitly argued for their need to have political representation, as in Henry Arncliffe-Sennett's *An Englishwoman's Home* and Margaret Wynne Nevinson's *In the Workhouse.* The latter play reveals the absurdity of the law that allowed unmarried women all rights to their children while the children of married women belonged to their fathers. Evelyn Glover's *A Chat with Mrs. Chicky* and Evelyn Glover's *Miss Appleyard's Awakening* demonstrate how illogical the anti-suffrage position could be. Bessie Hatton's *Before Sunrise,* set in 1867, the year when John Stuart Mill attempted to include women in the bill that enfranchised many men, develops the connection between women's political powerlessness and their limited choices in marriage and careers. By contrast, Mary Cholmondeley's *Votes for Men* depicts a futuristic world in which women have all the political power and men are forced to make a convincing argument for their enfranchisement. The arguments men had used against women's enfranchisement were then turned against them. Cicely Hamilton and Christopher St. John's *How the Vote Was Won* humourously dramatizes the logical consequences of the law that made men responsible for their female relatives. The actual implementation of the law would be so burdensome for men that, acting in their own self-interest, they would give women the vote to rid themselves of the burden. Cicely Hamilton's *A Pageant of Great Women* argued for the vote in a more serious way. By parading women artists, warriors, scholars, monarchs, and saints across the stage, the play answers the charge that women lack the intelligence to enter into political life by noting that history is replete with gifted and talented women. *A Pageant of Great Women*, one of the most popular of the suffrage plays, was performed all over England.

CICELY HAMILTON AND CHRISTOPHER ST. JOHN

HOW THE VOTE WAS WON:
A PLAY IN ONE ACT

[London: National Women's Social and Political Union, (1909)]

[First produced at the Royalty Theatre, London, 13 April 1909.]

CHARACTERS
Horace Cole (a clerk, about 30)
Ethel (his wife, 22)
Winifred (her sister)
Agatha Cole (Horace's sister)
Molly (his niece)
Madame Christine (his distant relation)
Maudie Spark (his first cousin)
Miss Lizzie Wilkins (his aunt)
Lily (his maid-of-all-work)
Gerald Williams (his neighbour)

Scene: *Sitting-room in* HORACE COLE'S *house at Brixton. The room is cheaply furnished in a genteel style. The window* (L.C.) *looks out on a row of little houses, all of the Cole pattern. The door* (C.) *leads into a narrow passage communicating at once with the front door. The fireplace* (L.) *has a fancy mantel border, and over it is an overmantel, decorated with many photographs and cheap ornaments. The side-board* (R.), *a small bookcase* (R.), *a table* (L.C. *up stage*), *and a comfortable armchair* (C. *by table*) *are the chief articles of furniture. The whole effect is modest, and quite unpleasing.*

Time: *Late afternoon on a spring day in any year in the future.*
When the curtain rises, MRS. HORACE COLE *is sitting in the comfortable armchair* (C.) *putting a button on to her husband's coat. She is a pretty, fluffy little woman who could never be bad-tempered, but might be fretful. At this minute she is smiling indulgently, and rather irritatingly, at her sister* WINIFRED, *who is sitting by the fire* (L.) *when the curtain rises, but gets up almost immediately to leave.* WINIFRED *is a tall and distinguished looking young woman with a cheerful, capable manner and an emphatic diction which betrays the public speaker. She wears the colours of the NWSPU.*[1]

WINIFRED: Well, good-bye, Ethel. It's a pity you won't believe me. I wanted to let you and Horace down gently, or I shouldn't be here.

ETHEL: But you're always prophesying these dreadful things, Winnie, and nothing ever happens. Do you remember the day when you tried to invade the House of Commons from submarine boats? Oh, Horace did laugh when he saw in the papers that you had all been landed on the Hovis wharf by mistake! "By accident, on purpose!" Horace said. He couldn't stop laughing all the evening. "What price your sister Winifred," he said. "She asked for a vote, and they gave her bread." He kept on— you can't think how funny he was about it!

WINIFRED: Oh, but I can! I know my dear brother-in-law's sense of humour is his strong point. Well, we must hope it will bear the strain that is going to be put on it to-day. Of course, when his female relations invade his house—all with the same story, "I've come to be supported"—he may think it excruciatingly funny. One never knows.

ETHEL: Winnie, you're only teasing me. They would never do such a thing. They must know we have only one spare bedroom, and that's to be for a paying guest when we can afford to furnish it.

WINIFRED: The servants' bedroom will be empty. Don't forget that all the domestic servants have joined the League and are going to strike, too.

ETHEL: Not ours, Winnie. Martha is simply devoted to me, and poor little Lily *couldn't* leave. She has no home to go to. She would have to go to the workhouse.

WINIFRED: Exactly where she will go. All those women who have no male relatives, or are refused help by those they have, have instructions to go to the relieving officer. The number of female paupers who will pour through the workhouse gates to-night all over England will frighten the Guardians into blue fits.

ETHEL: Horace says you'll never *frighten* the Government into giving you the vote.

WINIFRED: It's your husband, your dear Horace, and a million other dear Horaces who are going to do the frightening this time. By to-morrow, perhaps before, Horace will be marching to Westminster shouting out "Votes for Women!"

ETHEL: Winnie, how absurd you are! You know how often you've tried to convert Horace and failed. Is it likely that he will become a Suffragette just because—

WINIFRED: Just because—? Go on, Ethel.

ETHEL: Well, you know—all this you've been telling me about his relations coming here and asking him to support them. Of course I don't believe it. Agatha, for instance, would never dream of giving up her situation. But if they did come Horace would just tell them he *couldn't* keep them. How could he on £4 a week?

WINIFRED: How could he! That's the point! He couldn't, of course. That's
why he'll want to get rid of them at any cost—even the cost of letting
women have the Vote. That's why he and the majority of men in this
country shouldn't for years have kept alive the foolish superstition that
all women are supported by men. For years we have told them it was a
delusion, but they could not take our arguments seriously. Their method
of answering us was exactly that of the little boy in the street who cries
"Yah—Suffragette!" when he sees my ribbon.

ETHEL: I always wish you wouldn't wear it when you come here.... Horace
does so dislike it. He thinks it unwomanly.

WINIFRED: Oh! does he? To-morrow he may want to borrow it—when he
and the others have had their object-lesson. They wouldn't listen to
argument...so we had to expose their pious fraud about woman's place
in the world in a very practical and sensible way. At this very minute
working women of every grade in every part of England are ceasing
work, and going to demand support and the necessities of life from
their nearest male relatives, however distant the nearest relatives may be.
I hope, for your sake, Ethel, that Horace's relatives aren't an exacting
lot!

ETHEL: There wasn't a word about it in the *Daily Mail* this morning.

WINIFRED: Never mind. The evening papers will make up for it.

ETHEL: What male relative are you going to, Winnie? Uncle Joseph?

WINIFRED: Oh, I'm in the fighting line, as usual, so our dear uncle will be
spared. My work is with the great army of women who have no male
belongings of any kind! I shall be busy till midnight marshalling them
to the workhouse.... This is perhaps the most important part of the
strike. By this we shall hit men as ratepayers even when they have
escaped us as relatives! Every man, either in a public capacity or a private one, will find himself face to face with the appalling problem of
maintaining millions of women in idleness. Will the men take up the
burden, d'ye think? Not they! (*Looks at her watch.*) Good heavens! The
strike began ages ago. I must be off. I've wasted too much time here
already.

ETHEL (*looking at the clock*): I had no idea it was so late. I must see about
Horace's tea. He may be home any minute. (*Rings the bell* L.)

WINIFRED: Poor Horace!

ETHEL (*annoyed*): Why "poor Horace"? I don't think he has anything to complain of. (*Rings again.*)

WINIFRED: I feel some pity at this minute for all the men.

ETHEL: What can have happened to Martha?

WINIFRED: She's gone, my dear, that's all.

ETHEL: Nonsense. She's been with me ever since I was married, and I pay
her very good wages.

(*Enter* LILY, *a shabby little maid-of-all-work, dressed for walking, the chief effect of the toilette being a very cheap and very smart hat.*)

ETHEL: Where's Martha, Lily?

LILY: She's left, m'm.

ETHEL: Left! She never gave me notice.

LILY: No, m'm, we wasn't to give no notice, but at three o'clock we was to quit.

ETHEL: But why? Don't be a silly little girl. And you musn't come in here in your hat.

LILY: I was just goin' when you rang. That's what I've got me 'at on for.

ETHEL: Going! Where? It's not your afternoon out.

LILY: I'm goin' back to the Union. There's dozens of others goin' with me.

ETHEL: But why—

LILY: Miss Christabel—she told us. She says to us: "Now look 'ere, all of yer—you who've got no men to go to on Thursday—yer've got to go to the Union," she says; "and the one who 'angs back"—and she looked at me, she did—"may be the person 'oo the 'ole strain of the movement is restin' on, the traitor 'oo's sailin' under the 'ostile flag," she says; and I says, "That won't be me—not much!"

(*During this speech* WINIFRED *puts on a sandwich board which bears the inscription: "This way to the Workhouse."*)

WINIFRED: Well, Ethel, are you beginning to believe?

ETHEL: Oh, I think it's very unkind—very wicked. How am I to get Horace anything to eat with no servants?

WINIFRED: Cheer up, my dear. Horace and the others can end the strike when they choose. But they're going to have a jolly bad time first. Good-bye.

(*Exit* WINNIE, *singing the "Marseillaise."*)[2]

LILY: Wait a bit, Miss. I'm comin' with yer (*sings the "Marseillaise" too*).

ETHEL: No, no. Oh, Lily, please don't go, or at any rate bring up the kettle first, and the chops, and the frying-pan. Please! Then I think I can manage.

LILY (*coming back into the room and speaking impressively*): There's no ill-feeling. It's an objick lesson—that's all.

(*Exit* LILY. ETHEL *begins to cry weakly; then lays the table; gets bread, cruet, tea, cups, etc., from the cupboard* (R.) LILY *re-enters with a frying-pan, a kettle, and two raw chops.*)

LILY: 'Ere you are—it's the best I can do. You see, mum, I've got to be recognized by the State. I don't think I'm a criminal or a lunatic,[3] and I oughtn't to be treated as sich.

ETHEL: You poor little simpleton. Do you suppose that, even if this absurd plan succeeds, *you* will get a vote?

LILY: I may—you never know your luck; but that's not why I'm giving up work. It's so as I shan't stop them as ought to 'ave it. The 'ole strain's on me, and I'm goin' to the Union—so good-bye, mum.

(*Exit* LILY.)

ETHEL: And I've always been so kind to you! Oh, you little brute! What *will* Horace say? (*looking out of the window*). It can't be true. Everything looks the same as usual. [(HORACE's *voice outside*): We must have at least sixteen Dreadnoughts[4] this year. (Williams' *voice*): You can't get 'em, old chap, unless you expect the blooming colonies to pay for 'em.] Ah, here is Horace, and Gerald Williams with him. Oh, I hope Horace hasn't asked him to tea! (*She powders her nose at the glass, then pretends to be busy with the kettle.*)

(*Enter* HORACE COLE—*an English master in his own house—
and* GERALD WILLIAMS, *a smug young man stiff with self-consciousness.*)

ETHEL: You're back early, aren't you, Horry? How do you do, Mr. Williams?

GERALD WILLIAMS: How do you do, Mrs. Cole? I just dropped in to fetch a book your husband's promised to lend me.

(HORACE *rummages in book-shelves.*)

ETHEL: Had a good day, Horry?

HORACE: Oh, much as usual. Ah, here it is—(*reading out the title*)— "Where's the Wash-tub now?" with a preface by Lord Curzon of Kedleston,[5] published by the Men's League for Opposing Women's Suffrage. If that doesn't settle your missus, nothing will.

ETHEL: Is Mrs. Williams a Suffragette?

GERALD: Rather; and whenever I say anything, all she can answer is, "You know nothing about it." Thank you, old man. I'll read it to her after tea. So long. Good-bye, Mrs. Cole.

ETHEL: Did Mrs. Williams tell you anything this morning ... before you went to the City?...

GERALD: About Votes for Women, do you mean? Oh, no. Not allowed at breakfast. In fact, not allowed at all. I tried to stop her going to these meetings where they fill the women's heads with all sorts of rubbish, and

she said she'd give 'em up if I'd give up my footer matches; so we agreed
to disagree. See you to-morrow, old chap. Good-bye, Mrs. Cole.

(*Exit* GERALD WILLIAMS.)

HORACE: You might have asked him to stop to tea. You made him very welcome—I don't think.

ETHEL: I'm sorry; but I don't think he'd have stayed if I *had* asked him.

HORACE: Very likely not, but one should always be hospitable. Tea ready?

ETHEL: Not quite, dear. It will be in a minute.

HORACE: What on earth is all this!

ETHEL: Oh, nothing. I only thought I would cook your chop for you up here
to-day—just for fun.

HORACE: I really think, Ethel, that so long as we can afford a servant, it's
rather unnecessary.

ETHEL: You know you're always complaining of Martha's cooking. I thought
you would like me to try.

HORACE: My dear child! It's very nice of you. But why not cook in the
kitchen? Raw meat in the sitting-room!

ETHEL: Oh, Horry, don't!

(*She put her arms round his neck and sobs.*
The chop at the end of the toasting-fork in her hand dangles in his face.)

HORACE: What on earth's the matter? Ethel, dear, don't be hysterical. If you
knew what it was to come home fagged to death and be worried like
this.... I'll ring for Martha and tell her to take away these beastly chops.
They're getting on my nerves.

ETHEL: Martha's gone.

HORACE: When? Why? Did you have a row? I suppose you had to give her a
month's wages. I can't afford that sort of thing, you know.

ETHEL (*sobbing*): It's not you who afford it, anyhow. Don't I pay Martha out
of my own money?

HORACE: Do you call it ladylike to throw that in my face....

ETHEL (*incoherently*): I'm not throwing it in your face ... but as it happens I
didn't pay her anything. She went off without a word ... and Lily's gone,
too.

(*She puts her head down on the table and cries.*)

HORACE: Well, that's a good riddance. I'm sick of her dirty face and slovenly
ways. If she ever does clean my boots, she makes them look worse than
when I took them off. We must try and get a charwoman.

ETHEL: We shan't be able to. Isn't it in the papers?

HORACE: What *are* you talking about?

ETHEL: Winifred said it would be in the evening papers.

HORACE: Winifred! She's been here, has she? That accounts for everything. How that woman comes to be your sister I can't imagine. Of course she's mixed up with this wild-cat scheme.

ETHEL: Then you know about it!

HORACE: Oh, I saw something about "Suffragettes on Strike" on the posters on my way home. Who cares if they do strike? They're no use to anyone. Look at Winifred. What does she ever do except go round making speeches, and kicking up a row outside the House of Commons until she forces the police to arrest her. Then she goes to prison and poses as a martyr. Martyr! We all know she could go home at once if she would promise the magistrate to behave herself. What they ought to do is to try all these hysterical women in camera[6] and sentence them to be ducked— privately. Then they'd soon give up advertising themselves.

ETHEL: Winnie has a splendid answer to that, but I forget what it is. Oh, Horry, was there anything on the posters about the nearest male relative?

HORACE: Ethel, my dear, you haven't gone dotty, have you? When you have quite done with my chair, I—(*He helps her out of the chair* C. *and sits down.*) Thank you.

ETHEL: Winnie said that not only are all the working women going to strike, but they are going to make their nearest male relatives support them.

HORACE: Rot!

ETHEL: I thought how dreadful it would be if Agatha came, or that cousin of yours on the stage whom you won't let me know, or your Aunt Lizzie! Martha and Lily have gone to *their* male relatives; at least, Lily's gone to the workhouse—it's all the same thing. Why shouldn't it be true? Oh, look, Horace, there's a cab—with luggage. Oh, what shall we do?

HORACE: Don't fuss! It's stopping next door, not here at all.

ETHEL: No, no; it's here. (*She rushes out.*)

HORACE (*calling after her*): Come back! You can't open the door yourself. It looks as if we didn't keep a servant.

(*Re-enter* ETHEL, *followed after a few seconds by* AGATHA. AGATHA *is a weary looking woman of about thirty-five. She wears the National Union colours,*[7] *and is dowdily dressed.*)

ETHEL: It *is* Agatha—and such a big box. Where can we put it?

AGATHA (*mildly*): How do you do, Horace. (*Kisses him.*) Dear Ethel! (*Kisses her.*) You're not looking so well as usual. Would you mind paying the cab-man two shillings, Horace, and helping him with my box? It's rather heavy, but then it contains all my worldly belongings.

HORACE: Agatha—you haven't lost your situation! You haven't left the Lewises?

AGATHA: Yes, Horace; I left at three o'clock.

HORACE: My dear Agatha—I'm extremely sorry—but we can't put you up here.

AGATHA: Hadn't you better pay the cab? Two shillings so soon become two-and-six. (*Exit* HORACE.) I am afraid my brother doesn't realise that I have some claim on him.

ETHEL: We thought you were so happy with the Lewises.

AGATHA: So were the slaves in America when they had kind masters. They didn't want to be free.

ETHEL: Horace said you always had late dinner with them when they had no company.

AGATHA: Oh, I have no complaint against my employers. In fact, I was sorry to inconvenience them by leaving so suddenly. But I had a higher duty to perform than my duty to them.

ETHEL: I don't know what to do. It will worry Horace dreadfully.

(*Re-enter* HORACE.)

HORACE: The cab *was* two-and-six, and I had to give a man twopence to help me in with that Noah's ark. Now, Agatha, what does this mean? Surely in your position it was very unwise to leave the Lewises. You can't stay here. We must make some arrangement.

AGATHA: Any arrangement you like, dear, provided you support me.

HORACE: I support you!

AGATHA: As my nearest male relative, I think you are obliged to do so. If you refuse, I must go to the workhouse.

HORACE: But why can't you support yourself? You've done it for years.

AGATHA: Yes—ever since I was eighteen. Now I am going to give up work, until my work is recognised. Either my proper place is the home—the home provided for me by some dear father, brother, husband, cousin or uncle—or I am a self-supporting member of the State who ought not to be shut out from the rights of citizenship.

HORACE: All this sounds as if you had become a Suffragette! Oh, Agatha, I always thought you were a lady.

AGATHA: Yes, I *was* a lady—such a lady that at eighteen I was thrown upon the world, penniless, with no training whatever which fitted me to earn my own living. When women become citizens I believe that daughters will be given the same chances as sons, and such a life as mine will be impossible.

HORACE: Women are so illogical. What on earth has all this to do with your planting yourself on me in this inconsiderate way? You must see, Agatha, that I haven't the means to support a sister as well as a wife. Couldn't you go to some friends until you find another situation?

AGATHA: No, Horace. I'm going to stay with you.

HORACE (*changing his tone and turning nasty*): Oh, indeed! And for how long—if I may ask?

AGATHA: Until the Bill for the removal of the sex disability is passed.

HORACE (*impotently angry*): Nonsense. I can't keep you, and I won't. I have always tried to do my duty by you. I think hardly a week passes that I don't write to you. But now that you have deliberately thrown up an excellent situation as a governess and come here and threatened me— yes, threatened me—I think it's time to say that, sister or no sister, I will be master in my own house!

(*Enter* MOLLY, *a good-looking young girl of about twenty. She is dressed in well-cut, tailor-made clothes, wears a neat little hat, and carries some golf-clubs and a few books.*)

MOLLY: How are you, Uncle Horace? Is that Aunt Aggie? How d'ye do? I haven't seen you since I was a kid.

HORACE: Well, what have you come for?

MOLLY: There's a charming welcome to give your only niece!

HORACE: You know perfectly well, Molly, that I disapprove of you in every way. I hear—I have never read it, of course—but I hear that you have written a most scandalous book. You live in lodgings by yourself, when if you chose you could afford some really nice and refined boarding-house. You have most undesirable acquaintances, and altogether—

MOLLY: Cheer up, Uncle. Now's your chance of reforming me. I've come to live with you. You can support me and improve me at the same time.

HORACE: I never heard such impertinence! I have always understood from you that you earn more than I do.

MOLLY: Ah, yes; but you never *liked* my writing for money, did you? You called me "sexless" once because I said that as long as I could support myself I didn't feel an irresistible temptation to marry that awful little bounder Weekes.

ETHEL: Reginald Weekes! How can you call him a bounder! He was at Oxford.

MOLLY: Hullo, Auntie Ethel! I didn't notice you. You'll be glad to hear I haven't brought much luggage—only a night-gown and some golf-clubs.

HORACE: I suppose this is a joke!

MOLLY: Well, of course that's one way of looking at it. I'm not going to support myself any longer. I'm going to be a perfect lady and depend on my Uncle Horace—my nearest male relative—for the necessities of life. (*A motor horn is heard outside.*) Aren't you glad that I am not going to write another scandalous book, or live in lodgings by myself!

ETHEL (*at the window*): Horace! Horace! There's someone getting out of a motor—a grand motor. Who can it be? And there's no one to answer the door.

MOLLY: That doesn't matter. I found it open, and left it open to save trouble.

ETHEL: She's got luggage, too! The chauffeur's bringing in a dressing-case.

HORACE: I'll turn her into the street—and the dressing-case, too.

(*He goes fussily to the door and meets* MADAME CHRISTINE *on the threshold. The lady is dressed smartly and tastefully. Age about forty, manners elegant, smile charming, speech resolute. She carries a jewel-case, and consults a legal document during her first remarks.*)

MADAME C.: You are Mr. Cole?

HORACE: No! Certainly not! (*wavering*). At least, I was this morning, but—

MADAME C.: Horace Cole, son of John Hay Cole, formerly of Streatham, where he carried on the business of a—

(*A motor horn sounds outside.*)

HORACE: I beg your pardon, but my late father's business has really nothing to do with this matter, and to a professional man it's rather trying to have these things raked up against him. Excuse me, but do you want your motor to go?

MADAME C.: It's not my motor any longer; and—yes, I do want it to go, for I may be staying here some time. I think you had one sister Agatha, and one brother Samuel, now dead. Samuel was much older than you—

AGATHA: Why don't you answer, Horace? Yes, that's perfectly correct. I am Agatha.

MADAME C.: Oh, are you? How d'ye do?

MOLLY: And Samuel Cole was my father.

MADAME C.: I'm very glad to meet you. I didn't know I had such charming relations. Well, Mr. Cole, my father was John Hay Cole's first cousin; so you, I think, are my second cousin, and my nearest male relative.

HORACE: (*distractedly*): If anyone calls me that again I shall go mad.

MADAME C.: I am afraid you aren't quite pleased with the relationship!

HORACE: You must excuse me—but I don't consider a second cousin exactly a relation.

MADAME C.: Oh, it answers the purpose. I suddenly find myself destitute, and I want you to support me. I am sure you would not like a Cole to go to the workhouse.

HORACE: I don't care a damn where any of 'em go.

ETHEL (*shocked*): Horry! How can you!

MADAME C.: That's frank, at any rate; but I am sure, Cousin Horace, that in spite of your manners, your heart's in the right place. You won't refuse me board and lodging, until Parliament makes it possible for me to resume my work?

HORACE: My dear madam, do you realise that my salary is £3 10s. a week— and that my house will hardly hold your luggage, much less you?

MADAME C.: Then you must agitate. Your female relatives have supported themselves up till now, and asked nothing from you. I myself, dear cousin, was, until this morning, running a profitable dressmaking business in Hanover Square. In my public capacity I am Madame Christine.

MOLLY: I know! I've never been able to afford you.

HORACE: And do you think, Madame Christine—

MADAME C.: Cousin Susan, please.

HORACE: Do you think that you are justified in coming to a poor clerk and asking him to support you—you could probably turn over my yearly income in a single week! Didn't you come here in your own motor?

MADAME C.: At three o'clock that motor became the property of the Women's Social and Political Union. All the rest of my property and all available cash have been divided equally between the National Union and the Women's Freedom League. Money is the sinews of war, you know.

HORACE: Do you mean to tell me that you've given all your money to the Suffragettes! It's a pity you haven't a husband. He'd very soon stop your doing such foolish things.

MADAME C.: I had a husband once. He liked me to do foolish things—for instance, to support him. After that unfortunate experience, Cousin Horace, you may imagine how glad I am to find a man who really is a man, and will support me instead. By the way, I should *so* much like some tea. Is the kettle boiling?

ETHEL (*feebly*): There aren't enough cups! Oh, what shall I do?

HORACE: Never mind, Ethel; I shan't want any. I am going to dine in town and go to the theatre. I shall hope to find you all gone when I come back. If not, I shall send for the police.

(*Enter* MAUDIE SPARK, *a young woman with an aggressively cheerful manner, a voice raucous from much bellowing of music-hall songs, a hat of huge size, and a heart of gold.*)

MAUDIE: 'Ullo! 'ullo! who's talking about the police? Not my dear cousin Horry!

HORACE: How dare you come here?

MAUDIE: Necessity, old dear. If I had a livelier male relative, you may bet I'd have gone to him! But you, Horace, are the only first cousin of this poor orphan. What are you in such a hurry for?

HORACE: Let me pass! I'm going to the theatre.

MAUDIE: Silly jay! the theatres are all closed—and the halls too. The actresses have gone on strike—resting indefinitely. I've done my little bit towards that. They won't get any more work out of Maudie Spark, Queen of Comédiennes, until the women have got the vote. Ladies and fellow-relatives, you'll be pleased to hear the strike's going fine. The big drapers can't open to-morrow. One man can't fill the place of fifteen young ladies at once, you see. The duchesses are out in the streets begging people to come in and wash their kids. The City men are trying to get taxi-men in to do their typewriting. Every man, like Horry here, has his house full of females. Most of 'em thought, like Horry, that they'd go to the theatre to escape. But there's not a blessed theatre to go to! Oh, what a song it'll make. "A woman's place is the home—I don't think, I don't think, I don't think."

HORACE: Even if this is not a plot against me personally, even if there are other women in London at this minute disgracing their sex—

MAUDIE: Here, stop it—come off it! If it comes to that, what are *you* doing—threatening your womankind with the police and the workhouse.

HORACE: I was not addressing myself to you.

AGATHA: Why not, Horace? She's your cousin. She needs your protection just as much as we do.

HORACE: I regard that woman as the skeleton in the cupboard of a respectable family; but that's neither here nor there. I address myself to the more lady-like portion of this gathering, and I say that whatever is going on, the men will know what to do, and will do it with dignity and firmness. (*The impressiveness of this statement is marred by the fact that* Horace's *hand, in emphasising it, comes down heavily on the loaf of bread on the table.*) A few exhibitions of this kind won't frighten them.

MAUDIE: Oh, won't it! I like that! They're being so firm and so dignified that they're running down to the House of Commons like lunatics, and black-guarding the Government for not having given us the vote before! (*Shouts outside of newsboys in the distance.*)

MOLLY: Splendid! Have they begun already?

MADAME C.: Get a paper, Cousin Horace. I know some men never believe anything till they see it in the paper.

ETHEL: The boys are shouting out something now. Listen.

(*Shouts outside.* "Extry special. Great strike of women. Women's strike. Theatres closed. Extry special edition. *Star! News!* 6.30 edition!")

MOLLY: You see. Since this morning Suffragettes have become women!

ETHEL (*at window*): Here, boy, paper!

> (*Cries go on.* "Extra special *Star*. Men petition the Government.
> Votes for Women. Extry special.")

Oh, heavens, here's Aunt Lizzie!

> (*As* ETHEL *pronounces the name* HORACE *dives under the table. Enter* AUNT
> LIZZIE *leading a fat spaniel and carrying a bird-cage with a parrot in it.* MISS
> ELIZABETH WILKINS *is a comfortable, middle-aged body of a type well known to
> those who live in the less fashionable quarter of Bloomsbury. She looks as if she
> kept lodgers, and her looks do not belie her. She is not very well educated, but
> has a good deal of native intelligence. Her features are homely and her clothes
> about thirty years behind the times.*)

AUNT L.: Well, dears, all here? That's right. Where's Horace? Out? Just as
well; we can talk more freely. I'm sorry I'm late, but animals do so hate a
move. It took a long time to make them understand the strike. But I
think they will be very comfortable here. You love dogs, don't you, Ethel?

ETHEL: Not Ponto. He always growls at me.

AUNT L.: Clever dog! he knows you don't sympathise with the cause.

ETHEL: But I do, Aunt; only I have always said that as I was happily married I
thought it had very little to do with me.

AUNT L.: You've changed your mind about that to-day, I should think! What
a day it's been! We never expected everything would go so smoothly.
They say the Bill's to be rushed through at once. No more broken
promises, no more talking out; deeds, not words, at last! Seen the
papers? The press are not boycotting us to-day, my dears. (MADAME C.,
MOLLY, *and* MAUDIE *each take a paper.*) The boy who sold them to me put
the money back into Ponto's collecting box. That dog must have made
five pounds for the cause since this morning.

> (HORACE *puts his head out and says* "Liar!")

MOLLY: Oh, do listen to this. It's too splendid! (*Reading from the paper*)
"Women's Strike–Latest: Messrs. Lyons and Co. announce that by special
arrangement with the War Office the places of their defaulting waitresses
will be filled by the non-commissioned officers and men of the 2nd Battal-
ion Coldstream Guards. Business will therefore be carried on as usual."

MADAME C.: What do you think of this? (*Reading*) "Latest Intelligence.—It is
understood that the Naval Volunteers have been approached by the
authorities with the object of inducing them to act as charwomen to the

House of Commons."

AUNT L. (*to* ETHEL): Well, my dear! Read, then, what the *Star* says.

ETHEL (*tremulously reading*): "The queue of women waiting for admission to Westminster workhouse is already a mile and a half in length. As the entire police force are occupied in dealing with the men's processions, Lord Esher has been approached with a view to ascertaining if the Territorials can be sworn in as special constables."

MAUDIE (*laughing*): This is a little bit of all right. (*Reading*) "Our special representative, on calling upon the Prime Minister with the object of ascertaining his views on the situation, was informed that the Right Honourable gentleman was unable to receive him, as he was actively engaged in making his bed with the assistance of the boot-boy and a Foreign Office messenger."

AUNT L.: Always unwilling to receive people, you see! Well, he must be feeling sorry now that he never received us. Everyone's putting the blame on to him. It's extraordinary how many men—and newspapers, too—have suddenly found out that they have always been in favour of woman's suffrage! That's the sensible attitude, of course. It would be humiliating for them to confess that they changed their minds. Well, at this minute I would rather be the man who has been our ally all along than the one who has been our enemy. It's not the popular thing to be an "anti" any more. Any man who tries to oppose us to-day is likely to be slung up to the nearest lamp-post.

ETHEL: (*rushing wildly to the table*): Oh, Horry! my Horry! (HORACE *comes out from under the table.*)

AUNT L.: Why, bless the boy, what are you doing there?

HORACE: Oh, nothing. I merely thought I might be less in the way here, that's all.

AUNT L.: You didn't hide when I came in by any chance!

HORACE: I hide from you! Aren't you always welcome in this house?

AUNT L.: Well, I haven't noticed it particularly; and I'm not calling to-day, you understand, I've come to stay. (HORACE, *dashed and beaten, begins to walk up and down the room, and consults* ETHEL.) Well, well! I won't deny it was a wrench to leave 118a, Upper Montagu Place, where I've done my best for boarders, old and young, gents and ladies, for twenty-five years— and no complaints! A home from home, they call it. All my ladies had left before I started out, on the same business as all of us—but what those poor boys will do for their dinner to-night I don't know. They're a helpless lot! Well, it's all over; I've given up my boarding-house, and I depend on you, Horace, to keep me until I am admitted to citizenship. It may take a long time.

HORACE: It must not take a long time! I shan't allow it. It shall be done at once. Well, you needn't all look so surprised. I know I've been against it, but I didn't realise things. I thought only a few howling dervishes wanted the vote; but when I find that you—Aunt— Fancy a woman of your firmness of character, one who has always been so careful with her money, being declared incapable of voting! The thing is absurd.

MAUDIE: Bravo! Our Horry's waking up.

HORACE: (*looking at her scornfully*): If there are a few women here and there who are incapable—I mention no names, mind—it doesn't affect the position. What's going to be done? Who's going to do it? If this rotten Government think we're going to maintain millions of women in idleness just because they don't like the idea of my Aunt Lizzie making a scratch on a bit of paper and shoving it into a ballot-box once every five years, this Government have reckoned without the men— (*General cheering.*) I'll show 'em what I've got a vote for! What do they expect? You can't all marry. There aren't enough men to go round, and if you're earning your own living and paying taxes you ought to have a say; it's only fair. (*General cheering and a specially emphatic "Hear, hear" from* MADAME CHRISTINE.) The Government are narrow-minded idiots! (MADAME C.: Hear! hear!) They talk as if all the women ought to stay at home washing and ironing. Well, before a woman has a wash-tub, she must have a home to put it in, mustn't she? And who's going to give it her? I'd like them to tell me that. Do they expect *me* to do it? (AGATHA: Yes, dear.) I say if she can do it herself and keep herself, so much the better for everyone. Anyhow, who are the Government? They're only representing *me*, and being paid thousands a year by *me* for carrying out *my* wishes. (MOLLY: Oh, er—what ho! Horace *turns on her angrily*) I like a woman to be a woman—that's the way I was brought up; but if she insists on having a vote—and apparently she does (ALL: She does! she does!)—I don't see why she shouldn't have it. Many a woman came in here at the last election and tried to wheedle me into voting for her particular candidate. If she has time to do that—and I never heard the member say then that she ought to be at home washing the baby—I don't see why she hasn't time to vote. It's never taken up much of *my* time, or interfered with *my* work. I've only voted once in my life—but that's neither here nor there. I know what the vote does for me. It gives me a status; that's what you women want—a status. (ALL: Yes, yes; a status.) I might even call it a *locus standi*.[8] If I go now and tell these rotten Cabinet Ministers what I think of them, it's my *locus standi*—(MAUDIE: That's a good word.)—that will force them to listen to me. Oh, I know. And, by gum! I'll give them a bit of my mind. They shall hear a few home truths for once. "Gentlemen," I shall say—well, that won't be true of all of them to start with, but one must give 'em the benefit of the doubt— "gentlemen, the men of England are sick and tired of your policy. Who's driven the women of England into this? *You*—(*he turns round on* ETHEL, *who jumps violently*)—because you were too stupid to know that they meant business—because you couldn't read the writing on the wall. (*Hear, hear.*) It may be nothing to you, gentlemen, that every industry in this country is paralysed and every Englishman's home turned into a howling wilderness—(MOLLY: Draw it mild, Uncle. HORACE: A howling wilderness, I repeat)—by your refusal to see what's as plain as the nose on your face; but I would have you know, gentlemen, that it *is* something to us. We aren't slaves. We never will be slaves—(AGATHA: Never, never!)—and we insist on reform. Gentlemen, conditions have changed, and women have to work. Don't men encourage them to work, *invite* them to work? (AGATHA: Make them work.) And women are placed in the battle of life on the same terms as we are, short of one thing, the *locus standi* of a vote. (MAUDIE: Good old *locus standi*!) If you aren't going to give it them, gentlemen, and if they won't go back to their occupations without it, we ask you, how they're going to live? Who's going to support them? Perhaps you're thinking of giving them all old age pensions and asking the country to pay the piper! The country will see you damned first, if, gentlemen, you'll pardon the expression. It's dawning upon us all that the women would never have taken such a step as this if they hadn't been the victims of gross injustice. (ALL: Never.) Why shouldn't they have a choice in the laws which regulate the price of food and clothes? Don't they pay for their food and clothes? (MAUDIE: Paid for mine all my life.) Why shouldn't they have a voice in the rate of wages and the hours of labour in certain industries? Aren't they working at those industries? If you had a particle of common sense or decent feeling, gentlemen—"

(*Enter* GERALD WILLIAMS *like a souvenir of Mafeking night.*[9] *He shouts incoherently and in a hoarse voice. He is utterly transformed from the meek, smug being of an hour before. He is wearing several ribbons and badges and carrying a banner bearing this inscription: "The men of Brixton demand votes for women this evening."*)

WILLIAMS: Cole! Cole! Come on! come on! You'll be late. The procession's forming up at the town hall. There's no time to lose. What are you slacking here for? Perhaps this isn't good enough for you. I've got twelve of them in my drawing-room. We shall be late for the procession if we don't start at once. Hurry up! Come on! Votes for Women! Where's your banner? Where's your badge? Down with the Government! Rule Britannia! Votes for Women! D'you want to support a dozen women for the rest of your life, or don't you?... Every man in Brixton is going to Westminster. Borrow a ribbon and come along. Hurry up, now! Hooray! (*Rushes madly out crying "Votes for Women!" Rule Britannia; Women never, never shall be slaves! Votes for Women!*)

(*All the women who are wearing ribbons decorate* HORACE.)

ETHEL: My hero! (*She throws her arms round him.*)
HORACE: You may depend on me—all of you—to see justice done. When
you want a thing done, get a man to do it! Votes for Women!

(AGATHA *gives him a flag which he waves truimphantly.*)

(*Curtain tableau:* HORACE *marching majestically out of the door,
with the women cheering him enthusiastically.*)

CURTAIN.

VOTES FOR MEN

[*The Romance of His Life and Other Romances.*
Freeport, New York: Books for Libraries Press, 1972. First published in
1909.]

Two hundred years hence, possibly less.

EUGENIA, *Prime Minister, is sitting at her writing table in her library. She is a tall, fine looking woman of thirty, rather untidy and worn in appearance.*

EUGENIA (*to herself, taking up a paper*): There is no doubt that we must carry through this bill or the future of the country will be jeopardized.

HENRY (*outside*): May I come in?

EUGENIA: Do come in, dearest.

HENRY (*a tall, athletic man of thirty, faultlessly dressed, a contrast to her dusty untidiness*): I thought I could see the procession best from here. (*Goes to windows and opens them.*) It is in sight now. They are coming down the wind at a great pace.

EUGENIA (*slightly bored*): What procession?

HENRY : Why the Men's Reinfranchisement League, of course. You know, Eugenia, you promised to interview a deputation of them at 5 o'clock, and they determined to have a mass meeting first.

EUGENIA: So they did. I had forgotten. I wish they would not pester me so. Really, the government has other things to attend to than Male Suffrage at times like this.

(*The procession sails past the windows in planes decked with the orange and white colours of the league. The occupants preserve a dead silence, saluting* EUGENIA *gravely as they pass. From the streets far below rises a confused hubbub of men's voices shouting "Votes for men!"*)

HENRY : How stately the clergy look, Eugenia! Why, there are the two Archbishops in their robes heading the whole procession, and look at the bevy of Bishops in their lawn sleeves in the great Pullman air car behind. What splendid men. And here come the clergy in their academic gowns by the hundred, in open trucks.

EUGENIA: I must say it is admirably organised, and no brawling.

HENRY : Why should they brawl? I believe you are disappointed that they
don't. They are all saluting you, Eugenia, as they pass. They won't take
any notice of me, of course, because it is known I am the President of the
Anti-Suffrage League. The doctors are passing now. How magnificent
they look in their robes! What numbers of them! It makes me proud I
am a man. And now come the lawyers in crowds in their wigs and gowns.

EUGENIA: Every profession seems to be represented, but of course I am well
aware that it is not the real wish of the men of England to obtain the
vote. The suffragists must do something to convince me that the bulk of
England's thoughtful and intelligent men are not opposed to it before I
move in the matter.

HENRY : I often wonder what would convince you, Eugenia, or what they
could do that they have not done. These must be the authors and artists
and journalists, and quite a number of women with them. Do you notice
that? Look, that is Hobson the poet, and Bagg the millionaire novelist,
each in their own Swallow planes. How they dart along. I should like to
have a Swallow, Eugenia. And are all those great lumbering tumbrils of
men journalists?

EUGENIA: No doubt.

HENRY : It is very impressive. I wish they did not pass so fast, but the wind is
high. Here come all the trades with the Lord Mayor of London in front!
What hordes and hordes of them! The procession is at least a mile long.
And I suppose those are miners and agricultural labourers, last of all, trying to keep up in those old Wilbur Wrights and Zeppelins. I did not
know there were any left except in museums.

(*The procession passes out of sight.* EUGENIA *sighs.*)

HENRY : Demonstrations like this make a man think, Eugenia. I really can't
see, though you often tell me I do, why men should not have votes. They
used to have them. You yourself say that there is no real inequality
between the sexes. The more I think of it the more I feel I ought to
retire from being President of the Anti-Suffrage League. And all the men
on it are old enough to be my father. The young men are nearly all in
the opposite camp. I sometimes wish I was there too.

EUGENIA: Henry!

HENRY : Now don't, Eugenia, make any mistake. I abhor the "brawling
brotherhood" as much as you do. I was quite ashamed for my sex when I
saw that bellowing brute riveted to the balcony of your plane the other
day, shouting "Votes for men."

EUGENIA (*coldly*): That sort of conduct puts back the cause of men's reinfranchisement by fifty years. It shows how unsuited the sex is to be trusted with
the vote. Imagine that sort of hysterical screaming in the House itself.

HENRY : But ought the cause to be judged by the folly of a few howling dervishes? Sometimes it really seems, Eugenia, as if women were determined to regard the brawling brotherhood as if it represented the men who seek the vote. And yet the sad part is that these brawlers have done more in two years to advance the cause than their more orderly brothers have achieved in twenty. For years past I have heard quiet suffragists say that all their efforts have been like knocking in a padded room. They can't make themselves heard. Women smiled and said the moment was not opportune. The press gave garbled accounts of their sayings and doings.

EUGENIA: Your simile is unfortunate. No one wants to emancipate the only persons who are confined in padded rooms.

HENRY : Not if they are unjustly confined?

EUGENIA (*with immense patience*): Dear Henry, must we really go over this old ground again? Men used to have votes as we all know. In the earliest days of all, of course, both men and women had them. The ancient records prove that beyond question, and that women presented themselves with men at the hustings. Then women were practically disfranchised, and for hundreds of years men ruled alone, though it was not until near the reign of Victoria the First that by the interpolation of the word "male" before "persons" in the Reform Act of 1832 women were legally disfranchised. Men were disfranchised almost as suddenly in the reign of Man-hating Mary the Second of blessed memory.

HENRY : I know, I know, but....

EUGENIA (*whose oratorical instincts are not exhausted by her public life*): You must remember I would have you all—I mean I would have you, Henry, remember that men were only disfranchised after the general election of 2009. It was the wish of the country. We must bow to that.

HENRY : You mean it was the wish of the women of the country, who were a million stronger numerically than men.

EUGENIA: It was the wish of the majority, including many thousands of enlightened men, my grandfather among them, who saw the danger of their country involved in continued male suffrage. After all, Henry, it was men who were guilty of the disaster of adult suffrage. Women never asked for it—they were deeply opposed to it. They only demanded the suffrage on the same terms that men had it in Edward the Seventh's time. Adult suffrage was the last important enactment of men, and one which ought to prove to you, considering the incalculable harm it did, that men, in spite of their admirable qualities, are not sufficiently far-sighted to be trusted with a vote. Adult suffrage lost us India. It all but lost us our Colonies, for the corner-men and wastrels and unemployed who momentarily became our rulers saw no use for them. The only good result of adult suffrage was that women, by the happy chance of their numerical majority, and with the help of Mary the Manhater, were able to combine, to outvote the men and so to seize the reins and abolish it.

HENRY : And abolish us too.

EUGENIA: It was an extraordinary *coup d'état*, the one good result of the disaster of adult suffrage. It was a bloodless revolution, but the most amazing in the annals of history. And it saved the country.

HENRY : I do not deny it. But you can't get away from the fact that men did give women the vote originally. And now men have lost it themselves. Why should not women give it back to men—I mean, of course, only to those who have the same qualifications as to property as women voters have? After all it was by reason of our physical force that we were entitled to rule, at least men always said so. Over and over again they said so in the House, and that women can't be soldiers and sailors and special constables as we can. And our physical force remains the greater to this day.

EUGENIA: We do everything to encourage it.

HENRY : Without us, Eugenia, you would have no army, no navy, no miners. We do the work of the world. We guard and police the nation, and yet we are not entitled to a hearing.

EUGENIA: Your ignorance of the force that rules the world is assumed for rhetorical purposes.

HENRY : I suppose you will say brain ought to rule. Well, some of us are just as able as some of you. Look at our great electricians, our shipbuilders, our inventors, our astronomers, our poets, nearly all are men. Shakespeare was a man.

EUGENIA (*sententiously*): There was a day, and a very short day it was, when it was said that brain ought to rule. Brain did make the attempt, but it could no more rule this planet than brute force could continue to do so. You know, and I know, and every schoolgirl knows, that what rules the birth-rate rules the world.

HENRY (*for whom this sentiment has evidently the horrid familiarity of the senna*[10] *of his childhood*): It used not to be so.

EUGENIA: It is so now. It is no use arguing; it is merely hysteria to combat the basic fact that the sex which controls the birth-rate must by nature rule the nation which it creates. This is not a question with which law can deal, for nature has decided it.

(*Henry preserves a paralysed silence.*)

EUGENIA (*with benignant dignity*): I am all for the equality of the sexes within certain limits, the limits imposed by nature. But the long and the short of it is, to put it bluntly, no man, my dear Henry, can give birth to a child, and until he can he will be ineligible by the laws of nature, not by any woman-made edict, to govern, and the less he talks about it the better.

Sensible men and older men know that and hold their tongues, and women respect their silence. Man has his sphere, and a very important and useful sphere in life it is. The defence of the nation is entrusted to him. Where should we be without our trusty soldiers and sailors, and, as you have just reminded me, our admirable police force? Where physical strength comes in men are paramount. When I think of all the work men are doing in the world I assure you, Henry, my respect and admiration for them knows no bounds. But if they step outside their own sphere of labour, then—

HENRY : But if only you would look into the old records, as I have been doing, you would see that Lord Curzon and Lord James and Lord Cromer, and many others employed these same arguments in order to withhold the suffrage from women.

EUGENIA: I dare say.

HENRY : And there is another thing which does not seem to me to be fair. Men are so ridiculed if they are suffragists. *Punchinella*[11] always draws them as obese disappointed old bachelors, and there are many earnest young married men among the ranks of the suffragists. Look at the procession which has just passed. Our best men were in it. And to look at *Punchinella* or to listen to the speeches in the House you would think that the men who want the vote are mostly repulsive old bachelors stung by the neglect of women. Why only last week the member for Maidenhead, Mrs. Colthorpe it was got up and said that if only this "brawling brotherhood" of single gentlemen, who had missed domestic bliss, could find wives they would not trouble their heads about reinfranchisement.

EUGENIA: There is no doubt there is an element of sex resentment in the movement, dear Henry. That is why I have always congratulated myself on the fact that, you, as my husband, were opposed to it.

HENRY : Personally I can't imagine now that women have the upper hand why they don't keep up their number numerically. It is their only safeguard against our one day regaining the vote. It was their numerical majority plus adult suffrage which suddenly put them in the position to disfranchise men. And yet women are allowing their number to decline and decline until really for all practical purposes there seems to be about two men to every woman.

EUGENIA: The laws of nature render our position infinitely stronger than that of men ever was. We mounted by the ladder of adult suffrage, but we kicked it down immediately afterwards. It will never be revived. Men had no tremors about the large surplusage of women as long as they were without votes. Why should we have any now about the surplusage of men?

HENRY : Then there is another point. You talk so much about the importance of the physique of the race, and I agree with all my heart. But there are so few women to marry nowadays, and women show such a marked disinclination towards marriage till their youth is quite over, that half the men I know can't get wives at all. And those who do, have almost no power of selection left to them, and are forced to put up with ill-developed, sickly, peevish, or ugly women past their first bloom rather than remain unmarried and childless.

EUGENIA: The subject is under consideration at this moment, but when the position was reversed in Edward the Seventh's time, and there were not enough men to go round, women were in the same plight, and men said nothing then about the deterioration of the race. They did not even make drunkards' marriages a penal offence. Drunkards and drug-takers, and men dried up by nicotine constantly married and had children in those days.

HENRY : I can't think the situation was as difficult for women as it is now for men. I was at Oxford last week, and do you know that during the last forty years only five percent of the male Dons and Professors have been able to find mates. Women won't look at them.

EUGENIA: In the nineteenth century, when first women went to Universities and became highly educated, only four per cent of them afterwards married, and then to schoolmasters.

HENRY : And I assure you the amount of hysteria and quarrelling among the older Dons is lamentable.

EUGENIA: I appointed a committee which reported to me on the subject last year, and I gathered that the present Dons are not more hysterical than they were in Victorian days, when they forfeited their fellowships on marriage. You must remember, Henry, that from the earliest times men and women have always hated anything "blue" in the opposite sex. Female blue stockings[12] were seldom attractive to men in bygone days. And nowadays women are naturally inclined to marry young men, and healthy and athletic men, rather than sedentary old male blue stockings. It is most fortunate for the race that it is so.

HENRY (*with a sigh*): Well, all the "blue" women can marry nowadays.

EUGENIA: Yes, thank heaven, *all* women can marry nowadays. What women must have endured in the eighteenth and early part of the nineteenth century makes me shudder. For if they did not marry they were never spared the ridicule or the contemptuous compassion of men. It seems incredible, looking back, to realise that large families of daughters were kept idle and unhappy at home, after their youth was over, not allowed to take up any profession, only to be turned callously adrift in their middle age at their father's death, with a pittance on which they could barely live. And yet these things were done by educated and kindly men who professed to care for the interests of women, and were personally fond of their daughters. Over and over again in the biographies of notable women of the Victorian and Edward the Seventh's time one comes across instances of the way in which men of the country-squire type kept their daughters at home uneducated till they were beyond the age when they could take up a profession, and then left them to poverty. They did not even insure their lives for each child as we do now. Surely, Henry, it is obvious that women have done one thing admirably. The large reduction which they have effected in their own numbers has almost eliminated the superfluous, incompetent, unhappy women who found it so difficult to obtain a livelihood a hundred years ago, and has replaced them by an extra million competent, educated, fairly contented men who are all necessary to the State, who are encouraged, almost forced into various professions.

HENRY : Not contented, Eugenia.

EUGENIA: More contented, because actively employed, than if they were wandering aimlessly in the country lanes of their father's estates as thousands of intelligent uneducated women were doing a hundred years ago, kept ferociously at home by the will of the parent who held the purse-strings.

HENRY : I rather wish I had lived in those good old times, when the lanes were full of pretty women.

EUGENIA: But you, at any rate, Henry, had a large choice. I was much afraid at one time that you would never ask me.

HENRY : Ah! But then I was a great heir, and all heirs have a wide choice. Not that I had any choice at all. I had the good luck to be accepted by the only woman I ever cared a pin about, and the only one I was sure was disinterested.

EUGENIA: Dearest!

HENRY (*tentatively*): And yet our marriage falls short of an ideal one, my Eugenia.

EUGENIA (*apologetically*): Dear Henry, I know it does, but as soon as I cease to be Prime Minister I will do my duty to the country, and, what I think much more of, by you. What is a home without children? Besides, I must set an example. When you came in I was framing a bill to meet the alarming decline of the birth-rate. Unless something is done the nation will become extinct. The results of this tendency among women to marry later and later are disastrous.

Henry: And what is your bill, Eugenia?

EUGENIA: That every healthy married woman or female celibate over twenty-five and under forty, members of the government excepted, must do her duty to the State by bringing into the world—

HENRY : Celibate! Bringing into the world! Eugenia! and I thought the sanctity of marriage and home life were among your deepest convictions. Just think how you have upheld them to—*men.*

EUGENIA: Patriotism must come first. By bringing into the world three children, a girl and two boys. If her income is insufficient to rear them, the State will take charge of them. One extra boy is needed to supply the wastage of accidents in practical work, and in case of war. I shall stand or fall by this bill, for unless the women of England can be aroused to do their duty—unless there is general conscription to motherhood, as in Germany, England will certainly become a second-class power.

HENRY : Perhaps when there are two men to every woman we shall be strong enough to force women to do justice to us.

EUGENIA: Men never did justice to us when they had the upper hand.

HENRY : They did not. And I think the truth lies there. Those who have the upper hand cannot be just to those who are in their power. They don't intend to be unfair, but they seem unable to give their attention to the rights of those who cannot enforce them. Men were unintentionally unjust to women for hundreds of years. They kept them down. Now women are unjust to us. Yes, Eugenia, you are. You keep us down. It seems to be an inevitable part of the *rôle* of "top dog," and perhaps it is no use discussing it. If you don't want your plane, would you mind if I borrow it? I promised to meet Carlyon at four above the Florence Nightingale column in Anne Hyde's park, and it is nearly four now.

EUGENIA: Good-bye, Henry. Do take my plane. And I trust there will be no more doubt in your dear head as to your Presidency of the Anti-Suffrage League.

HENRY : None. I realise these wrigglings of the under dog are unseemly, and only disturb the equanimity and good-will of the "top dog." Good-bye, Eugenia.

[CURTAIN]

BEFORE SUNRISE

[London: Privately Printed, 1909]

[First performed at the Albert Hall Theatre, London, 11 December 1909.]

Mr. William Sewell (a man of 60)
Mrs. Bertha Sewell (his wife—58)
Caroline (his daughter—24)
Mary Swayne (35)
Jane
Tom Bullock (a man of 28)

Period: 1867

Scene: *Breakfast-room in Mr. William Sewell's house in Kensington.*
The furniture is all early Victorian. Large steel chandelier. Steel grate. India-
rubber plant in window. At R. the breakfast table laid for two. L. upholstered seat.
C. window looking on to street. Window practical. Entrances R. from Hall—
L. to House.
Mr. William Sewell and Mrs. William Sewell discovered at breakfast.
Mr. Sewell is reading "The Times."

MRS. S: (*Pouring the tea.*) Any news this morning, Will?

MR. S: No, my love. I merely note that John Stuart Mill's amendment to the Representation of the People Bill,[13] which is now before Parliament, has been defeated, 81 voting for and 202 against it.

MRS. S: Oh! You are referring to this stupid female suffrage business? (*Passes tea.*)

MR. S: (*Taking cup.*) Yes, Mill's amendment was that instead of the word "man," the word "person" should be used to the suffrage under the act. Ah! it's a great pity that he was returned as M.P. for Westminster two years ago. These silly women will be sending in another petition to Parliament again, I suppose—(*tasting tea and making a wry face*). Sugar, Bertha, sugar!

MRS. S: Sorry, dear. (*Rises and helps HIM to sugar.*) I take no interest in politics, in fact I never think of reading a newspaper. I haven't the time, what with all my domestic work and the jam this family eats. Why, I am preserving forty pounds of plums to-day!

MR. S: You are right, Bertha. The great affairs of the state do no concern women at all. They have not the brain capacity to tackle them, but I must confess I was surprised to find that after John Stuart Mill was returned as Member for Westminster, a women's suffrage petition, signed by over a thousand women, was presented to Parliament.[14]

MRS. S: Really! How ridiculous!

Strumming heard on a distant piano.

Caroline is getting on nicely with the "Maiden's Prayer."

MR. S: (*Nods and moves HIS head in time with the music.*) By the way, Caroline is to give her answer to Tom Bullock to-day?

MRS. S: Yes, he is calling at twelve o'clock.

MR. S: An extremely rich man, my dear! A little wild perhaps—fond of the Turf—but the sort of man who settles down into a model husband.

MRS. S: I think it an excellent match for her. When a woman is twenty-four years of age, she can no longer pick and choose.

MR. S: Of course you have spoken to Caroline on the subject?

MRS. S: Yes.

MR. S: And in what light does she view the matter?

MRS. S: The girl is naturally flattered. She does not quite know her own mind, but I shall speak to her again before Tom comes, and I don't think we need entertain any uneasiness on the score of her acting contrary to our wishes in this matter.

MR. S: Glad to hear it, my love. The girl is lucky to have such a clever, tactful mother.

MRS. S: (*Smiling.*) Delighted that you should think so, dear. There is one little matter upon which I want your advice. I have been wondering whether you would allow Caroline to have a few months' tuition at Miss Cripp's Finishing School for Young Ladies?

MR. S: (*Astonished.*) Why, what can have put such an idea into your head? God bless my soul, I never heard of such a thing. You can't give a matured woman lessons at a finishing school! (*Crosses L.*)

MRS. S: (*To HIM, gently.*) Don't be angry, dear. The girl has lately felt that she is insufficiently educated. I suppose her friendship with Miss Mary Swayne has made her discontented.

MR. S: Don't encourage her in such foolishness, Bertha. Mary Swayne is a blue-stocking. I really don't approve of the friendship at all. Besides, Caroline is well educated. She can play and sing nicely, writes a neat ladylike hand, speaks a little French, sews and embroiders, and no one expects any more from a woman.

MRS. S: I know that men won't marry clever women, and I for one don't blame them.

MR. S: Of course not. A woman comes into the world to bring forth children, and to be man's comforter and help-mate. Man rules and woman obeys; so it has ever been, so will it be always. (*Crosses R.*)

MRS. S: (*Kisses HIM humbly.*) Yes, my dear. One other little thing I want to ask you. Do you think we can really afford to send Robert to Rugby[15] this year?

MR. S: (*Indignantly and pompously.*) My son shall have the finest education England can give him. A boy must have every chance, in order to become later on a bulwark of the State, a worthy inheritor of this great England!

MRS. S: (*Meekly.*) Yes, dear William.

MR. S: Never let any decision of mine be questioned again, my love. To Rugby he goes, and later to the University.

MRS. S: Oh, Willie, don't be cross. You make me feel so faint! (*Gasps.*) (*Crosses to sofa.*)

MR. S: Don't be alarmed, my love! (*Places HER on seat and fans HER.*) Women are tender plants. They thrive only under the shelter of the sterner sex. (*ENTER CAROLINE*)
Caroline, see to your mother, she feels faint.

CAROLINE: Oh, not again, Papa? That is the second time to-day.

MR. S: (*Pompously.*) Silence, if you please! Fetch her vinaigrette and smelling salts.

MRS. S: (*Faintly.*) They are on the mantel-piece in my key-basket, Caroline.

MR. S: (*After business with smelling salts, etc.*) Good-bye, my love, I am due in the city. I shall be back in time to see Mr. Bullock. Meanwhile, be a ministering angel to your mother, Caroline!

EXIT MR. SEWELL, R.
CAROLINE goes to open the window.

MRS. S: Don't open the window! A draught, and I go to my death!

CAROLINE: Mary Swayne says that we close up our houses too much.

MRS. S: I don't want to know the opinions of that mannish young woman. What interests me more is the answer you intend to give Tom Bullock to-day.

CAROLINE: (*Timidly.*) Oh, mother, I don't want to marry him.

MRS. S: Why?

CAROLINE: For several reasons—

MRS. S: For instance?

CAROLINE: He is very plain.

MRS. S: Handsome is as handsome does! He is very rich—

CAROLINE: (*Timidly.*) Yes, but I don't want riches—I—

MRS. S: (*Interrupting—after having examined HER attentively.*) Caroline, your waist, my dear, is huge. Are you wearing those new stays from Madame Debrand?

CAROLINE: Yes, and they hurt dreadfully—

MRS. S: Nonsense! Pride must suffer pain! Pull them in. When I was your age, though I had been married some years, I had a waist that measured eighteen inches. (*Coyly.*) I remember your father's hands more than spanned its circumference. Pray don't let Mr. Bullock see you with such an awkward figure!

CAROLINE: (*Piteously.*) Mother, don't—don't make me marry Mr. Bullock!

MRS. S: I see what is going to happen to you, Caroline. You are going to be an old maid—

CAROLINE: (*Hysterically.*) Oh, mother, mother, don't say such an awful thing. Don't, I beg of you—

MRS. S: (*Relentlessly.*) An old maid! Why, you are four and twenty. Another year, and no man will look at you—

CAROLINE: (*Beginning to cry.*) I can't marry him—I don't love him.

MRS. S: (*To HER.*) Listen to me, Caroline. You don't realize what it means to be an old maid. To live your life alone. In a few years your Papa and I will be in our graves. Life for a woman alone is impossible—think what people will say? You will have to live with your aunt in Oldham.

CAROLINE: (*Sobbing.*) Mother, I don't love him!

MRS. S: (*Shocked.*) Caroline, I don't think it is quite modest to allude to such a very delicate and personal matter as love.

ENTER JANE, very excited.

JANE: Miss Mary Swayne, Mum, and please (*beaming*), she druv up in a hansom![16]

MRS. S: A hansom? Good gracious!

ENTER MARY SWAYNE, a woman about 35.

MARY: How are you, Mrs. Sewell?

CAROLINE: (*Running to HER and kissing HER.*) Oh, Mary, I am so glad to see you, but how dare you drive through London in a hansom alone?

MRS. S: (*Severely.*) It is considered very bad taste for a young woman to be in a hansom alone, Miss Swayne.

MARY: Is it? Well, I think it is very good taste. I had a delightful drive—

MRS. S: (*Icily.*) Indeed!

JANE: (*Clearing table.*) Please, Mum, I have picked all the fruit over, and it is ready for cooking. (*Crosses to door.*)

MRS. S: I am coming, Jane.

EXIT JANE, with tray.

MARY: Still making jam, Mrs. Sewell?

MRS. S: (*Icily.*) Yes, Miss Swayne, I am still attending to my house.

EXIT MRS. SEWELL.

MARY: Your mater seems particularly cross, Carrie, and your eyes are red. What is it, my child?

CAROLINE: Tell me first, dear Mary, whether your new book has been accepted?

MARY: Hush! If your mother ever knows that I earn my living by my pen under a male pseudonym, she won't allow me in the house again. Well, congratulate me—my book is accepted!

Crosses to sofa. CAROLINE sits on footstool.

CAROLINE: (*Enthusiastically embracing HER.*) Oh, I am so glad!

MARY: I made all arrangements by letter, as I don't want the publisher to know that "John Cheviot" is a woman.

CAROLINE: Awful mistake being a woman, isn't it, Mary?

MARY: (*Dreamily.*) We are handicapped at present, but the sun will rise some day. We may not be here to see the wonderful dawn of the new era, but I can already hear the bugle that is heralding the great awakening. Women will be of finer physique in the time to come—tall and straight and strong, active at sports. I can see them too, making magnificent headway in great professions, as doctors, writers, artists. They are taking high honours at the colleges and universities of their country. It is all distant, but we have a great champion in Parliament—one, John Stuart Mill, and his voice will sound even more powerfully in the days to come than it does now!

CAROLINE: (*Who has listened with intense interest.*) Do you really think that the day will ever come when we shall have even a little freedom, Mary?

MARY: We ourselves shall see great changes if we live the three score years and ten allotted to man. Your daughters will be free women, Caroline.

CAROLINE: (*Sadly.*) Oh, Mary, I don't want to marry. I haven't seen you lately to tell you that Mr. Tom Bullock has proposed for my hand, and to-day I have to give him an answer.

MARY: (*Visibly distressed.*) Tom Bullock! (Rises.) Oh, you musn't marry him.

CAROLINE: You see I am twenty-four and Mamma says that I shall be an old maid in another year—

MARY: Well, what of that?

CAROLINE: An old maid! Think of it! Everyone will say that I have had no offers—and I shall have to live alone—

MARY: So much better than living with someone you don't love.

CAROLINE: (*Kneels.*) Do you think it indelicate to speak about love, Mary?

MARY: Indelicate to speak about the most beautiful thing in the world?—why, of course not.

CAROLINE: (*Wonderingly.*) If you think Love the most beautiful thing in the world, why don't you marry?

MARY: My dear, people who love the most often don't marry. To pass our lives by the side of the man we love is not the splendid fortune of all women. No, many of us who have known love, have to fight through the hot day alone, and some of us are glad when evening brings us rest; but though we find not his most precious gift on God's earth, shall we therefore pine and fret and waste our measure of days and sunshine? Those women, who in the future are going to win the freedom of our sex, will teach woman that there is a full life of usefulness, and high endeavour and great happiness open to her, though she is mateless and alone.

CAROLINE: (*Musingly.*) I wish that I could know the love you speak of, Mary. I have never felt love for any man—

MARY: (*Tenderly.*) My child, you are so young, far younger than your years. You will meet someone whom you can love one day, and that is why I don't want you to fling yourself away on Tom Bullock.

CAROLINE: Oh, Mary, if you knew what my life is! Surely life with him cannot be worse than life here. (*Rises, crosses to fireplace.*) I am a woman, yet I have no freedom, hardly any money. I am never allowed out unaccompanied, I am obliged to go with mother everywhere. There seems to me to be only one road to everything like freedom, and that is marriage!

MARY: (*Goes to HER.*) But you musn't marry for freedom, or money, or any worldly considerations. You must marry for love. Wait patiently, you have all your best days before you. Don't listen to people who tell you that you are losing your youth or your attractions. Bear with your lack of freedom for a time. This everlasting sacrifice of the young to the old, the children to the parents, can't last—(*Suddenly*) Look here, my child, I am off to my old rooms in Paris—come and live with me for a time—

CAROLINE: (*With great delight.*) You really mean it?

MARY: Of course.

CAROLINE: I will come with all the gratitude and thankfulness that is in me. (*They embrace.*) But—(*all HER enthusiasm going*), they will never let me—(*proudly*), besides, how can I be a burden on you?

(*Up C. to window.*)

MARY: I should not allow you to be a burden. You must work. I can obtain you several engagements to give English lessons in Paris.

CAROLINE: My dear Mary, I can't give English lessons—why, I can't even spell. I am hopelessly ill-educated.

MARY: But you were at school?

CAROLINE: At Miss Smith's Seminary for Young Ladies—where I learned the Child's Guide to Knowledge, and how to write a neat ladylike hand—a smattering of French, and how not to play the piano—and when I was sixteen my parents very wisely took me away.

MARY: Your brother is being well educated, no doubt.

CAROLINE: Yes. Mother says that a boy must be well educated in order to be able to choose a profession and to earn his living—a girl must make marriage her profession—

MARY: Poor girl! My dear little friend, your mother, forgive me saying so, talks very lightly about marriage. Well, you must come with me on a visit, and then, if you care to stay longer, I will myself prepare you to be a governess.

CAROLINE: Oh, you are good! I will work hard. (*Apprehensively*) Will you speak to mother? I am half afraid she won't let me—she has set her heart on my marrying Mr. Bullock.

MARY: (*Sternly.*) You mustn't marry Tom Bullock. I will speak to Mrs. Sewell at once—

CAROLINE: Oh, my dear, dear friend, do rescue me from this marriage. I can't tell you how I dislike him—

MARY: Yes, do tell me—How does he affect you?

CAROLINE: When I see him something comes over me. I am no longer myself, I am someone else, and then he looks at me, and soon I can only see his eyes, and I know that nothing in the world can save me from being his wife, and I tremble and feel faint, and so afraid—I—(*To chair L. of table.*)

MARY: But, Caroline, my child, Tom is a very ordinary sort of person to make you feel all this—

CAROLINE: Well, you see, I know so little of men. I am never myself in their presence—

MARY: We women find it impossible to be our real selves at all. Not our fault. The fault of the false conditions under which we live. Our minds are enveloped in moral stays, just as our bodies are pinched and tortured to take on an unnatural and ugly shape—

CAROLINE: Hush! Here's mother!

ENTER MRS. SEWELL, in large pickling apron, her sleeves rolled up.

MRS. S: Caroline, Mr. Bullock will be here directly—please put your hair straight, and remember what I told you a little while ago—

CAROLINE: Yes, Mamma.

EXIT CAROLINE.

MARY: Mrs. Sewell, will you let Caroline come to Paris with me for a month or two? I have some nice rooms there?

MRS. S: My dear young lady, I hope Caroline will very soon be married.

MARY: She doesn't seem quite happy about this proposed marriage. I was wondering whether you would let her live with me in Paris for a time. I could obtain several engagements for her to give English lessons in private families.

MRS. S: (Haughtily.) Did I hear aright? You are proposing that my daughter should go out as a governess?

MARY: I am sure the change would benefit her, and to earn a little money for herself would give her the moral tonic of which she is in need—

MRS. S: I really don't think that you can be in your right mind, Miss Swayne, to propose that my daughter shall go out and earn money! I must absolutely refuse to allow her to accompany you to Paris at all—

MARY: (Sadly.) I am very grieved at your decision, Mrs. Sewell, but I do beseech you not to allow this engagement between Caroline and Tom Bullock to take place.

MRS. S: And what is your reason for such a request?

MARY: I have known Tom from his babyhood, and he is not the sort of man who should propose marriage to a pure young girl.

MRS. S: Please speak plainly.

MARY: Tom Bullock has run a course of low, common profligacy!

MRS. S: Can I believe my ears? Miss Swayne, these are subjects which I refuse to discuss with anyone. I am simply aghast with surprise and anger to think that you dare approach me on such a matter! What have we women to do with the past of the men who marry us?

MARY: Everything! I—

MRS. S: (Putting up HER hand for silence.) I am so horrified, so disgusted to think that a single woman has dared to speak to me on a subject, which wife and mother as I am, I have never in my life discussed, not even with my own husband.

MARY: I can only say that the sooner wives do discuss these matters with their husbands, the better it will be for the generations of unborn men and women who come after them.

MRS. S: (Faints.) (Gasping.) I have never been spoken to like this in my life before.

MARY: I have no patience with married women, who mistake ignorance for innocence, and when shown their duty, plead modesty.

MRS. S: (Staggering.) I feel so faint. (Staggers to bell and pulls it violently.)

ENTER CAROLINE.

MRS. S: (Weakly.) Caroline, my smelling bottle!

CAROLINE finds it and holds it to MRS. SEWELL'S nose.

MARY: Caroline, your mother will not listen to our little plan—I am so
   sorry—
CAROLINE: Oh, mother!
MRS. S: Quite impossible, Caroline. I could not entertain such an idea for a
   moment. Two single women living alone in Paris!

ENTER JANE, R.

JANE: Mr. Bullock is waiting to see you in the drawing room, Ma'am.

CAROLINE clutches MARY'S arm.

MRS. S: (*Recovering HER strength at once.*) I must go and take off this apron.
   Say I will be with him immediately, Jane.

JANE EXITS.

MRS. S: Good-bye, Miss Swayne. I shall expect an apology for your indescrib-
   able behavior—
CAROLINE: Mother! Mary—
MRS. S: Caroline, don't forget that Mr. Bullock has called to see you.

EXIT MRS. SEWELL.

MARY: I mustn't keep you, my dear little girl—I am deeply grieved at having
   failed in my attempt to help you, but your mother wouldn't listen to me.
   She is very angry—I think I had better go now.
CAROLINE: Oh, dear Mary—I knew we were dreaming....
MARY: Good-bye, my little friend, and should you ever want my help, write to
   me in Paris, and if Mary Swayne is still on earth, there is nothing she will
   not do for you. Good-bye.
CAROLINE: Good-bye, my dear, dear friend.

EXIT MARY.
CAROLINE goes to window, opens it, and waves handkerchief.
Pause—ENTER MR. SEWELL.

MR. S: I do hope your blue-stocking friend has gone for good, Caroline.

CAROLINE is wiping her eyes.

Come, come, my dear, if you allow this hysteria to conquer you, it will be a very bad look out for those who have got to live with you. It seems to me that you are always crying.

CAROLINE hastily puts her handkerchief in her pocket.

CAROLINE: I am so miserable, Papa!

MR. S: Well, I am the bearer of cheering news—I wish to tell you that Mr. Bullock has my consent to propose marriage to you. Can you see him now?

CAROLINE: Oh, Papa, must I marry him?

MR. S: I think he is a very suitable match. Your parents are not rich, and it would make us happy to see you settled in life. Besides, you are no longer very young, and the life of an old maid is a very sad and bitter one. Believe me, Carrie, it is more amusing to marry any sort of a man than to be an old maid.

CAROLINE: (*Meekly.*) Yes, Papa.

MR. S: Now, take my advice. Tom Bullock is a good fellow, and I am sure you will never regret marrying him.

ENTER JANE.

JANE: Mr. Bullock.

ENTER TOM BULLOCK, a young man about 28, faultlessly dressed. HE has a coarse mouth, and rather a red face.

MR. S: Ah! here is Tom!

TOM: (*Going towards CAROLINE with outstretched hands.*) Ah, Miss Caroline, how charming you are looking this lovely morning—

CAROLINE: (*Allows HIM to take HER hand, SHE is very shy and awkward.*) It is kind of you to come, Mr. Bullock.

MR. S: Well, I will leave you young folks for a few minutes.

EXIT MR. SEWELL.
(*Both sit.*)

TOM: I am afraid you are upset at Mary Swayne's departure. She is a nice creature.

CAROLINE: The best I know in all the world—because she thinks about other people and tries to help them.

TOM: Miss Caroline, I would delight in helping you, if you will let me—

CAROLINE: (*Timidly.*) It is difficult for a man to help a girl—

TOM: The easiest thing in the world. There is nothing I can't do for you. I have money and youth, and permit me to say it, an intense and overpowering admiration and love for you—(*takes HER hand*). Miss Caroline, I want you to be my wife—

CAROLINE: But—I—I—Mary Swayne wanted me to go to Paris with her—

TOM: I will take you to Paris for our honeymoon. Caroline, can't you answer me to-day? I have had a talk with your mother—she tells me that although you are so shy, she knows from things you have told her that you are very attached to me—

CAROLINE: Does mother say so?

TOM: Yes.

ENTER MRS. SEWELL.

MRS. S: (*In her most coaxing manner.*) Well, is it all settled? May I congratulate my son and daughter?

TOM: (*Uneasily.*) Caroline has not honoured me with an answer, Mrs. Sewell, yet—

MRS. S: Poor girl, she is so shy—a most affectionate disposition, my dear Tom, but young girls, you know, are always bashful. It is their great charm. (*Looks at Caroline, who is visibly wiping away her tears—quietly signs to TOM to leave the room.*) Come back in a few minutes.

EXIT TOM.

(*Going to sofa.*) Caroline, control yourself—what is the meaning of this?

CAROLINE sobs.

Do you know what you are doing? You are losing the best chance you will ever have. (*Looks round warily at door through which TOM made his exit.*) Come, come, my dear, be a good girl—(*Coaxingly*) Don't you want to please your Papa and Mamma, who love you so much—and who have made such sacrifices for you?

CAROLINE: (*Throwing her arms round HER passionately.*) Mother!

MRS. S: There, there, control yourself. What a fortunate girl you are! Tom has the engagement ring in his pocket—such a beauty—rubies and diamonds. When you are married you will ride in your carriage—just think of it!

CAROLINE: (*Raising HER head.*) Oh, mother, must I marry him?

MRS. S: (*Sternly.*) Caroline, you must.

CAROLINE bows her head.

ENTER TOM. MRS. SEWELL signs to HIM to come forward. SHE quietly places CAROLINE in his arms.

TOM: My dear Caroline!

CURTAIN.

A Pageant of Great Women

[London: Marian Lawson, 1948]

[First produced at the Scala Theatre, London, 10 November 1909.]

CAST:
JUSTICE
PREJUDICE
WOMAN

THE LEARNED WOMEN[17]
Hypatia
St. Teresa
Lady Jane Grey
Madame de Staël
Madame Roland
Madame de Scudéry
Jane Austen
George Sand
Caroline Herschell
Madame Curie
Graduate

THE ARTISTS
Sappho
Vittoria Colonna
Angelica Kauffmann
Vigée le Brun
Rosa Bonheur
Margaret van Eyck
Nance Oldfield

THE SAINTLY WOMEN
St. Hilda
Elizabeth Fry
Elizabeth of Hungary
Catherine of Siena

THE HEROIC WOMEN
Charlotte Corday
Flora Macdonald
Kate Barlass
Grace Darling

THE RULERS
Victoria
Elizabeth
Zenobia
Philippa
Deborah
Isabella
Catherine the Great
Tsze-Hse-An

THE WARRIORS
Joan of Arc
Boadicea
Agnes of Dunbar
Emilie Plater
Ranee of Jhansi
Maid of Saragossa
Christian Davies
Hannah Snell
Mary Ann Talbot
Florence Nightingale

JUSTICE (*enthroned.*)

(*To her enters* WOMAN, *pursued by* PREJUDICE. *She kneels at the foot of* JUSTICE.)

JUSTICE: Why dost thou cling to me? What dost thou ask?
WOMAN: I cling to Justice and I cry for freedom!
JUSTICE: Is it not thine already?
WOMAN: No and no!
JUSTICE: Art thou not worthy freedom?
WOMAN: Yea and yea!
PREJUDICE: Goddess, she speaks but stammering foolishness,
            Not knowing what she asks.
WOMAN: I know and long—

PREJUDICE: She weeps for that she is not fit to have;
She is a very child in the ways of the world,
A thing protected, covered from its roughness—
WOMAN: Have I not felt its roughness, suffered and wept?
JUSTICE: Let him speak on—let him accuse—then answer.
PREJUDICE: Freedom is born of wisdom—springs from
wisdom—
And when was woman wise? Has she not ever
Looked childlike up to man? Has she not ever
Put the outward show before the inward grace?
Scorned learning, lest it dim the light of her eye?
Shunned knowledge, lest long study pale her
cheek?
Is not her day a day of petty cares,
Of petty hates and likings? When has she
Stood godlike in her wisdom, great of soul?
What is her prize in life—a kiss, a smile,
The right to claim caresses! Yet she cries
For freedom! An she had it, she would sell it
For a man's arm round her waist!
WOMAN: Oh, well, indeed, well does this come from you,
Who held the body as all, the spirit as naught—
From you who saw us only as a sex!
Who did your worst and best to quench in us
The very spark and glow of the intellect:
Who blew a jeer at the leap and glimmer of it
And smothered it with laughter!... This from you
Who praised a simper far above a thought—
Who prized a dimple far beyond a brain!
So were we trained to simper, not to think:
So were we bred for dimples, not for brains!
Not souls, but foolish flesh—so you desired us
And, God have pity, made us!... Shall you cry
Contempt on your own doing? Then you cry
Contempt upon yourself! Had never woman
Been more than roseleaf cheek and pouted lip,
You should be dumb before her meanness—you
Who ask no more of her... Oh, think you well
What you have done to make it hard for her
To dream, to write, to paint, to build, to learn—
Oh, think you well! And wonder at the line
Of those who knew that life was more than love
And fought their way to achievement and to fame!

(The Learned Women *enter.*)

Hypatia	Hypatia, she whose wisdom brought her death,
	Heads the brave line; and see the saintly nun,
St. Teresa	Teresa, guide and leader unto God,
	Writer of living words! Thou ten days queen,
Lady Jane Grey	Poor little maid, the pawn of guiltier minds,
	Thy learning had put many a man to shame!
Madame de Staël	What of the keen De Staël, quick of tongue,
	Polished of pen? Of Manon Roland, what—
Madame Roland	Leader of men, unconquered even in death?
	Boast of romancers—'twas a woman's hand
Mlle. de Scudéry	That penned a novel first—de Scudéry's!
	And on her follow her disciples twain,
Jane Austen	English Jane Austen and George Sand of France.
George Sand	See one who helped to map the stars of heaven—
Caroline Herschell	Caroline Herschell! And where is the man
	Stands higher in the ranks of science to-day
Madame Curie	Than Madame Curie! Last of all the train
	Comes the girl graduate of a modern day,
Graduate	Working with man as eagerly and hard—
	And oft enough denied a man's reward.
	And though you barred from us the realms of art—
	Decreeing Love should be our all in all—
	Denying us free thought, free act, free word—
	Yet some there have been burst the silken bonds
	(Harder to burst than steel) and lived and
	wrought.

(The Artists *enter.*)

Sappho	Thy voice, oh Sappho, down the ages rings!
	Woven of passion and power, thy mighty verse
	Streams o'er the years, a flaming banner of song!
Vittoria Colonna	Inspiring others and herself inspired,
	Vittoria Colonna sweeps us by—
Angelica Kauffmann	Poet and noble dame ... Ah, Madame Kauffmann,
	In your day were our painters more gallant,
	Admitting women to due share of honour!
Vigée Le Brun	Vigée le Brun, your sitters live for us
	From far-off years ... A man? No—Rosa Bonheur!
Rosa Bonheur	Back from the horse fair, virile in her garb
	As virile in her work! Who follows? Sure

	A painter too, and one of no mean fame—
Margaret Van Eyck	'Tis that Van Eyck, that Margaret, who shared
	A brother's glory!.. Lo, Camargo comes—
Camargo	A dancer, a dancer, a poem—a song herself!
	Lyric of movement, ballad of gliding grace;
	Rhythm of lifted hand and poised foot—
	Music made manifest!.. Come we last of all
	To the living art of the actor—
Nance Oldfield:	By your leave,
	Nance Oldfield does her talking for herself!
	If you, Sir Prejudice, had had your way,
	There would be never an actress on the boards.
	Some lanky, squeaky boy would play my parts:
	And, though I say it, there'd have been a loss!
	The stage would be as dull as now 'tis merry—
	No Oldfield, Woffington, or—Ellen Terry!
WOMAN:	Have I not answered him?
JUSTICE:	Thou hast answered well!
	How sayst thou—art thou still of the same mind?
PREJUDICE:	She is unworthy. In her narrow life,
	Cramped round and centred in her man, her child,
	Is room for no wide love of the outer world—
	Is room for no stern duty to her kind.
	She only serves the lips that touch her own;
	She only serves those who go in and out
	At the door of her daily life—being small of heart.
WOMAN:	It is not so!
PREJUDICE:	I cry for proof!
WOMAN:	Shalt have it!

(The Saintly Women *enter.*)

	Oh, saintly women, were ye small of heart?
St. Hilda	Thou Mother in God, St. Hilda, answer him!
	Abbess and ruler in thy northern home,
	Was no wider love of the outer world in thee?
Elizabeth Fry	O, thou, dear Friend that wast a friend indeed
	To all that sorrowed, being in chains and sin,
	Thou sweet Elizabeth, thou saint of the gaol,
	Not narrow was the door of thy daily life!
Elizabeth of Hungary	Thou rose-lapped princess, daughter of Hungary,
	Thy days were perfumed with a glory of love

	And stainless in their pure humility!
St. Catherine of Siena	And thou, high Catherine, Siena's child,
	Maker of peace 'twixt princes, humbly bred,
	Do we not count thee 'mongst the mighty dead?
	So pass my saints—not cramped nor mean of soul!
	Nor do they pass alone!

(The Heroines *enter*.)

	See where they come,
	Those who have loved a cause, been loyal to it,
	Striven and suffered nobly rather than fail
	In a hard duty ...
	Look on her who wears
Charlotte Corday	The blood-red garb of the condemned—on her
	Who took the knife in her small woman's hand
	Who laid the stain of murder on her soul
	And met death smiling—steadfast, unashamed!
Flora Macdonald	And what of her, the Highland lass, the maid
	Whose love unfaltering led a hunted prince,
	Whose faith, unbroken, saved a broken man?
Kate Barlass	Or her, that dauntless Kate, her countrywoman,
	Who barred the assassin's pathway with her arm?
Grace Darling	And was her deed unworthy of a man—
	The frail lone girl who fought through wind and wave,
	Risking her own, her brethren's life to save?
JUSTICE:	Art answered yet?
PREJUDICE:	Nay, hear me, goddess, hear me!
	Give her her freedom, she will strive to rule.
	Her brain will reel beneath the sense of power—
	She will grow dizzy, grasp at what she knows not!
	'Tis man's to reign, 'tis woman's to obey.
	The steady outlook, the wide thought are man's
	So Nature has ordained—she cannot rule.

(The Queens *enter*.)

	WOMAN:
Queen Elizabeth	Here's Royal Bess to give the lie to him—
	He had not dared to speak it to her face!
	And see, the little maid of eighteen years
Queen Victoria	Who, on a summer morning, woke to find

Herself a queen, to reign where Bess had reigned.
You shall not put her, nor shall you put Bess,
Below the wisest of our line of kings!

Zenobia Behind, Zenobia of the hero's heart;
Phillipa of Hainault And that Philippa, wise and merciful,
Who ruled a kingdom for her absent lord
And knelt in pity for a humbled foe.

Deborah And thou, O Deborah, judge in Israel,
Rise up and bear me out! And thou, O Queen,
Isabella of Spain Grave Isabella, prince of proud Castile,
Thou who gav'st ear unto a sailor's dream
To his eternal honour and thine own!

Maria Theresa And when Theresa reigned in Hungary;
Catherine II of Russia And when great Catherine wore the Russian Crown;
Who stood more high than they, who ruled more
kingly?

Empress of China And was there any in the Flowery Land
That dared its cunning Empress to outface—
Tsze-Hsi-An Born slave, then monarch of a countless race!

PREJUDICE: All these have ruled because men let them rule,
And not against his will. Come we to that,
Force is the last and ultimate judge: 'tis man
Who laps his body in mail, who takes the sword—
The sword that must decide! Woman shrinks from it,
Fears the white glint of it and cowers away.

WOMAN: O bid him turn and bid him eat his words
At sight of those who come to bear out mine—
Captains and warrior women!.. Look on her

(The Warriors *enter.*)

Joan of Arc Brave saint, pure soldier, lily of God and France,
Whose soul fled hence on wings of pain, of fire!
Boadicea Oh, look on her who stood, a Briton in arms,
And spat defiance at the hosts of Rome!
Black Agnes See there, the black-browed Agnes of Dunbar
Who held her fortress as a soldier should
And capped the cannon's roaring with a jest—
Maid of Fit comrade for the girl who, when the guns
Saragossa Thundered at Saragossa, took her stand
Upon the walls and fired her countrymen
With her own burning courage—or for her,
Emilia Emilia Plater, Poland's heroine,

Plater	Leader and patriot, dauntless in despair!
	Thou dark-eyed princess of an eastern land,
Ranee of Jhansi	Ruler of Jhansi, captain proved in war
	Though but a child in years, thou tak'st thy rank
	Among thy fellows ... These, and many more,
	Have nobly fought where need there was to fight—
	Have nobly died where need there was to die—
	All these, and many more, some named, some
	nameless,
	Have risked their lives as blithely as a man.
	And, come to that, we've rough-and-tumbled it!
Christian Davies	Where's Christian Davies, Chelsea pensioner,
	Who shouldered musket for a dozen fights?
Hannah Snell	Where's Hannah Snell, stout private of the line?
Mary Ann Talbot	And little Talbot, drummer of King George?
	And see, she comes, our Lady of the Lamp!
Florence Nightingale	No soldier she, yet not unused to war
	Nor fearful of its horrors—death and wounds
	And pestilence—well hast thou fought them, well,
	O Lady on whose shadow kisses fell!
JUSTICE:	There falls a silence.
WOMAN:	Goddess, he is dumb!
JUSTICE:	Dost thou not speak?
WOMAN:	Goddess, he slinks away!

(PREJUDICE *goes out.*)

JUSTICE:	Is it e'en so?
WOMAN:	Yes, I have silenced him:
	O give me judgment, give it!
JUSTICE:	I give thee judgment—and I judge thee worthy
	To attain thy freedom: but 'tis thou alone
	Canst show that thou art worthy to retain it.
	O Woman with thy feet on an untried path,
	O Woman with thine eyes on the dawn of the world,
	Thou hast very much to learn.
WOMAN:	But I shall learn it!
JUSTICE:	Yes, truly; but with suffering.

(The WOMAN *kneels before her silent.*)

Go forth
To achieve with tears; and bear within thy heart

This word of mine—That soul alone is free
Who sees around it never a soul enslaved.
Go forth: the world is thine ... Oh, use it well!
Thou hast an equal, not a master, now.

WOMAN (*rising*): I have an equal, not a master now.
I will go speak with him as peer with peer,
Free woman with free man.

JUSTICE: Then let thy words
Be just and wise.

WOMAN: They shall be wise and just;
Free words, and therefore honest ... Thus I'll speak
him!
I have no quarrel with you; but I stand
For the clear right to hold my life my own:
The clear, clean right! To mould it as I will,
Not as you will, with or apart from you.
To make of it a thing of brain and blood,
Of tangible substance and of turbulent
thought—
No thin, grey shadow of the life of man!
Your love, perchance, may set a crown on it;
But I may crown myself in other ways—
(As you have done who are one flesh with me).
I have no quarrel with you; but henceforth,
This you must know: The world is mine, as yours,
The pulsing strength and passion and heart of it:
The work I set my hand to, woman's work,
Because I set my hand to it. Henceforth
For my own deeds myself am answerable
To my own soul.
                    For this in days to come
You, too, shall thank me. Now you laugh, but I
Laugh too, a laughter without bitterness;
Feeling the riot and rush of crowding hopes,
Dreams, longings and vehement powers; and
knowing this—
'Tis good to be alive when morning dawns!

LEARNED WOMEN

Hypatia: Born at Alexandria about 370 A.D. Neoplatonist philosopher. Lectured in her native city, thereby incurring the enmity of the Christians, who feared her great influence. Murdered by a mob of her enemies 415 A.D.

*St. Teresa:*1515-1582. Spanish saint, writer and reformer. The only woman upon whom the title of Doctor of the Church has ever been conferred.

Lady Jane Grey: 1537-1554. A pupil of Roger Ascham. "Versed in the Greek, Latin, Italian and French languages and had some acquaintance with Hebrew and Arabic." Nominal queen of England for 10 days; deposed and executed at the age of 17.

Ann Louisa de Stael-Holstein: 1766-1817. Author and politician. Principal works: "Corrine," "De l'Allemague," "Considerations sur la Revolution Française."

Manon Roland: 1756-93. One of the leading intellects of the French Revolution. Shared the fall of the Girondists and died on the scaffold.

Madelène de Scudéry: 1607-1701. Author of "The Grand Cyrus" and other romances. The first person to receive the "Prix d'Eloquence" from the Académie Française.

Jane Austen: 1775-1817. Author of "Sense and Sensibility," "Pride and Prejudice," "Emma," "Mansfield Park," "Northanger Abbey," "Persuasion."

George Sand (Amantine Aurore Dudevant):1804-76. Author of "Consuelo," "La Comtesse de Rudelstadt," "Mauprat," "Horace," and numerous other novels; also plays.

Caroline Herschell: 1750-1848. Astronomer. Discovered five new comets.

Marie Curie (born Sklodowska): One of the foremost of living scientists. The discoverer of radium and polonium. Born 1867.

ARTISTS

Sappho: Born in Lesbos about 630 B.C.; died about 570 B.C. Poet; styled by Plato "the tenth muse."

Vittoria Colonna: 1490-1547. Poet and friend of Michael Angelo.

Maria Angelica Kauffmann: 1742-1807. Painter and engraver. One of the original members of the Royal Academy.

Marie Louise Elizabeth Vigée Lebrun: 1755-1842. Portrait painter and litterateur.

Rosa Bonheur: 1822-99. The famous painter of animals.

Margaret Van Eyck: Flemish painter. Flourished about 1430.

Marie Anne Cuppi Camargo: 1710-70. A famous opera dancer.

Nance Oldfield: 1683-1730. One of the earliest and most celebrated of English actresses. Played at Drury Lane and the Haymarket Theatres.

SAINTS

St. Hilda: 614-80. Founder of Whitby Abbey and Abbess of Hartlepool and Whitby.

Elizabeth Fry: 1780-1845. Philanthropist. Founder of the Association for the Improvement of the Female Prisoners in Newgate. Effected great reforms in prison conditions. A member of the Society of Friends.

St. Elizabeth of Hungary: 1207-31. Daughter of the King of Hungary, wife of the Landgrave of Thuringia. Renowned for her piety and wonderful charity.

St. Catherine of Siena: 1347-80. Saint and politician. Sent by the Tuscan people on an embassy to the Pope to procure removal of ban of ex-communication. Helped to bring about the return of the Pope from Avignon to Rome.

HEROINES

Charlotte Corday (Marie Anne Charlotte de Corday d'Armand): 1768-93. The self-appointed executioner of Marat. Died on the scaffold.

Flora Macdonald: 1720-90. The guide and saviour of Prince Charles Edward after his defeat at Culloden.

Kate Barlass: The name given to Catherine Douglas, who thrust her arm into the staples of a bolt in a vain endeavour to save James I of Scotland from his murderers (1437).

Grace Darling: 1815-42. Was instrumental in saving the crew of the "Forfarshire," wrecked on the Farne Islands in 1838.

QUEENS

Elizabeth: 1533-1603. Queen of England, 1558.

Victoria: 1819-1901. Queen of Great Britain, 1837.

Zenobia: Queen of Palmyra from 267 A.D. to 273 A.D. A courageous and accomplished woman; defeated by the Emperor Aurelian, she was carried captive to Rome.

Philippa of Hainault: 1314-69. Wife of Edward III. of England. Froissart gives her credit for organising the army which defeated the Scots at Nevile's Cross during her husband's absence from England. Remembered for her intercession in favour of the burghers of Calais.

Deborah: "The children of Israel came up to her for judgment."

Isabella of Spain: 1450-1504. Queen of Castile in her own right, joint ruler of Spain with her husband; one of the wisest of Spanish sovereigns. The patron of Columbus.

Maria Theresa: 1717-80. Queen of Hungary in her own right; Empress of Austria by marriage. One of the foremost rulers of the eighteenth century.

Catherine II, called the Great: 1729-96. Empress of Russia in her own right— the right of the strongest—1762.

Tsze-hsi-an: Empress of China, born 1834. Her extraordinary force of character obtained for her the position of actual ruler of China. She died in 1908.

WARRIORS

Joan of Arc: 1410-31. The deliverer of France from the English. Burnt at Rouen.

Boadicea: Queen of the Iceni. Led the British forces against the Romans under Suetonius Paulinus and took poison rather than survive defeat (A.D. 61).

Black Agnes: 1312-69. Countess of March. Defended the castle of Dunbar against the English, 1338.

Maid of Saragossa: The name bestowed upon Agostina, a young girl who distinguished herself at Saragossa when the town was besieged by the French, 1808-09.

Emilia Plater: 1806-31. A Polish heroine who took a prominent part in the struggle of her country to throw off the yoke of Russia.

Ranee of Jhansi: 1838-58. Killed fighting against the British in the Indian mutiny. Said to have been "the best man on the other side."

Christian Davies: 1667-1739. Enlisted as Christopher Welsh. Fought at Blenheim, wounded at Ramillies, pensioned 1712.

Hannah Snell: 1723-92. Served both in the army and navy; wounded at Pondicherry; out-pensioner of Chelsea Hospital, 1750.

Mary Ann Talbot: 1778-1804. Served in Flanders as a drummer boy, 1793; wounded and pensioned.

Florence Nightingale: Born 1820. The organiser of hospital nursing in the Crimea; the first woman to be decorated with the Order of Merit.

AN ENGLISHWOMAN'S HOME: A PLAY IN ONE ACT

[London: Actresses' Franchise League, (1911)]

CHARACTERS:
Bates
Maria
John
Young Woman

Scene.—*Interior of a half-cottage in a suburb of London. A sort of kitchen living-room— dingy and poor-looking. Walls decorated with grocer's cheap calendar pictures. One or two clotheslines with washing, screen L. corner, from dresser to L. Corner. Wash-tub (resting on chair) from stool, down L. Scrubbing-board in tub, also clothes and steaming water, showing that washing is now going on. Fire-place with fender—general air of being used. Mantel-shelf, with irons and such knick-knacks on. Cheap clock—time about 8 p.m. Dirty-looking calendar picture of "Home, Sweet Home," or something similar, above mantel-shelf. Gas bracket coming from mantel-shelf—gas lit. "Penny-in-slot" meter to be near. Door R. above fireplace. Window R.C. with old and torn blind down. Water-tap and sink, about C. Door L.C. Kitchen dresser L., with variety of useful props on. Door L. Table R. C. Chair L. of table.*
At Rise of Curtain, enter MARIA *door R., with tray, bearing debris of lodger's supper; a pair of dirty and formidable-looking boots dangling from right hand, which is also supporting tray.*

BATES: (*Off stage.*) Mrs. Jenkins!
MARIA: (*Pausing in doorway.*) Yessir.
BATES: (*Off.*) Could ye let's 'ave a jug of 'ot water to wash me 'ed.
MARIA: (*In doorway.*) Yes sir, I dessay—'alf a minnit. (*She brings tray down to table—puts boots on fender.*) Boil 'is 'ed! I wish 'e'd a-let it go for a day. More trouble than it's worth, I should think. 'E's a faddy in some ways.
VOICE: (*Off door L.—a toy would do for this.*) Ma! Ma! Ma! Ma! (*not too long*).
MARIA: Stop crying this minnit, or you'll wake your brother Ted. Now you be a good girl, an' don't utter another sound, an' I'll give you a nice snack—jest 'alf a minnit. (*She proceeds to cut piece of lodger's bread and butter,*

then to forage in plate; holding up in her left hand skeleton of kipper, while she picks up tiny atoms from plate, and carefully puts them on the piece of bread and butter.) 'E do love 'is relish. It 'ud want a bloomin' telescope to find any tit-bits as 'ad escaped 'is beagle heye. (*Going to door L.*) Ah, well, poor devil! I expec' 'e don't get too much 'isself—jest like the rest of us. (*She goes off door L. and continues speaking off stage.*) There now, when you've 'ad that, you must keep quiet and get to sleep, and let me get on with my work. (*She re-enters and goes to table.*) I don't know when I shall get done at this rate. (*Puts her hand to her back.*) In some ways I feel done already. (*Opens lid of tea-pot, and with one eye shut, looks critically inside.*) It's a blessin' 'e don't care for tea-leaves. I shall be able to 'ave a cup bye-and-bye. (*Pours water in from kettle, and puts tea-pot on hob.*)

BATES: (*off stage.*) I say, Mother Jenkins, wot price the 'ot water?
MARIA: Comin', sir, comin'—I clean forgot it! 'Alf a minnit.
BATES: (*Off stage.*) And if you've a bit of soda—
MARIA: Aint got a bit left. (*She takes jug of hot water, which she has poured out of kettle, and goes off door R.*)

(*Off stage.*) Sorry I forgot.

BATES: Awright, missus, better late than never.

(MARIA *re-enters.*)

BATES: (*Off stage.*) Don't forget—breakfus at six and a 'alf sharp.
MARIA: (*At doorway.*) Awright, you shall 'ave it. I won't be late again. Them there workmen's trains *is* early.
BATES: (*Off stage.*) Yus. They're the early bird wot catches the worms.
MARIA: Ha, ha, ha! that's good! (*Closes door and comes down stage.*) Ha, ha, ha! *Worms* is good. Funny man 'e is—will 'ave 'is joke. What amuses *me* is, that though 'e 'as to catch the early train, 'e never thinks of gettin' up unless I knock's 'im. 'E don't seems to regard it as 'umanly possible that I should oversleep *my*self, although I'm workin' as a rule, long after 'e's in bed. (*During the above, she has resumed work at the wash-tub.*)
Bibulous voice heard off, singing "Rule Britannia."
'Ere come my *purtecter*!

Enter JOHN JENKINS, *slightly "sprung." He stands at door R.C. to finish last line.* MARIA *continues working furiously without looking up.*

JOHN: "Britons never, never, never shall be slaves!" (*After pause, cheerily.*) Well, Maria, 'ere I ham, you see.

MARIA: (*Without looking up.*) Oh, yes, I *see!* *I'm* not blind, if *you* are!

JOHN: Blind? 'Oo's blind? You get very (*hic*) 'culiar fancies. Can't a man shing "Britons never shall be slaves" wi'out bein' blind? (*After a pause.*) I shay, it's dishgrasheful—I shay—

MARIA: Don't say any more. Go an' sit down, and be quiet.

JOHN: Jus' as you like, but I shay—I shay—I shay— "Britons never, never,— shall be shlaves!"

MARIA: Well, that must be right, if you say so, I suppose.

JOHN: It's right, whether I say so or not. Right is right, an' can't be no different.

MARIA: (*After a pause.*) Is females Britons?

JOHN: Females? Of course! Wot do you think? Wot's the good of askin' such a silly question?

MARIA: Well, 'ow was I to know what the arrangement was? And if it comes to that, what *is* slavery, I should like to know?

JOHN: (*Pompously.*) Well, I'll tell yer. If you was a slave, you'd 'ave to work for some man without any wages. Just for your food and lodgins, like.

MARIA: Oh, Rule Britannia! Fancy that! *'E* would *provide* my food and lodging!

JOHN: But when 'e didn't want yer, 'e could sell yer off to some other man!

MARIA: Instead of jus' going off nobody knows where, an' leavin' yer all 'appy an' comfortable to get yer livin' as best yer may!

JOHN: I dunno what you're talking about. It's always the way with you women—you can't think imperially!

MARIA: Not when the rent is owin', an' the children cry for food, an' she works from mornin' to night an' is only able to keep body an' soul together, an' 'as a *man* to keep as well, 'oo does nothing to 'elp.

JOHN: (*After a pause.*) It's awright, Maria. I'm not angry with yer. (*Goes over to table.*)

MARIA: I s'pose if you 'ad a-been you'd 'ave expected me to 'ave drownded myself in the wash-tub from feelins of remorse.

JOHN: (*Looking over the tray at table.*) 'Ave yer got annythink to eat 'andy?

MARIA: No. There's not a morsel of aught in the 'ouse.

JOHN: (*Uneasily.*) Well, I suppose there would be no 'arm in takin' a *snick* off the lodger's bread and butter?

MARIA: Yes, there would. I've 'ad a *snick* off it already.

JOHN: Well, what am *I* to do?

MARIA: Get some work, and keep out of the pubs.

JOHN: Don't go to no pubs. I was at the club.

MARIA: You was to come and take Mrs. Rawlins' washing 'ome, but I 'ad to waste my time takin' it myself, in the middle of my work.

JOHN: Well, you know, old girl, this is election time.

MARIA: 'Lection time or any other time, it's all the same—anythin' except work.

JOHN: I'm *willin'* to work—I may say *anxious* to work, but work don't come. You can't make work, you know.

MARIA: You pretty well can, if you're willing an' anxious. You *might* 'ave kept that odd job Mrs. Rawlins got for yer, until somethin' better turned up.

JOHN: What! Me do *women's* work? Clean grates, scrub steps, and such? Me? A master carpenter?

MARIA: But if there aint no carpenter's work to be got?

JOHN: But—but there *may* be—some day. I'm not down-'earted, Maria.

MARIA: Not you—cos you've got a roof to shelter you, and nothing to pay for it.

JOHN: There you go—naggin' again! Why can't you be cheery, like me?

MARIA: (*Breaking down.*) 'Cos I feel sometimes nearly done. As if body and soul was goin' their separate ways and I couldn't hold 'em together no longer. What's to become of the children if I breaks down, and 'as to go to the 'orspital? I tell yer it just scares me when I feel bad. The thought of lyin' 'elpless in one o' them 'orribly tidy 'orspital rooms— thinkin' of the 'ome breaking up, an' the children in the streets—

JOHN: There now, don't cry—cos it makes me feel uncomfortable!

MARIA: (*Through her sobs.*) You're terribly unselfish, aren't yer?

JOHN: Yes, Maria, I may 'ave faults, but I *ham* unselfish. After all, things aint so bad. Yer've got this 'ere lodger by the name of Bates. 'E don't pay much, but perhaps 'e's a sticker. Then you've got three days a week charing, and some washing to do at 'ome besides; and you've 'ad several other odd jobs promised yer. *I* don't see no cause for yer to be down-'earted.

MARIA: But where do *you* come in?

JOHN: (*Airily.*) Oh; I shall 'ope on—'ope hever! Don't you fret about me. "Never say die" is my motter!

MARIA: It'll be the last thing yo'll *do*, that's certain.

JOHN: It's a pity you aint got a motter, Maria. A motter's a wonderful 'elp in time o' trouble.

MARIA: If you think o' one that'll be some 'elp when the landlord calls agen for 'is rent, you might let me know it. I'm goin' down to the grocer's before he shuts. He'll let me pay 'im on Saturday, and I 'ave to get a hegg for Mr. Bates's breakfast.

JOHN: Awright, old gal, don't be too long, cos I promised Joe Williams I'd meet 'im at the club later.

MARIA: (*Indignantly.*) What!

JOHN: An' I'll tell yer what I'll do while yer gone. I'll brush the lodger's boots for yer!

MARIA: Well, that'll be better than nothing. Every little 'elps. And perhaps the breath of fresh air'll do me good.

JOHN: That's right, ole girl—look on the bright side.

MARIA: But if there aint none?

JOHN: Oh, there is—there is!

MARIA: Yes, at the club, perhaps.

Exit MARIA *door R.C.*

JOHN: (*Shakes his head and sighs.*) What a pity it is that women ain't got no sense o' humour. O' course, poor things, they *reckons* ter 'ave, but even then—as far as my experience goes—it's a nasty *sour* sort o' 'umour that don't do nobody no good an' leaves a man tired—an' thirsty. Ah! Well! (*Taking out a pipe and small screw of tobacco, and moving towards fireplace.*) They can't 'elp it. It aint in their constitutions. (*Stands filling his pipe and gazing moodily down at the boots on the fender.*) Talkin' o' humour, why the 'ell don't Bates brush 'is own boots? Things 'as come to a fine pitch when a master carpenter 'as to brush another man's boots—specially dirty clod-hoppers like them. (*Takes chair and sits, then lights his pipe and smokes, looking moodily at boots.*) I wonder 'ow 'e gets 'em in such a 'orrible mess—seems as if 'e must 'ave done it a purpose! he's jest the sort that would. Never once *yet* said "Jenkins, 'ave you a mouth?" Not that I want 'is *drink*—it's the compliment. It would 'ave showed a friendly feeling as *man* to *man*. (*Rising wrathfully.*) An' now if you please I'm to brush 'is boots. Damn 'is boots, I say. (*Picks up poker and putting it inside the boots, slides them one after another, to C. of stage.*) And damn '*im* too!

BATES: (*Off stage.*) Mrs. Jenkins! Mrs. Jenkins!

JOHN: (*Opening door R.*) The missus is aht, but she'll be in in a jiffy.

BATES: (*Off stage.*) Let's have 'alf a jug more 'ot water, guv'nor; I can't get the soap out of me 'ed. It's in my eyes, too. 'Urry up, for Gawd's sake.

JOHN: Aw-right, I'm your man. 'Alf a mo'. (*Rushes about for jug. Picks up one thing, then another. At last takes a basin, and rushes over to kettle.*)

VOICE: (*Off door L.*) Ma! Ma! Ma! Ma!

JOHN: (*Starts to pour water from kettle to basin and turns head round to door L. growling.*) Quiet there, will yer? Go to sleep. (*With a yell, he drops basin, having burnt his hand.*)

(*A knocking at door R.C.*)

BATES: 'Urry up, gov'nor, 'urry up!

VOICE: Ma—ma—ma—ma!!

(JOHN *rushing up and down stage, shaking his hand, blowing on it, and howling.*)

(*Knocking repeated. Door is opened and a* YOUNG WOMAN *enters.*)

YOUNG WOMAN: Is anybody at home?

JOHN: Oh, Crikey! I should think we was at 'ome! Wish I wern't.

VOICE: (*Off stage.*) Ma! Ma! Ma! Ma!

JOHN: I'll come and give you "Ma, ma, ma, ma" if you're not quiet.

BATES: (*Off stage.*) You are a corker, gov'nor! Look slippy with the 'ot water!

JOHN: You can't 'ave it. I've burnt me 'and, an' smashed the basin, and all through your foolin' about with that fat 'ead of yourn.

BATES: (*Off stage.*) You are a cove, and no mistake!

Y. WOM.: What has happened? Can I be of any help?

JOHN: Oh, it's nothink. Me 'and's nearly burnt off, that's all.

Y. WOM.: Do let me see it—I could go and get something to put on it.

(JOHN *holds hand out.*)

Oh, I don't really think that's serious.

(JOHN *very indignant.*)

Although of course, I can see it must be very painful!

BATES: (*Off stage. Puts head—covered with towel—out of door.*) This soap must be rotten! What am I to do with my 'ead?

JOHN: Bury it, my son, bury it! Out of sight, out of mind.

BATES: (*Off stage.*) I say, it's a bit thick, you know! (*Withdraws his head.*)

JOHN: Yes, I should say so, too!

Y. WOM.: Poor man, what has he done?

JOHN: Oh, it's awright. 'E's only the lodger.

Y. WOM.: Has he a vote?

JOHN: 'E's only bin with us three weeks. I'm the only one as 'as a vote 'ere. I s'pose you're what they calls canvassin'. Now what side may you be for? I likes to 'ear what women think o' these things. What's your politics?

Y. WOM.: (*Loudly.*) "Votes for Women."

JOHN: (*Gasping.*) What! How dare you? You most presumptoo-us—(*hesitates, then repeats emphatically*) presumptoo-us! To-to-enter this 'ere 'ouse! 'Ow dare you, I says!

Y. WOM.: Why, you said you liked to have a woman's view.

JOHN: So *I do*—when I agrees wi' 'em.

Y. WOM.: And you don't agree with women having votes?

JOHN: Not 'alf!

Y. WOM.: Why not?

JOHN: Never you mind. I got my reasons.

Y. WOM.: What does your wife think?

JOHN: Nothin'! She aint got no time to *amuse* 'erself wi' thinkin'.

Y. WOM.: But is her work never done?

JOHN: No, never. Well, yer see, that's just it with *women's* work. It's what you might call casual labour, and goes on all the time.

Y. WOM.: I see. Man's work is of man's life a thing apart.

JOHN: That's it! That's the difference. Men 'ave *time* to think imperially—women 'avent.

Y. WOM.: You don't believe then, that what's sauce for the goose is sauce for the gander?

JOHN: I dunno nothin' about goose's sauce, cos we don't 'ave none. What I do know is that I am the responsible party for the rent, rates, and taxes of this 'ere 'ouse and—

MARIA: (*Who had entered door R.C.*) You don't find the money, John.

JOHN: Maria! 'Ow dare you!

MARIA: It's gospel, aint it?

JOHN: It don't matter 'oo finds the money. I 'ave the vote.

Y. WOM.: Well, I say that isn't fair.

JOHN: Why not? I'm willin' an' *anxious* to find the money, but I'm unfortnit. I 'ave been temporarily unemployed for the last four or five years.

MARIA: (*Who has picked up* BATES'S *boots, and holds them in her hand.*) Now, 'oo may you be, Miss, when you're at 'ome?

Y. WOM.: My name is—

JOHN: This is one of them sufferajetty wimmen—come, if you please, to ask me to 'elp 'em to the vote. Nice, aint it? I should like to see me takin' my polertics from wimmen. H'anything but that!

MARIA: You're right, John, I don't know nothink else that you wouldn't take. What about these 'ere boots? You 'ave brushed 'em nicely! No mistake, when you say you'll do a thing you do it well.

JOHN: It's all the fault of this 'ere "Votes for Women" party. If she 'adn't a-come in they'd a-been polished like glass.

(*Light goes down to a peep. Should go down slowly.*
If quick it makes audience think something is wrong.)

Y. WOM.: What's happened? What the matter with the light?

MARIA: The meter's give out. It's a penny in the sloter.

(*Light right down at this.*)

JOHN: Hah! The blasted gas down again!

BATES: (*Off stage.*) This 'ere gas is chronic—it's shrunk again!

MARIA: (*Who has been feeling in all her pockets.*) Oh, lor' I don't believe I've got a penny. John, where's the tuppence you 'ad yesterday?

JOHN: (*Feeling in his pockets in a guilty sort of way.*) I—I dunno. I must 'ave lost it!

MARIA: No wonder you come 'ome h'intoxicated. They get a lot for tuppence at the club, Miss.

Y. WOM.: (*Who has opened her purse.*) Here are some coppers, if you want some.

MARIA: Oh, a penny, Miss, if you would be so kind. Thank you, Miss. (*Taking a coin.*) It's a penny-in-the-slot meter as we 'ave. (*Puts penny in meter, and after a second, the gas goes up.*) And we don't get much for a penny.

(*Gas up.*)

BATES: (*Off stage.*) I say, it's a bit thick, yer know. It gives me the fair jumps.

MARIA: (*At door.*) I'm very sorry, Mr. Bates—it wont 'appen again.

BATES: (*Off stage.*) Awright, missis—still, it *is* thick.

Y. WOM.: (*To herself.*) I do wish he wouldn't insist on the *thickness* of everything.

MARIA: Well, I'm very much obliged to you, Miss.

Y. WOM.: Not at all—it's nothing.

MARIA: An' if you'll excuse me, Miss, I should like to try an' understand somethin' about this "Votes for Women" business. Could you explain it a little?

Y. WOM.: We have a meeting starting now at the Hall. It wouldn't take you long, and you would hear it all explained. It's the Women's League of Liberty. *Do* come down.

JOHN: Certainly not. 'Ow dare you suggest such a thing?

MARIA: How long would I be?

Y. WOM.: Come away as soon as you like. Come down with me now, and I'll bring you back in less than an hour.

MARIA: I'll do it.

JOHN: Maria—'ow dare—

MARIA: Women's League of Liberty! I like the name, John, don't you?

JOHN: I think it's disgustin'. 'Ussies, I call 'em—screamin', scratchin 'ussies. You leave polertics to me, my gal. Don't go and meddle in things you don't understand.

MARIA: Seems to me I understand most things as well as you, an' I'm goin' to 'ave a whack at polertics. Now Miss, if you're ready.

Y. WOM.: Come along then, we must make haste. (*Going to door.*)

JOHN: You won't do nothing of the sort, Maria.

MARIA: Yes, I will. An' if you'll brush the boots as you promised, I shall be much obliged.

JOHN: But you've your washin' to do.

MARIA: Well, 'ave a go at that, when you've done the boots.

JOHN: You impudent woman, 'ow dare—

MARIA: Lead on, Miss League o' Liberty, and I will follow you.

Y. WOM.: Bravo! Come on then.

(*Exit* Y.W.)

JOHN: (*Aghast.*) Well I'm damned.
MARIA: P'raps you are an' p'raps you aint.
JOHN: (*Quickly.*) What!
MARIA: Well—you never can be quite sure.

(*Exit.*)

JOHN: Impertinent *impidence*! A nice thing—I *don't* think. A man's whole evening to be ruined by this tommy-rot—Votes for Women! Pure unadulterated damned selfishness, *I* call it. Not even left a penny for the meter in case the gas does out. An' me got such a thirst on me—
BATES: (*Heard off, humming to himself in harsh unmusical tones.*) "Put me among the girls"!
JOHN: (*With great scorn.*) Put 'im amongst the girls!! Put 'im amongst the suffragettes, *I* say! Perhaps *they'd* make something of him.
BATES: (*Heard singing again.*)
JOHN: (*Reflectively.*) Wonder why 'e's always so light-'earted when 'e's washed 'is 'ead? Just as if a load was took off 'is mind! (*After a pause.*) Sounds a bit light-'eaded! Oh, I can't stop 'ere all night listenin' to a silly fool cryin' to be put amongst the girls. (*Loudly.*) Better leave well alone, my lad. You stop at 'ome and put yer 'air in curls. I don't see as 'ow it wants two of us to look after a little place like this. 'Specially as 'e's such a nice reliable young feller. (*Gets his cap—then goes to Bates's door R.*) I say, cockey! Are you goin' to be in for a bit?
BATES: (*Off stage.*) Wha' do yer mean?
JOHN: The missus is out, an' I've a very particular engagement at the club. Would you mine jes' givin' a heye to things?
BATES: (*Off stage.*) 'Ere, I say, what are you talking about?
JOHN: If the kids calls out, see to 'em. I 'aven't a minnit to stop. I wont forget yer—I trusses yer. I'm leavin' yer in charge of *heverythink*!

(*Rushes off door R.C.*)

BATES: (*Off stage—in alarmed voice.*) 'Ere, 'arf a minnit! 'Oo are yer gettin' at? I don't know nothin' about kids! What's the game?

(BATES *enters on last line, looking as ridiculous as possible; his hair all sticking out from having been washed—no collar or tie on—cheap gaudy slippers—towel in one hand— "Star" newspaper in other hand. After a pause and look round, he speaks.*)

Blowed if he ain't bally well been an' done it! Lef' me in charge! This is comin' it a bit thick!

VOICE: (*Off stage.*) Ma!!!

BATES: (*Looks terrified in direction of voice, and shrinks back slowly as if some apparition were rising.*) (*In hoarse whisper.*) 'Evvens above! What's that?

VOICE: (*Off stage.*) Ma! Ma!

BATES: (*With solemn conviction.*) No bloomin' error! *This* is thick!!

VOICE: Ma! Ma! Ma!

BATES: Alone in the 'ouse wiv a yellin' kid.

(CHILD *off,* "*Ma, ma.*")

Blow me tight I've 'alf a mind to go for the perlice.

("*Ma, ma, ma, ma!*")

Oh! Criley!—'ere's a go.

("*Ma, ma, ma!*")

All right, popsy wopsy, her ma's comin' back.

("*Ma, ma, ma, ma!*")

(*At door R.*) There, don't be frightened—it's only yer pore ol' Uncle Jim—don't ye know yer ol' Uncle Jim.

("*Ma, ma,*" *more fretful, but more reassured.*)

There, there, yer don't min' now it's only pore Uncle Jim—Gawd 'elp 'im—what wouldn't 'arm nobody.

("*Ma, Ma.*")

There—there!

(*Exit door R. and speaking off.*)

If I nurses yer for a bit will yer go to sleep? Come on then, but ye must go to sleep as ye've promised,—there ye are.

(*Re-appears at doorway, carrying something like a child with bed clothes and coverlet trailing on the ground as if he had lifted the lot together.*)

BATES: Now ye're a bit of all right, an' so am I—I don't think. 'Ush! (*Walks up and down nursing child and singing "Put me among the girls."*) When I come 'ere I was promised all the comforts of 'ome, an' sure enough I'm getting' 'em. (*Resumes "Put me among the girls." Stops near door R.*) I do believe I've done it. Asleep! I shall pop 'er back again and chance it.

(*Exit softly on tip-toe.*)
(*Knock at door C. twice.*) (*After pause enter* YOUNG WOMAN.)

Y. WOM.: Gracious! nobody here. I wonder where Mr.—what's his name is—? What's that?

(BATES *enters from door R. backwards on tip-toe.*)

Y. WOM.: Who are you?

(*Bates turns round startled.*)

I beg your pardon, I didn't know. Can I see Mr.—?
BATES: (*Grotesquely mysterious.*) 'Ush!

(*Y. Wom. is astonished. Bates glances nervously at door R.—then mysteriously in stealthy grotesque melodramatic fashion, approaches Y. Wom., takes her by the arm and leads her down stage a few steps, then whispers intensely.*)

BATES: It's asleep!
Y. WOM.: (*In terrified whisper.*) Wha-what is?
BATES: The kid! Their kid! (*Solemnly.*) I've been *a-nursin'* it.
Y. WOM.: (*Relieved.*) Oh! But how splendid!
BATES: I'm the lodger. It's a bit—
Y. WOM.: No, no, not—not thick. It *can't* be.
BATES: (*Astonished.*) Why not?
Y. WOM.: Well, it doesn't seem quite—quite you know—the right word, does it? Suppose we said fat.
BATES: It aint fat.
Y. WOM.: I'm so sorry. I wish it were.
BATES: It don't signify. *Fat or no fat.* I clears out o' these 'ere digs.
Y. WOM.: Oh, don't say that. Think of poor Mrs. Jenkins. She was so anxious about her poor little home, that nothing would satisfy her but that I should come back at once to see if it was all right. I shall tell her how nobly you've behaved. But where is Mr. Jenkins?

BATES: 'E 'ad a *partikler* hengagement he says, an' 'e offs wiv 'imslef leavin' me in charge.

Y. WOM.: But how good of you. What a kind generous nature you must have. You will never leave Mrs. Jenkins—promise me you will never leave Mrs. Jenkins.

BATES: That's a bit fat—I mean *thick.*

Y. WOM.: No, no, it isn't—it isn't really. Do promise.

(*Row outside.* MR. *and* MRS. JENKINS *heard approaching wrangling.*)

Y. WOM.: What's that?

BATES: 'Ere they come—love birds—no mistake.

JENKINS: (*Off.*) I tell ye I didn't.

MRS. J.: (*Off.*) What did ye come for?

JENKINS: (*Off.*) Why shouldn't I?

MRS. J.: (*Off.*) You 'ad no business to leave the washin'.

JENKINS: (*Off.*) Am I never to get out?

(*Enter* JENKINS, *excitedly, holding dirty handkerchief to his face.*)

JENKINS: A woman what leaves 'er washin' aint fit to 'ave a vote.

(*Enter* MRS. JENKINS.)

MRS. J.: An' a man as disgraces 'isself aint fit to 'ave one either.

Y. WOM.: (*Quickly.*) What has happened? What's the matter?

JENKINS: I tell ye I were doin' nothin'.

BATES: (*Quickly.*) Yus, but 'ow did ye do it?

JENKINS: I jest asked to see my wife.

MRS. J.: An' pushed yer way through an' made a dreadfu' row.

JENKINS: Nothin' o' the sort, I tell ye I was shoved. An' when I shoved back, I got landed one on the eye an' thrown out o' the 'all. An' ye call yersels *Women*!!

BATES: Serves ye bloomin' well right for sneakin' off an' leavin' me 'ere all alone by myself wi' a cryin' kid. I tell ye what, it aint good enough, an' I shall *git.*

MRS. J.: Oh, Mr. Bates, try an' overlook it. It won't 'appen again. I'll never leave me 'ome *no more.*

BATES: Orl right, Missus.

JENKINS: (*At tub bathing his eye.*) What about my eye? What's goin' to be done about my eye?

MRS. J.: Ye're doin' all that can be done, but it's rough on the washin'.

Y. WOM.: (*To* MRS. J.) I'm so sorry you had to come away from the meeting.

JENKINS: I've 'ad anough o' you an' your meetins. Wot I says is, an Englishman's 'ome is 'is Castle, an' this is *my* Castle, see? An' I don't want you 'ere any more.

BATES: Oh! Come off it. Talk sense.

MRS. J.: (*To* Y. WOM.) Nice thing in Castles aint it? Can't say I feel much like a Duchess.—Oh, of course, *I* am the Royal Prisoner. As this is my prison, I'd be glad for you to look in sometimes. What prisoner wouldn't like to 'ear o' a league o' *liberty*.

Y. WOM.: Then I shall come again.

BATES: Bravo!

Y. WOM.: And tell you all about it, for I am afraid you heard nothing tonight.

MRS. J.: Oh, yes I did. It was fine. That tall 'aughty lookin' lady was speakin', an' o' my, didn't she let 'em 'ave it. It was splendid.

BATES: What did she say?

MRS. J.: She said—she said.

JENKINS: *Damn* Politics! I shan't be able to go out for weeks.

(MRS. JENKINS *laughs.*)

BATES: Good job too; but what did the lidy say?

Y. WOM.: Yes, what was it?

MRS. J.: She said—*Home was the place*—for *Men!*

Curtain

JENKINS *at tub bathing his eye and groaning.*
Mrs. Jenkins *and* Y. WOM. *laughing and shaking hands as if saying good-bye.*
BATES *at door of his room looking round at* JENKINS.

MARGARET WYNNE NEVINSON

IN THE WORKHOUSE:
A PLAY IN ONE ACT

[London: The International Suffrage Shop, 1911]

[Produced by Edith Craig's Pioneer Players, Kingsway Theatre, 8 May 1911.]

AUTHOR'S PREFACE.

In writing this play (I make no apology for its realism except that it is true) I have tried to show the parlous condition of twentieth century womanhood under the unjust Gilbertian muddle of uni-sexual legislation: "the truth shall make you free," and it seems sometimes as if the lamp of truth turned upon the dark places and cruel habitations of the earth, like radium upon some foul sore, will heal these wrongs.

For most of these wrongs the ridiculous and antiquated law of coverture is mainly responsible, and until it is wholly abolished, new reforms only seem to create new absurdities; it is merely tinkering at a rotten system and pouring new wine into old bottles. It has been said that "the four Married Women's Property Acts are a record of the hesitation and dulness of members of Parliament. Parliament tried to reform the law in accordance with ideas borrowed from equity, and some of the lawyers, by whom Parliament was guided, did not understand the principles of equity they were meant to follow."

It has ever been so. I suppose in private life our legislators claim to be gentlemen and sportsmen, but in the game of law-making for women they seem to be lost to all sense of decency and fair play, and the only excuse for the stupidity and lack of imagination in these male lawyers is that made long ago for all human dulness and brutality on the Cross of Calvary, "Father, forgive them for they know not what they do."

Under the law of coverture the wife has no separate existence whatever; like an infant, she is entirely under the custody and control of her husband. He is the sole parent and guardian of all children born in marriage, and has power to fix their religion and education; and under the Poor Law it is a common thing to see whole families dragged about at the will of a drunken, brutal and lazy male, their cries stifled in the dust.

Some three years ago all England was startled at its own laws on reading that an able-bodied woman, willing and anxious to earn her own living, and knowing a trade, was compelled to remain in the workhouse, a dead weight round the necks of the ratepayers, because the drunken scoundrel of a husband, who had brought his family there, "has power by his marital authority to detain his wife in the workhouse." Questions were asked in Parliament; distinguished lawyers wrote saying that such detention is an infringement of the great Law of Habeas Corpus. (Undoubtedly that is so, for even under the Poor Law a wife cannot be compelled to enter the workhouse; but, once there, it is easy to keep her.) Suffragette tongues spread the story and the woman was allowed to leave; but the order still stands in Glen's Poor Law Orders, and no doubt in our free England up and down the country married women are still in captivity at the will of some worthless husband.

By the same law a married woman is compelled to follow her husband wherever he goes, and the Liberal Government which gave us the Children's Charter and interests itself in infant mortality, either in ignorance or indifference, still permits wives and babes to be turned out in all weathers, to wander without food or shelter, should the husband choose to leave the workhouse, sometimes nominally to look for work, sometimes merely to enjoy a day's drinking.

Under the law of coverture a woman under seventy married to an old age pensioner may not receive parish relief, though she has a separate digestive apparatus. "Relief given to the wife is relief given to the husband," and the wife must either starve till she is seventy or the husband must forfeit his pension.

On the other hand, a husband under seventy married to a State pensioner may receive parish relief, he being an independent citizen.

Under the same law British women married to foreigners are counted aliens and shut off from old age pensions, though foreign women married to Britishers receive the pension without demur.

Again, a deserted wife, not being a parent, has frequently to suffer the agony and humiliation of having her children taken away from her, protected by the Guardians, and sent away to workhouse schools. By the sin of the male, without any fault of her own, she is deprived not only of a husband but also of the children of her body.

The law of coverture, however, is quietly dropped when there is money to be got out of a woman; a wife can be compelled to contribute to the support of a lazy, drunken or dissolute husband in workhouse, infirmary or lunatic asylum.

It is not legal to tax married women, for the law of 1842 has never been repealed, but the Inland Revenue has always done so, subsequently counting the wife's income as the husband's, and so increasing their revenue on the aggregate.

Mr. Lloyd George is also bringing in a law waiving again the law of coverture and compelling wives to return their income for the Super Tax.

In this little play I have attempted to illustrate from life some of the hardships of the law to an unrepresented sex, the cruel punishment meted out to women, and to women only, for any breach of traditional morality, the ruin of the girl, the absolute immunity of the male, the brutality that attacks an idiot, the slavery of the married women, the singular advantage a clever woman can take of laws apparently made for the maintenance of wickedness and vice and the punishment of virtue.

No wonder the marriage rate is declining and we hear that more and more throughout the country free unions are on the increase, particularly in the industrial parts of England. The shrewd and self-supporting younger generation hesitate before they accept wedlock on the present terms and endure the wrongs they have seen their mothers suffer. Added to this the persistent rumours of legislation limiting the work of married women in factories does not encourage the young to put their heads beneath the yoke of such tyranny. Will this be for the making of a great nation?

These facts told to a street corner audience invariably arouse great indignation, for the poor know by bitter experience that they are true; to bring them to the knowledge of our legislators is harder. If only men knew, we feel that "these laws that blaspheme and tyrannies that fetter" would be swept away and we could sing without hypocrisy "Rule Britannia," a song which sounds to many of us a hideous blasphemy of the truth.

"For the hurt of the daughter of my people am I hurt...astonishment hath taken hold of me. Is there no balm in Gilead; is there no physician there? Why then is not the health of the daughter of my people recovered?"[18]

CHARACTERS:
Lily, a red faced, Cockney girl.
Wilhelmina, thin and worn, about 40.
Monica, idiot girl, about 18.
Mrs. Jarvis, middle-aged, drunken and coarse.
Ethel, refined and pretty parlour maid.
Penelope Law, a handsome, voluptuous woman, about 30.
Mrs. Cleaver, respectable, middle-aged matron.
Infants.

A workhouse ward. Yellow washed walls with a few texts about: "In everything give thanks," "Blessed are the pure in heart for they shall see God," "Little children love one another." Bedsteads and cots covered with red coverlets. INFANTS, LILY, MRS. JARVIS, WILHELMINA, *and* MONICA *discovered. All are in pauper dress: dark blue cotton gowns, ill-fitting, with white caps and aprons.* LILY *is rocking her baby.*

MONICA *is standing by the window, singing. She has her baby in her arms.*

(*Before the curtain rises*)—
"All things bright and beautiful,
All creatures great and small,
All things wise and wonderful,
The Lord God made them all."

(*At the rise of curtain*)—
"The tall trees in the green wood,
The meadows where we play,
The rushes by the water,
We gather every day."

(*In the middle of the song* ETHEL, *with open letter in her hand, runs in and flings herself on the bed, sobbing.*)

LILY: (*A coarse red-faced young woman, walks up and down the ward, trying to soothe a wailing* Infant; *Cockney accent*): There, there, did 'ums, then! Don't cry, my beauty! We're going out tomorrow, my pet! And father's going to marry us.

WILHELMINA: (*A wasted consumptive looking woman, about 40; Yorkshire accent*): Don't be too sure, my wench. There's many a slip 'twixt the cup and the lip, and fathers don't always turn up you know on these occasions.

LILY: (*Sharply*): The mission lady's seeing to it; she's bought a ring and put up the banns, and H'augustus says she's promised him a sovereign if he turns up at the church door punctual at ten. She's got another lidy to mind biby, too, whilst I am in church, so as not to shime me. Can't tike you to my wedding, duckie, can I now?

WILHELMINA: The sovereign may do the trick, but men are slippery cards to the likes of us, as no doubt you know. I remember well how I stood in the church at Foxearth, up on the moors, waiting for my child's father, the parson in his surplice ready to make us one, and poor mother a-running up and down the street outside, a-cocking her head into all the pubs to try and find 'im. But 'e ain't turned up neither then or since, and that is nigh on twenty year ago.

(*Elderly woman with twins, babies on each arm, walks up and down.*)

Your twins are restless to-night, Mrs. Jarvis. Seems cruel 'ard on a mother to bring forth a pair of superfluous twins, and no father between 'em. What's the law of the land on this matter? Do you get 5s. each or are you held responsible for the extra one?

MRS. JARVIS: None of your lip, Wilhelmina; I'm a married lidy, that's what I
am, and I'll thank you to remember it.

WILHELMINA: I'm sure I beg your pardon, Mrs. What's-a-name, only I understood you to say as Mr. Jarvis 'ad been dead some years.

MRS. JARVIS: Well, and if 'e 'as? Ain't I got the ring and the lines just the
same? Makes all the difference, my gal, I can tell you between my position and you bad women in 'ere.

WILHELMINA: There, there, keep your 'air on! Don't you know it is an unwrit-
ten law in these state-rooms that pots don't call kettles black?

MONICA: (*Squint-eyed and with wide grin from ear to ear gives a shrill cry of ecsta-
cy*): I do love my biby!

WILHELMINA: That's a mercy, my dear, as no one else ain't likely to. Who's
the baby's father, Monica?

MONICA: (*With another broad grin*): Bill.

WILHELMINA: What's baby's name?

Monica: Bill.

WILHELMINA: Got any more babies, Monica?

MONICA: Ess, two bibies, two Bills, three Bills; love my Bills.

Wilhemina: And where are the other Bills?

MONICA: (*With an extra grin*): I dunno.

WILHELMINA: Well, I ain't a saint myself, but I do think as the propagation of
idiots ought to be stopped.

MONICA: (*Sings to her* BILL):
  "All things bright and beautiful,
  All creatures great and small,
  All things wise and wonderful,
  The Lord God made them all."

(*On a bed behind the door* ETHEL *sits crying, her apron over her head.* LILY *pauses
in her walk to speak to her, takes her hand kindly and tries to soothe her; but her
attempts at consolation meet with no result, and she shrugs her shoulders and
resumes her walk up and down the ward.*)

WILHELMINA: Dear, dear! what's the matter with that poor soul?

LILY: The organisation lady outside has written and told her mother where
she is, and she's terrible upset. Poor Ethel! she's a different sort to us.
Father's a coachman in an earl's family, and she was keeping it quiet
from them, hoping her young man would marry her afore they knew; but
now her mother's written to 'er very cruel, and it's about broke 'er 'eart.
She feels disgracing them—quite natural, too.

WILHELMINA: (*Rising and going towards* ETHEL): A dirty bit of busybodying, I
call that! There, there, my wench! don't 'ee cry, dearie; it's 'ard, I know,
the first time, cruel 'ard, but we gets used to it. Don't 'ee cry, dearie.

(BABY *in cot yells wildly.* LILY *picks it up and rocks the two of them.*)

LILY: Did it want its mother, my lamb? 'Ere, Pennyloaf, take your young
monkey, it's waking the crew of 'em just as they were going off nicely.

(*A tall, handsome woman enters the ward and takes the infant silently in her arms.*)

PENELOPE: (*Sitting down*): Ain't Mrs. Cleaver back yet?

LILY: Not yet; she's gone to appear afore the Board. She gave in 'er discharge two or three days ago, but 'er husband says as she got to stop 'ere
with 'im, and Master says that's the law of the land; so, not believing such
nonsense, she's gone to complain on 'em both to the Board.

WILHELMINA: And a fine dose she's 'aving. I hate appearing afore them Committees; last time I went I called the lady "Sir" and the gentleman "Mum,"
and my 'eart went pitter-patter in my breast so that you might have
knocked me down with a feather.

MONICA: (*Sings*):
"The purple-headed mountain,
The river running by,
The sunset and the morning,
That brighten up the sky."

WILHELMINA: Just 'ark to that—purple-headed mountains and sunsets. Lor',
child, 'old your row; turns me creepy in my inside to 'ear of such things
in 'ere, we who never goes out year in year out. Doing time is better than
this; even in 'Olloway ye runs round the yard and sees a bit of sky for one
hour. Lord, how it makes me think of Yorkshire 'earing that there 'ymn.
Why, 'ere's Mrs. Cleaver. Well, my dear, and you do look bad. Sit ye down
and tell us all about it.

MRS. CLEAVER: (*A middle-aged woman, very over-heated sinks down on the end of a
bed panting and fanning herself vigorously with her apron*): Them Committees
allus turns me dead-sick, and my boots feel too tight for me, and I goes
into a perspiration and the great drops go rolling off my forehead. Well,
'e's kept 'is word and got the law and right of England behind 'im.

(*Sensation in the ward. The other women gather round* MRS. CLEAVER; *infants are
patted and dandled and soothed with much vigour.*)

Well, I went afore the Committee and I says "I want to take my discharge,"
I says. "I applied last week to Master, but mine got at 'im first, and Master
up and says, 'No, Mrs. Cleaver, you can't go,' he says; 'your 'usband can't
spare you,' 'e says; 'wants you to keep 'im company in 'ere,'" he says.

(*Sensation and exclamations of horror.*)

"Is that true, Master?" says the little man wot sits lost in a big chair. "That is so, sir," says Master, and then 'e out with a big book and reads something very learned and brain-confusing that I did not rightly understand, as to 'ow a 'usband may detain 'is wife in the workhouse by his marital authority.

WILHELMINA: Good 'evens! Is that the law of England?

MRS. CLEAVER: That's what the little lady-guardian said, 'er that comes up here dressed so shabby. "'evens!" she says, same as you; "is that the law of England?" Then they all began talking at once most excited, and the little man in a big chair beat like a madman on the table with a 'ammer, and no one took the slightest notice; but when some quiet was restored the little man asked me to tell the Board the circumstances. So I says 'ow 'e lost 'is work through being drunk on duty; which was the lying tongue of the perlice, for 'his 'ead was clear, the drink allus taking 'im in the legs, like most cabmen, and the old 'oss keeps sober. It was a thick fog, and 'e'd just got off the box to lead the 'oss through the gates of the mews, and the perliceman spotted 'is legs walking out in contrary directions, though 'is 'ead was clear as daylight, and so the perlice ran 'im in, and the beak took 'is licence from 'im and 'ere we are. Now I've got over my confinement, and the child safe in 'eaven after all the worrit and starvation, I thought I'd like to go out and earn my own living. I'm a dressmaker by trade, and my sister will give me a 'ome. I 'ate being 'ere, living on the rates, and 'e not having done better for us than this Bastile—though I allus says as it was the lying tongue of a perliceman—it seems fair I should go free. The lady wot comes round Sundays told me I ain't got no responsibility for my children, being a married lady with the lines.

WILHELMINA: That's quite true—you can 'ear the Suffragette ladies a-saying that at any street corner.

MRS. CLEAVER: Well, it is time the Guardians learnt it; but the little man in the big chair flew out most violent: "Don't talk like that, my good woman; of course you have responsibility for your children; you must not believe what ignorant people tell you." Then I 'eard the tall ginger-'aired chap—'im wot sits next the little man, as you unmarried girls go before to try and father your babies—I 'eard him say quite distinct: "The woman is right, sir—married women are not responsible for their children; but I believe the husband is within his rights in refusing to allow her to leave the 'ouse without him." Then they told me to retire and I should know the result later. O Lord! I'm that 'ot and upset with the worry of it, I feel I'll never cool again. (*Sits back on the bed, wipes her face and fans herself with her apron.*)

PENELOPE: Single life has its advantages: you with the lines ain't been as perlite as might be to us, who ain't got 'em, but we 'as the laugh over you really. I'm taking my discharge to-morrow morning, and not one amongst them dare stop me. I don't have to appear afore Boards and be worried and upset with 'usbands and Guardians and things before I can take myself off the parish and eat my bread independent.

WILHELMINA: But why weren't you married, Pennyloaf? Not for want of asking, I'll be bound.

PENELOPE: No, it wasn't for lack of asking. Fact is, I was put off marriage at a very early age. I 'ad a drunken beast of a father, as spent 'is time a-drinking by day and a-beating mother by night. One night 'e overdid it and killed 'er. He got quad for life, and we was put away in them workus schools; it would 'ave been kinder of the parish to put us in the lethal chamber as they do cats and dogs as ain't wanted. But we grew up somehow, knowing as we weren't wanted, and then the parish found me a place, under-housemaid in a big 'ouse, and then I found as the young master wanted me, the first time since Mother died as any human soul had taken any interest in me, and Lord! I laughs now when I think what a 'appy time it was. Since then I've had five children and twenty-five shillings a week coming in regular besides what I can make at the cooking.

LILY: How do you manage to get the five shillings a week; the lawyer chaps don't seem to do much for us.

PENELOPE: I don't bother with lawyer chaps. I make my own arrangements and not one man has gone back on 'is promise. I lives clean and respectable—no drinking, no bad language—my children never see and 'ear what I saw and 'eard and they are mine—mine—mine. I always come into the 'ouse for confinement, liking quiet and skilled medical attention. I never gets refused; the law dare not refuse such as me—it's you married ladies as can't get in 'ere. I always leave the coming in till the last moment, then there are no awkward questions, and when they begin to "enquire as to settlement" I'm far away. All the women in our street are expecting next week; their 'usbands all out of work and not a pair of sheets or the price of a pint of milk between them; all lying in one room too, as I don't consider decent, but having the lines it's precious 'ard for them to get taken in 'ere, and besides 'alf on 'em daren't even try, for fear he and some one else will sell up the 'ome whilst they are away.

MRS. JARVIS: Yes, that's quite true; the law seems agin us respectable women. You remember the lady as died last week up in the lying-in. Well, she told me she tried to get in 'ere weeks ago, 'er 'usband being out of work all right and she feeling very queer and low, but the Board said as she was the wife of an able-bodied man and 'e was responsible for 'er and must find work. But she got 'ere in the end spite of 'em all, for 'er 'usband swore at 'er so fearful for having twins, that the Doctor nearly fought 'im for being a brute, and he ordered 'er in 'ere out of 'is way, but what with

all the upset and the starvation whilst she was carrying of 'em, it was too
late to save 'er; she took fever and snuffed out like a candle, and it was
fearful to 'ear 'er raving and crying out to 'im not to beat 'er till the
child was born.

MRS. CLEAVER: If I'd my time over again I'd not marry, not I.

LILY: What? Mrs. Cleaver, you say that?

MRS. CLEAVER: Yes, and I means it, too. The idea of keeping me 'ere with
that there drunkard when I knows a trade. And look how us married
lidies 'as to turn out if 'e chooses to tike 'is discharge and wander about
with the kiddies in the rain and snow with no clothes nor decent boots
for them. I remember Mrs. Page and her four children coming back
looking like death last Christmas time. Page had been out to look for
work, but 'e never went further than the King of Bohemia to find it, and
all day, whilst he was drinking, they had been shivering outside in the
rain. In the old days there was the shelter of the bar, but now there ain't
that any longer. Only 'Arry kept dry, being over fourteen. Mrs. Page told
me a gentleman stood 'er a 'alf-quartern of gin, but the children 'ad
nothing all day, and they was 'alf dead with cold and 'unger. Massacring
of the hinnocents I call it, for all the children, except 'Arry, were laid up
in the Infirmary next day, the biby died the next week of bronchitis, and
Mrs. Page took a heavy cold on 'er chest, and now she's coughing 'er
poor 'eart out in the 'tysis ward with the wall taken out on one side and
the winds and the fogs coming in shameful; this is the truth, for I used to
scrub in the 'tysis ward.

WILHELMINA: Mrs. Kemp 'ad 'em all nicely over that. Kemp wanted a day off
to look for work, though being such a cripple 'e ain't got no chance, and
when 'e took his discharge Master told 'er she and the children 'ad got
to go too. She says as she warn't going out to wander the streets with no
clothes and no 'ome, and then Master tells 'er as she got to go, the law
being that them two are one, and e's the one, and if she wouldn't go
quiet she'd be put out by force. Then Mrs. Kemp went off in one of 'er
tantrums, flying out at 'im most fearful; "Well, then, you shall 'ave the
truth," she says, "which I've been keeping quiet for shame. I ain't married to Kemp—never 'ave been—my first 'usband deserting me and
going off with another woman, leaving me starving at one-and-twenty
with two children and another coming. Kemp offered me a 'ome then
and 'e's been a sight better to me than Johnson, who went to church and
swore to be faithful, but couldn't manage to keep his oath not even for
three years. We'd never 'ave been in here if the motor car 'adn't run over
Kemp a-crippling 'im for life, but I shan't take out my children to die of
cold, not for 'im nor no man, and now you know I'm a bad woman perhaps I may be left in peace." And she was.

PENELOPE: That's just what I was a-telling you. The law is all on the side of us bad 'uns. I'm going back to-morrow to my next little 'ome, which my lidy-help is minding for me, to my dear children and my regular income, and I can't say as I envies you married lidies either your rings or your slavery.

WILHELMINA: But don't the neighbours find out, Pennyloaf?

PENELOPE: Not they; they don't know as I'm a bad woman. I generally moves afore a confinement, and I 'as a 'usbnd on the 'igh seas. Besides that, I 'as a good connection cooking dinner parties in the West End. If your cooking's good, I find there's no nasty questions about your morals.

LILY: (*Walking up and down with her baby*): I think we won't get married, my pet! better keep single, I says, after what we've 'eard to-night. What I've heard to-night is a lesson to me. I'll not get married, not I. Just look at Mrs. Cleaver, an honest married woman. All 'er 'usbnd 'as done for 'er is to bring 'er and the kids to the 'Ouse, and now they say she can't even go out to earn her living. Then look at Pennyloaf, free and rich and prosperous, and the kids 'er own. The bad 'uns wins, my pet! Vice triumphant, I says!

MONICA: (*Gives an ecstatic shriek*): I do love my biby!

Graham Moffat

The Maid and the Magistrate: A Duologue in One Act

[London: Actresses' Franchise League, (1912)]

Note: *The sketch is arranged so that it may be performed on any platform and without scenery, although an appropriate setting helps it very considerably.*
The double seat at L. may be arranged, should the correct piece of furniture not be available, by placing two chairs on a slant up the stage, the one nearest the footlights facing, and the other with its back to the audience. The chairs should be so placed that anyone seated on the chair furthest L. would be seen in profile when speaking to another on the stage. If possible dance music should be heard "off" before the sketch opens and towards the end, but very faintly, so as in no way to interrupt the action, or distract the attention of the audience.

Enter R. A lady and gentleman in evening dress. The lady is much younger than her companion—she is excited and happy. The gentleman is middle-aged, clean shaven, and has mannerisms that betoken the successful lawyer. At present he is fatigued with recent exertions in the ball-room and for a while speaks somewhat breathlessly.

SHE: (*As they enter.*) Oh, no, thanks, Mr. Potter, I don't want refreshments. The buffet is crowded and I've been there three times already. How nice and cool it is here!

HE: I shall be glad of the rest. That last dance fairly winded me. Jig time too! But for you I should never have attempted it.

SHE: I am afraid you are getting old.

HE: I hope you don't really look upon me as a "fogey," Miss Smith? After all, I'm just in my prime—not more, I should think, than twenty years your senior.

SHE: Oh, we won't go into that. You lawyers are so clever at ferreting out secrets.

HE: Won't you sit down?

SHE: No, thank you. I'm too restless to-night. I shan't think you rude, however, if you collapse into the chair. You are quite worn out.

HE: Very well—I'll sit and look at you. (*He sits at L., back to audience, but speaking to her is seen in profile. She walks up and down.*)

SHE: You may tell me what you think of my frock.

HE: That's quite out of my line. I'll tell you what I think of the lady in the frock.

SHE: Excellent. The lady in the frock will be delighted to see herself reflected in your criticisms. But be a true mirror—you must neither flatter nor distort. Shall I stand before my glass?

HE: No! Go on walking about.

SHE: Then it's the frock you'll see to advantage.

HE: Let me think. Miss Smith, how long is it since your first season?

SHE: Oh, don't begin and calculate.

HE: Well, I won't. Do you know, you are delightfully feminine.

SHE: You think so—really?

HE: Most decidedly. You have all the little feminine weaknesses that I, like most men, sincerely admire.

SHE: Indeed.

HE: Yes—you are simply charmed with yourself in that frock and you are afraid that I may find out how old you are.

SHE: I don't want to be admired for my weaknesses—there! As for my age—I'm twenty-nine.

HE: Miss Smith, I only meant that I like a woman to be womanly.

SHE: It isn't fair to sum up our faults and call them feminine and womanly and delightful—as if woman had nothing strong and good in her nature. Self-sacrifice is as feminine a quality as love of dress, and far more worthy of admiration.

HE: Yes, yes, I know. I meant no disparagement, I assure you. Miss Smith, I admire your spirit—it is a new side to your character and it becomes you. Yes, I must say I like it. Do you know you are very much changed since last we met.

SHE: Since three months ago?

HE: Yes. There's something different about you and it puzzles me.

SHE: Don't you think I'm looking well?

HE: You always look charming—to-night you are a picture.

SHE: Then I'm a sort of picture puzzle.

HE: Quite so.

SHE: And what particular kind of metamorphosis do I appear to have undergone?

HE: You seem to me to have wakened up.

SHE: Perhaps I've been a sort of caterpillar and I'm only just finding my wings.

HE: You appear to have recovered the life and spirits you had during your first season.

SHE: Ah, that was before I grew sick of being useless.

HE: Useless?

SHE: Yes! What sort of life do we women lead. We ladies who work so hard dressing and dancing and eating, holding receptions and going to theatres. Oh, it hardly took me a season to get bored to death. What a sham and a waste of energy it all is while there is real work for women to do.

HE: (*Rising.*) But you appear to have recovered your taste for this sort of thing.

SHE: Not really—I can enjoy it as a recreation although I have given it up as an occupation—and to-night I'm happy.

HE: Indeed! And may I enquire why?

SHE: No, you are not to ask me. You'll find out soon enough.

HE: Won't you give me a hint?

SHE: Shall I? Well, it's because I've done something. Now, that's all you are going to be told.

HE: Perhaps I could guess the rest.

SHE: You mustn't try. And I shan't answer you if you do.

HE: If my guess is correct it becomes my duty to congratulate someone—although I shall grudge the lucky fellow his good fortune.

SHE: What are you talking about?

HE: Ah, then you're not engaged?

SHE: Certainly not. Whatever made you think of such a thing?

HE: Well, you said that you had "done something" and I naturally concluded that you had become engaged. Miss Smith, I can only think of one reason why you should be so happy.

SHE: Indeed!—and that reason is—

HE: Love.

SHE: So you think that nothing can make a woman happy—even for a day—but love?

HE: No! Not as you are to-night. It is the only thing that accounts for the new light in your eyes and the joyousness you import to every movement. I wonder who he is?

SHE: There is no one.

HE: Are you sure of that. Then it may be—After all why shouldn't I?

SHE: Oh, please don't.

HE: Why not?

> He either fears his fate too much
> Or his deserts are small
> Who will not—

SHE: Change the subject. (*She crosses L. and sits in chair he has vacated.*) You haven't told me what you think of my frock.

HE: I'm afraid I'm no judge.

SHE: That won't hinder them from making you one some day.

HE: Not a judge of frocks at any rate. By the way that reminds me. (*Crosses to her.*) You haven't congratulated me.

SHE: No, what about? Are you engaged?

HE: I've been made a magistrate. (*Sitting beside her.*)

SHE: A magistrate—you? One of those dreadful men?

HE: What's this? Pardon me—I see nothing dreadful.

SHE: (*Goes R.*) No—oh no, of course not. A magistrate of all things.

HE: It was announced in all the papers. Strange you didn't notice it.

SHE: Oh, I've been away from home. So you are a magistrate—and, oh dear! I'm talking to you here just as though you were an ordinary man. What fun!

HE: I quite fail to understand you, Miss Smith. It sounds like sarcasm. A magistrate is an important man no doubt—but he *is* an ordinary man, after all. As to the fun, I don't see where that comes in.

SHE: It *will* come in though. Tell me, Mr. Potter, have you ever tried any women?

HE: Oh yes, plenty.

SHE: Any suffragettes?

HE: Suffragettes? Well, no; that is, not yet. But I believe a number of them are to come up before me to-morrow morning.

SHE: Not the women who were arrested at Downing Street to-day?

HE: (*Rising.*) Yes, but how did you know? The affair has only just happened. I heard of it as I came along. The women are out on bail.

SHE: Oh, I read about it in the papers. I understand that some of them are perfect ladies.

HE: It is monstrous. These women are holding all our (*walking about*) leading public men up to ridicule. Such absurd, outrageous tactics are driving the entire British Cabinet distracted. It must be put down.

SHE: What will you do with them?

HE: I'll give them all three months.

SHE: You're a brute. (*She crosses L. and sits facing audience. He comes behind her chair.*)

HE: Ah! Miss Smith, you don't understand. These women belong to a different world from you. Don't think—ah, don't think I am lacking in respect to all true womanly women. You are my ideal of all that a woman ought to be—So good, so gentle and flowerlike.

SHE: Flowerlike? Ah yes, as a man wants a woman to be, with nothing to do but look sweetly pretty til some enterprising man comes to pluck her—and being plucked she is taken home and left to wither in the matrimonial cold water.

HE: It is not like you to be cynical. Miss Smith, I have watched you with delight to-night. It's no doubt absurd but I am speaking now in the hope that this change in you has something to do with me.

SHE: You are mistaken—the change in me has quite another source.

HE: Then that's my answer. I'll try to bear it. Shall we return to the ball-room?

SHE: No we won't. You're a silly old stupid, and I didn't give you any dismissal.

HE: You didn't—Ah! Phyllis!

SHE: As to your proposal—You did propose didn't you?

HE: Well, I hardly know. Perhaps not quite—I was coming to the point.

SHE: I can't give you an answer now. I do like you very much. You poor dear magistrate, you don't know how sorry I am for you.

HE: Sorry! Why should you be?

SHE: Oh you'll find out soon enough. Meantime you must wait.

HE: How long must I wait?

SHE: I don't know. You see it doesn't depend upon me. I'm going away for awhile.

HE: Not for long I hope?

SHE: Well it might be—three months.

HE: You mean to go for a holiday?

SHE: Not quite—let us say for a rest.

HE: Doubtless you intend to spend some time at a Hydro.

SHE: Y-e-s—something of that sort.

HE: And may I hope that when you return—?

SHE: When I return! Listen to me—you say that you remember when I came out in society years ago?

HE: Radiant as you are to-night.

SHE: You noticed how quickly I became dull and depressed—that was because I was as indolent and useless as my own pet poodle. I did no good by "coming out" so I've determined to "go in" for awhile—and when I return, when I "come out" this time I mean to begin life all over again on a new plan.

HE: In Society? A sort of second *debut?*

SHE: No! I mean to work in the world.

HE: Ah Phyllis how splendid you are! You have indeed wakened up! Every word you utter adds to my admiration! I love to see you so courageous who are yet so womanly! Let us be fellow workers?

SHE: Oh, if you had been anything but a magistrate. But no, it won't do—our ways lie far apart.

HE: You are passing a cruel sentence upon me.

SHE: A cruel sentence—three months?

HE: Eh? Ah, you mean that I must wait till you return from your holiday?

SHE: Perhaps after all we could settle the matter now. Will you do me a favour?

HE: I am yours to command.

SHE: Oblige me by sitting here. (*Points to chair centre.*)

HE: (*Sits.*) Certainly.

SHE: Now please suppose you are in the court at Cannon Row and that the suffragettes are being brought before you.

HE: (*Rising.*) What! The suffragettes again—really Phyllis.

SHE: Now do please sit still. I want to know what it feels like.

HE: (*Sits.*) What what feels like? I feel like a fool.

SHE: To be sentenced by a magistrate.

HE: (*Rises.*) Oh tut-tut! It's too absurd.

SHE: Now do oblige me. I certainly shan't marry you if you don't.

HE: Oh well, if you put it that way. (*Sits.*)

SHE: Now look majestic.

HE: (*Staring at her.*) Majestic?

SHE: Yes—remember that you are invested with all the majesty of the law— say to yourself "the dignity of man must be maintained at all costs."

HE: Miss Smith! Phyllis! You are laughing at me.

SHE: Not at all. It will require all your manly dignity to carry it off. You are to try fifteen helpless women who pay taxes, but are kept outside the Constitution. You are to try them for claiming the freedom of citizens, which should have been their birthright. You are to try them by laws which no woman had any part in framing. So you may demonstrate in your hearing and by your wisdom what superior creatures men are.

HE: Phyllis, I am amazed. Do you actually *sympathise* with these viragoes?

SHE: I rather think I do. (*She crosses R. and goes behind a chair.*) Now then, supposing I am the prisoner.

HE: Oh it's quite preposterous. Suppose someone were to come in from the ballroom and find us at this ridiculous game!

SHE: If you won't do as I ask you I absolutely refuse to marry you.

HE: Well, well, go on.

SHE: Presuming that I am the prisoner—what happens?

HE: The prisoner is usually brought in by a policeman.

SHE: We'll imagine a policeman—what then?

HE: The charge being read over, it is my custom to ask the policeman what he knows of the case.

SHE: He will probably reply (*steps from behind chair, stands still and erect in imitation of a policeman*) "The woman, sir, chained herself to the Prime Minister's door-knocker— with her companions she held the door for fifteen minutes, notwithstanding the efforts of the police. Almost the entire British Cabinet were obliged to listen while she held them up to the ridicule of the mob." (*Returns behind chairs.*) Now sentence me please.

HE: Phyllis, what an extraordinary girl you are. I must admit it is an excellent joke.

SHE: Sentence me!

HE: Oh, no, no (*much amazed*), I couldn't do it even in fun.

SHE: You'd better—for you'll have to do it in earnest to-morrow.

HE: What? Why you don't mean to tell me that all that mad tale was true? (*Rises.*)

SHE: Every word of it! I'm going to begin and live now—to live and fight for the Freedom of my sex!! (*Crosses L.*)

HE: (*Comes down R.*) And you are to come up before me to-morrow morning? And I shall be obliged to send you—the girl I love—to prison.

SHE: For three months.

HE: (*Walking about.*) Oh, I couldn't do it. It would be a crime.

SHE: Hear, hear! You see that now when it is brought home to you. Every one of them is a refined, delicately nurtured woman. It is only when it is your own sister or sweetheart or wife who is to suffer for her convictions that you realise how criminal your treatment of such women has become.

HE: You of all women! What made you do this mad act? Have you not a good home? Are you not loved and protected?

SHE: Yes! So are pet poodles.

HE: I can't even think what you want a vote for.

SHE: Because it is my right. But do you imagine I am thinking only of myself? *I* may be loved and protected but there are thousands of women who need the vote, to right the wrong they endure through man's neglect and their own helplessness. We women want equality of opportunity. It's not the vote, it's what it means to us.

HE: Oh don't make speeches. My only thought now is how to save you—how, how.

SHE: I'm not asking to be saved. I want to save my sisters—my sister, for instance, the sweated worker whose condition has grown steadily worse since Tom Hood wrote "The Song of the Shirt." Why, even the shirt on your own back may have been made by some poor woman at a shilling a dozen.

HE: Rubbish! I buy my shirts in Regent Street and pay sweetly for them.

SHE: That proves nothing. We know that even West-end establishments—

HE: I refuse to discuss the subject. Phyllis, I am thinking of the disgrace you are bringing upon yourself and your people. Ah, think of your father—your brothers and sisters.

SHE: Oh, don't distress yourself about them. They are all converted. Why the whole family will be proud of me when I win my Holloway medal. Even dad has joined the Men's League.

HE: Then think of me, Phyllis, think of my feelings.

SHE: Yes, it is awkward for you I admit.

HE: And of yourself. Prison. Do you realise what that means? The degrading dress—oh, I can't bear to think of it.

SHE: I shall be so proud to wear it—far, far prouder than I am of this frock.

HE: And then the food—the loathsome horrible food.

SHE: Ah the simple life—shouldn't wonder if it did me good.

HE: I give it up. You are beyond me. Women are simply incomprehensible. (*Sits L. back to audience.*)

SHE: To men they are—that's why men are unfit to legislate for us.

HE: You don't reason. If I could only get you to think.

SHE: Why it is just because I have begun to think that I've wakened up as you call it. (*She rests her arm on back of chair adjoining his.*) Now listen. You thought you understood me when you used to feed me with chocolate cream and treated me as a society doll— something to flirt with, to love and protect if you will, but not capable of thinking an earnest thought or discussing a serious problem. Well, you will have to revise your opinion of your loving Phyllis. (*Walks R.*)

HE: (*Rises.*) My—loving Phyllis?

SHE: Yes, but perhaps you don't want me to love you now.

HE: Oh yes I do. I believe I want you more than ever.

SHE: That's good.

HE: And to-morrow I'll pay your fine myself.

SHE: If you dare do anything of the kind I'll never speak to you again.

HE: Very well, I won't. But I'll let you off with an admonition.

SHE: Then you'll have to let all the others off too.

HE: Oh no, I couldn't do that. The law must be maintained.

SHE: Mr. Magistrate, you will take your instructions from me.

HE: No, don't think of it, Phyllis. (*Sits L. facing audience.*) It would be a gross abuse of my official position. I can't possibly let you all off.

SHE: No, you are not brave enough for that, I suppose. Still you must listen to me, dear.

(*She comes behind him, puts her arms about his neck and her head beside his.*)

HE: (*Delighted—strokes her hand.*) Well, well—and what do you—advise?

SHE: That you give us a fortnight each in the first division,[19] and come to Holloway gate and meet me when I "come out."

HE: Well, I'll take it to avizandum.[20]

SHE: How romantic it will be.

HE: And when shall we be married?

SHE: Oh let us return to the ball-room (*going*). I must have one more dance before I lose my liberty.

HE: Not till you answer me.

SHE: I can't possibly fix a time for our wedding. It may have to be postponed for years. You see it doesn't depend upon me at all. Perhaps you'd better ask—

HE: I'll ask your father of course.

SHE: Oh no—not Dad—you should ask Mr. Asquith.

HE: Indeed—why should I?

SHE: Because it is a government question. Until women gain their freedom I have better work to do than getting married. My mind is fully made up—remain a spinster till we get the vote.

(*They exit arm in arm—he protesting.*)

CURTAIN

A CHAT WITH MRS. CHICKY:
A DUOLOGUE

[London: Actresses' Franchise League, (1913)]

[Originally performed at the Rehearsal Theatre, London,
20 February 1912.]

Mrs. Chicky—A Charwoman.
Mrs. Holbrook—An Anti-Suffrage Canvasser.

Scene: *Room in the house of* MRS. HOLBROOK'S BROTHER. *Window L. with desk and writing chair in front of it. Door L.C. Fireplace R. with armchair (on castors) drawn towards it, facing audience. Bookshelf R.C. Table up C. One small chair on top of another L. of desk. Fender drawn away from hearth. Broom leaning against wall. Pail of water, flannel, dustpan and brush, hearthbox with hearthcloth, scouring-stone, blacking brushes, old gloves, etc., up near door. Desk, table, bookshelf and armchair covered with dust-sheets.*

N.B.: *Although the effect of this duologue is much enhanced by the setting, it can quite well be played without it on small platforms, etc. Where this is desired,* MRS. HOLBROOK *should be discovered on rising of curtain, seated at a table with paper and pencil. She says, "Come in!" in answer to a knock at the door, and* MRS. CHICKY *appears, saying, "Sarah said you wanted to speak to me, 'M." MRS. HOLBROOK answers: "So I do, Mrs. Hicky. Sit down," and the duologue proceeds as written, except that instead of asking* MRS. CHICKY *to go on with her work,* MRS. HOLBROOK *says "I won't keep you from your work more than a few moments." Subsequent chance references to the "turning-out" would, of course, be omitted.*

On rising of curtain MRS. CHICKY, *with sleeves rolled up, skirts pinned high, etc., is discovered scattering tea-leaves from a jar over the carpet. She stops short as* MRS. HOLBROOK, *in outdoor things, bustles into the room.*

MRS. H: Oh, you're here, Mrs. Hicky! I just want to—
MRS. C: (*Briefly.*) Chicky.
MRS. H: What do you say? Oh, Chicky—yes, of course. You're not the same

charwoman my brother employed last time I came to see him, are you?

MRS. C: I couldn't say.

MRS. H: Ah! but I remember. I've such a memory for faces. She was short and stout, and—

MRS. C: (*Interrupting.*) If you're alludin' to Martha Buggins, 'M., she 'ad a cock-eye.

MRS. H: Oh, poor woman, yes. She had a *slight* squint.

MRS. C: Ope I may never see a severe one, then!

MRS. H: (*Ignoring remark.*) My brother said I might have a little chat with you, Mrs. Chicky.

MRS. C: (*Setting jar on table, pulling down sleeves, and looking round at general disorder.*) Shall I come into the 'all, 'M.?

MRS. H: No, no! I haven't come to keep you from your work. Please go on with it just as if I wasn't here—I shan't interfere with you. (*Laughs pleasantly.*) You and I are the sort of women who like to stick to our own work and not interfere with other people's aren't we?

MRS. C: I'll answer for meself.

MRS. H: It's a pity everybody can't say as much. (*Looks round for somewhere to sit down.* MRS. C. *takes up small chair, puts it C. and dusts it with apron.*) Ah, thank you! (*Sits down.*) Now please go on with whatever you're doing. We can talk just as well while you're working.

MRS. C: (*Takes up broom leaning against wall.*) Thank you, 'M.

MRS. H: (*As* MRS. C. *begins to sweep round the room.*) That's right. Well, I'm trying to collect opinions wherever I go on a subject that a handful of women are making a great fuss about just now. I wonder if you know what I mean by Women's Suffrage?

MRS. C: (*Looks thoughtfully at* MRS. H., *then shakes her head and goes on sweeping.*) No, 'M.

MRS. H: All the better! You haven't got time to trouble your head bout politics, have you?

MRS. C: (*Sweeping tea-leaves and dust almost into* MRS. H.) I don't interfere with what don't interfere with me!

MRS. H: (*Gathering skirts round her and putting feet on chair-rail.*) Splendid! Well, the fact is, Mrs. Hicky—

MRS. C: Chicky!

MRS. H: Chicky—I beg your pardon. The fact is that a few women who haven't got anything else to do have some ridiculous idea that they ought to have votes, and do men's work instead of their own and interfere with the government of the country, and if you and I and millions of other women who know better don't stop them at once we shall simply have England going to rack and ruin!

MRS. C: (*Pauses, leans on broom, and asks as if seeking light.*) Then I 'ave got to trouble me 'ead about pollytics after all?

MRS. H: Oh, no! Let me put it a little differently! If you don't want a thing you certainly oughtn't to be made to have it, ought you?

MRS. C: (*Giggling as she goes on sweeping.*) That's what John Joseph says when 'e sees me with 'is lickrice powder. 'E's my third, is John Joseph.

MRS. H: (*Coughing as dust rises, but evidently determined not to show irritation.*) And a credit to you, I'm sure. Well, what we want to do is to show every-body that by far the greater number of women *don't* want votes, and I'm doing my part by asking a hundred women, taken as far as possible from every station in life, and putting down their replies so that I can send the result to a newspaper.

MRS. C: An' 'ow might you be getting' on, 'M.?

MRS. H: Oh—er—of course one can't quite tell till one's got to the end. But when once we show in figures that most women are against having the vote, of course nobody can go on saying anything in favour of it.

MRS. C: Well I 'ope you won't be disappointed 'M., I'm shore. But some people are that obstinate you can't make 'em see nothin'.

MRS. H: Oh those kind of people needn't be considered at all.

MRS. C: No 'M. (*Stops sweeping again*) Why if you took one o' them lists o' yours, down our Court to find out 'ow many wanted to wash theirselves every day I could tell you before 'and which side you'd 'ave a big balance on, an' yet I dessay you'd find some folks pig-'eaded enough to go on sayin' as they all orter use soap and water.

MRS. H: (*Looks sharply at* MRS. C. *whose face remains impassive.*) Please don't let me stop your work, Mrs. Chicky. I don't think we need to go into the question of your neighbours' cleanliness this afternoon. I merely want to know if I may put you down on my list as being against votes for women?

MRS. C: (*Still pausing.*) Well o' course 'M., if I was to set out to explain to you—

MRS. H: (*Patiently*) I don't want *you* to explain anything to *me*, Mrs. Chicky. I'm here to explain things to *you* this morning. (MRS. C. *still hesitates.*) You'd like to hear something more from me about it before you say yes, perhaps?

MRS. C: I should, 'M.

MRS. H: I thought so. Well, I can make the whole thing clear to you in a few minutes. Yes, please go on. (MRS. C. *begins to sweep again.*) You see we think that women have their own special work to do in their homes, and of course some of them have a Council vote already about things they can understand, like lighting streets and making roads.

MRS. C: (*Encouragingly.*) Yes 'M. (*For the next few minutes she takes* MRS. H's *chair as the goal towards which her tea leaves, etc., are to be swept, till she has finally collected little heaps all around it.*)

MRS. H: Well isn't it better for them to leave the Army and Navy and wars with other countries to the men who know all about them? If women had the brains to understand the things men settle in Parliament it might be different, but they haven't. They're clever in another way. You can't combine politics and domestic matters. You— (*turns first one way and then the other in chair to follow* MRS. C. *who is now sweeping behind her*) you see what I mean, don't you?

MRS. C: (*Pausing again.*) You mean as 'ome's one spere an' Parlyment's another, an' they didn't orter be mixed up?

MRS. H: (*Much pleased.*) Exactly!

MRS. C: (*Reflectively.*) It just shows you oughtn't to believe 'alf you 'ear! (*Crosses L. as she sweeps again.*)

MRS. H: (*Smiling.*) What nonsense have you been hearing?

MRS. C: (*Pausing.*) Why I remember Marier Jackson down our Court tellin' me—oh it's some time back now—when 'er baby got pewmonier from sleeping in a banana box, as she didn't never take it to bed with 'er because Parlyment 'ad made a lor about it. I'll give it 'er proper for 'avin' me on like that! (*Sweeps vigorously again.*)

MRS. H: (*Hurriedly.*) Oh but I think she was quite right, Mrs. Chicky. At least I know there has been some Act passed by Parliament in connection with poor children getting smothered in that way.

MRS. C: (*Pausing in surprise.*) You don't say, 'M.! Why you'd a' most think it was a-mixin' itself up with the 'ome if you didn't know different, wouldn't you?

MRS. H: (*Hotly.*) It's a splendid thing that such a law *has* been passed by men!

MRS. C: Oh yes 'M., an' I'm not sayin' that pewmonier an' the Docter's certif'kit aint a sight more respectable than overlayin' an' the Crowner. I 'ope the dust don't worry you 'M.? (*as* MRS. H. *coughs again.*) Of course I like to see a woman 'ave a voice in settlin' what's best for children meself, but I know some ladies thinks diff'rent. (*Sweeps gradually R., crossing behind* MRS. H.)

MRS. H: You don't understand, Mrs. Chicky! Nobody could feel more strongly than I do that the care of children is a woman's work above everything.

MRS. C: She may care till she's black in the face, but she won't do much good if she's got the lor against 'er!

MRS. H: My dear Mrs. Chicky, you talk like an ignorant woman! How *could* the law be against her caring for her children?

MRS. C: (*A little huffily.*) Ho, it's not for me to set my opinion against yours, 'M., bein', as you say, an ignorant woman. An' of course she's got the care of 'em right enough if she aint got 'er marriage-lines. It's on'y if she's kep' respectable as she can be 'ampered somethin' crool!

Mrs. H: You seem to have got some extraordinary ideas in your head!

Mrs. C: Yus I 'ave. The lor's put 'em there, wot's more.

Mrs. H: Now my good woman just tell me your difficulties and let me explain them away!

Mrs. C: (*Pauses again and delivers speech very clearly.*) Difficulties? Well I guess many a married woman finds it a bit difficult not bein' 'er own child's parent—goin' by the lor, that is. It's a bit difficult for 'er as the lor don't give 'er no voice in 'er child's schoolin' nor religin' nor vaccinatin' nor such like, in the or'nary way. It's a bit difficult for 'er as 'er 'usband can pretty nigh starve 'er an' it if 'e's the mind, but she's got to go the lenth of leavin' 'im before she can get a maint'nance order, an' it's often none too easy to get *that* carried out. It's a bit—

Mrs. H: (*Interrupting.*) But where have you read all this? I'm quite sure it's nonsense!

Mrs. C: (*With a laugh.*) Read it? Bless your 'eart, 'M., women like us don't 'ave to *read* about the lor like you ladies! We're too busy knockin' up against it, as you might say. I don't serpose any o' *your* lady friends comes before the Magistrit onst in a lifetime, but it's diff'rent with mine, though I've kep' clear so far meself, thanks be! (*Begins to poke broom vigorously under Mrs. H's chair which is surrounded by a ridge of tea-leaves.*) Don't you move, 'M.! I can sweep under you quite comfortable.

Mrs. H: (*Hastily.*) No, no, thank you! (*Gets up and steps gingerly over tea-leaves to armchair R. and sits down.*) But even if you're right, those difficulties would only arise where a husband and wife weren't doing their duty of living happily together.

Mrs. C: (*Setting broom aside and picking up dust-pan and small brush.*) Well, the lor aint made for turtle-doves! (*Goes down on knees and begins to sweep leaves into pan.*)

Mrs. H: Of course not. But we were talking about votes, weren't we? All this has nothing to do with them.

Mrs. C: Votes wouldn't give women a bit of a voice in drorin' up the lors about their own affairs, then?

Mrs. H: Oh my dear Mrs. Hicky—

Mrs. C: Chicky!

Mrs. H: —er—Chicky, if the women of England had a voice even in such a roundabout way as that in making laws, what would the homes of England be like?

Mrs. C: Maybe you're right 'M. 'Twouldn't never do for those as know most about 'omes to 'ave anythin' to do with fixin' rules for 'em.

Mrs. H: (*Testily.*) You don't understand what I mean. Fancy giving any woman such a terrible responsibility!

Mrs. C: Yes 'M. You can understand some of 'em wantin' to shirk it, can't you? (*Goes on hurriedly as Mrs. H. looks annoyed.*) But after all, there's

many would say I 'and't much call to trouble my 'ead about England!
(*Gets up slowly.*)

MRS. H: (*Rising indignantly.*) Anybody who would say such a thing to an Englishwoman ought to be ashamed of themselves!

MRS. C: Yes 'M. But I aint an Englishwoman.

MRS. H: You're not an Englishwoman?

MRS. C: (*Serenely.*) No 'M. (*Faces MRS. H. with dustpan in one hand and brush
in the other.*) I'm French.

MRS. H: (*In bewilderment.*) *French?*

MRS. C: Yes 'M. My name's Chicky.

MRS. H: (*Puzzled.*) How do you spell it?

MRS. C: Well my 'usband 'e used to spell it C-h-i-q-u-é-with-a-mark.

MRS. H: (*Crossing L.*) Oh, *Chiqué!*

MRS. C: Yes 'M, 'e did call it like that onst, but the men in the fact'ry always
called 'im "Chicky" and some'ow we got to writin' it like the poultry, too.
'E was French right enough though, Gawd rest 'im! Talk the langwidge
beautiful, 'e could!

MRS. H: But that doesn't make *you* French!

MRS. C: Oh yes 'M. it does, more's the pity. I don't serpose they'd give me
one o' these 'ere votes if I wanted one. They won't let me 'ave one for
the Council. 'E's been dead this four year, 'as my 'usband, but 'e never
nateralised 'isself, you see.

MRS. H: But why havn't you got a Council vote?

MRS. C: (*Wearily.*) Cos I'm French, as I'm tellin' you.

MRS. H: But you're *not!* (*Crosses R.*)

MRS. C: Oh yes 'M, the gentleman what come round to arsk Annie Mills to
vote for 'im— she's the room below ours—'e explained it to me. 'E said a
wife's what 'er 'usband is—she don't count sep'rit.

MRS. H: But you're a *widow!*

MRS. C: 'E said that didn't make no diff'rence. I 'ave to be what Chicky was.
(*Puts brush and pan aside and gets hearthbox.*)

MRS. H: (*Moves down towards fireplace.*) That does seem rather peculiar, certainly.

MRS. C: Yes 'M. (*Comes down R. with hearthbox.*) I don't feel French!

MRS. H: (*Hurriedly.*) Of course not—of course not. (*Pauses, leaning elbow on
mantlepiece as MRS. C. shakes out hearthcloth, spreads it and kneels down to
grate.*) Of course if one thinks a moment one sees the beautiful idea at
the back of it. A husband and wife are one, you know.

MRS. C: (*Docilely.*) Yes 'M. Which one? (*Puts on dirty kid gloves and begins to
black grate.*)

MRS. H: (*Confusedly.*) Oh—er—just *one.* (*Sits down.*) Let's go back to what we
were talking about. I was trying to make you see, wasn't I, that all these
ideas of women doing men's work are ridiculous.

MRS. C: Well that's as plain to me as (*looks round*) you 'M., sittin' in that chair. I've no patience with the way you'll 'ear some folk settin' women against men as if they was oppersite sides in a battle!

MRS. H: (*Much pleased, leaning forward.*) I felt sure you were a sensible woman!

MRS. C: Yes 'M., thank you 'M. There was a lady at my door it'll be a fortnight come Monday, an' me up to my elbers in soap-suds, talkin' a lot o' that nonsense, but she went off quicker'n she'd come, I can tell you!

MRS. H: (*Leaning more forward excitedly.*) I'm very glad to hear it!

MRS. C: Yes, 'M. "Woman's spere this, an' Man's spere that," I says. "Goin' on for all the world as if one 'ad got four legs an' the other two! The Lord 'E started 'em fair when 'E cremated 'em" I says "an' 'E didn't lay down no rules about speres, nor make no diff'rence in their jobs. An' I guess those 'oo go tryin' to parcel 'em off sep'rit" I says "'ave more'n one muddle to answer for!"

MRS. H: I—I don't quite—

MRS. C: (*Glorying in recollection of her own eloquence, waves blacking-brush to emphasise it and hits* MRS. H. *who starts back in annoyance.*) "Besides" I says—oh, beg pardon 'M., I'm shore!—"besides" I says "women are doin' men's work, an' men women's, as you call it, all over the shop, an' if you want their speres to be diff'rent at this time o day" I says "you've got to do more undoin' than'll larst your time an' mine." She'd got a paper with 'er as she wanted me to put my name to, but I told her straight as I couldn't 'ave no truck with such silliness. (*Gets up and crosses L. to fetch pail of water.*)

MRS. H: (*Much perturbed.*) But Mrs. Chicky, you probably misunderstood her entirely. I—I more than suspect she was *against* votes for women!

MRS. C: She was against common-sense, whatever she was. (*Carries pail across R. and sets it down near hearth.*)

MRS. H: And you know it's all nonsense to say women can do men's work. Women can't fight.

MRS. C: (*Significantly, rolling sleeves higher.*) Try 'em!

MRS. H: (*Coldly.*) I was alluding to fighting for their country.

MRS. C: Lor bless you, 'M., I guess you an' me wouldn't be so far be'ind the men in that, neether, if it come to the point! (*Kneels down, wrings out flannel in water and proceeds to wash over hearthstone.*) I'm the last in the world to be-little soldierin'—I'm proud to 'ave two brothers in that line meself—but the way some folks talk about men fightin' you'd think as there wasn't a man in England as didn't stand up to be shot at onst a week! It's a good job they don't 'ave the bearin' of the childring, or they'd be that set up at riskin' their lives so constant there'd be no 'oldin' of 'em in!

MRS. H: You get so confused, Mrs. Chiqué—

MRS. C: Chicky!

MRS. H: What I mean is that if women were soldiers and sailors there'd be something at once for them to have a vote *for*.

MRS. C: Do soldiers 'ave the vote, then? Well I might 'ave knowed! They will 'ave their joke, will George an' Albert! If you'd 'eard 'em larst Election goin' on like bears with sore 'eads because they 'adn't a vote same as most o' their pals you'd never 'ave serspected it was just a do the 'ole time!

MRS. H: You mean your brothers? Oh but it's quite likely that they hadn't.

MRS. C: 'Ow's that, 'M.?

MRS. H: Well you see to get a vote a man has to be a householder and pay rates and taxes, or a lodger, and stay in the same place a year and—oh, various things that most soldiers and sailors can't do.

MRS. C: Oh then the vote *'asn't* got nothin' to do with fightin' for your country, after all?

MRS. H: (*Testily.*) I never met a woman more difficult to explain things to! Can't you see that the right to vote really depends on physical force— strength, you know—and that women havn't got that? (MRS. C. *finding* MRS. H. *in her way gets up and pushes her, chair and all, a foot or so C. with perfect ease.*)

MRS. C: (*Returning R. and kneeling down to hearth again.*) Thank you 'M.—I couldn't quite get to this 'ere corner. Strenth, is it? There's a parrylised man down our Court what's wheeled to the poll regler. I pushed 'im there meself larst Election, wishin' to oblige.

MRS. H: Yes, yes, but you musn't take everything I say too strictly.

MRS. C: I'm not doin'. (*Dips scouring-stone into water and begins to scour hearth.*)

MRS. H: What I want you to see is the broad principle of the thing. A woman's place is in her home, you know.

MRS. C: (*Sitting back on her heels.*) Am I to understand as your brother's not requirin' of me no more?

MRS. H: Oh really, Mrs. Chiqué—Chicky, then! (*as* MRS. C. *begins to correct her*) please don't go on narrowing everything I say down to particular cases! Of course I don't mean that you ought to stop going out charing!

MRS. C: Bad job for *my* 'ome if I did!

MRS. H: (*With brilliant inspiration.*) Yes, but don't you see how it all works back to what I said at first? You'd never have time for voting *and* charing, would you?

MRS. C: Well I should say it took me a quarter of a 'our to wheel Tom Welford to the poll an' it was on my way to my work. 'E was took back by moter because 'e'd said 'e wouldn't vote unless. (*Smooths hearthstone over with wet flannel.*)

MRS. H: Ah, but it's not just the voting! Look how this Mr. Welby had probably *studied* the question, and how he— (MRS. C. *emits strangled sounds*) what's the matter?

MRS. C: On'y—on'y you'll eggscuse me larfin' 'M., but Tom Welford can't read. '*E* couldn't do no studyin'. My Josephine runs in now an' 'again to read 'im the football news—they say 'e was a rare player in 'is young days, pore feller—but 'e don't care to listen to nothin' else. (*The hearth finished, she puts fender back into place and tidies up.*)

MRS. H: Very kind of her I'm sure. Well, to go back to what we were talking about—

MRS. C: Yes 'M., we don't seem to be getting' much forrader, do we? (*Carries hearth box and pail up L.*)

MRS. H: But I don't think there's any need for us to argue when in your heart you agree with all I've said. I only wanted to be satisfied that I could put you down as being against votes for women.

MRS. C: An' are you satisfied?

MRS. H: Quite. There are hundreds of sensible hardworking women like you who merely want to have the thing simply explained to them and they see its dangers at once. (*Rises and crosses L.*) I don't think I've anything more to ask you Mrs. Chicky, thank you.

MRS. C: (*Coming down C.*) Then can I arsk *you* somethin' 'M.?

MRS. H: (*A little surprised.*) Certainly.

MRS. C: Well, it's this. What are you worritin' about 'em for?

MRS. H: About whom?

MRS. C: Why this little 'andful of women you've been a-tellin' me about. What 'arm can they do?

MRS. H: Oh they've grown—I don't say they havn't grown. They've such a dangerous way of getting hold of people. You see they promise excitement and bands and processions— we can only offer dull things like looking after one's children and caring for one's home. (*Crosses R. again.*)

MRS. C: (*Sharply, as she removes dust-sheet from table.*) I've never found lookin' after my childring dull, though (*looking meaningly at* MRS. H.) I know it's what some ladies calls it! (*Folds dust-sheet and places same on table.*)

MRS. H: You will keep misunderstanding me! I say that the women who want votes think looking after children dull. I believe they'd like to make all women fond of politics instead of children!

MRS. C: (*Uncovering desk and folding its dust-sheet.*) Will they make you vote, then, whether you've the mind or not? (*Places dust-sheet on table.*)

MRS. H: (*Dramatically, as she crosses L.*) Never! (*After a little pause.*) I'm not saying that some of us might not think it right to use a vote if it was forced upon us, so that we might counteract all the harm the other women would be doing.

MRS. C: (*Proceeding to uncover bookshelf and place its dust-sheet on table.*) Would they all vote the same way, then?

MRS. H: Oh women always herd together!

MRS. C: (*With puzzled expression, as she uncovers armchair.*) But if you an' your lady friends was all votin' the other way, it don't look as if women *would* be 'erdin' together?

MRS. H: (*Cornered, crossing R.*) I—I—oh it's no use trying to explain!

MRS. C: (*Folding last dust-sheet and putting it on table.*) Seems to me this 'ere vote's mighty difficult to understand!

MRS. H: (*Triumphantly*) *Too* difficult—for a woman!

MRS. C: (*With apparent relief.*) Oh then you don't understand it, neether?

MRS. H: (*With annoyed little laugh.*) My good Mrs. Chicky, all that I don't understand is why any woman should be so ridiculous as to want it!

MRS. C: (*Quickly.*) You don't?

MRS. H: I certainly don't!

MRS. C: (*Comes down C., gazes at* MRS. H. *for a moment, and then speaks as if on a sudden thought.*) Now I wonder if it would 'elp you if you saw it writ?

MRS. H: If I saw what written?

MRS. C: (*Raises her skirt, dives into under-pocket with difficulty, and finally produces red handkerchief knotted at corner, keeping up running comments the while.*) It must be 'ere somewhere. I don' know I'm shore why it didn't come to me sooner as I'd got it on me. I know I put it in me 'andkercher to keep it away from 'Eneryett cos she was wantin' to suck it all the time the lady was a-talkin'—she's my fourth, is 'Eneryett. Never give it a thought till this minit, I didn't. 'Ere it is! Funny 'ow if you onst put a thing in your 'andercher it can go there for days! (*She undoes knot in handerchief with her teeth, Mrs. H. watching her in bewilderment, and discloses small crumpled handbill which she smooths out and from which she proceeds to read.*) "WHY WOMEN WANT THE VOTE"—that's on top—"A FEW PLAIN REASONS IN PLAIN WORDS"—I could 'ave give 'em a few more if they'd 'ave arsked me, but these is put very distink—very distink indeed they are. Praps you'd like to—

MRS. H: (*Splutters interruption in horrified amazement.*) You—you—you're a *Suffragist?*

MRS. C: (*Looking up from paper with something approaching grin.*) What do *you* think?

MRS. H: (*Furiously, flopping into chair.*) You told me you knew nothing about Women's Suffrage!

MRS. C: (*Sweetly.*) Oh no 'M. You arsk me if I knew what you meant by it, an' I says no. (*Goes on hurriedly as* MRS. H. *gives angry exclamation.*) I was a-startin' to tell you as I knew what I meant meself right enough, but you stop me. You said you was 'ere to explain things to *me!*

MRS. H: (*Crosses L. speaking hotly.*) D' you suppose I'd ever have wasted my time over you if I'd known? We—we don't want to talk to people who are against us!

MRS. C: I'm sorry, 'M., I'm shore. You see (*tapping handbill*) this lot's so dif-
f'rent. Seems to revel in talkin' to them as don't agree with 'em, they do!

MRS. H: (*Looking at paper as if it were poisonous.*) May I ask where you got
that?

MRS. C: I bring it away from a meetin' larst Tuesday. Praps you'd like to bor-
rer it, 'M.?

MRS. H: (*Waving it hastily away.*) Oh, if you're going to be taken in by all you
hear at meetings—

MRS. C: (*Interrupting quickly.*) Taken in? No 'M., no one don't do no takin'
in when Elizer Chicky's about, thankin' you kindly! Why we've 'ad two
ladies down our street tryin' to stuff us with argyments that my own cat
wouldn't 'ave swallered, an' 'e aint pernickety. "We've h'always got on
very well without women 'avin the vote" says one. "Yes" I calls back, "you
may 'ave, but what price us?"

MRS. H: (*Coldly.*) Mere selfishness never did anybody any good yet!

MRS. C: (*Apologetically.*) Well 'M, I didn't like to call out that for fear she'd
think I just wanted to sauce 'er.

MRS. H: (*Losing control.*) Stupid woman!

MRS. C: So I thought 'M. But praps she was a bit 'ard of 'earin', for she just
says over again, "We've always got on very well without women 'avin the
vote." "Splendid!" I calls back, "with some of us makin' blouses at one an'
a penny a dozen an' ackcherly managin' to earn six shillins a week for a
fourteen hours day! We all keeps our kerridges!"

MRS. H: But my good woman— (*Crosses R.*)

MRS. C: (*Unheedingly.*) "Ho" says she, "there's a lady in the ordyance what
makes the mistake of thinkin' the vote's a-goin' to raise women's wages!"
"No" I says, very prompt, "the lady 'oo's makin' a mistake aint in the
ordyance" I says "but there's a woman there" I says "'oo's got the sense to
see that if 'er sex 'as got a vote what's useful to the men they're more
likely to listen to 'er than if it 'and't!"

MRS. H: But my good woman—

MRS. C: (*Interrupting earnestly.*) Look 'ere 'M., I arsk you before an' I arsk
you again— what are you doin' it for?

MRS. H: Doing what?

MRS. C: Carryin' on this 'ere 'obby of yours—cerlectin' names?

MRS. H: Why, I want to help to stop this movement! (*Crosses L.*)

MRS. C: You might as well try to stop a leak in a saucepan with sealin'-wax!

MRS. H: But my good woman—

MRS. C: Yus you might! You take it from me 'M. The first time I 'eard a lady
at a street corner sayin' as women orter 'ave votes, I listens for a bit 'an I
says "I'm on this job" I says. I says "She knows. She's talkin' gorspel. She
aint sat in no drorin'-room an' *read* about us" I says. "She knows." (MRS.
H. *tries to interrupt with little indignant exclamations all through this speech, but*

MRS. C. *once fairly started, refuses to be baulked.*) She didn't waste no time tellin' women out workin' to keep body an' soul together as they orter be queens of their 'omes! She didn't go talkin' about a man's 'ome for all the world as if 'e orter knock at the door n' arsk 'is wife's leave every time 'e wanted to get inside it! (*Mrs. H. crosses R.*) She didn't waste no time tellin' women 'oo'd sent their lads off to fight with their own 'earts breakin' for all their lips were smilin', as women 'adn't no feelins for their country an' didn't understand nothin' about war! She didn't waste no time tellin' sweated women drove on the streets—women 'oo's 'usbands give 'em a drib 'ere an' a drab there when they're sober, an' the childring goin' 'alf-naked— women 'oo's 'usbands take up with another woman, an' "I'm afrid the lor can't 'elp you my good woman" says 'Is Wushup, in nine cases outer ten—women 'oo get drove to despair with facin' their trouble alone while the man 'oo's brought 'em to it gets off scot free— women 'oo'll take on their 'usband's job when 'e's ill, to keep the 'ome goin', an' get eight or ten shillins docked off for the same amount of work cos they aint men—she didn't waste no time, I say, jorin' to women like that about the splendid way their int'rests are perfected already! She *knew.* (MRS. H *crosses L.*) Oh I'm not sayin' this 'ere votes goin' to set everythin' right, but I do say as anythin' that's done without it'll be just patchin' an' nothin' more! It's goin' to make women *count*! It'll make 'em *'ave* to be reckoned with! I've nothin' against the men. (*Draws hand across eyes.*) I'd the best 'usband as ever stepped! I believe same as you do that the men want to do what's best for us, but—*you 'ave to be a woman yourself to know where things 'urt women*! It's Gawd's truth, that is, an' I say Gawd bless the ladies 'oo are 'elpin' us by stickin' out for it!

MRS. H: (*With satirical little smile.*) Well, I'm afraid you would be wasting less time scrubbing your floors than as an orator, Mrs. Chicky.

SERVANT'S VOICE: (*Heard off.*) Mrs. Chicky! Mrs. Chicky! You're wanted! (*Mrs. C. hesitates.*)

MRS. H: Oh pray go! Of course you won't understand my attitude, but nothing that you or anybody else could tell me would make me alter my mind!

MRS. C: (*Picking up hearthbox and dustsheets.*) Oh yes 'M., I've 'eard of that before. (*Pauses at door.*) You see 'M. my 'usband lived in France till just before we was married, an' *'e kep' MULES*!

(*EXIT.* MRS. H. *drops on to chair and stares after her in open-mouthed amazement.*)

CURTAIN

MISS APPLEYARD'S AWAKENING:
A PLAY IN ONE ACT

[London: Actresses' Franchise League, (1913)]

[First performed at the Rehearsal Theatre, London, 20 June 1911.]

CHARACTERS
Miss Appleyard
Mrs. Crabtree (her visitor)
Morton (her Parlourmaid)

DESCRIPTION OF SCENE
Small Chamber Set
Window, C.
Door, U, R, E.
Writing Table and Chair, C.
Table and Chair, D.R.
Sofa, L; Bell in Wall Down L. Below Sofa

SCENE—A Drawing-room.
TIME—During an Election.

MORTON *is discovered arranging blind, tidying up room, etc.*

(*Enter* MISS A. *in outdoor things.*)

MISS A: Oh Morton, I must have some tea now—I really can't wait till half-past four. I don't think there's anything in the world so tiring as canvassing! (*Sits at table, R.*).

MORTON: I hope you got a proper lunch 'm?

MISS A: (*Drawing off gloves.*) No, it wasn't at all proper—two stale sandwiches at Owen's—but I couldn't get home. The dinner hour was the best time for catching some of the men. Fancy, Morton. I've got three fresh promises for Mr. Sharp!

MORTON: How splendid, 'm! Were you up by the factory?

MISS A: Yes, in Dale Street and Quebec Street. I begin to think half the idiots in Mudford must have settled there judging from the intelligence of some of the voters I've been arguing with this morning!

MORTON: Won't you go and lie down a bit, 'm? You look tired out.

MISS A: Oh no, I shall be all right when I've had some tea. I should have been home earlier only I simply couldn't get through the crowd in Nevil Square where one of those dreadful Suffragists was speaking. I really could shake the whole lot of them!

MORTON: (*Evidently interested.*) I suppose she was talking about votes for women, 'm?

MISS A: Oh yes I suppose so—I didn't really listen. I heard something about some bill they wanted to get passed. The less women have to do with bills the better, to my mind— Parliamentary *and* other kinds.

MORTON: (*As if wishing to hear more.*) I daresay she'd plenty to say, 'm?

MISS A: (*Suppressing a yawn.*) I daresay she had, Morton. I wish I'd been near enough to tell her to go back and look after her home and leave Parliament to manage its own affairs! (*Pauses a moment, then speaks as if on a sudden recollection.*) Oh by the way, Morton, if you and Cook would like to go to Mr. Sharp's meeting at the Town Hall to-night I think the house might be shut up for a couple of hours. I can take my key in case I get back first.

MORTON: Thank you, 'm, we should very much.

MISS A: Well tell Cook, then. You could manage to get off by half-past seven, couldn't you, as I'm having dinner earlier? She'll have no washing up to speak of.

MORTON: Oh yes, 'm.

MISS A: Don't leave it later because the place is going to be crowded. (*Looks at her hands.*) I'm too dirty to eat—those factory chimneys were simply raining blacks! I'll be ready in two minutes! (*Crosses L, and Exit.*)

(*Exit* MORTON *and returns with tea cloth, putting it on table, R, and humming "March of the Women." While she is doing this a bell rings outside. She ignores it, and it rings again.*)

MORTON: All right—all right! Somebody else has got things to do as well as you!

(*Exit, to reappear almost immediately and usher in a visitor.*)

MORTON: (*About to leave room.*) What name shall I say, please?

MRS. C: (*Crosses to R on entrance.*) Miss Appleyard wouldn't know my name. Just say that a lady from the Anti-Suffrage Society would be much obliged if she could speak to her.

MORTON: Thank you, 'm. (*Crossing to door L.*)

MRS. C: (*Sitting down R.*) I won't keep her more than a moment or two. Oh—er—(MORTON *stops.*) I shall be asking her to allow you and your fellow-servants to sign a petition I've got with me. How many of you are there?

MORTON: (*Evidently surprised.*) Two, 'm.

MRS. C: (*Disappointedly.*) Not more? Still, two names are something.

MORTON: (*Hesitatingly.*) What is the petition about 'm?

MRS. C: (*As though she thought the question unnecessary.*) About?—Oh it would take rather long to explain. But you don't want women to sit in Parliament and leave their homes to go to rack and ruin, do you?

MORTON: Oh no, 'm.

MRS. C: And you don't want every woman in England to have a vote so that they can swamp the men and govern the country themselves?

MORTON: That's never what the Suffragists want, it is 'm?

MRS. C: Oh they'll all *tell* you they don't, but of course they do really. When a woman leaves her own duties to take up a man's she soon loses her sense of truth and everything else.

MORTON: Really, 'm?

MRS. C: Why this very petition you were asking about is against a set of women, who pretend that they don't think their sex ought to meddle with politics and yet they're working themselves in this Election as hard as they can!

MORTON: Oh that doesn't seem right 'm does it?

MRS. C: Right? It's very wicked and deceitful, of course, but that's just an example of the sort of thing that happens when a woman interferes with—(*She stops short as* Miss Appleyard *enters the room and looks round inquiringly.*)

MORTON: A lady to see you, 'm. (Exit.)

MRS. C: (Rising.) Good afternoon, Miss Appleyard. I hope I'm not disturbing you? I'm afraid you're just going out?

MISS A: No, I've just come in. Please sit down.

MRS. C: (*Seating herself again.*) I won't detain you more than a few minutes. My name is Crabtree—Mrs. Crabtree. I've come as a delegate from the Mudford ASS—I understand that you belong to it?

Mrs. A: (*Puzzled.*) The ASS? (*Sitting on sofa.*)

MRS. C: The Anti-Suffrage Society.

MISS A: (*Laughing.*) Oh, I beg your pardon. I didn't recognise those rather unfortunate initials for the moment. Yes, I've been a member for nearly a year, I think. A friend of mine gave me no peace till I said she might send in my name.

MRS. C: We have one or two noble proselytizers! They stop at nothing!

MISS A: Oh, I'd no real objection—I've always steadily declined to listen to anything on the subject of Women's Suffrage.

MRS. C: I wish there were more like you! I've really come to ask if you would be good enough to sign a petition that some of us are getting up?

MISS A: Oh certainly. I never refuse my name to any Anti-Suffrage Petition. I should think I've signed four this last month.

MRS. C: (*Looking at her admiringly.*) How splendid of you! And yet Suffragists say we don't work for our cause!

MISS A: Oh but Suffragists will say anything! I suppose you've read the accounts of the disgraceful disturbances in Liverpool last night.

MRS. C: (*Indifferently.*) No. Were there any? I can't say that I trouble my head much about that sort of thing.

MISS A: (*Astonished.*) But don't you think it's abominable?

MRS. C: There are worse things in connection with the Suffrage movement than disturbances.

MISS A: Worse?

MRS. C: (*Impressively.*) Very much worse.

MISS A: But what *could* be worse?

MRS. C: Oh my dear Miss Appleyard, if a woman's in a policeman's arms—of course it's very deplorable, but at least you know where she *is*!

MISS A: Certainly—but—

MRS. C: (*Interrupting.*) And if she's shouting in the market-place like the female I saw addressing crowds in Nevil Square just now—at all events she's fighting you in the open!

MISS A: (*Puzzled.*) Of course.

MRS. C: Even if she's never done anything for her side but join a Suffrage Society—well, you do know she's against you.

MISS A: Certainly, but I'm afraid I don't quite see what you mean to imply.

MRS. C: (*Drawing her chair closer to* MISS A. *and lowering her voice.*) What should you say to *traitors within the camp*?

MISS A: (*In bewilderment.*) Traitors within the camp?

MRS. C: Traitors within the camp, Miss Appleyard. Women who join *Anti*-Suffrage Societies and under the cloak of such a membership go about propagating the very ideas they pretend to abhor!

MISS A: (*Incredulously.*) You can't possibly be serious!

MRS. C: (*Triumphantly.*) I thought I should startle you. My firm belief is that they're in the pay of the Suffragists.

MISS A: But how perfectly disgraceful! I hadn't the slightest idea that such a thing existed! Surely it can be stopped?

MRS. C: We hope so—we believe so. That is the object of the petition I'm asking you to sign. (*Draws paper from long envelope.*) We want some pronouncement from headquarters in London that will make treachery of this kind impossible.

MISS A: That's an excellent idea. I'll sign it with pleasure.

MRS. C: Thank you very much. And I hope you'll allow your servants to do the same?

MISS A: (*A little astonished.*) My servants?

MRS. C: Well it swells a list of signatures so beautifully—especially if a large staff is kept. Lady Carter's signed to the boot-boy!

MISS A: I'm afraid I don't keep a boot-boy and I have only two servants. I've really never asked them their views on the Suffrage.

MRS. C: Their views? I didn't ask my servants their views. I merely sent the petition to the kitchen for signatures. Nobody will think we're in earnest if we don't get plenty.

MISS A: Well to be quite frank with you, one rather hesitates—I mean it might be a little difficult for a servant to refuse her mistress, mightn't it?

MRS. C: Refuse? (*She is apparently about to go on, then looks at MISS APPLEYARD again and checks herself.*) Of, of course I don't press the point for a moment, Miss Appleyard. We shall be only too pleased if you will give us your own signature.

MISS A: May I have the petition? (*Takes paper from MRS. CRABTREE and goes to writing table, where she sits down, picks up a pen and examines it.*) I always write particularly badly when I inscribe my name on a public document. Do you want full Christian names? I'm afraid I've got four.

MRS. C: They would look imposing.

MISS A: (*Putting new nib in penholder and talking rather absently.*) As you say, treachery within the camp must be put down at any cost. One can hardly believe that women would stoop to it!

MRS. C: I'm surprised at nothing in connection with the Suffrage.

MISS A: I wonder if you're right in thinking that the Suffragists are responsible?

MRS. C: I'm convinced of it.

MISS A: (*Still manipulating penholder.*) Of course the quickest way to stop anything so flagrant would be to show it up in the papers. (*Draws petition towards her.*) If you'll give me a few particulars I don't in the least mind writing a letter to the *Spectator.*

MRS. C: Oh that would be splendid! There's every excuse for a woman to come out into the open in an exceptional case like this. Besides you could use a *nom de plume.*

MISS A: (*Rather surprised.*) I haven't the slightest objection to signing my name to any letter I write.

MRS. C: (*Hurriedly.*) Just as you like, of course. A name often does work wonders. I've got twenty-three to my petition already.

MISS A: (*Smiling.*) I'd better complete your second dozen before we discuss the matter further. (*Turns to petition again.*) After all, though one must make a stand against it, conduct of this sort is bound to defeat its own ends. Every decent-minded woman will turn from it in disgust.

MRS. C: (*Gloomily.*) How many decent-minded women will there be left in England if this Suffrage movement goes on?

MISS A: (*Laughing.*) Oh come, Mrs. Crabtree, we're not all going to bow the knee to Baal! I can't think that the Suffrage has made any open headway in Mudford and you must get this petition sent in in time to prevent any secret proselytizing.

MRS. C: (*Sighing significantly.*) Prevent? I wish we were in time for that!

MISS A: (*Sitting back in chair.*) You surely can't mean that there are any of these atrocious women among us?

MRS. C: I do, Miss Appleyard. I have only too good reason to believe that we are warming a viper in our bosoms!

MISS A: Tell me her name! Don't hesitate to mention a name in a case like this!

MRS. C: I don't know it yet unfortunately. I'm waiting to discover it before I denounce her openly.

MISS A: Nothing would give me greater pleasure than to help you!

MRS. C: I wonder if you could! Do you know anything of the streets behind the factory? (*Rises, and comes to writing table.*)

MISS A: What—Dale Street and Quebec Street do you mean?

MRS. C: Yes—with the little red houses where so many of the hands live.

MISS A: (*Excitedly.*) You don't mean to say she's dared to go there?

(Mrs. Crabtree *looks round, draws a little closer, and lowers her voice.*)

MRS. C: Miss Appleyard, I've just been told on excellent authority that a member of our own Anti-Suffrage Society was seen canvassing in Quebec Street and Dale Street this very morning!

(*There is a moment of absolute silence.* MISS APPLEYARD's *pen falls to the ground and she gazes at* MRS. CRABTREE *as if petrified.* MRS. C. *picks up pen, and gives it back to* MISS A. MISS A. *pulls herself together and ejaculates faintly.*)

MISS A: C-canvassing?

MRS. C: Dear Miss Appleyard, you evidently haven't grasped the brazen tactics of these women. They pretend to be Anti-Suffragists and they *canvass!*

MISS A: (*Much embarrassed.*) But surely I—they—

MRS. C: (*Excitedly.*) They subscribe—openly—to the tenet that woman is incapable of forming a political opinion, and they not only form one for themselves, but they go about trying to influence those of men!

MISS A: Yes, but you surely—

MRS. C: (*Working herself up and ignoring any interruption.*) They assert—with us—that woman's place is the home and spend long hours away from their own in the arena of politics!

MISS A: But do you seriously mean that an Anti-Suff—

MRS. C: (*Striking table with her hand.*) They profess to leave imperial matters to men with one hand and force their way into meetings at which such matters are discussed with the other!

MISS A: But is it possible that—

MRS. C: (*Still more heatedly.*) They proclaim that political activity tends to break up the harmony of the home and go straight out and address envelopes in Committee rooms by the hour! The insidiousness of it! Of course the ignorant women to whom they talk are drawn into politics in spite of themselves and the way is paved for the Suffragist who works openly! It's a far more dangerous crusade than the militant one, in my opinion, because it wears the guise of an angel of light!

MISS A: (*Faintly, as* MRS. CRABTREE *pauses for breath.*) I see what you mean, of course. But perhaps it hasn't occurred to them that they're doing—doing all you say!

MRS. C: (*With a snort.*) Don't tell me!

MISS A: Don't you think they might never have looked at it in that light?

MRS. C: (*A little impatiently.*) Oh my dear Miss Appleyard, one either is or isn't in favour of a thing. You can't do it in practice and denounce it in print, you know!

MISS A: I—I never thought of that. Of course it *is* inconsistent.

MRS. C: It's worse than inconsistent, to my mind. Personally I strongly disapprove of the way in which I'm sorry to say some of even the leaders of our party try to defend the municipal vote for women. I prefer to be honest and deplore the mistake which granted it to them.

MISS A: You don't think women should have the municipal vote?

MRS. C: Of course I don't! What is it but a smaller edition of the Parliamentary one? There's merely a difference of degree. The qualities that unfit a woman for one naturally unfit her for the other.

MISS. A: What qualities do you mean, exactly?

MRS. C: Why, Lord Cromer has told us. Hasty generalisation—vague and undisciplined sympathies—extreme sentimentality—I can't remember all he said, but it was in the papers. He said they were characteristic of the majority of the female sex.

MISS A: (*Grimly.*) Oh, did he?

MRS. C: Yes—at a meeting for men only, in Manchester.

MISS A: Perhaps it's as well that women weren't admitted.

MRS. C: Well, I believe there were a few on the platform, but I quite agree with you. I'm not at all in favour of women attending public meetings as a rule, though I *have* made an exception myself to hear Lord Cromer.

MISS A: Really?

MRS. C: He has such a marvellous grasp of this subject. There's Lord Curzon, too—of course you know his fifteen reasons against Women's Suffrage?

284 Literature of the Women's Suffrage Campaign in England

MISS A: No, I'm afraid I don't.

MRS. C: Oh, I must send them to you! I'm always meaning to learn them by heart. I know the first—(*shuts her eyes and repeats as from a lesson book*)— "Political activity will tend to take away woman from her proper sphere and highest duty, which is maternity."

MISS A: But we can't *all* be mothers.

MRS. C: Oh, he recognises that! Only no doubt he considers married women particularly because, as he says in a later reason, they, if any, are best qualified to exercise the vote.

MISS A: But I thought he said it would interfere with maternity?

MRS. C: So he did.

MISS A: Then how can he say that married women are best qualified to exercise it?

MRS. C: I don't altogether follow that myself, I admit. I'm content to leave it to a superior brain to my own.

MISS A: (*After a pause.*) And even in the case of mothers—of course I've never been in favour of their having votes, but supposing they *had*— would they be constantly engaged in political activity? Fathers aren't!

MRS. C: Men are political by nature—women are not. If women got votes they would have so much to learn that they'd never have time for anything else. (*Goes on as* MISS APPLEYARD *is evidently about to demur but thinks better of it.*) But you must read the reasons for yourself—that is if you think it advisable to go into the subject. They set forward so plainly the awful dangers of adding a host of unbalanced judgments to a logical male electorate.

MISS A: (*Dryly.*) I happened to be talking to one of the logical male electorate this morning. He's my chimney-sweep. He informed me that he was going to vote for Mr. Holland because his own wife is a Dutchwoman.

MRS. C: Really? Which is Mr. Holland?

MISS A: (*Curiously.*) Do you mean to say you didn't know that he was the Labour Candidate?

MRS. C: (*Indifferently.*) Oh, I must have seen the placards and heard people talking, of course. But I naturally don't take any interest in politics. I don't consider them to be a woman's concern.

MISS A: What do you consider to be a woman's concern?

MRS. C: (*Impressively.*) Her HOME! (*Crosses L, and sits on sofa.*)

MISS A: But—do excuse me—you're putting things in rather a new light to me. Don't vague sympathies and sentimentality and—what else did Lord Cromer say?—hasty generalisation?—matter in the home?

MRS. C: (*A little taken aback.*) Oh—er—well—of course it would be better *without* them, but as Lord Cromer says, most women *are* like that. I mustn't trespass longer on your time, Miss Appleyard. If I may have your signature I won't detain you any more.

MISS A: (*Taking up petition.*) I haven't really looked at the text of this—I'd only surmised it from what you told me. (*Scans paper in silence, then looks up.*) I see that it's a request to headquarters that some rule may be framed which shall debar any member of an Anti-Suffrage Society from canvassing.

MRS. C: We thought it better to confine ourselves to the canvassing to start with. Later we hope to attack more of these abominable tactics. (*A bell is heard outside.*)

MISS A: (*Folding up paper deliberately and handing it back.*) Well, Mrs. Crabtree, I may as well tell you quite frankly that you won't attack them through me. (*Rises.*)

MRS. C: (*In astonishment.*) Miss Appleyard—I don't understand you!

MISS A: I can't sign that paper.

MRS. C: May I ask why not? (*There is a tap at the door.*)

MISS A: Come in! (*Enter* MORTON.)

MORTON: Excuse my disturbing you a moment, please 'm.

MISS A: What is it, Morton? (*To* MRS. CRABTREE.) Excuse me, Mrs. Crabtree!

(MRS. CRABTREE *bows, and crosses over to R.*)

MORTON: (*at door—*MISS A. *goes up to her*) Miss Allbutt's called, 'm, and she won't come in, but she says could you kindly send word if it's ten or half-past that she's to go canvassing with you tomorrow.

(*There is a gasp from* MRS. CRABTREE *who stares at* MISS APPLEYARD *in absolute horror.* MISS APPLEYARD *after a moment's pause turns to* MORTON.)

MISS A: (*Firmly.*) Say ten o'clock, please.

MORTON: Yes 'm. (*Exit.*)

MISS A: I beg your pardon, Mrs. Crabtree. You were asking—

MRS. C: (*Very excitedly.*) I am answered, Miss Appleyard—I am answered! Little did I think when I denounced the women among us who are secretly undermining our influence that they had so far worked upon your feelings as to persuade you to join them!

MISS A: I really don't understand you. Nobody has worked on my feelings. I offered to help with canvassing this time as I did at the last Election. I was just going to tell you so when my maid came in.

MRS. C: (*Agitatedly.*) Then—then is it possible that you are the woman who was canvassing in Dale Street and Quebec Street this morning?

MISS A: (*Quietly.*) It's more than possible—it's a fact.

MRS. C: This—this is beyond everything! You consider yourself capable of forming a political opinion?

MISS A: Well—shall we say at least as capable as the gentleman whose going to vote for Mr. Holland because his own wife's a Dutchwoman!

MRS. C: (*Almost in a scream.*) You don't think that woman's place is the home?

MISS A: Place—certainly. Prison—no. You might as well say that a man's place is his office and blame him for coming home in an evening or taking an interest in his wife's duties or his children's lessons!

MRS. C: (*Solemnly and loudly.*) Man is Man and Woman is Woman!

MISS A: (*With a twinkle in her eye.*) Oh I'm quite prepared to concede that.

MRS. C: And conceding it, you actually think that a woman ought to meddle with politics?

MISS A: Meddle? How can any intelligent woman help taking an interest in the affairs of her country?

MRS. C: *Her* country? It's the country of the men who fight for it!

MISS A: You mean that only soldiers and sailors should be politicians?

MRS. C: This is ridiculous! It is only too easy to see what influences have been at work!

MISS A: (*Coldly.*) Would you kindly explain what you mean?

MRS. C: I mean that your line of reasoning is taken straight from the publications of the Suffrage Societies!

MISS A: The publications of the Suffrage Societies? I've never even seen any!

MRS. C: I cannot, of course, dispute your word. But Suffragists think that a woman should take what they call an intelligent interest in the affairs of her country! Suffragists maintain that a woman doesn't unsex herself by political activity. Suffragists declare that the average woman is as capable of forming an opinion in these matters as hundreds of the men voters of to-day!

MISS A: (*Defiantly.*) And so do I!

MRS. C: Then, Miss Appleyard, all I can ask is, what are you doing among *us*?

(*There is a silence.* MISS APPLEYARD, *after a moment's pause, turns down L below sofa, and is evidently nonplussed.* MRS. CRABTREE *prepares to leave and continues speaking.*)

I am glad that you see the absurdity of your position for yourself. It would be waste of time to argue further with you to-day, but I shall never rest until you are back within the true fold. (*Slowly and solemnly.*) I want every woman to be a perfect woman!

MISS A: (*Nettled.*) It seems to me that you want every woman to be a perfect fool!

MRS. C: (*After an indignant glance.*) Good afternoon, Miss Appleyard.

MISS A: (*Rings bell.*) Good afternoon, Mrs. Crabtree!

(*They bow stiffly. Exit* MRS. CRABTREE *with head in air.* MISS A. *stands in a listening attitude until an outer door bangs; then goes up to the door.*)

MISS A: (*Calls.*) Morton!

MORTON: I'm just bringing your tea 'm. (MORTON *enters with tea things on a tray, and puts on table, R.*)

MISS A: (*Coming down to table, R, and sitting.*) Morton, some papers came by post this morning—printed papers from a Suffrage Society. I put them in the waste-paper basket. I suppose they'll have been thrown away by now?

MORTON: No 'm, they've not. Cook and me have got them in the kitchen.

MISS A: I should rather like to have a look at them.

MORTON: I'll bring them, 'm. (*Hesitating.*) If you'll excuse my saying so, 'm. Cook and me think there's a deal of sound common-sense in this Suffrage business.

MISS A: (*Slowly.*) D'you know, Morton, I'm beginning to think it's quite possible that you may be right!

CURTAIN

NOTES

1 The colours of the Women's Social and Political Union were purple, white, and green.

2 "The Women's Marseillaise" was a marching song composed by F.E.M. Macaulay. The words are included in this book in the chapter on poetry and songs.

3 The Third Reform Act of 1884 enfranchised a majority of men. It excluded, among others, criminals and lunatics.

4 Heavily armed battleships.

5 George Curzon (1859-1925), a member of the Men's Committee for Opposing Female Suffrage, served in the House of Commons from 1886-98. He entered the House of Lords in 1908 where he led the Conservative Party from 1916-25.

6 A judge's private room or chamber.

7 The colours of the National Union of Women's Suffrage Societies were red and white. Green was added in 1909.

8 Literally "a place to stand on." It means the right to appear in court and argue a case. (Latin)

9 Mafeking night refers to a huge, boisterous celebration that took place on 18 May 1900 when England learned of the lifting of the siege of Mafeking, South Africa. During the Boer War, the British garrison there had been under siege for 217 days.

10 Dried leaves used medicinally as a cathartic.

11 *Punchinella* is a reference to a supposed female version of the publication *Punch*, which often satirized New Women and suffragettes.

12 Intellectual or scholarly women were called blue stockings. The term derived from the unconventional dress of members of a club in eighteenth-century London whose membership was predominately female.

13 In 1867 John Stuart Mill attempted to include a franchise for women in the Second Reform Act which gave the vote to almost all working men. His amendment was defeated.

14 In 1866 Mill and Henry Fawcett presented to the House of Commons a petition to extend the franchise to all male and female householders. It was signed by 1,499 women.

15 An exclusive private school for boys founded in 1567.

16 A two-wheeled, horse-drawn covered carriage.

17 The women who appear in the play are identified at the end of the play. The notes about the women were in the original publication.

18 Jeremiah 8:21-22: "For the heart of the daughter of my people am I hurt; I am black; astonishment hath taken hold of me. Is there no balm in Gilead; is there no physician there? Why then is not the health of the daughter of my people recovered?" (King James Version)

19 Political prisoners were placed in the first division in prison. These prisoners received better treatment than was given to criminals in the second or third divisions. Holloway was the prison in London to which many of the suffragette prisoners were sent.

20 A legal term for a judge's or court's private consideration of a case before giving judgment.

CHAPTER FIVE

SUFFRAGE FICTION

Suffrage fiction replicated the daily experiences of women involved in the campaign. It also dramatized defining events in their lives: their conversion to the suffrage cause, their participation in militant actions, their imprisonment and forcible feeding, and their solidarity with other women in prison and in marches. In many cases, real women and events, with slight modifications, were incorporated into the fiction. As was true of the women who worked for suffrage, the fictional women of suffrage literature varied greatly in their degree of commitment to the cause and in their willingness to participate in militancy. These women did not fit any stereotype and thus were not readily identifiable, hence the difficulty of anticipating and preventing their actions in public places.

Not all fiction dealing with women's suffrage supported it. Depending on the writer's point of view, the characterization of the heroines and depiction of their activities became propaganda for or against suffrage. The best-known antisuffrage novel is Mary (Mrs. Humphry) Ward's *Delia Blanchflower* (1914) which depicts suffragettes as man-hating viragoes. Delia, the eponymous heroine, rejects her suffrage friends with their violent ways in favour of marriage and domesticity by novel's end.

By jettisoning the obligatory marriage ending, prosuffrage fiction was able to portray a more complex view of women in the movement. Suffrage women's romantic interests were secondary to their political commitment. Male suitors were desirable candidates for marriage only if they embraced the suffrage cause or at least accepted their lovers' commitment to it. The fictional endings varied, but many were hopeful and even visionary, imagining a day when women would finally gain their political freedom by possessing the vote.

Fiction that focussed directly on suffrage had a brief existence; after women gained the vote such fiction was neglected and in many cases forgotten. Several factors may have contributed to this situation: the polemical nature of the fiction made it less engaging after women got the vote, World War I with its attendant horrors replaced suffrage in the country's consciousness, and modernism made the fiction's realism seem old-fashioned.

SHORT STORIES

Rebel Women by Evelyn Sharp is no doubt the finest collection of short stories written about the daily activities of ordinary suffragettes who, in their battle for the vote, willingly but uneasily place themselves before the public gaze. In so doing, they find themselves in situations ranging from the serious and frightening to the absurd and comic. By not naming her heroines and by depicting them as indistinguishable from ordinary women, Sharp turns them into universal figures who do not conform to the public's stereotyped perception of suffragettes. These women represent all suffragettes, most of whose names are not remembered but whose brave actions and years of devotion to the cause are memorialized in her stories. Sharp's "rebel women" are ordinary women transformed by their time and place into political rebels. Sharp herself was active in the suffrage movement and served time in prison for her activities.

Gertrude Colmore, best known for her novel *Suffragette Sally*, also wrote a group of suffrage stories that were first published in a variety of places and then collected as *Mr. Jones and the Governess and Other Stories*. "The Introduction," as did other suffrage stories, challenges the common perception that suffragettes are easily recognizable and romantically undesirable, while "The Magical Musician" contains a vision of the relationship between men and women as God intended it to be at the creation. William Leonard Courtney's "The Soul of a Suffragette" debates the justification for militant action and the usefulness of the sacrifice made by women who participate in violence.

Evelyn Sharp

"The Women at the Gate"

[*Rebel Women*, New York: John Lane Company, 1910, 7-19]

"Funny, isn't it?" said the young man on the top of the omnibus.

"No," said the young woman from whom he appeared to expect an answer, "I don't think it is funny."

"Take care," said the young man's friend, nudging him, "perhaps she's one of them!"

Everybody within hearing laughed, except the woman, who did not seem to be aware that they were talking about her. She was on her feet, steadying herself by grasping the back of the seat in front of her, and her eyes, non-committal in their lack of expression, were bent on the roaring, restless crowd that surged backwards and forwards in the Square below, where progress was gradually becoming an impossibility to the stream of traffic struggling towards Whitehall.[1] The thing she wanted to find was not down there, among the slipping horses, the swaying men and women, the moving policemen; not did it lurk in those denser blocks of humanity that marked a spot, here and there, where some resolute, battered woman was setting her face towards the gate of St. Stephen's;[2] nor was the thing she sought to be found behind that locked gate of liberty where those in possession, stronger far in the convention of centuries than locks or bars could make them, stood in their well-bred security, immeasurably shocked at the scene before them and most regrettably shaken, as some of them were heard to murmur, in a lifelong devotion to the women's cause.

The searching gaze of the woman on the omnibus wandered for an instant from all this, away to Westminster Bridge and the blue distance of Lambeth,[3] where darting lamps, like will-o'-the-wisps come to town, added a touch of magic relief to the dinginess of night. Then she came back again to the sharp realism of the foreground and found no will-o'-the-wisps there, only the lights of London shining on a picture she should remember to the end of her life. It did not matter, for the thing beyond it all that she wanted to be sure of, shone through rain and mud alike.

"Lookin' for a friend of yours, p'raps?" said a not unfriendly woman with a baby, who was also standing up to obtain a more comprehensive view of what was going on below.

"No," was the answer again, "I am looking at something that isn't exactly there; at least—"

"If I was you, miss," interrupted the facetious youth, with a wink at his companion, "I should chuck looking for what ain't there, and—"

She turned and smiled at him unexpectedly. "Perhaps you are right," she said. "And yet, if I didn't hope to find what isn't there, I couldn't go through with what I have to do to-night."

The amazed stare of the young man covered her, as she went swiftly down the steps of the omnibus and disappeared in the crowd.

"Balmy, the whole lot of 'em!" commented the conductor briefly.

The woman with the passionless eyes was threading her way through the straggling clusters of people that fringed the great crowd where it thinned out towards Broad Sanctuary.[4] A girl wearing the militant tricolour[5] in her hat, brushed against her, whispered, "Ten been taken, they say; they're knocking them about terribly to-night!" and passed noiselessly away. The first woman went on, as though she had not heard.

A roar of voices and a sudden sway of the throng that pinned her against some railings at the bottom of Victoria Street, announced the eleventh arrest. A friendly artisan in working clothes swung her up till she stood beside him on the stone coping, and told her to "ketch on." She caught on, and recovered her breath laboriously.

The woman, who had been arrested after being turned back from the doors of the House repeatedly for two successive hours, was swept past in the custody of an inspector, who had at last put a period to the mental and physical torment that a pickpocket would have been spared. A swirling mass of people, at once interested and puzzled, sympathetic and uncomprehending, was swept along with her and round her. In her eyes was the same unemotional, detached look that filled the gaze of the woman clinging to the railings. It was the only remarkable thing about her; otherwise, she was just an ordinary workaday woman, rather drab-looking, undistinguished by charm or attraction, as these things are generally understood.

"Now then, please, every one who wants a vote must keep clear of the traffic. Pass along the footway, ladies, if you please; there's no votes to be had in the middle of the roadway," said the jocular voice of the mounted constable, who was backing his horse gently and insistently into the pushing, struggling throng.

The jesting tone was an added humiliation; and women in the crowd, trying to see the last of their comrade and to let her know that they were near her then, were beaten back, hot with helpless anger. The mounted officer came relentlessly on, successfully sweeping the pavement clear of the people whom he was exhorting with so much official reasonableness not to invade the roadway. He paused once to salute and to avoid two men, who, having piloted a lady through the backwash of the torrent set in motion by the plunging horse, were now hoisting her into a place of safety just beyond the spot where the artisan and the other woman held on to the railings.

"Isn't it terrible to see women going on like this?" lamented the lady breathlessly. "And they say some of them are quite nice—like us, I mean."

The artisan, who, with his neighbour, had managed to evade the devastating advance of the mounted policeman, suddenly put his hand to his mouth and emitted a hoarse cheer.

"Bravo, little 'un!" he roared. "Stick to it! Votes for women, I say! Votes for women!"

The crowd, friendly to the point of admiring a struggle against fearful odds which they yet allowed to proceed without their help, took up the words with enthusiasm; and the mud-bespattered woman went away to the haven of the police station with her war-cry ringing in her ears.

The man who had led the cheer turned to the woman beside him, as though to justify his impulse. "It's their pluck," he said. "If the unemployed had half as much, they'd have knocked sense into this Government long ago!"

A couple of yards away, the lady was still lamenting what she saw in a plaintive and disturbed tone. Unconsciously, she was putting herself on the defensive.

"I shouldn't blame them," she maintained, "if they did something really violent, like—like throwing bombs and things. I could understand that. But all this—all this silly business of trying to get into the House of Commons, when they know beforehand that they can't possibly do it—oh, it's so sordid and loathsome! Did you see that woman's hair, and the way her hat was bashed in, and the mud on her nose? Ugh!"

"You can't have all the honour and glory of war, and expect to keep your hair tidy too," observed one of the men, slightly amused.

"War!" scoffed his wife. "There's none of the glory of war in this."

Her glance ranged, as the other woman's had done, over the dull black stream of humanity rolling by at her feet, over the wet and shining pavements, casting back their myriad distorted reflections in which street lamps looked like grinning figures of mockery—over the whole drear picture of London at its worst. She saw only what she saw, and she shuddered with distaste as another mounted officer came sidling through the crowd, pursuing another hunted rebel woman, who gave way only inch by inch, watching her opportunity to face once more towards the locked gate of liberty. Evidently, she had not yet given sufficient proof of her unalterable purpose to have earned the mercy of arrest; and a ring of compassionate men formed round her as a body-guard, to allow her a chance of collecting her forces. A reinforcement of mounted police at once bore down upon the danger spot, and by the time these had worked slowly through the throng, the woman and her supporters had gone, and a new crowd had taken the place of the former one.

"Oh, there's none of the glory of war in that!" cried the woman again, a tremble in her voice.

"There is never any glory in war—at least, not where the war is," said her second companion, speaking for the first time. His voice travelled to the ear of the other woman, still clinging to the railings with the artisan. She glanced round at him swiftly, and as swiftly let him see that she did not mean to be recognized; and he went on talking as if he had not seen her turn round.

"This is the kind of thing you get on a bigger scale in war," he said, in a half-jesting tone, as if ashamed of seeming serious. "Same mud and slush, same grit, same cowardice, same stupidity and beastliness all round. The women here are fighting for something big; that's the only difference. Oh, there's another, of course; they're taking all the kicks themselves and giving none of 'em back. I suppose it has to be that way round when you're fighting for your souls and not for your bodies."

"I didn't know you felt like that about it," said the woman, staring at him curiously. "Oh, but of course you can't mean that real war is anything like this wretched scuffle of women and police!"

"Oh, yes," returned the other, in the same tone of gentle raillery. "Don't you remember Monsieur Bergeret?[6] He was perfectly right. There is no separate art of war, because in war you merely practise the arts of peace rather badly, such as baking and washing, and cooking and digging, and travelling about. On the spot it is a wretched scuffle; and the side that wins is the side that succeeds in making the other side believe it to be invincible. When the women can do that, they've won."

"They don't look like doing it to-night, do they?" said the woman's husband breezily. "Thirteen women and six thousand police, you know!"

"Exactly. That proves it," retorted the man, who had fought in real wars. "They wouldn't bring out six thousand police to arrest thirteen men, even if they all threw bombs, as your wife here would like to see."

"The police are not there only to arrest the women—"

"That's the whole point," was the prompt reply. "You've got to smash an idea as well as an army in every war, still more in every revolution, which is always fought exclusively round an idea. If thirteen women batter at the gates of the House of Commons, you don't smash the idea by arresting the thirteen women, which could be done in five minutes. So you bring out six thousand police to see if that will do it. That is what lies behind the mud and the slush—the idea you can't smash."

A man reeled along the pavement and lurched up against them.

"Women in trousers! What's the country coming to?" he babbled; and bystanders laughed hysterically.

"Come along; let's get out of this," said the woman's husband hurriedly; and the trio went off in the direction of the hotel.

The woman with the passionless eyes looked after them. "He sees what we see," she murmured.

"Seems he's been in the army, active service, too," remarked the artisan in a sociable manner. "I like the way he conversed, myself."

"He understands, that is all," explained his companion. "He sees what it all means—all this, I mean, that the ordinary person calls a failure because we don't succeed in getting into the House. Do you remember, in 'Agamemnon'—have you read 'Agamemnon'?"[7]

It did not strike her as strange that she should be clasping iron railings in Westminster, late on a wet evening, talking to a working-man about Greek tragedy. The new world she was treading to-night, in which things that mattered were given their true proportions, and important scruples of a lifetime dwindled to nothingness, gave her a fresh and a whimsical insight into everything that happened; and the odd companion that chance had flung her, half an hour ago, became quite easily the friend she wanted at the most friendless moment she had ever known.

The man, without sharing her reasons for a display of unusual perception, seemed equally unaware of any strangeness in the situation.

"No, miss, I haven't read it," he answered. "That's Greek mythology, isn't it? I never learnt to speak Greek."

"Nor I," she told him; "but you can get it translated into English prose. It reminds me always of our demonstrations in Parliament Square, because there is a chorus in it of stupid old men, councillors, they are, I think, who never understand what is going on, however plainly it is put to them. When Cassandra prophesies that Agamemnon is going to be murdered—as we warn the Prime Minister when we are coming to see him—they pretend not to see what she is driving at, because if they did, they would have to do something. And then, when her prophecy comes true and he is murdered—of course, the analogy ends here, because we are not out to murder anybody, only to make the Prime Minister hear our demands—they run about wringing their hands and complaining; but nobody does anything to stop it. It really is rather like the evasions of the Home Office when people ask questions in Parliament about the prison treatment of the Suffragettes, isn't it?"

"Seems so," agreed her new friend, affably.

"And then," continued the woman, scorn rising in her voice "when Clytaemnestra comes out of the house and explains why she has murdered her husband, they find plenty to say because there is a woman to be blamed, though they never blamed Agamemnon for doing far worse things to her. That is the way the magistrate and the daily papers will talk to-morrow, when our women are brought up in the police court."

"That's it! Always put all the blame on the women," said the artisan, grasping what he could of her strange discourse.

Big Ben tolled out ten strokes, and his companion, catching her breath, looked with sudden apprehension at the moving, throbbing block of people, now grown so immense that the police, giving up the attempt to keep the road clear, were merely concerned in driving back the throng on four sides and preserving an open space round the cluster of buildings known to a liberty-loving nation as the People's House. The gentlemen, who still stood in interested groups behind the barred gates of it, found the prospect less entertaining now that the action had been removed beyond the range of easy vision; and some of the bolder ones ventured out into the hollow square, formed by an unbroken line of constables, who were standing shoulder to shoulder, backed by mounted men who made little raids from time to time on the crowd behind, now fast becoming a very ugly one. Every possible precaution was being taken to avoid the chance of annoyance to any one who might still wish to preserve a decorous faith in the principle of women's liberty.

Meanwhile, somewhere in that shouting, hustling, surging mass of humanity, as the woman onlooker knew full well, was the twelfth member of the women's deputation that had been broken up by the police, two hours ago, before it could reach the doors of the House; and knowing that her turn had come now, she pictured that twelfth woman beating against a barrier that had been set up against them both ever since the world grew civilized. There was not a friend near, when she nodded to the artisan and slipped down from her temporary resting-place. The respectable and sympathetic portion of the crowd was cut off from her, away up towards Whitehall, whither it had followed the twelfth woman. On this side of Parliament Square all the idlers, all the coarse-tongued reprobates of the slums of Westminster, never far distant from any London crowd, were herded together in a stupid, pitiless, ignorant mob. The slough of mud underfoot added the last sickening touch to a scene that for the flash of an instant made her heart fail.

"St. James's Park is the nearest station, miss," said the man, giving her a helping hand. "Don't advise you to try the Bridge; might find it a bit rough getting across."

She smiled back at him from the kerbstone, where she stood hovering a second or two on the fringe of the tumult and confusion. Her moment's hesitation was gone, and the sure look had come back to her eyes.

"I am not going home," she told him. "I am the thirteenth woman,[8] you see."

She left the artisan staring at the spot near the edge of the pavement where the crowd had opened and swallowed her up.

"And she so well-informed too!" he murmured. "I don't like to think of it—I don't like to think of it!"

Shortly after midnight two men paused, talking, under the shadow of Westminster Abbey, and watched a patrol of mounted police that ambled at a leisurely pace across the deserted Square. The light in the Clock Tower was out. Thirteen women, granted a few hours' freedom in return for a word of honour, had gone to their homes, proudly conscious of having once more vindicated the invincibility of their cause; and some five or six hundred gentlemen had been able to issue in safety from the stronghold of liberty, which they had once more proved to themselves to be impregnable. And on the morrow the prisoners of war would again pay the price of the victory that both sides thought they had won.

"If that is like real war too," said one of the men to the other, who had just made these observations aloud, "how does anybody ever know which side has won?"

"By looking to see which side pays the price of victory," answered the man who had fought in real wars.

EVELYN SHARP

"SHAKING HANDS WITH THE MIDDLE AGES"

[*Rebel Women*, New York: John Lane Company, 1910, 27-40]

"Going to be a good meeting, don't you think?" chatted one of the men wearing a steward's button to a woman dressed in black, who sat in the front row of the little block of seats reserved for ladies, just below the platform.

She gave an indifferent glance round the hall.

"Yes," she acquiesced; "I suppose it is. I've never been to a political meeting before."

"Really?" said the steward blandly. "Quite an experience for you, then, with a Cabinet Minister coming!"

He hurried away, unaware of the touch of condescension that had jarred indescribably, and spoke in an eager undertone to a large stout gentleman who was inspecting tickets at the ladies' entrance.

"It's all right," he said officiously. "I've just been talking to her. She isn't one of them."

The stout gentleman looked over his shoulder. "Who? That one next my wife? Oh, no! She's not their sort. Besides, they all wear green or purple, or both. I'm up to their dodges by this time—just had to turn away quite a nice little girl in a green hat—"

"My sister!" observed the other. "Oh, it don't matter; I let her in by the side door, and it won't do her any harm. They've got so out of hand, some of these canvassers, since the general election."

The large steward observed with an indulgent smile that one must make allowances. He did not say for what or for whom, but his meaning seemed to be clear to the other steward.

"The eternal feminine, eh?" he remarked with a knowing nod; and all the men standing round laughed immoderately. Under cover of this exhibition of humour, a girl in grey, with a fur cap and muff, was allowed to pass in without any special scrutiny. She moved deliberately along the front chairs, which were now filled, stood for an instant facing the audience while she selected her seat, then made her way to one in the middle of a row.

"Votes for women!" piped a wit in the gallery, reproducing the popular impression of the feminine voice; and the audience, strung up to the point of snatching at any outlet for emotion, rocked with mirth.

The girl in grey joined in the laughter. "Every one seems very jumpy tonight," she observed to her neighbour, a lady in tight black satin who wore the badge of some Women's Federation.[9] "I was actually taken for a Suffragette in the market-place just now."

"Were you, now?" returned the lady, sociably. "No wonder they're a trifle apprehensive after the way those dreadful creatures went on at the Corn Exchange, last week. You were there, perhaps?"

The girl in grey said she was there, and the Federation woman proceeded to converse genially. "Thought I'd seen your face somewhere," she said. "A splendid gathering, that would have been a glorious triumph for the Party, if it hadn't been for those—" She paused for a word, and found it with satisfaction—"females. Females," she repeated distinctly. "You really can't call them anything else."

"I suppose you can't," said the girl demurely. The sparkle lit up her eyes again. "Our minister called them bipeds, in the pulpit, last Sunday," she added.

"And so they are!" cried the lady in tight black satin. "So they are."

"They are," agreed the girl in grey.

In the front row of chairs, speculation was rife as to the possible presence of Suffragettes. The wife of the man at the door, a homely little woman with a pleasant face, was assuring everybody who cared to know that the thing was impossible.

"They've drafted five hundred police into the town, I'm told; and my husband arranged for thirty extra stewards at the last minute, because the detectives wired that two of them had travelled down in the London train," she informed a circle of interested listeners.

"Is that why there are so many men wearing little buttons?" asked the woman on her left. "I wondered if that was usual at political meetings."

"I think I heard you say you'd never been to a meeting before, didn't I?" said her neighbour pleasantly. "Neither have I, and I wouldn't be wasting my time here to-night if it wasn't to please my husband. He likes to see women take an interest in politics; it was him that got our member a hundred and twenty-eight canvassers, last election. Oh, he thinks a lot of women, does my husband; says he hasn't any objection to their having a vote, either, only they ought to be ashamed of themselves for going on so about it. I don't hold with votes myself. It's only men that's got all that idle time on their hands, and if they're respectable married men, there's nothing else to occupy them but politics. But for a woman it's work, work, work, from her wedding-day till her funeral, and how can she find time for such nonsense? 'You've got to be made to think, Martha,' he says to me, coming here to-night. Think? If a woman stops to think, she don't stop with her husband, chances are. Of course, he don't believe me when I say that. He's too sure of me, that's where it is."

"That is always where it is," said the women in black, quietly.

Her neighbour took out some knitting. "They laugh at me for bringing my knitting everywhere," she said. "I can't listen if I sit idle. Not that I want to listen," she concluded, as she settled down comfortably to the counting of stitches.

The organ boomed out a jerky tune with elephantine lightness, and the audience vented its impatience in a lusty rendering of some song about England and liberty. The music was uninspiring, the words were clap-trap, and seemed to convey the singular idea that freedom had been invented and patented within recent years by a particular political party; but the indifferent expression of the woman in black changed and softened as the chorus rose and fell, and a tall man with a lean, humorous face, who stood looking at her, gave her a smile of understanding as the echoing sounds died away. He too was wearing a steward's button, she noticed.

"There's a sort of barbaric splendour about that, isn't there?" he remarked.

She felt none of the irritation that had been roused by the conversational advances of the other steward. It was a relief, indeed, to talk about something ordinary with a man who, she felt instinctively, knew how to give even ordinary things their true values.

"It's the whole effect," she answered impulsively. "The cathedral outside, and this thirteenth-century interior, and then—this!" She looked round the magnificent old County Hall, and along the densely packed rows of restless modern men and women, and then back again, half whimsically, at the man who had spoken to her. "It is like reaching back to shake hands with the Middle Ages," she said.

"To fight with the Middle Ages," he amended, and they both laughed. "You will find," he added, narrowing his eyes a little to look at her, "that the Middle Ages generally win, when we hold political meetings here in the provinces."

There was a distant sound of cheering, and every one stiffened into attention. A stir ran round the hall; doors were closed with a good deal of noise, and the stewards, looking apprehensively at the little block of seats in the front, gradually closed round them until the gangways were entirely blocked at that end of the hall. One lady, who complained that she could not see the platform for stewards, instantly found herself placed under observation, and was only freed from suspicion when one of the gentlemen identified her as his aunt and pledged his word that she did not want a Parliamentary vote. Her neighbours congratulated her, but in accents that betrayed disappointment.

The stir was followed by an expectant hush. The tall man looked steadily at the fingers of the woman in black, which locked and unlocked ceaselessly, though she leaned back in her chair with a vast assumption of unconcern. Those tireless, nervous hands told him what he wanted to know.

The little officious steward was back at his side, whispering in his ear. He shook his head impatiently in reply.

"I'm not going to stay," he said shortly. "You've got enough without me, even to deal with two Suffragettes who may not be here; and—well, it's a sickening business, and I'd sooner be out of it."

He went, and all that was of her world seemed to the woman in black to go with him, as she looked after him, half disappointed, half contemptuous. Up to this point, the Middle Ages were certainly winning, she decided.

The next quarter of an hour was the longest she had ever lived through. Afterwards, looking back, she remembered every detail of what took place, all the impressiveness of it, all the ironic absurdity. At the time, it felt like holding one's breath for interminable minutes while unfamiliar things went on somewhere in the thick of a mist, as things happen in a bad dream that just escapes the final incoherence of a nightmare.

There was the roar that broke through the mist in a huge wave of sound, when the speakers walked on to the platform. Looking round at that swaying, white-faced multitude, mad with a hero-worship that lost not a jot of its attraction in her eyes because for her there was no hero, the woman in the front row, who had never been to a political meeting before, felt a moment's amazement at her own temerity in coming there, alone with one other, to defy an enthusiasm that had all the appearance of invincibility. Then the mist began to roll away, as somebody started the usual popular chorus. Translated in terms of jolly good-fellowship, hero-worship no longer appeared unconquerable.

To the woman in black it seemed as though a thousand chairs scraped, a thousand throats grated while the audience settled down, and the chairman delivered carefully prepared compliments, and the great man sorted slips of paper. Then two women out of the hundred or so who had been admitted because they did not appear to want the historic liberties they came to applaud, clenched lips and hands as the roar burst out once more.

The great man was on his feet, facing it with a gratified smile. To one at least of his audience that smile restored a courage that was in full flight the minute before. That he should strike so egregiously the wrong note, that a fine situation should be met with affability, argued something wrong with the situation or something wrong with the man. There was a false note, too, in that second roar, and it stopped so unexpectedly that one man was left cheering alone in a high, falsetto voice, provocative of instant derision. The fineness had gone out of the situation, and the immediate future of the woman in black, full as it was of unfamiliar fears, came back into some sort of a line with the present.

The absolute silence that greeted the opening period of the ministerial oration had something abnormal in it. It was a silence that almost hurt. The smallest movement put stewards on the alert, made heads go round. The speaker felt the strain, shuffled his notes, stumbled once or twice. Yet, as the tension tightened to breaking-point, the woman in the front row knew the grip over her own nerves to be strengthening by minutes. In the mental commotion around her, she felt the battle already half won that she had come to fight.

A man's voice, challenging a fact, caused a sensation of relief out of all proportion to the slightness of the interruption. Some wag said amiably, "Turn him out!" and there was laughter. The man, a well-known local Socialist, repeated his objection, and was supported this time by several other voices. There was quite a little stir, and the great man put out his hand benevolently.

"No, no, gentlemen, let him stay!" he adjured the stewards, none of whom had shown one sign of wishing to do otherwise. "I stand here as the champion of free speech—"

The rest of his sentence was drowned in a spontaneous outburst of applause, during which it was to be supposed that he dealt with the objection that had been raised, for when his words again became audible he had gone on to another point. His next interrupter was a Tariff Reformer, at whose expense he was courteously humorous. The emotional audience rewarded him with appreciative laughter, in which the Tariff Reformer joined good-humouredly. Speaker and listeners were rapidly coming into touch with one another.

The great man, growing sure of his ground, made an eloquent appeal to the records of the past. The woman, who had never heard a politician speak before, leaned forward, hanging on every word. She felt strangely elated, strangely sure of herself, now. This man, believing all that about liberty, seeing all that behind the commonplace of democracy, should surely understand where others had failed even to tolerate. She felt disproportionately irritated by the click of knitting-needles, wondering how any woman could occupy mind and fingers with wool while eternal principles of justice were being thundered over her head. Then there came a pause in the thunder; and sight and sound were blotted out as she took the opportunity, rose to her feet, and stared up blindly at the spot where she knew the speaker to be standing.

"Then give all that to the women," she said, in a voice she never seemed to have heard before. "If you think so much of justice and freedom for men, don't keep it any longer from the women."

For a little space of time, a couple of seconds, probably, her eyes went on seeing nothing, and her ears drummed. She thought she had never known what it really meant to be alone until that moment. She was a woman who had known loneliness very early, when it came to her in an uncongenial nursery; she knew it still, in some houses, where everything was wrong, from the wall-papers to the people. But the meaning of utter isolation she had never learnt until that moment when clamour and confusion reigned around her and she saw and heard none of it.

Then her senses were invaded by the sound and the look of it all; and to her own perplexity she found herself on the point of smiling.

She thought of a hundred things, many of them irrelevant, as she tried in vain to walk to the door, and was obstructed at every step by stewards, who fought to get hold of some part of her in their curious method of restoring order and decorum. She wondered why the meeting was interrupting itself with such complete success, because one woman had made the mistake of thinking that the hero they had welcomed with bad music was a man who meant what he said. She thought of plays she had seen, dealing with the French Revolution, very bad plays most of them, she reminded herself as she was dragged this way and that by excited gentlemen, divided in opinion as to the door by which she was to be ejected. The sea of distorted faces past which they took her, the memory of the knitting-needles, even the intolerable smile of the great man as he made little jokes about her for the amusement of the platform—all this was very suggestive of the French Revolution, as portrayed in a badly written play. In all the plays she had seen, however, she did not remember that there had ever been women who cried a little, or men who sat silent and ashamed, yet not sufficiently ashamed to put a stop to what was going on. These two things appeared to be really happening, here and there among the audience; and she supposed this was why they hurt the most.

She thought of the fastidiousness that made her a jest of her friends, as she felt her hat knocked sideways, looked down and saw the lace at her wrists dangling in rags. The blow that some one aimed at her, as she was dragged unresisting by, seemed a little thing in comparison with those torn strips of lace. Apparently, she was not alone in this eccentric adjustment of proportions; for the little fussy steward who, unbalanced to the point of irresponsibility, had struck the blow, was apologizing clumsily the next minute for treading on her skirt. He did not seem to understand when she told him gently that he was the man who had boasted of protecting women since the world began.

Sky and stars looked very remote when at last by circuitous ways they brought her to a door and thrust her out into the night. A final push from the gentleman who liked to see women take an interest in politics, sent her stumbling down stone steps into a moonlit market-place. Everything looked very big, very still, out there, after the banality and the bad staging of the play from which she had just made her unrehearsed exit. In the clearness of thought that came to her, freed at last of hands that dragged at her and voices that coarsened to say things to her that she only now dimly began to comprehend, she knew what it was that had made women, ordinary quiet women like herself, into rebels who were out to fight for the right to protect themselves even against their protectors.

A cheer greeted her from the farther side of the market-place, where the police kept back a crowd that had waited all the evening to see the two Suffragettes from London, and not, as the local paper afterwards somewhat flamboyantly put it, to "worship from afar the apostle of progress and democracy, almost as the servants of the gods might wait at Olympic banquets for crumbs to fall from the rich man's table." It was a friendly cheer, she noticed, though this did not matter much. Nothing seemed to matter much, just then, except that the black mass of the cathedral towered overhead and looked unshakable.

A little altercation floated down to her from the top of the steps, as she leaned motionless against the worn stones of the old balustrade.

"Martha! You of all people! Disgracing me like that! However did you come to be mistaken for one of those screaming—?"

"Well, I couldn't stand the humbug of it, there! Talking about free speech and all that fal-lal nonsense, and then—! I wouldn't let my cat be treated as they treated her, all for nothing—"

"Nothing, do you call it? Coming here on purpose to interrupt—"

"So did that ranting Socialist you think so much of! So did Mr. What's-his-name with the husky voice. Why didn't they tear *them* to pieces? Now, you listen to me, James. You brought me here to-night because you said I'd got to be made to think. Very well. I've been made. If you don't like it, you should ha' let me stay at home, as I wanted to."

She stuffed a mass of dropped stitches into a torn work-bag, and went down the steps, her chin in the air. "If that's politics," she called back to him from the pavement, "then it's time women got the vote, if it's only to put a stop to them!"

The girl in grey came round the corner of the building and joined her comrade, who still waited in the shadow cast by the cathedral. Her muff was gone, her cap lopped over one eye, and she held her hand to her throat where the collar had been wrenched at; but her eyes shone with their unalterable courage and spirit. She knew better than any one that every skirmish in the battle they were out to fight was always won before a single blow was struck.

"All right, are you? You did splendidly, for a first shot! Come along to the Martyrs' Cross; the police say we may hold a meeting there. Oh, I know you never have, but you can come and try. Any *idiot* can speak after being chucked out of a Cabinet Minister's meeting!"

Encouraged by this quaint process of exhaustion to regard herself as an orator, the woman who had never been to a political meeting till she went to be thrown out of one, walked across the market-place to shake hands with the Middle Ages on a spot where men and women were made to die, centuries ago, for having been born too soon.

She found the girl in grey cheerfully assuring an interested crowd that she stood there as the champion of free speech.

GERTRUDE COLMORE

"THE INTRODUCTION"

[*Mr. Jones and the Governess and Other Stories*,
London: The Women's Freedom League, (1913), 62-67]

He stood on Mrs. Fairfield's lawn and looked about him.

He was rather florid, with a tall, well set-up figure and a superior carriage. His hair was fair and inclined to curl, his eyes were blue—a light blue; his nose was prominent, his mouth a trifle coarse. Men said he was manly; women—some women—said he was masterful; others described him as masculine. The women who called him masterful admired him; those who called him masculine, didn't.

He was a well-known and rather important person in the neighbourhood, and was generally supposed to have a future. He was a young Liberal; spoke at local meetings, and acted as steward at gatherings addressed by Cabinet Ministers. He had a comfortable income, was unmarried, and knew that he could marry any day he pleased.

He stood and looked about him. There were girls he knew—many; and girls he didn't know—a few. There was one unknown to him whom he thought he would like to include in his acquaintance. He strolled over to his hostess.

"Will you be so kind as to introduce me—over there—the girl in blue, with her arm in a sling?"

"Oh certainly, of course; but I don't know—that er—well, that she's altogether your style."

He smiled. "She's a style I like the look of anyhow. May I persist?"

"Delighted, of course. Will you come now?"

He followed his hostess across the lawn. The girl in blue was talking to another girl; very earnestly. "About clothes, of course," he said to himself.

It was usually considered rather a feather in a girl's cap if he asked to be introduced to her; this girl hardly seemed properly to appreciate the feather; she looked almost vexed at the interruption to her conversation.

"Miss Laurie, Mr. Brewster wishes to be introduced to you. Mr. Brewster—Miss Laurie"; and the hostess moved away.

The girl half-turned in her chair and bowed; then a sudden alertness came into her eyes and face, and she stood up. She stood up and, standing, looked intently at the man before her.

"I'm afraid I interrupt," he began. "I asked Miss Fairfield to introduce me—"

"It was unnecessary. We have met before."

He smiled; it was not the first time that he had been remembered by girls he had forgotten. "You have the advantage of me."

"I almost think I have," she answered, slowly.

"May I ask—er—where—?"

"At the Liberal meeting at Torchester."

"When Mr. FitzJames was speaking?"

"Precisely."

"Ah, yes, I was one of the stewards."

"I know you were."

"Ah, I see; that is how—. It is kind of you to remember me."

"Not kind; I could hardly fail to remember."

She was really rather queer. He was used to being flattered, made much of, but in a flirtation he was accustomed to take the lead. He would give her a slight set-back, make the conversation less personal. "We had a bit of a row that night," he said. "Were you there all the time?"

"Not quite. I left before the end."

"Perhaps you were so fortunate as to avoid it, then?"

"Do you mean when the stewards went for the woman who asked questions? No, I was there."

"They were outrageous, were they not?"

"The stewards?"

"No, the women—if you call them women—hysterical, struggling—"

"They were one to six, you see; and the stewards were like wild beasts."

"You can't judge. To you, looking on, perhaps—"

"I was not looking on."

"Then—"

"You broke my arm," she said.

"I—I—I don't remember," was all he found to say.

"No, I know you don't. You remember nothing of what you did, or said, or looked like. You were so carried away, you and your fellows, by hysterical fury, that you had no idea what you were doing. You were madmen—without a keeper."

"I—I'm sure I—are you sure? I can't believe that—the arm—. Are you sure?" he stammered.

"Quite sure." She turned and walked away, but, having gone a yard or two, half-turned again and looked back at him; on her face was a half-smile. "You see," she said, "it was *my* arm."

GERTRUDE COLMORE

"THE MAGICAL MUSICIAN"

[*Mr. Jones and the Governess and Other Stories,*
London: The Women's Freedom League, (1913), 55-61]

He came in amongst the crowd almost unperceived; and, indeed, there was but little to distinguish him from the bulk of the people, gathered in mass together.

Some there were to whom he was utterly unlike—rich, well-dressed, well-nurtured, and well-bred; others, neat and clean, in their best clothes and their best manners; but many were ragged as he was, ill-kept, with worn, unlovely faces. He was in no way different from these, with his mottled skin and sodden features; in no way different, save that he carried a fiddle-case under his arm, and that his eyes were dreamy.

All over the splendid park and gardens the people streamed and were encouraged to stream; and there were refreshments, and games, and a band that played from time to time, and speeches. It was a great political gathering, and the people for miles around were to be instructed and entertained.

Fed and pleased, with some of the rich man's luxuries and a peep at his privacy vouchsafed to them, by-and-by they were gathered round platforms, from which, at intervals, speeches were to be delivered; speeches short and simple, according to the intentions of the organisers, and according to the ideas of the speakers, and not very brief and not very easy to follow to most of those who listened. They listened at first, then their thoughts and their eyes wandered, and the tongues of those not close to the platform began to wag in whispers; many on the fringe of the audience stole away, back to the refreshments.

But presently there was a rush of returning, for the Great Man was to speak, the Cabinet Minister. He would be different, surely, from other men; though the gaping crowd did not define their expectations, they looked for a more compelling personality, a greater power of speech.

He was there, on his feet, the Great Man, with a row of supporters on either side, and he hummed a little and hawed a little, and settled himself into the stride of his periods. He spoke of liberty; for all; even the poorest in that favoured land of England was to be endowed to the uttermost with political privilege.

"And what of the women?"

The crowd was no longer stolid; the sporting instinct was aroused. Of far greater interest than the Great Man, of real, living interest, was the Interrupting Woman. It was as exciting as a fox or an otter hunt to see her disposed of. No fear now of success of the meeting; the crowd was all agog, for at any moment another woman might offer herself to the fury of the stewards, to the sport of the spectators.

Another did, and another yet.

The Great Man was flustered; he stumbled in his speech, even when the woman—the third—had been swept quite away; lost the thread of his thoughts, hesitated, paused.

There was hardly silence. As his voice stopped, a thin, clear note slid out and held and embraced the stillness. At the back of the platform stood the man with the sodden face and the ragged clothes and the fiddle-case. The case lay at his feet and the fiddle rested near his heart, and the dreamy eyes were alight.

He played; a music strange and very sweet, that carried no tune known to any there, but breathed a spell on all who heard; a music of magic. It was a magic that opened inner eyes, and for a space the crowd, as they listened, saw.

Dim and hazy, far back it lay, and far back into it they were borne, to the Garden of God. In that Garden they saw man in the abstract, as God meant him in perfection to be; and beside him, neither beneath nor above, but on his level, woman; differing the two in their bodies, physical, emotional and mental, but in harmony; companions, lovers, friends.

Moans came into the music, and the people saw darkness and sorrow; women made slaves and toys and prostitutes, women grown vain and foolish and afraid.

The measure of the music changed. It was a march that was played, and the air of it might be known to those who had Irish blood in them. And the crowd, listening, saw the roll of the ages, and through the ages women marching, hand in hand. A few there were at first, and often with broken ranks; then, as the time drew later, more and more. Away in the far past, some could see their faces, but ever, as age followed age, the faces grew clearer, till, in the days that are now, the faces were fully seen. The magic of the music made those faces plain, and in the marvel of them showed a meaning. Pale they were, most of them, and many worn and drawn, but on every one was a smile; not akin to laughter, not of the lips, but lifting the whole countenance, a radiance; and in the eyes of all a light of courage and hope and the splendour of victory.

Past they went, and past, and amongst them were three faces recently seen; not agonised now, nor torn and bruised, but rapt like the other faces, beyond fear. On and on; you could almost hear their footsteps; and in a strange silent way they seemed to sing with the magic music of the magical musician.

The bow is still and the music stops, and the people on the platform and the crowd about it are astir.

How did he get here? What negligence on the part of somebody! He must be drunk. Hustle him away!

So he goes, the magical musician, his eyes no more alight, but only dreamy.

The stewards are alert; the supporters of the party gather together; the Great Man continues his speech. Gross darkness is again upon the people.

Yet for a little while they saw; for a very little while some of them understood.

W.L. [WILLIAM LEONARD] COURTNEY

"THE SOUL OF A SUFFRAGETTE"

[*The Soul of a Suffragette and Other Stories*,
London: Chapman and Hall, 1913, 3-44]

She was just Una Blockley—a militant suffragette. As she stood up in the
Court to receive her sentence in the midst of an unfriendly crowd, an
unfriendly bar, and a judge who only just succeeded in tempering his
unfriendliness by a strict sense of justice, she looked a poor thing enough,
perhaps at most thirty years of age, rather thin and meagre, with a wistful
prettiness of her own and the blue eyes of an idealist, chin and nose equally
obtrusive, and rather fine and expressive hands. She has said very little in the
course of her trial, for, indeed, what was there to say? The evidence against
her was overwhelming. She had been taken red-handed in the act of throwing a bomb through the window of a Cabinet Minister's house, whereby she
had grievously endangered the lives of a caretaker and his wife, living in the
basement (the Cabinet Minister being away from London), together with two
cats and a canary. It was not much of a bomb and it made an ineffective sort
of explosion. No one was killed; but that was not the fault of Una Blockley,
who, for aught she knew to the contrary, might have brought the existence of
the Cabinet Minister's caretaker to a summary end. A mad, reckless, diaboli-
cal act—so it was argued by the prosecution and echoed by the judge—of
which only a Mænad[10] could have been capable. Suffragettes of this criminal
militancy must be taught what such awful disregard of laws human and divine
really meant. They must be dealt with like anarchists and enemies of the
human race. And so to the prisoner, who stood with lips tightly closed, blue
eyes wide open and staring, and clasped hands—expressive hands, as has
been already said, which could not help but tremble—came the sentence of
the Court, delivered in icy tones by the offended majesty of the Law. Two
years' imprisonment with hard labour. Something between a gasp and a cry,
succeeded by a faint suggestion of applause, and then Una Blockley disappeared from the view of the spectators to endure the sentence which, according to general opinion, she had so richly deserved.

* * * * *

It had come at last—the martyrdom of which Una Blockley had dreamed, and
towards which she had aspired through many anxious months. She had long

ago felt the call, ever since, as a matter of fact, she had listened to a woman with a quiet, patient face and grey hair, who had explained to her and many others of her sex in Hyde Park what was the imperative duty resting on womanhood. All the conditions of the time, she heard, were wrong, and unjust to women—the social conditions, the political conditions, the economic conditions, to say nothing of the legal enactments which man had made in his own behoof and without any thought of the partners who were joined to him by such inequitable bonds. How came it that women's work was paid so badly? How was it that woman was defrauded of the proper reward of her toil? Not because she was inefficient, not because her work was not as good as any other's, but because there were so many women, and women's work was a drug in the market. And this, too, she understood in some dim fashion, was the fault of man, who, in the guise of careless and reckless fatherhood, had added carelessly and recklessly to the population, and even where he had not neglected the education of his girls, had sent them out into the world far less equipped for the struggle than his male offspring. How came it that woman was so indifferently represented on all those Boards which were supposed to look after the health and welfare of the community? How came it that in some prisons there were only one or two female warders—far too few, at any rate, to look after female prisoners? At police stations the case was far worse, for there only rough men were in attendance, short-tempered, more than a little brutal, apparently devoid of all feelings of compunction or pity. And then there were the marriage laws, which weighed so heavily on women. And the whole machinery of law, which was designed, it would appear, altogether in the interest of the male, inasmuch as it had been created by the colossal egotism of the masculine intelligence.

Una Blockley listened to all this, and many other suggestions, with greedy ears. She did not understand all that was said, nor had she any experience or knowledge to check or control afterwards the eloquent words of the orator. But her soul was set on fire with the idea of a championship, a cause, a wonderful new gospel for femininity, something which would redress the uneven balance and bring greater justice and fairer dealing in the world. And there was one thing which strangely appealed to her warm, emotional nature. The path to the future reform led through much present suffering, and the women who took the burden on their shoulders were not only apostles of the new evangel, but also only too likely to be martyrs. That was something glorious, to suffer in the cause of humanity! Una dreamed of a great sisterhood, united in aims, fervent and unwearied in well-doing, always ready for sacrifice, never leaving one another in the lurch, struggling with whatever bodily weakness or disadvantage they possessed, but also with unfailing resolution, towards a distant and shining goal.

She was the daughter of a successful shopkeeper at Wandsworth, and she was quite aware that all the influence of the great middle-class that surrounded her was dead against her. What her father had said, with no little coarseness, when he heard that she intended to become a suffragette; what her brother had said, with still greater plainness of speech, when he learnt that she was prepared to break windows in public thoroughfares; what her mother's tears and expostulations had meant—of all this she was full aware. But she was prepared to take the risk, as she had already counted the cost. In her youth she had fed greedily on biographies—biographies, especially of the Saints, of great women like Saint Teresa and Joan of Arc, or great heroines like Berengaria and Queen Eleanor.[11] She mixed them all up, these great women of the olden time, and dimly conceived them as feminists and suffragettes, prematurely born to kindle the torch for their far-off successors. Dimly there worked in her little brain visions of what, even in this dull and drab century, might be done by fervent and enthusiastic and great-hearted saints to change the whole aspect of things and realise the millennium.

Once, too, she was transported utterly beyond herself. She listened to a young girl speaking from a platform in Trafalgar Square,[12] a fair, beautiful girl, with a wonderfully persuasive eloquence, who, heckled by the crowd, answered them back, and in her quiet self-possession seemed to be greater than all those who surrounded her. A born leader of women, she said to herself, and if circumstances helped her and stubborn hearts were changed, even a born leader of men. This slim, fair orator of the Square, standing on the pedestal of Nelson's Column, had told her and the rest of the audience that the one thing necessary for feminine salvation was the possession of the vote. Equal electoral facilities for women—that was the beginning of the grand and beneficent revolution. Then woman would have her hand on the great machinery of Parliament, and become in reality a fully qualified citizen of the State. That was clearly the thing to work for, Una Blockley said to herself. It was the necessary preliminary for all the future stages of progress, because the vote meant power, and electoral power would lead to several things, perhaps even a share in the Government itself.

So Una sat and dreamed at home, and nursed her great ambitions, which she dared not share with any of those who were her kith and kin. She felt strangely uplifted, as though a mandate had come to her from some great spiritual energy. She was young and inexperienced; she had not read much, nor, indeed, was she capable of much consecutive thought; but she had a great heart and a wonderful capacity for dreams. What were the ordinary ambitions of her sex compared with aspirations like these? Love, marriage, motherhood—these were elements in a fatal bondage, means by which crafty man had hitherto ensnared all womankind. The New Woman had nothing to do with these, or, at least, could put them away into some dim background while the great drama was being played. That was a drama indeed, a drama of liberty and emancipation, and deliverance from slavery, the enlightenment and the uprising of the greater half of humanity itself. So Una Blockley enrolled herself a member of the militant section of the W.S.P.U. and waited for its commands.

* * * * *

There was one thing, however, which troubled her with a palsying doubt. Would she ever have the courage to go through the test? It was all very well to have splendid visions, but in the actual moment of danger, when something had to be done before the very eyes of an authority prompt to coerce and punish—surely that must be a terrible ordeal. It meant a physical trial, and she was more than a little doubtful of her physical strength. She might be able to train her muscles, but could she control her nerves? Would she not die of fear and behave like a craven when the pinch came? This was an agonising thought with which, in the early days of her novitiate, she struggled through many anxious hours. "If I can imagine what it would be like," she said to herself, "and try to realise exactly what might happen, surely, then, I shall not be surprised at anything, and therefore I shall be brave." But in her secret heart she was dimly aware that courage is not a matter of prevision and forethought, but a question of temperament, of instinct, of prompt answer to stimulus, which can only be possessed and cannot be acquired. How terrible it would be if she should fail! And once she did fail. She was part of a crowd of women trying to force their way into the House of Commons, seeking an interview with a Cabinet Minister. For a while all went well. The women were in a compact body, and each could support her neighbour. Then came ugly rushes on the part of a jeering crowd of spectators, and skilful manœuvres on the part of the police who were breaking up their army into little isolated detachments. In one horrible moment Una Blockley found herself alone. By some miracle she eluded the grab of a policeman, and then she turned and fled. "Coward, coward, coward," she murmured, when at last she found herself in safety; "shall I ever be able to bear the burden and win the crown?" She could have beaten herself for very shame.

Yet once she had managed affairs not so badly. With many others she had been ordered to patrol Bond Street, and to watch her opportunity of doing as much damage as she could to the shop-windows. It was after five on a winter's afternoon; the lights had been lit for some time and there was some fog in the air. The orders were that the women should distribute themselves throughout the street so that at half-past five—the time that had been arranged—simultaneous attacks should take place at intervals of about twenty yards. Each woman carried a muff or a bag in which a hammer was concealed. If possible, the women—who were straitly enjoined not to wear suffragette colours and to dress as quietly and unostentatiously as they could—were to rendezvous at six o'clock at a given place of meeting, so that they might report what they had done. But, of course, if they were pursued, they were to take their own course to avoid capture.

Una's heart was beating fast as she took her stand opposite a fashionable haberdasher's shop, pretending to look with interest at the scarves and gloves and white shirts displayed in the windows, while her hand was nervously playing with the hammer in her muff. She kept her eyes fixed on the clock inside the shop. Would the time never come? And would her nerves play her the same trick as they had done on a previous occasion? She set her teeth hard, and her square, obtrusive little jaw was rigid and tense with emotion. Slowly the minute hand reached the half-hour, and then Una, with a half-suppressed cry, pulled out the hammer and dealt one resounding blow on the plate-glass. How hard and tough it was! She struck again and again with vicious and determined blows, but even so she only managed to make a great star on the window-pane with cracks reaching here and there from the centre of the impact. Meanwhile she heard around her a growing cry of excitement and anger; the men were coming out from the shop: the crowd were collecting round her: there were loud shouts for the police. Everywhere the signs of danger were manifest: yet Una stood rooted to the spot, paralysed and numb, wholly incapable—so it seemed to her—of taking a single step. What happened then? She hardly knew. She was conscious of some strong arms round her, of some loud voices of anger and hate, to which her preserver made quick reply. And then she was bundled anyhow into a cab—she was distinctly aware that it was a hansom[13] and not a taxi—and was rapidly driven off down some side street. She was safe, at all events. Harassed and confused as she was, she realised that she was delivered from the danger of capture and that the man who had saved her was sitting beside her, urging the cabman to still greater speed. That was something to be grateful for. It was curious how kind an individual man could be, albeit that men as a whole were so horrid and hateful! For this man, whoever he might be, had clearly interposed himself between her and the deadly imminent peril. And she felt that the least she could do was to thank him.

* * * * *

There was a silence between the pair for some time, as the hansom was driven rapidly westwards. At last Una became conscious that brown eyes—soft brown eyes, as she subsequently confessed to herself—were bent upon her in a serious, investigating gaze.

"Forgive me," said a kindly voice, "but whither are we driving?"

She looked up, startled. Evidently her senses were keenly alert to every impression, for she noted the little pedantry of the word "whither." It pleased her somehow, as a possible indication of refinement. But the situation was so absurd that she could not help smiling. Here were a man and a woman, who had never met until ten minutes ago, driving together into space, without a thought as to destination.

"Oh, forgive me," she said. "Take me to any Tube station—Marble Arch will do. Or perhaps we might go up to Edgware Road station. That would be still more convenient." She never knew how it came about, but in a minute or two she found herself talking quite easily and readily with this stranger. He had told her that he was a schoolmaster—"Ah, that accounted for 'whither,'" she said to herself. And she had told him that she lived in a suburb.

"It is unnecessary to ask what your interests are," he said, in his even, pleasant voice. "I suppose you are very keen about this Suffrage movement."

"It is my religion," she said, simply.

He passed the answer over, without comment. "Well, I hope if you are again in trouble it may be my good fortune to rescue you once more."

"It is our duty to get into trouble," she answered. "We have to do what our leaders tell us to do."

He looked a little pained, she thought, or perhaps it was merely that he was sympathetic.

"I suppose I must not ask what is the next item on your programme?"

"Nothing very serious just at present," Una replied. "Let me see. Oh, I go on Monday to the usual meeting of the WSPU at the Pavilion."

"The Pavilion?" He arched his eyebrows. "Surely that is a music hall?"

"Yes; in Piccadilly Circus. We listen to speeches and pass resolutions in favour of the Cause."

"I wonder if I might come?"

"Any one can come who is sympathetic," she replied.

"I mean, may I come with you?"

She wondered afterwards why she said "Yes" so simply, without thinking. But reflection came very soon. How could this stranger, whose name she had learnt was Tom Bateson, accompany her? Where were they to meet? What business had she to suppose that he was interested in the Movement? They were close to Edgware Road station, and she looked perplexed. Tom Bateson grasped the knotty problem in his quiet way.

"Perhaps I may come to call, if you will give me your address," he said. "I live at Harrow. And you?"

"85 Acacia Road, Wandsworth." She spoke without hesitation. Probably it was because the hansom was drawing up in Chapel Street, and that the ride was so obviously finished, that she gave the desired information so easily.

"Thank you," he said. "Let me see, to-day is Tuesday. I will call on Thursday afternoon."

"Will you let me pay half the cab fare?" said Una, hesitatingly and nervously. "You must remember that I believe in equal rights between men and women."

Bateson laughed out at this, a rich, comfortable laugh.

"Certainly," he said. "I will take a shilling. For, after all, I forced you into the cab, which makes my contribution to this journey stand at one-and-six—as compared with yours at a shilling."

For some reason she, too, laughed joyously as she gave him the coin.

Altogether a strange experience for Una Blockley—especially as a sequel to a window-breaking foray.

* * * * *

The odd intimacy between Tom Bateson and Una Blockley, begun in so unexpected a fashion, seemed to progress of its own accord during the next few days. When Bateson duly presented himself at Acacia Road, he was, to his own surprise, received with open arms. There was in reality nothing astonishing in this, however much the recipient of the welcome might have wondered at the proffered cordiality. For Bateson seemed to represent the dawn of commonsense, the return—for the much-afflicted home circle in Acacia Road—of something approaching sanity and right reason. If Una had, in the eloquent phraseology of her brother Sam, "picked up a young man," then it was obvious that she could not be so abnormal after all. Mrs. Blockley, who had often wept in secret over her daughter's aberrations, felt quite a flutter of maternal interest over Una's "young man." She had always maintained that if Una were left alone and not worried by excessive domestic criticism, she would be sure to "come right," and fall in love with some decent male who added to his other recommendations the possession of an adequate balance at his banker's. John Blockley, provision merchant, a Conservative, a Tariff Reformer, and a stout opponent of Lloyd-Georgeism in all its prodigal varieties of mischief, naturally included among the patent signs of national decadence, which obsessed his mind whenever he could spare time to think about them, the portentous phenomenon of women clamouring for the vote and accompanying their demands by open violence. When, therefore, he was informed by Mrs. Blockley that a young man was to be imported into the family circle, he was inclined to believe that Providence had specially interposed on his behalf. He laughed noisily and boisterously. "A young man, did you say, Maria? A young man come after Una?"—he shook his portly sides—"Thank 'Eaven, say I! I hope he will knock all this damned nonsense out of her head—though what any young man can see in Una, with all her whims and fandangoes, fairly beats me. She is a plain-looking article, too—not half so good-looking as you were, Maria, at her age!" And he laughed again.

Mrs. Blockley smiled, and, delighted to find her lord in so unusually good a temper, carefully refrained from saying anything.

Thus Tom Bateson was greeted with marked kindness and warmly pressed to look in whenever he found himself "round this way." It was not his custom, of course, to visit Wandsworth with marked frequency, but that was a misfortune which could easily be remedied. The worst of it was, that the greater the cordiality of the family, the greater, also, grew the discomfort of poor Una. For she could not mistake the reason of the welcome—especially as her brother Sam did not fail to improve the occasion by many winks and sly witticisms. She was afraid that Mr. Bateson would realise the situation: and she was so piteously anxious that he should not confuse her attitude towards him with that of her kinsmen that her natural shyness often made her manner cold and awkward. He did not seem to notice anything, however, or if he did, he kept his own counsel. Una Blockley interested him—partly, it must be confessed as a psychological curiosity, and only partly as a woman. How, out of such surroundings, could so strange a product of idealism and dreams have been evolved? Was this really a specimen of the New Woman, of whom he had heard so much? And was it true that modern femininity had thrown behind itself all the old trivialities of romance? Or perhaps transferred the romance from persons to a Cause? The analysis of so strange a soul piqued his curiosity—stirred, possibly, some dumb, unconscious instinct in him of masculine assertiveness. It might be that the New Woman was only the Old Eve, metamorphosed a little by the passage of the centuries. Besides, he liked what he had seen of Una: he liked her simple faith, her warm-hearted enthusiasm, her Quixotry. Therefore, without hesitation, he did his best to improve the acquaintance. The family might think what it pleased, and if Blockley *père* treated him with a familiarity which, in the circumstances, was quite uncalled for, and Mrs. Blockley sometimes looked at him in a melting mood, with actual tears in her eyes, he could, at all events, be quite frank and open with Una. She certainly could not mistake his friendliness for any warmer feeling. He always was *bon camarade*, a "pal" and nothing more. Thus, by degrees, her shyness wore off, and their intimacy grew apace. She did not reveal all her secrets to him, but she told him a good deal, and in many ways learnt to depend on his obvious sincerity and straightforwardness.

Sometimes, it is true, she gave him unpleasant shocks. One day, while they were walking—they had got into the habit of taking walks at least once a week—they wandered close to a golf course. Over the hedge they could see one of the greens, disfigured by straggling black marks roughly indicating the legend "Votes for Women." These had evidently been burned by some corrosive acid, and, as obviously, the work of destruction was due to militant suffragettes. Tom Bateson stopped, pointed to the ruined green, and, with a note of sternness in his voice, said, "Do you defend that sort of thing?"

Una hesitated a moment. They had been talking about theatres and operas, and her companion had interested her deeply in some of the Wagner stories and the Russian Ballet. It seemed such a pity that their conversation should be abruptly suspended by so untoward and ugly an accident—so far removed from the glittering regions of Romance. But, after a pause, she answered bravely enough.

"Yes; I have myself helped to do similar things."

Bateson shrugged his shoulders impatiently.

"And to destroy or deface other people's letters in a pillar-box, I suppose you think that a legitimate game also?"

"Yes," said Una meekly.

"Look here, Una"—in his excitement he was not aware that he had called her by her Christian name, but she winced and blushed—"I have found you a reasonable and level-headed woman, with whom it was a real pleasure to converse on all kinds of subjects. But really, if you defend this kind of thing, you remind me of what I heard a man say once about your sex, which at this moment seems to me profoundly true. Asked to explain why a woman did some extraordinary or unusual thing—I forget what it was at this moment—he said: 'You must remember that the average woman is not a gentleman.' That seems to me to hit the nail on the head."

"What precisely do you mean?" asked Una coldly.

"Well, according to our masculine code, there are some things that are fair and some that are unfair. Even if you dislike a man, you must not say evil about him behind his back. If you are having a fight, you must not hit below the belt. Wars are conducted according to certain principles of courtesy and chivalry. When your enemy is badly wounded he ceases to be your enemy and becomes your friend, and you staunch his wounds and carry him on your back out of the zone of danger. In a properly conducted club, the man who talks lightly or scandalously about a woman is held to be a cad. But you women seem to have no code of honour. You want the political vote, and *therefore* you try to spoil a purely social sport. You want to have the right to elect members of Parliament, and *therefore* you destroy quite harmless people's correspondence."

Bateson had worked himself up into quite a temper.

Una looked at him a little forlornly. There was a suspicion of tears in her eyes.

"You don't understand," she said. "No—don't interrupt me, let me speak. First, as to myself. I am a soldier in an army and I must carry out orders. No one knows better than you that an army is useless for offensive purposes unless it has strict discipline. What would happen if private soldiers began to question and discuss the commands given them by their leaders? It is not my business to argue. I have been enrolled in a militant force, and I should be a deserter if I refused to obey. Next, as to the character of the campaign— which I can discuss with you, of course, though not with my superior officers. Every extension of the franchise in this country—and probably also in others, but England is good enough for my purpose—has been won by violence. It has been extorted out of the ruling caste, it has never been voluntarily conceded. The political kingdom, like the Kingdom of Heaven, 'suffereth violence and the violent take it by force.'[14] The democracy of England has gained the right to help in the government of the country—by what? By burning castles, by pulling down park railings, by wide-spread destruction of all kinds—in short, by making itself a nuisance and so at last enforcing attention to its needs. We women are not physically strong enough to pull down railings, like you men. But we, too, can make ourselves a nuisance in whatever way is open to us. And as to your fine codes of honour in fighting and never hitting below the belt—well, we women believe ourselves to be more logical, if not so romantic. Do you remember how the peasants fought against the knights in the Peasants' War in the sixteenth century? It was the etiquette in fighting against a knight to strike only at the horseman. But the peasants had no silly scruples of this sort. They struck at the horses—and down came the knights! That is how we carry on our campaign. We know that real fighting is not done with kid gloves and that revolutions are not made with rose water. We don't hesitate to break eggs for our omelette!"

Una spoke passionately. Her friend had touched a sore point and she was up in arms to defend her creed. There was silence for a few seconds. Then Bateson spoke gravely.

"Very well. We must agree to differ, I suppose. Our walk is spoilt, anyhow—like" (he smiled grimly) "those golf-greens. I will see you home."

They walked side by side without saying a word.

* * * * *

Tom Bateson kept away for two or three weeks after this episode, nursing his resentment, or perhaps thinking that the medicine of absence would not hurt either of them.

It was then that Una suddenly discovered to her dismay that this man counted for something in her life, and that she had learned to depend on his friendly companionship. She was shocked at herself: the discovery of her weakness was a keen humiliation for her. Was she, despite her years of self-discipline, only an ordinary woman after all? And her gospel of militancy—could it be that it was not so sacred a thing as she had thought? No—no—a thousand times no! She prayed on her knees that she might never lose faith, never play the coward, never abandon the holy cause of womanhood. She even prayed that some trial might be vouchsafed her, some test of her constancy and her courage, so that she might the better surmount her weakness. The answer to her prayer came sooner than she expected. At the very next meeting of the WSPU a call was made for volunteers for a particularly difficult and dangerous piece of work. It had been decided that a bomb should be thrown into a Cabinet Minister's house during his temporary absence from town. There was no intention of destroying life—for this was one of the principles of the campaign. But there was quite sufficient peril in the adventure, an obvious risk of immediate capture, and the practical certainty of a severe sentence if the offender was brought up in a court of law. Una, without hesitation, sent in her name with three others. The names were drawn by lot, and it was hers which was selected. With something like exultation Una accepted the responsibility. She thanked Heaven that she had not been considered too unworthy to have this great honour entrusted to her. In ten days' time the deed had to be done and it was with a glow of triumphant pride that the girl made her way home.

Then came the reaction. The spirit, indeed, was willing, but the flesh was weak. The horrible interval of ten days' inaction was more than she could bear. If only she could have done the thing at once, how much easier it would have been! But this period of waiting was agonising. The necessary preparation for the deed, the instructions of her leaders, the practice required for throwing a heavy weight, and finally the actual acquisition of the bomb and its careful secretion—all these things became a positive torture for her nerves. She could not sleep, she could scarcely eat. Her hands shook with apprehensive tremors, her breath came quick with prescient dread. And then suddenly she thought of Tom Bateson. At least, now that her fate was fixed, she might see him once more. Perhaps he would come to her if she wrote to him. She had better not tell him anything, of course, but she could see him, at all events, and talk to him and hold, if only for a moment, his hand—his loyal, manly hand—in hers. She longed for a sight of his frank face: she remembered how good and kind he had been to her. He was her best, her only friend. Surely, she had a right, on the ground of their friendship, to see him again. He would not, he could not, refuse. So the letter was sent, a strangely cold little letter, for she was afraid of giving herself away. "Please come and see me next Tuesday, if you find it possible. I shall be glad if you can. Next Tuesday at 4 would suit me, and, I hope, you also." That was all. It was not exactly a love-letter, but Una felt uncomfortable about it, after it had been posted. However, it fulfilled its purpose. At the appointed hour Tom Bateson came.

* * * * *

Of course, she had decided to say nothing to her visitor of the enterprise that lay before her. But such self-denial was impossible. Tom Bateson came to her, the embodiment of health and sanity and good temper, on a day which seemed to afford the natural sunny background to his high spirits. He appeared to have forgotten the misfortune of their last encounter and to be determined to prove to Una that not a single cloud had ever chequered their happy relationship. Poor Una struggled to keep her secret to herself, but that was a heroic resolve which transcended her strength.

"I can't say you are looking well," he said.

"No, I have been sleeping badly," she returned.

"Dyspepsia or Conscience?" he asked, gaily.

"Both, I think," said Una, with a wan smile.

Bateson suddenly looked grave. "Not something to do with the Cause?" (a pause). "Won't you tell me?" (another longer pause). "Come, come, little woman," and his hand sought hers. Indeed, he had never been so affectionate before. "You might tell your old friend."

"No, no," she wailed. "I must not, I must not!"

And then she told him. Bit by bit, the whole story was revealed; and while her hand still rested in his she even went back to their quarrel and explained how, in her penitent remorse, she had volunteered for the great adventure— to prove her faith and her loyalty.

His face grew very serious before she had finished. She looked so white and fragile, so inadequate an instrument to carry out a woman's vengeance upon a stubborn Cabinet, that he longed to take her in his arms and ask her, then and there, to relinquish all her dreams and be his wife. But in the back of his head he knew that any such action on his part would startle and wound her, and perhaps defeat the very object he had in view.

"Una," he said, and his voice was tender and quiet, "if you must do this, will you let me come with you?"

She smiled faintly at this. "What about your own creed?" she said.

"My own creed be blowed!" he cried heartily.

She looked at his eager, flushed face, and then she knew, with a sudden pang at her heart, that she loved him. But she could not say a word.

"Look here, Una," he went on—the name had become quite familiar on his lips by this time—"you know you are not strong enough to do what they ask of you. There must be stronger women than you, much better fitted for violence of this kind. Say you are ill, say that you are kept a prisoner at home, say anything you like, but get out of this. You really must! I suppose you could not say that—that—your heart fails you?"

Una shook her head. She felt terribly weak and every pulse in her body was beating and jarring in a sort of agony, but she would not confess that she was a coward. But how good and kind he was to her, how infinitely tender! Some women in this topsy-turvy world must be very lucky if they owned a friend, a brother, a husband like this!

Then he made his great appeal.

"Dear Una," he spoke just above a whisper and his brown eyes looked straight into her "blue eyes of an idealist," while he clasped her hand in both in his, "I will not say that this act of yours is a folly. I will not utter one word of criticism. I will not rebuke those leaders of yours who have condemned you to this horrible trial. On their conscience be it, with all its only too probable consequences. No—I am going to make this a personal matter—something just between you and me. I am your friend and you are my friend. We have been loyal and frank comrades, have we not? And our comradeship is very dear to both of us. In the name of our friendship, I ask you not to do this thing. Una—Una, will you refuse—for my sake?"

She was terribly shaken and her breast was rent with sobs. Her piteous tears ran down her face and dropped on his hands. "I must, I must!" she moaned. "I must keep my oath!"

"For my sake, Una, for my sake," he pleaded. "Will you not refuse, just because I ask you? It is not because I am selfish, dear. If you like, I will not see you again. But I want to save you, to know that you are safe—because—because you are dear to me!"

The sweetness of his manner, his face, his words, went through her like a dividing sword. The burden of her oath and her allegiance to the Cause seemed impossible to bear. She shivered. But her little heart was brave. "For the sake of Womanhood no sacrifice is too great," she murmured—the words that her great leader had given her to help her in times of trial. And when she said them once more aloud, Tom Bateson knew that his appeal had failed.

A few days later the bomb had been thrown, and Una Blockley, militant suffragette, by the sentence of the Court, had become a martyr in the cause of "Votes for Women." At her special request Tom Bateson had absented himself from the proceedings before the magistrate and the subsequent trial, and only in the evening newspapers had learnt that for the crime of bomb-throwing his friend had been condemned to two years' imprisonment with hard labour.

* * * * *

There is much waste in Nature and in Life. Wastefulness is indeed Nature's characteristic method in carrying out her evolutionary processes. Just as she squanders hundreds of acorns in order to produce a single oak, so too many human lives are sacrificed in the effort to secure an isolated reform. Who shall say, therefore, that fanatics are wrong or martyrs thrown away in the great processes whereby Humanity or the Immanent Will works out its obscure destinies?

Did Una Blockley waste her life?

The usual dreary incidents followed her incarceration—hunger-strike, forcible feeding, the long struggle between the authorities and the audacious rebel. Then came the doctor's report and the Home Secretary's order to set her free. Many friends greeted her on her release from prison—Tom Bateson among the foremost. But they could hardly recognise the anæmic, emaciated woman, who came out from her great adventure with her health hopelessly impaired and nothing to look forward to except the pitiful career of the chronic invalid. Did Una Blockley throw away her life? Did she do aught to help the Woman's Cause? She never knew. Perhaps it did not matter very much, after all. For examples count for something in this world. At least she had proved the rare constancy, the ardent faith which could illumine a Suffragette's Soul.

NOVELS

In the novel *No Surrender* by Constance Maud, Jenny Clegg, a young mill worker from the north of England, joins the suffrage movement. (Her experiences bear some resemblance to those of Annie Kenney.) After her first imprisonment for suffrage activity, she does not return to the mill, choosing instead to devote all her time to working for the Women's Social and Political Union. She is again imprisoned, this time "for holding a protest meeting outside the grim walls of a Midland county jail, where some of their companions were, they considered, undergoing a most unjust sentence" (253). Placed in a cell in the second division, to which ordinary criminals were sentenced, rather than in the first division, reserved for political prisoners, Jenny decides to protest. In her first act of defiance, she uses a hairpin and her own blood to write "Votes for Women" on the wall.

The novel *Suffragette Sally*, by Gertrude Colmore, tells the story of three women from quite different social classes—the maid Sally Simmonds, middle-class Edith Carstairs, and the aristocrat Lady Geraldine Hill—all committed to getting the vote for women. The novel demonstrates the impact of the call to participate in the suffrage movement on their personal lives, particularly on their relationships with men. The women hold differing opinions on the desirability of militant action. Sally and Geraldine, as suffragettes, believe that militancy is necessary and are willing to go to prison if need be, while Edith, as a suffragist, holds back from militant action. Suffragettes, who favoured militancy, were generally associated with the Pankhursts and their organization, the WSPU; suffragists were committed to obtaining the vote through more constitutional methods.

CONSTANCE ELIZABETH MAUD

FROM *NO SURRENDER*

[New York: John Lane Company, 1912]

FROM CHAPTER XII, "BEHIND PRISON BARS"

But she [Jenny] was not to have much solitude that day, for presently the door opened again, this time to admit the sewing-mistress, a pleasant, sweet-faced little woman, accompanied by a third-class prisoner, carrying a large basket of cut-out needlework.

"Well, Number Seventeen, how are you getting on?" she inquired with a smile. Then her eye fell on the wall, and her tone changed to one of dismay. "Oh dear, what have you been doing? I'm afraid you'll get into fresh trouble."

Jenny laughed at her concern.

"Don't worry about me," she said. "As well be hanged for a sheep as a lamb!" She held up her work. "I've done my best, but I'm a poor hand, I'm afraid. You see, I've worked all my life at the mill—I can manage my four looms all right, but needles ain't much in my line."

The sewing-mistress examined the work carefully.

"Not so bad—you're improving, Number Seventeen. You'll go out knowing something more than when you came in, which is more than most can say."

"Thanks to you," answered Jenny warmly. "You don't know how I look for your coming every morning. Have you read this week's *Votes!*"[15]

"Yes"—the mistress lowered her voice and spoke quickly. "I've news for you—good news. The magistrate has given the case against those Visiting Justices who ordered the water-hose to be turned on that Suffragette prisoner in her cell—it's a wonderful victory for you women."

Jenny's face shone with pleasure.

"Don't say you women," she said, "say *us*, for you're one of us now, you know."

"Oh yes, I'm with you," the little woman answered, smiling. "You've converted me—made me feel proud to be a woman—which I can't say I'd ever been before."

The third-class prisoner listened with blinking eyes. They spoke in an unknown tongue to her.

"Oh, I tell you it's a glorious thing to be a woman," Jenny went on with eager enthusiasm. "And it's a glorious thing to be in this movement—to be one of this great Sisterhood...."

A wardress passed the half-open door, and the little sewing-mistress said hurriedly:

"I must be going, or I'll get into hot water—and as to you...."

"For me it will be boiling—bubbling and boiling," laughed Jenny, as her friend nodded and went out, closing the door.

She had hardly been gone a minute when the door banged open once more, and another voice announced:

"The Governor!"

A tall, dignified gentleman, with iron grey hair and keen soldierly features, surveyed the prisoner sternly.

"Complaints again, Number Seventeen?" he said in his deep, quiet voice, and you felt that at this man's hands you would at least get justice, according to his lights. "You women," he continued, "would be better employed obeying and keeping rules, let me tell you."

Jenny stood before him, her work in hand, looking the very embodiment of well-conducted womanhood. She answered respectfully:

"We only make complaints against injustice, sir. We feel it our duty to protest against being treated as second-class criminals—we have committed no crime."

The Governor's eye was fixed on the inscription on the wall. He answered in tones of deep displeasure:

"You *are* criminals, and most troublesome ones. How could you venture to deface the prison wall in that manner?"

"I've nothing else to write on," Jenny answered simply. "If I was in the first class, where I ought to be accordin' to justice, I'd have writing-paper and no occasion to use the wall."

"No occasion to use the wall! Now look here, my good girl—you must be crazy—absolutely crazy. It is the most charitable, and I am beginning to believe, the true view, to take of your case. Now, take my advice and give up these people who have got hold of you—quit the whole silly business—do as you are told while you are here, and then go home quietly and do your duty in that state of life to which it has pleased God to call you."

With these words he turned and went out, sincerely hoping they would take effect. It really seemed to him a thousand pities such a bright, intelligent-looking young woman should have found her way into prison at all.

"How can he know, or anyone else, what God's Voice has been calling to me," said Jenny to herself, as she sat down again on her stool of penance. "You've got to be very still to hear that Voice yourself—but once you have heard it, you've got to listen and heed It well—and that's just what I'm doing and why I'm here—"

The cold was penetrating. Jenny's hands were blue and her feet stung with cold, not only from lack of exercise, but a naturally poor circulation and somewhat weak action of the heart. She rose and taking off the great thick, ill-fitting shoes, which had blistered both her heels, tried to warm her feet on the hot-water pipe which passed along one side of the wall; but not with much success. Outside in the yard, by mounting the stool and standing on tip-toe, she could see the prisoners doing their daily exercise. Round and round in a never-ending circle they trudged, a yard or so apart to prevent any opportunity of interchanging a word. Those who were strong and active going round the outer path, the feeble and aged round the inner one. Oh, the grey life! the grey flagstones, the grey sky overhead, and the grey, grey faces of the trudging women! Yet Jenny longed to be out there walking with them and breathing in the foggy mist, instead of the close bad air of the narrow cell.

Slowly the hours dragged on. The snow had ceased to fall, giving place to a chill, grey drizzle.

At twelve o'clock the key turned in the lock, and the wardress and third-class prisoners entered with dinner, consisting to-day of a lump of suet pudding, two potatoes, and a small brown loaf. Jenny knew she would need this food to stoke up for the future. She eat quickly, for now was the wardresses dinner-hour, and there was no time to be lost. Presently she heard four taps on the wall, and a voice that seemed to come from a long way off called out the Suffragette signal.

Jenny knelt down by the hot-water pipe and answered vigorously:

"I'm ready—"

"It will mean the punishment cell for all of us," came the voice through the wall.

"And we're all ready," answered Jenny cheerfully.

"The only protest left then will be the Hunger Strike.—Oh, Jenny, I don't like that for you—I am certain your heart is none too strong."

"Faith in God and our Cause gives us all strong hearts—never fear for me," was Jenny's reply.

She went to the opposite wall and sung out in a high, clear voice:

"Ready?"

"Ready," came the answer.

Then Jenny, shoe in hand, mounted her stool.

"Here goes," she cried, and with a good swing of her strong young arm, smash went three out of the four small thick panes of glass. And like an echo went the sound of breaking glass to right and to left down all the length of the corridor.

"Good and clean, if it is damp." Jenny drew in long draughts of the grey, damp, winter air gratefully. But retribution was already on foot. Bang, bang,

bang came the sound of opening doors, followed by loud, angry voices and hurrying footsteps.

Jenny's door was flung wide and the wardress burst in, panting and purple with indignation:

"'Ooligans!" she gasped, "'ooligans! that's what you are—three—four— five panes smashed!" She gazed up at the window, but could not see clearly for rage. "You'll 'ear of this, you disgraceful, unsexed creatures you."

"It's our protest at bein' deprived of fresh air," said Jenny, still standing near the broken window. "We *had* to do something, or you and the newspapers would have sworn we were quite content to be treated as criminals— can't have you sayin' that, you know!"

"Well, you'll come up before the Governor an' the magistrates for this little turn. They'll let you know whether they're quite content, Miss 'Ooligan. We'll see 'ow a punishment cell'ull suit you." With that she bounced out of the cell, and Jenny heard the cry of "'Ooligans!" starting next door.

But another voice now came ringing through the air—a giant voice from outside.

"Courage—courage, brave friends of the Cause! Victory is in sight. All goes well. Your broken windows are a symbol—the light and air are let in." The loud, hoarse tones of the megaphone came from the open window of a house opposite, which overlooked this side of the prison.

"It is her voice—our splendid young Captain!" cried Jenny joyfully. She caught up the prison clothes on which she had been at work, and waved them out of the broken window.

"How they just think of everything, those leaders of ours," she cried with enthusiasm. "The little things, like cheering us in prison, as well as the big things that's going to change the world for women—aye, and men too. Never were such women as our leaders—never in all the world."

"No surrender," pealed in glad, exultant tones from the broken windows all along the line.

"No surrender," echoed the giant voice of the megaphone. Then it continued so that all those in the cells could hear:

"Good news, friends. Splendid news—we've won the by-election at Bermondsey. Grand meeting at the Star Music Hall two nights ago. Our women carried vote against the Government unanimously. What did it was the Government's treatment of the working women. Fine Liberals releasing the two ladies because of weak hearts, tested by specialist—but no testing for the working women, and no weak hearts!—Well, it lost the Liberals Bermondsey!"

"Hurrah! hurrah! hurrah!" came through the broken windows.

"It'll lose them scores more seats before we've done with them—the sham Liberal Government—sham friends of the people!" cried the megaphone.

"Silence there, you disgraceful creatures—not women at all, you ain't," shrieked the wardress, appearing again at the door. "Come down this minute," she commanded Jenny.

But Jenny, still standing and waving, did not even hear her.

"No surrender, indeed!" cried the wardress, "we'll see about that—'Ooligans!" and out she went in search of higher authority and power, while Jenny and her companions, standing at their broken windows, burst into the Suffragette Marseillaise, other voices from the house opposite joining in:

"To Freedom's cause till death
We swear our fealty.
  March on, march on,
   Face to the dawn—
The dawn of liberty."

[For her actions, Jenny Clegg, along with the other prisoners who participated in breaking windows, is sentenced to the punishment cell. One of these prisoners, Mary O'Neil, lies on a plank bed in the bitter cold of the cell, exhausted by five days and nights of fasting.]

FROM CHAPTER XIII, "IN THE PUNISHMENT CELL"

Mary already loved her fellow-prisoners. There was the girl who looked up at her from her scrubbing as she passed and gave her a smile like that of an innocent country girl—a smile which went straight to her heart, claiming her as a comrade and a prison-sister. And the young mother exercising in the prison yard, her baby in her arms, that baby born in prison, but who crowed and snatched at his mother's prison cap as if it had been a flower, and she a princess walking in her garden. Was the baby incorrigibly bad? He was certainly as impudently happy as though he had been born in the "purple" instead of the prison.

Yes, it was easy enough to love these, but how hard not to hate those others—the hard, blind bigots whose bad laws and bad systems built up and perpetuated all the misery. The selfish, arrogant men who would not hear the cry of the prisoners, nor the pleading of those who would save them, or at least make better conditions for the children still to be born.

"Yet they too are victims, though they do not know it," reflected Mary, as she lay stretched on her bed of pain through those long dark hours, "and truly 'they know not what they do.' Divine love," she prayed, "teach me to say 'Father, forgive them.'[16] Only when I can say that from my heart can I ever know the real meaning of the love of Christ Who gave Himself for a world which rejected Him. He saw right through the hard stony surface, deep, deep into the depths of each poor human heart, and there lay the divine germ waiting to be quickened into life—and the only thing to quicken it is love. I suppose, after all, there is not one of those hard-looking wardresses and officials, not one of those Cabinet Ministers so bitterly opposed to the idea of doing justice to women, who would not cheerfully die to save someone they love."

And with this thought, her eyes closed, and her spirit soared away, far above the grey walls of the prison, the grey mists of earth.

[The final chapter of *No Surrender* describes a suffrage march that took place in London. No doubt the account is based on the huge march of 17 June 1911 which included a large contingent of women who had been prisoners, all wearing white. They carried wands topped by arrows, which were the identifying symbols of prison dress. At the time of the actual march about 700 women had been imprisoned for their suffrage activities. These former prisoners marched behind the suffrage leaders and in front of the pageant of famous women from history.

In the following fictional account of the march, Alice Walker, who has gradually become sympathetic to the suffrage cause, is watching the parade with her American friend Penelope Otis, who considers the whole topic of suffrage to be tiresome and boring. A young Indian, a lawyer of the Brahmin caste who is studying in London, wanders onto the balcony where the two women are seated to view the parade, and he watches it with them. The parade includes, along with fictional women from the novel, actual women who were active in the suffrage movement; while they are not named, they can be readily identified.]

From L'Envoie, "The Passing of the Women"

Louder and louder roared the cheers and rolled the drums. The mounted police pushed back the surging crowd round Hyde Park Corner, and on down Piccadilly wound the great living river of women. It appeared endless, like a stream that had its source away in the heights of some far mountain.

Leading the way, with banners gleaming in the sunshine, marched the veterans. A gallant little company of women in the evening of life, whose valiant spirits, like bright, well-worn swords, had most of them well-nigh worn out the frail scabbard. But their tired eyes were bright with hope to-day, their step showed no sign of faltering or weariness, for at last the goal was surely within sight. Of how many times they had already believed it in sight they did not think. These were those who had borne the toil and heat of life's long day— working, digging, ploughing, sewing, since early womanhood. Side by side with these marched their younger sisters, the gallant leaders of the great Social and Political Union, whose heroic courage and devotion, even to the death test, had lifted the question of Woman's Enfranchisement at last into the arena of practical politics.

And now surely the hour of dawn was nearing. Strong men and true had rallied round them. The Conciliation Committee[17] had been formed, and the claims of the women would never more be allowed to be pushed aside. However reluctant the Government might be to keep their pledges, the staunch Committee would see to it there was no more shuffling and shirking. Not that their hope rested mainly on their men friends, however; no, it was in the great Movement itself, of which each woman felt she was an integral part, moving on like a wave with the irresistible tide, before which every obstacle must before long give way.

Next in order came a white-clad band of women and girls of all classes, bearing proudly as the very crown and glory of their womanhood, the prisoner's badge of disgrace, a wand surmounted by the broad arrow. All eyes turned on the woman who led them. She had the face of one whose eyes "have seen the glory of the coming of the Lord." She walked unconscious of the cheering crowd, her feet scarcely seeming to touch the solid ground.

Just behind her, four abreast with her companions, walked Mary O'Neil.

"There's Mary," cried Alice excitedly. "The one at this end."

"Isn't she sweet?" cried Penelope Otis; "one wouldn't be surprised to see a halo shine right out round her any moment."

But the young Brahmin was following the leader of the band with wrapt, intent gaze:

"That woman is like a high priestess," he said, half to himself.

Alice caught the words.

"She would lay down her life for this Cause," she said warmly.

"She *has* laid down her life," the Indian answered quietly.

"Do you know her?" asked Penelope.

"I do not know her as you would say 'know,'" he answered simply, "but with her the soul is written on the face."

"You are quite right," said Alice, bending forward and speaking in low eager tones, "quite right. You know what she did not long ago? She had been arrested with some working women for an open protest against the Government, but the Home Secretary ordered her release at once on the plea of a weak heart, the real reason being that she belongs to a well-known family of our aristocracy. She determined to show this up by disguising herself as a workgirl, and getting arrested again. This is what she did, and proved that the same heart in a workgirl did not procure her release from this Liberal Government. There was no other way—for they had indignantly denied making any differences when they had been accused of it."

"Wasn't it splendid," said Penelope.

The Indian said nothing, but his luminous eyes spoke his keen interest.

"They treated her," went on Alice, "well, just exactly as they did the other unfortunate working women, little thinking who she was. When at last their suspicions were aroused as to her identity, they at once took fright and released her."

"Well, it baffles me how she ever managed to deceive them for a day. Her class is just stamped all over her," said Penelope, who had heard the story when all England rang with it.

"One such a woman is enough to ensure the success of any movement," remarked the Indian; "she radiates, and her light is reflected on each one of those who follow her."

"All very well, you know," said a man's voice behind, "but this show is pure play-acting. You women love it—now own up, don't you?"

"I don't know about play-acting—personally, however devoted I was to theatricals, I should draw the line at prison," a woman's voice answered lightly.

"Not if you thought you were going to be made into a heroine—come now?"

"I'd rather sleep comfortably in my own bed than be a Holloway heroine, thank you," replied the lady.

Alice Walker also had caught that look on the face of the woman who walked first in the prisoners' contingent, and was pondering the Indian's words.

"What a lot of them have been in prison—old and young—and such awfully sweet-looking women some of them too. It is a curious country, this old England of yours," observed the American girl, as the six hundred prisoners marched by, and the cheers grew warm with enthusiasm from the crowd below—this crowd which two or three years before would have assembled only in their hundreds, with but jeers and rotten eggs for these same women. The broad arrow, like the cross, had already worked the miracle.

And now marched past the long deputation of women doctors and University students in caps and gowns and hoods—a goodly company with strong, firm step, and young, frank, fearless faces full of purpose.

"Ought to have been men, they ought," said an elderly woman just below the Lyceum balcony: "takin' the men's work—'tain't fair, I say." Her voice rang with resentment.

"Takin' men's work? That it ain't," retorted a younger woman. "Doctorin' women is women's work, and so is teaching the girls—that's what I say. It's the men 'as taken *our* work, and doin' it all the time too! What business 'ave they sellin' ribbons and laces and doin' ladies' 'air, I'd like to know?"

"'Ere, someone, get this lady a tub to stand on," cried the crowd jester, "begin again, Miss, do...." The rest was lost in the laughter of those round them.

Above the army of women, and linking past and present into one great Sisterhood, floated the banners bearing the names or portraits of the great company of those who had gone before—those pioneers down the ages who had fought for Freedom, Justice, and Truth in some form or other, whether in religion, politics, science or art. Prophetess, Priestess, Saint, Martyr, Queen, Scientist and Artist. Each section bore aloft their own special patron. Brightest among these constellations, blazing with the oriflamme of France,[18] shone the immortal name of Jeanne d'Arc. Those who followed were too numerous to note, but among them one caught an occasional flash which sent one's thought back to ancient days of Egypt, Greece and Rome. Down through the centuries followed the lineal descendants of Miriam, Deborah, Sappho, Hypatia, Boadicea, down to recent times of such as Elizabeth Fry, Mary Wollstonecraft and Mrs. Somerville, the latter proudly borne aloft by the caps and gowns. The writers held up to the sun such golden names as Vittoria Colonna, Jane Austen, George Sand, George Eliot, Charlotte and Emily Brontë, Elizabeth Barrett Browning. The artists with the palettes and brushes walked under the portraits of Angelica Kaufmann, Mme. Le Brun and Rosa Bonheur.[19] Beneath the banner of their patron saint, Florence Nightingale, walked the long line of hospital nurses in their small, neat bonnets and long cloaks. These women, with their cheery smile and gentle, patient skill, appealed specially to the spectators; few among them had not had reason to bless them.

"Hooray for the Women," shouted a small boy with a pale little face which bespoke his experience.

"My, ain't they a dandy lot," said a soldier, with enthusiasm.

Then followed the long regiment of toilers in great factories and industries—the women who make the wheels go round. The mothers of this band had lived under such conditions of slavery as made their own hard lives seem bright in comparison, for they had not had the bare human right to their own pitiful earnings, the husband legally claiming every penny. One of those devoted women, who took part in the twenty years' fight to win this inestimable boon for her sisters, looked out on the procession to-day as it passed by her windows. And her eyes, grown dim, lit with the old light of battle and of victory, as she noted to what a mighty host the women's army had grown—that army once a mere handful, on and ever on, still they came in their thousands.

Textile workers from Lancashire and Yorkshire in their shawls and clogs. Swarthy, strong-limbed Welsh women from the pit's mouth; sweated tailoresses, doing Government work on sailors' and soldiers' uniforms at half men's pay; post office clerks, who had also experienced the bitter difference between justice as meted out to those with the vote and those without; chain-makers from Cradley-Heath, hat-makers, bottle-makers, match-makers, jelly-makers, each bearing on a banner the emblem of their trade; on and on they came. Many held their babies in their arms and returned the greetings of the crowd of spectators with beaming friendly smiles to right and left. A look of steadfast purpose and hope shone on all these workers' faces, old and young alike. And still they passed—the interminable miles and miles of women.

Alice caught sight of Jenny as she marched foremost among the Lancashire textile workers. Jenny was to be married to Joe Hopton next month.

He had thrown himself with his usual dogged fixity of purpose into the Women's Cause, and never intended resting, or letting others rest, until every sex disability had been removed, and justice done to women. Poor Maggie's awful sentence had been commuted to three years penal servitude, a period which it had been whispered might, by great circumspection on the prisoner's part, possibly be shortened another six months.

Mrs. Wilmot had touched the spring and set a great machinery in motion. The veteran leader of the Freedom League had rallied to her aid with all the forces at her disposal, and the result had been a monster petition to the Home Secretary with signatures both of a number and of a significance impossible to disregard.

Alice Walker, on hearing from Jenny of her poignant interest in the case, had worked too in a quiet way. A quiet way perforce on her parents' account, but still real enough to make her partake not only in the anxiety but in the joy of the reprieve. Great forces were working and seething in Alice's formerly complacent and easygoing little soul. She watched herself as through a looking-glass, and wondered what she would find herself obliged to do next. The motive power came from inside, a gradual unfolding, like that of a green shoot. Resistance and opposition, which would have combated outside influence, was useless here, as Alice, with her usual philosophy, fully realised.

The procession continued—more, and always more, to come. Among the banners flashed the legends, "No vote no tax," "Courage is the mother of all the virtues," "Stone walls do not a prison make," "Dare to be free"; and occasional reminders to the "Antis" and laggards, such as: "Six million women workers need the vote," "Rise ye women that be at ease," etcetera.

Then came some of the "protest banners," recalling the lines along which the Militant Movement had passed—"The Police-Court protests," "The Tax-resistance," "The Picketers"—"729 hours spent picketing the House of Commons to exercise the subject's historic right of petitioning the King's Ministers." Such weary hours, standing there at the closed gates in heat and cold, rain and snow, day after day, week after week, to be ridiculed and scorned by the Noël Crowleys of the House, execrated by the Boulders and Blathertons, pitied half contemptuously by the more kindly Weir-Kemps! Other banners told other tales, which the young Brahmin and the American girl spelt out with dispassionate interest and curiosity, while Alice Walker listened and watched, absorbing all in silence.

And now the crowd below were making merry over a new diversion—a small delapidated trail of sandwich men, whom the stream was bearing on its fringe like the straws and sticks of debris on the edge of a flood. Their boards bore the comic announcement, in letters of dull red on a ground of grimy white: "Women do NOT want the Vote!"

The mud, that a few years before would have been flung at the women, had found a new target. Gladly the poor sandwiches would have hidden their diminished heads, such was the uproarious merriment they excited. But they were starving, poor creatures, and the men who hired them expected the work to be done for which they paid. It was typical of the "Anti" that he, or she, should do their propaganda by deputy, and such deputies. Only when Lord Wimperdale, Mr. Crowley, Mrs. Prendergast and Miss Selina Crompton begin to parade their own sandwich boards, as the Suffragist women so often have done, will they convince the men and women in the street, or on the fence, of the sincerity of their purpose, let alone the righteousness of their Cause.

"Why don't the bloomin' 'Antis' carry their own boards?" cried one of the crowd.

"Chuck it, Joe—game's up, my boy," laughed another.

"I'll paint you a fresh board, Bill," said a stout, pleasant-faced woman with a child in her arms. "Men do *not* want their supper—t'would be about as true."

"Here's a fine banner coming," cried Penelope, "John Stuart Mill—and why, I declare here are a lot of men," she added, as the deputation of Members of the Men's League followed the banner of their great precursor.

"That's Hopton—one of the Labour Members—bearing the standard," said a guest on the balcony. "The women are getting no end of those fellows to join them."

Alice leant forward just in time to get a good view of Joe Hopton as he stepped bravely forward, making this public declaration of his new-found faith.

"Well, I do call this one of the most interesting and dramatic scenes I have ever witnessed," remarked Penelope Otis after, for her, a long silence.

Alice Walker started up suddenly.

"I want to get out," she said, "will you please let me pass?"

"You want to go inside? You're feeling the sun?" inquired her friend, making way for her. "Shall I come with you?" she asked, as Alice went inside the Club.

"No thank you," Alice called back, "you stay where you are. I simply can't— not another minute."

Down the staircase she rushed and out into the crowded street. Her eyes sparkled, her cheek was flushed. A girl stood near the Club steps selling ribbons inscribed "Votes for Women." Alice pushed a shilling into her hand and seizing the ribbon, twisted it rapidly round her broad Panama hat with its plain white satin bow.

She threaded her way through with such quiet insistence, all made way for her instinctively. A regiment of women were passing at the moment, led by a distinguished, erect figure, frail and spare and immaterial as a flame, her face finely cut as a cameo. On her silver-grey hair she wore a black lace veil. Every inch a leader, she held her head high, her eyes had a light, a flash, that told of battles won and battles still to win. Before her was borne aloft a banner on which showed a pair of silver wings springing from a heart. She herself seemed more spirit than body, and quite ready for her own wings, but the sweet grey eyes smiled on the people who pressed forward, giving a special volley of cheers to greet her as she passed, with a look of warm, human sympathy.

"God bless you."

"Good luck to you."

"Here's the old warrior."

"Stick it Missus."

"Good luck to you"—came from all sides as the men held up their caps and women waved their handkerchiefs to one whose invisible sceptre swayed over their hearts in a way exercised by no crowned sovereign.

Alice Walker darted towards her like a lost child who on a sudden sees a haven.

"May I walk behind you? Do you mind?" she gasped out breathlessly.

The kind grey eyes smiled down on this unexpected companion.

"Do, my dear—do walk with us. Where did you come from?"

Alice fell into line as she answered with a little laugh which was almost a sob:

"I was looking on just as an outsider, till I couldn't bear being an outsider another minute—I want to belong!"

Suddenly she remembered Penelope, and turning, saw her bending over the balcony waving a handkerchief.

Alice waved back and then disappeared from her friend's sight, swallowed up by the river of women.

"Well—that's really very interesting," observed Penelope to the young Brahmin. "You never can quite tell what these English women are going to do—can you now?"

"They cannot tell that themselves. They obey a Voice," said the Indian; "and they are carried forward on the bosom of the onward flowing river."

GERTRUDE COLMORE

FROM *SUFFRAGETTE SALLY*

[London: S. Paul, 1911 (Reissued as *Suffragettes: A Story of Three Women.*
London: Pandora Press, 1984)]

[In the first excerpt, Edith and her friend Agatha Brand are soliciting signatures for a suffrage petition at the entrance to the local town hall on election
day.]

FROM CHAPTER III, "FANTASY AND FACT"

At first she [Edith] had much ado to prevent herself from running away; still
more ado, when man after man turned from her and her request with rude
refusal or coarse gibe, to keep herself from bursting into tears. Oh, for the
lane and the chivalrous knights who wandered with her there! Oh, for shelter, alike from rough tongues and cutting winter wind! Oh, for a fire or a brisk
trot to set the circulation going in her numbed feet! It would be unwomanly,
she supposed, to run round the market-place. A suffragette no doubt would
do it if she were cold, in spite of the crowd; but she was a suffra*gist*, and must
show the men of England—the men who, as her mother pointed out, had the
power to give or withhold the vote, and who must be propitiated, therefore,
and not incensed or defied—must show them that it was possible to be womanly and at the same time—determined? Was that the word Agatha Brand
had used? Yes, determined.

Poor Edith! She felt far from determined as she stood, tapping now and
again a cold foot against the colder pavement, putting out a timid hand, forcing a faltering voice to say, with little gasps between the words: "Please, will
you sign—a petition—to give the vote to those women—who pay rates and
taxes?"

There were men who grunted, there were men who snarled, there were
men who pushed her aside in contemptuous silence; men who told her that
her place was the home (could they but know how she wished herself in that
place!); men who told her she ought to get married; men who told her—a
gentleman one of these, according to his own estimate of himself—that what
she and all women wanted was a husband. A perfect nightmare of men, with
manners so different from the manners of the drawing-room and the tennis-
court!

Beside these, the yokels, brought in in motor loads from outlying districts, seemed comparatively kind; yokels who scratched their heads and had never heard tell of votes for women; who did not rightly understand what was the use of a vote after all; who did not want their "missuses" to get the upper hand; who did not know—dear, generous, open-minded souls!—but what there might be something in it. Couldn't write, some said, but if the lady would put down their names, they'd put a cross, same as inside on the voting paper; and this illiterate support, though hardly establishing the theory of the superiority of the male mind *qua* male mind, was nevertheless encouraging to a girl whose chief desire at the moment was the accumulation of signatures on a petition paper, where finger-marks seemed to gather more quickly than names.

After the first hour, even Mrs. Alick Brand, dainty and indomitable, showed signs that her courage, if not weakened, was put to the strain. Yet she stood firm, though, as she confessed afterwards, had it not been for shame and for the friendly policeman who guarded the entrance to the Town Hall, directing the voters and incidentally keeping a protecting eye on the petitioners, she must have fled.

"It's the beginning that's the worst," she said. "It will get better as the day goes on."

"Yes, I suppose so; oh yes, of course."

"You've got to get used to it. I believe there's a knack about it, somehow."

"I'm afraid I haven't got it."

"Look at Miss Liddon. She's getting on splendidly."

Miss Liddon was the head of a girls' college in Charters Ambo. She had taken an honour degree at Cambridge, and she stood in the street, asking for the signatures of men who could not read or write, a smile on her face, amused rather than embittered by the irony of the situation.

Somehow it did get better. A friendly tradesman with whom Edith had frequently exchanged, across a counter, trite remarks as to the seasonableness or unseasonableness of the weather, signed the petition with alacrity, making her feel that when her next allowance became due, she would betake herself to that same counter, and there spend the whole of it; and after that, names were scrawled on the paper at more frequent intervals. When at one o'clock Edith went to partake of mince-pies and coffee and warm her feet in a room hired for the purpose, she had turned her second page, and felt, compared with the mood of the morning, almost elated.

It was hard to go back. The room with the fire in it was so cosy and so quiet, and, as the day wore on, the streets and the market-place became noisier and more crowded, the voters more boisterous and more beery. Nevertheless, in spite of the beer, it was to the working-class voters that Edith continued to turn with the greater confidence; they were more boorish, but less offensive than the better dressed men.

"How are you getting on? Better isn't it," asked Agatha Brand.

"Yes, much, though lately I've had rather a slack time."

In truth there had been a period during which Edith had secured not a single signature, and discouragement was once again enfolding her.

"I must make more effort," she thought. "I must explain more—argue. The next that comes my side—Oh dear, here come two men in tall hats! They're *sure* to be rude."

But they were not rude; neither were they voters; they sauntered along, observing the crowd, talking together, but did not enter the portico. As they paused, however, by the pillar close to which Edith stood, she felt bound to make her appeal.

"Will you sign—a petition—to give votes to those women—who pay rates and taxes?"

She knew the formula very well now, yet still could not reel it off without little panting pauses.

"I shall be delighted," the elder man said.

He had what Edith called a jolly face; it was round and rubicund, with little close-cut white whiskers halfway down the cheeks.

"Oh, thank you!"

The younger man raised his hat. "May I sign too?"

"Oh please!" Edith looked up with a half-smile. "You don't know what a comfort it is to come across somebody who's in favour."

"I can't conceive of an intelligent being who isn't. The principle is incontrovertible. It's the methods of some of—"

"Oh, we're suffra*gists*, not suffra*gettes*, who are here to-day."

"I felt sure you couldn't be a suffragette."

"You think they really do harm to the cause?"

"The Amhurst lot? Haven't a doubt of it. They've put up the backs of the whole Liberal party; and who's going to give the vote if we don't? Men who haven't logical minds and can't stick to a principle, get put off from the whole thing by the outrages called militant tactics. It's people of your kind who will win the day."

"You think it will be won?"

"Sooner or later—certainly."

The young man—for he was young; about three-and-thirty, Edith judged him to be—raised his hat again and passed on.

Edith turned to her petition and read the two signatures. Gillingham was the first, without initial. Lord Gillingham, of course; she knew he was staying in the neighbourhood and had been speaking on behalf of Mr. Bradley, the Liberal candidate. The second signature, in a very distinct, straightforward handwriting was Cyril Race; a nice name she thought, like its owner's face, which was keen, with well-cut features and stamped with the easy self-assurance of the man of the world.

[The lives of the three principal women in the novel, Geraldine Hill, Edith Carstairs, and Sally Simmonds, converge by chance at Littlehampton, a sea-side town. As a result of overwork and illness, Sally is recovering at the Home of Rest for Working Women in Littlehampton. Geraldine (Lady Henry Hill), a committed suffragette, is temporarily in charge of the home. Edith is stay-ing in the town with relatives. One evening, the paths of Geraldine and Edith cross while both are walking on the beach.]

FROM CHAPTER VI, "SALLY HAS A THOROUGH CHANGE"

The tide was turning and it was time for Geraldine to turn too; she faced round and set out westwards, homewards. She loved the grey-brown expanse with the sunlight on it, the sparkling sea, the soft sound of the tiny waves as they fell gently; baby waves, she thought, making their first efforts to be break-ers. This morning the space was not all her own; a figure was following the path she had trod, and drew towards her now that she had turned; a woman's figure she saw while it was yet far off; a girl's as it drew nearer. Passing close, two solitary beings on the wide wet sand, they glanced at each other as they passed. Geraldine liked the face she saw, with its pallor, that was a healthy pal-lor, tanned faintly by the sun, its blue-grey eyes and dark soft hair; a taking face and a sensitive one.

Turning her eyes westward again from this glimpse of a face, Geraldine perceived ahead of her, lying on the sand, a small white object, a handker-chief she saw, as she came close to it. Perhaps—had she dropped it, that girl? Probably. Geraldine picked it up, turned, and pursued the retreating figure.

The girl was sauntering and it was not difficult to overtake her.

"I beg your pardon; I thought—is this your handkerchief?"

"Oh, thank you! How kind of you! Yes, it's mine. So stupid of me. I hope you haven't come back far?"

"Oh no, not far." Then, because she liked the face, Geraldine continued to stand and look at it. "It's a lovely place to walk, isn't it?" she said with easy friendliness, "so wide and open."

"Yes, yes it is. But I walk mostly in a lane—when I'm at home, that is—and the width of this and the flatness, makes me feel as if—as if I were naked."

Geraldine laughed. "I think I know what you mean. This isn't your home then? You don't live here?"

"Oh no, I came yesterday to stay a week with an uncle and aunt—at the Beach Hotel, I suppose—" The girl looked at a watch on her wrist—"I sup-pose I ought to be going back to them."

"Let's walk together then, if you're really turning back.

"I'm on a visit also," Geraldine went on, as the two set out side by side, "and I come here every morning; sometimes heavenly early when it seems as if there wasn't a living thing on land or sea, sometimes later. It depends of course, upon the tide."

"Do you like loneliness so much?"

"Not loneliness, but wide lonely places—for a time, for a change. I feel as if the width and the solitariness of a space like this, for instance—well, as if it sort of washed out my soul and made it fresh again."

The girl glanced at the face beside and above her. "You hardly look—" she began, then paused and smiled.

"Oh, but I do, I assure you. One gets horribly besmudged and begrimed at the work I do, even though it's a labour of love and love is supposed to keep you clean."

"Is it amongst the poor—in the slums, your work?"

"Yes, and the rich. My work is for all women, and it brings me into conflict with all—no, not all, but most, men."

"The suffrage, is it? I work for that too; oh, only in a small insignificant sort of way, but still—Some of it's *hateful.*" The girl spoke with emphasis; in her mind was the picture of a portico before a Town Hall, and a throng of contemptuous men. "Men are horrid to deal with," she went on; then added: "At least, not all."

"No, not all."

"It's the militants who turn them against us."

"You think so?"

"Certain of it. That's why I'm a suffra*gist* and not a suffra*gette.* I've been told, by a member of Parliament, that the Government will never do anything for us so long as they behave as they do."

"I've been told that too—by members of both Houses."

"It seems such a pity. Doesn't it?"

"Have you ever watched the tide come in?" asked Geraldine. "When it's far out, a long way from the shore, it ripples along gently, as the woman's movement did for fifty years; a very lady-like tide; and nobody heeds it—nobody on the shore, I mean. But when it gets to the beach, and the slope is steep and there are stones and rocks which stem the force, the irresistible force of it, then the smooth waves change to breakers, and the nearer it comes to its destined goal, the fiercer the conflict."

"But—" Edith said, and stopped.

"But it comes in all the same."

"It was coming in just as fast, wasn't it, when it moved quietly?"

"Because there was nothing to stem it. The rocks—if I may credit the rocks with intelligence—or the lack of it—the rocks, seeing it so far away, so unobtrusive, so patient, imagined in complacency that it would never reach them, or that, if it ventured near, it would be easy to beat it back."

"Then you—do you approve of the militants?"

"If I didn't, I should still stand up for them, since it is they, undoubtedly who have brought on the movement to where it stands to-day."

"But in the fifty years you spoke of—"

"Oh yes, I know, women, splendid, patient, persevering women gave their strength and time and intelligence to dragging it through the initial stage, the stage when the tide was creeping over the level sands; and men like John Stuart Mill gave their brains and influence to speeding it on. With what result? The men were disregarded, the women ridiculed—that was all in those first days. It was as it is with all causes that have life in them. They begin almost tentatively; the waves are just ripples; and are disregarded, laughed at, by those who represent the rocks—the rocks that the tide is going to overtake. It is only when it begins to rouse antagonism, anger, bitterness, that you may be sure a cause is gaining ground."

"Do you think then that nothing is to be done without aggression?"

"Almost, I am inclined to think so. But what makes the thing that is called aggression? Not the steady unfolding of a new phase of the world's develop-ment—and all movements of progress are just that—but the opposition which is offered to the unfolding. It is the rocks which make the breakers, it is the rocks round which the in-coming tide eddies and swirls. You cannot blame the sea, which inevitably follows the law laid down for it."

"The rocks make the breakers, you say. Yes—perhaps," added the girl slow-ly; "but it is the waves that are broken."

"Individual waves: but the tide comes in. And individual women have been and will be broken: but woman will reach her destined place."

"It may be—" The words came haltingly and after a pause—"it may be that you are right—in theory. You argue better than I do. But in practice—"

"I argue better than you do because I have thought more precisely and have got my ideas into clearer form; for that reason and no other. As for prac-tice—do you remember how all this began?"

"Hardly. It—there was some trouble at the meeting, wasn't there?"

Geraldine smiled. "Some trouble; that's rather vague. Who and what caused it is the question."

"There were women—who interrupted—surely? I remember hearing about it at the time."

Lady Henry turned and looked at the girl beside her, the girl whose colour had risen, whose eyes had a doubtful look.

"It's evident that you don't know what actually happened. Do you care to know? Shall we turn back a little, or sit a few minutes on this breakwater? Or—must you go?"

"I'm afraid I must; Aunt Bessie—and my uncle is rather particular. But I *should* like to hear what you were going to tell me."

"Although I'm a *gette* and not a *gist?*" The eyes that looked at Edith had laughter in them.

"You really are then, a militant?"

"I forgot to put my badge on this morning, or you would have been warned at once. Yes, I belong to the WSPU. Well, is it all over between us, or are we to meet again?"

"Please let us meet again! I should so like it, and to hear—To-morrow, about the same time.—Are you likely to be here?"

"Most likely—or a little later, because of the tide you know, and looking out for you. Au revoir then."

"Au revoir."

"Oh, I'd better tell you my name, perhaps; Lady Henry Hill."

"And I am Edith Carstairs."

"I'm going to sit here a minute before I go on. Till to-morrow!"

Edith walked away, but before she turned the bend of the beach, she stopped for a moment and glanced back. Lady Henry had not moved from the breakwater; she sat, a still figure, slender and tall, with a blue motor scarf fluttering in the breeze: a militant suffragette.

[Geraldine Hill later describes to Edith the scene that took place in 1905 in the Free Trade Hall in Manchester when Christabel Pankhurst and Annie Kenney tried to speak and were thrown out of the meeting; this event, Geraldine explains, was the beginning of the militant movement. Despite the power of Geraldine Hill's argument for militancy, Edith continues to resist it because of her attraction to Cyril Race, a member of the very government that the women oppose. Nevertheless she is often conflicted about the non-militant course she has chosen.]

FROM CHAPTER XIII, "THE SIGN OF THE CROSS"

For her [Edith Carstairs] the woman's cause carried no call to arms; the methods by which to win it, by which undoubtedly it would be won, were methods of patience, of peace, of confidence in the men—gentlemen, states-men—at the helm of political events. Such methods being right, the others, the methods of obstruction, of violence, must be wrong; and moreover unwise. It was unwise to hamper and harass a Government whose hands were so full, who had so many obligations which they were pledged to fulfil; it was wrong to distrust and persecute a Cabinet of which Cyril Race was a member. Persecute was Race's word and Edith has accepted it. The by-election policy, the disturbing of Ministers' meetings, these things came under the heading of persecution; they were, in themselves, repugnant to her, besides being, as Race had pointed out, tactically unwise. If you want a Government to give you something, why put its back up? he had asked; and Edith had found no answer to the question, though she had tried to find an answer.

With the scene that Lady Henry had painted on the mist still vivid in her mind, with the sound of angry shouts and the calling of a girl's voice, "The question, the question! Answer the question!"[20] still mingled with the breaking of tiny waves that fell upon her inward ears, she had asserted that the policy he combated had taken its rise in injustice and brutality. But Cyril Race had argued that all men make mistakes, that two wrongs do not make a right, and that it was ungracious, as well as illogical, to pursue a whole Cabinet with petty persecutions because some members of it were opposed to a measure of which the majority were actually in favour.

Edith had ended by agreeing with him, and it was delightful to find her heart and her head working in conformity. People did make mistakes, both men and women; even the leaders of the WSPU were not infallible. There were parts of their programme which, in spite of admiration for their pluck, of the comprehension of their motives and objects which Lady Henry had engendered in her, Edith could not but condemn; incidents in their policy of which even their own members—so she had been assured—did not wholeheartedly approve. If allowances were to be made, they should be made all round....

Edith, who had watched the spring come often, and knew its every step, forgot herself, forgot the suffrage and its problems, forgot Cyril Race, in beholding the signals of its presence. A gleam of sunshine fell upon the ploughed surface of the fields that ran down from the trees, showing the mauve tint which lurks in the brown of Dawnshire clay; ahead, where the woods paused and left the sky-line free, the clouds were breaking.

She was nearing the bridge now, with the railway line below running north and south, parallel with the main road which lay but a field's breadth away. The road she was on ran down from the bridge in a slope to meet it, widening at its issue into a space large enough to leave room in the centre for a plot of grass; to the left of the grass, uphill, was the way towards London; to the right, downwards, you went through Pagnell to the University town some seventeen miles away.

As Edith came towards the bridge, the thoughts which had been banished by the promises of the spring came back to her. She could not support the militant movement; that she had decided some time ago; but she would work for the suffrage nevertheless, as hard, as faithfully, as any militant; but in a way that would bring no discredit on the cause; in the way that Cyril Race declared to be worthy of women, the way that was void of violence.

She was near the main road now, and she saw it branching right and left, and saw the patch of grass which split the by-road into two. And on that grass she saw a cross. It stood, white against the hedge on the thither side of the road, one arm stretched out towards the north, the other southwards. Of all the many times that she had come across the bridge, never had she seen it till now. A sign-post stood there always, pointing out the way; but to-day for the first time she saw it in the form of a cross.

An omen was it, or just the outcome of her thoughts? for peace, surely, was the message linked with that sign, peace and goodwill. Nay, but there were other words: "I come not to bring peace, but a sword."[21]

[To distract attention from the activity of other suffragettes, Sally Simmonds throws a bottle into a Cabinet Minister's car. She is arrested and imprisoned. When she is denied bail, and thus forced to spend Christmas in prison, she refuses to eat the prison food and breaks the windows in her cell.]

From Chapter XXXIX, "The Long Night"

The next morning Sally was taken before the visiting magistrates. It was true that she had broken windows; but Sally, on her side, had charges to bring against the prison officials. They had no right to treat her as she had been treated while she was on remand.

Yes, said the magistrates, the wardresses were justified in what they had done.

Sally tried again. They had no right to threaten her with forcible feeding while she was on remand.

Then back to the cell; and the second day was as long and as lonely as the first; but a worse day, taking it as a whole, because of the evening.

In the evening several wardresses came to Sally in her cell.

"You are to come to the doctor's room."

"I ain't coming; not of my own will."

"You had best come quietly. You'll have to come."

"I ain't comin'."

Foolish Sally to resist the irresistible! What is the good of it? None, in a sense; in another sense, it was sticking to the protest against being treated other than as a political prisoner. To give in would mean to sanction the treatment awarded to suffragette prisoners, would mean to fail in carrying out the plan of campaign; "them ladies" would never submit; no more would Sally.

"I ain't comin'," she said.

The wardresses had been upheld by the visiting magistrates, the wardresses could do as they would. They dragged her to the foot of the stairs, with her hands handcuffed behind her; then, face downwards, they carried her by the arms and legs to the doctor's room. After all, they had to do as they were bid, these wardresses; their task was to bring Sally from her cell hither; they had accomplished their task. Or part of their task, for there was more to do yet. The prisoner had to be placed in a chair, the handcuffs removed and her arms held firmly, so that she could not move, while the doctor and his assistant forced down the stomach-tube into the prisoner's stomach, and then poured in the food.

It is well to feed the hungry, and so, and thus, in His Majesty's prisons, in the years of grace 1909 and 1910, prisoners, who adopted the hunger strike, were fed.

The feeding over, Sally was handcuffed once more and walked to the head of the stairs. Strange that she, who had looked with shrinking dread from the attic window in Brunton Street, across roofs and chimney-pots to Holloway Gaol, and had told herself then that prison was a thing she could not face, strange that now, after the worst that prison could bring her, she still had some spirit left.

"I ain't goin' back to that there cell," said Sally.

There were three wardresses with her: two seized her by the shoulders, the third kicked her from behind. So she went down the stairs, till she reached the bottom step, and at the bottom step the wardresses relaxed their hold. Then, with her hands secured behind her and no means of resisting the impetus of her descent, she fell forward, on her head.

That was the end of the trouble, so far, at any rate, as the wardresses were concerned. Sally made no further resistance; indeed, she lay quite still. The wardresses picked her up and carried her to her cell....

Sally lay in her cell; awake, because the hunger pangs would not let her sleep. The feeding had made her sick and had added pain to faintness; her throat was swollen and sore; her mouth was dry. If only she had somebody to give her a drink as she, in past days, had given drinks to thirsty little Bilkeses!

The night was very long, as nights are in December, and the day, when it came, always lagged in forcing its way into that dark place. Sally lay and thought of those who were thinking of her: of Miss Carstairs with her delicate face, of Lady 'Ill. Those two together always led to Littlehampton. What a time she had had there! a rippin' time. Perhaps, when she came out of prison, she might be able to go to Littlehampton again. She would need what she had gone there for before; a thorough change. To walk along the sands with Lady 'Ill and watch the tide come in! That would make up for all the loneliness, all the suffering. The tide; that was what Lady 'Ill had said about the Cause. "Nobody can hold the waves back, Sally. In the end the tide must come in."

"We can't hold it back," she had said, "but we can help it on by clearing away the rocks."

She, Sally, was helping it now, perhaps. Perhaps; but the night was very long.

[Gertrude Colmore completed her novel in early 1911, not knowing how the suffrage drama would end. But her confidence in the justice of God and in women's ultimate victory is evident in her final chapter, given here in its entirety. The lines are from "The Battle Hymn of the Republic," written by Julia Ward Howe during the American Civil War.]

CHAPTER LIII

"He has sounded forth the trumpet that shall never call retreat,
He is sifting out the hearts of men before His judgment seat;
Oh, be swift, my soul, to answer Him! be jubilant, my feet!
OUR GOD IS MARCHING ON."
Julia Ward Howe

NOTES

1 A London street lined with government buildings.

2 One of the entrances to the Houses of Parliament.

3 Westminster Bridge crosses the Thames River and is adjacent to the Houses of Parliament. Lambeth is the area across the Thames from Parliament. Lambeth Palace is the official residence of the Archbishop of Canterbury.

4 A street adjacent to Parliament Square and Westminster Abbey.

5 The "militant tricolour" would be purple, white, and green, the colours of the WSPU.

6 Jules Henri Martin Bergeret (1830-1905), a French general during the siege of Paris and the Commune in 1871.

7 In Aeschylus's play, *Agamemnon,* the king of Mycenae and leader of the Greek forces against Troy is murdered by his wife Clytemnestra on his return home. Cassandra, the captive princess whom he takes back with him, prophesies his death.

8 Concerning the thirteenth woman, Emmeline Pankhurst states the following in *My Own Story:* "We had endeavoured to force the authorities to make good their threat to charge us under the obsolete Charles II 'Tumultuous Petitions Act,' which prescribes severe penalties for persons proceeding to Parliament in groups of more than twelve for the purpose of presenting petitions. It had been stated that if we were charged under that act our case would be given a hearing before a judge and jury instead of a police magistrate. Since this was exactly what we desired to have happen we had sent deputation after deputation of more than twelve persons, but always they were tried in police courts, and were sent to prison often for periods as long as that prescribed in the Charles II Act" (137).

9 The Women's Federations were organizations such as the Women's Liberal Federation and the Primrose League that worked to elect male party candidates.

10 A Mænad, a female member of the cult of Dionysus, behaved on occasion in a frenzied manner.

11 Saint Teresa (1515-82) was a mystic, administrator, and founder of the discalced (barefoot) Carmelites. Joan of Arc (*c.*1412-31) led the French Army against the English; she was burned at the stake. Berengaria was Princess of Navarre and Queen of England (thirteenth century), married to Richard the Lionhearted.

Queen Eleanor of Aquitaine (twelfth century) was Queen of France and later wife of Henry II of England.

12 Trafalgar Square in London, which celebrates Admiral Nelson's naval victory at Trafalgar in 1805, is an area where people often congregate and demonstrate. Nelson's Column is in the Square.

13 A two-wheeled, covered, horse-drawn carriage holding two persons inside. A taxi or taxicab would be a motorized vehicle.

14 A reference to Matthew 11:2: "And from the days of John the Baptist until now the kingdom of heaven suffereth violence, and the violent take it by force" (King James Version).

15 *Votes for Women* was the official organ of the WSPU. It was sold on the streets.

16 A reference to Luke 23:34: "Then said Jesus, Father, forgive them; for they know not what they do" (King James Version). Jesus spoke these words on the cross.

17 In 1910 a Conciliation Committee for Woman Suffrage was formed with members from the House of Commons. They were to find a solution to the woman suffrage question that all political parties would accept; while they deliberated the women called off all militant action. However, despite support in the House, Prime Minister Asquith killed the Conciliation Bill.

18 The oriflamme of France, the red or orange-red flag of the Abbey of Saint-Denis, was used as a standard by early French kings when setting out for war.

19 Most of these women are identified in the notes at the end of the play *A Pageant of Great Women*, included in this text (see pp. 229-232).

20 When Christabel Pankhurst and Annie Kenney interrupted the political meeting at the Free Trade Hall in Manchester in 1905 to ask if the Liberal Government would give the vote to women, none of the politicians present would answer. Pankhurst and Kenney were dragged out of the meeting, still shouting "The question, the question! Answer the question!"

21 In Matthew 10:34, Jesus says, "Think not that I am come to send peace on earth: I came not to send peace, but a sword" (King James Version).

BIBLIOGRAPHY

PRIMARY SOURCES

Arncliffe-Sennett, Henry. *An Englishwoman's Home.* London: Actresses' Franchise League [1911].

Bennett, Arnold. *The Lion's Share.* New York: George H. Doran Company, 1916.

Cholmondeley, Mary. *Votes for Men* in *The Romance of His Life and Other Romances.* 1909; Freeport, NY: Books for Libraries Press, 1972.

Colmore, Gertrude. *Mr. Jones and the Governess and other stories.* London: Women's Freedom League [1913].

———. *Suffragette Sally.* London: S. Paul, 1911.

Courtney, W.L. *The Soul of a Suffragette and Other Stories.* London: Chapman and Hall, 1913.

Despard, Charlotte, and Mabel Collins. *Outlawed: A Novel on the Woman Suffrage Question.* London: Henry J. Drane, 1908.

Fawcett, Millicent. *Women's Suffrage: A Short History of a Great Movement.* London: T.C. and E.C. Jack, [1912].

Glover, Evelyn. *A Chat with Mrs. Chicky: A Duologue.* London: Actresses' Franchise League, [1913].

———. *Miss Appleyard's Awakening: A Play in One Act.* London: Actresses' Franchise League, [1913].

Hamilton, Cicely. *Diana of Dobson's.* Eds. Diane F. Gillespie and Doryjane Birrer. 1925; Peterborough, ON: Broadview Press, 2003.

———. *Life Errant.* London: J.M. Dent and Sons, 1935.

———. *A Pageant of Great Women.* London: The Suffrage Shop, 1910.

———, and Christopher St. John. *How the Vote Was Won.* London: Woman's Press, [1909].

Hatton, Bessie. *Before Sunrise.* London: Privately printed, 1909.

Johnson, Harry. *Mrs. Warren's Daughter.* New York: Macmillan Company, 1920.

Kenney, Annie. *Memories of a Militant.* London: Edward Arnold and Co., 1924.

Lytton, Constance. *Prisons and Prisoners: The Stirring Testimony of a Suffragette.* London: Heinemann, 1914.

Maud, Constance Elizabeth. *No Surrender.* New York: John Lane Company, 1912.

McPhee, Carol, and Ann FitzGerald, eds. *The Non-Violent Militant: Selected Writings of Teresa Billington-Greig.* London and New York: Routledge and Kegan Paul, 1987.

Mitchell, Geoffrey, ed. *The Hard Way Up: The Autobiography of Hannah Mitchell, Suffragette and Rebel.* London: Faber and Faber, 1968.

Moffat, Graham. *The Maid and the Magistrate: A Duologue in One Act.* London: Actresses' Franchise League, [1912].

Nevinson, Margaret Wynne. *In the Workhouse.* London: International Suffrage Shop, 1911.

Pankhurst, Christabel. *Unshackled: The Story of How We Won the Vote.* London: Hutchinson, 1959.

Pankhurst, Emmeline. *My Own Story.* New York: Hearst's International Library Co., 1914.

Pankhurst, E. Sylvia. *The Suffragette Movement: An Intimate Account of Persons and Ideals.* London, New York, Toronto: Longmans, Green and Co., 1931. Rpt. London: Virago, 1977.

——. *The Life of Emmeline Pankhurst: The Suffragette Struggle for Women's Citizenship.* Boston and New York: Houghton Mifflin Co., 1936.

Pethick-Lawrence, Emmeline. *My Part in a Changing World.* London: Victor Gollancz, 1938.

Robins, Elizabeth. *The Convert.* 1907; New York: Feminist Press, 1980.

——. *Votes for Women!* London: Mills and Boon, 1907.

——. *Way Stations.* New York: Dodd and Mead, 1913.

Sharp, Evelyn. *Rebel Women.* New York: John Lane Company, 1910.

Smyth, Ethel. *Female Pipings in Eden.* London: Peter Davies Limited, 1933.

Ward, Mary [Mrs. Humphry]. *Delia Blanchflower.* New York: Hearst's International Library, 1914.

Wells, H.G. *Ann Veronica, A Modern Love Story.* London: T. Fisher Unwin, 1909.

Woolf, Virginia. *Night and Day.* London: Hogarth Press, 1919.

——. *A Room of One's Own.* New York and London: Harcourt Brace and Co., 1929.

Secondary Sources

Bartley, Paula. *Votes for Women 1860-1928.* London: Hodder and Stoughton, 1998.

Blease, W. Lyon. *The Emancipation of English Women.* 1910; New York: Benjamin Blom, Inc., 1971.

Crawford, Elizabeth. *Women's Suffrage Movement: A Reference Guide 1866-1929.* New York and London: Routledge, 2001.

Eustance, Claire, Joan Ryan, and Laura Ugolini, eds. *A Suffrage Reader: Charting Directions in British Suffrage History.* London and New York: Leicester University Press, 2000.

Fletcher, Ian Christopher, and Laura E. Nym Mayhall. *Women's Suffrage in the British Empire: Citizenship, Nation, and Race.* London and New York: Routledge, 2000.

Hardie, Frank. *The Political Influence of Queen Victoria: 1861-1901.* London: Frank Cass and Co, 1963.

Holledge, Julie. *Innocent Flowers: Women in the Edwardian Theatre.* London: Virago, 1981.

Holton, Sandra Stanley. *Feminism and Democracy: Women's Suffrage and Reform Politics in Britain, 1900-1918.* Cambridge: Cambridge University Press, 1986.

——. *Suffrage Days: Stories from the Women's Suffrage Movement.* London and New York: Routledge, 1996.

John, Angela V. *Elizabeth Robins: Staging a Life, 1862-1952.* London: Routledge, 1995.

Liddington, Jill, and Jill Norris. *One Hand Tied Behind Us: The Rise of the Women's Suffrage Movement.* London: Virago Press, 1978.

MacKenzie, Midge, ed. *Shoulder to Shoulder: A Documentary.* New York: Vintage Books, 1988.

Marlow, Joyce, ed. *Votes for Women: The Virago Book of Suffragettes.* London: Virago, 2000.

Marcus, Jane, ed. *Suffrage and the Pankhursts.* London: Routledge and Kegan Paul, 1987.

Pugh, Martin. *The March of the Women: A revisionist analysis of the campaign for women's suffrage 1866-1914.* Oxford: Oxford University Press, 2000.

——. *The Pankhursts.* London: Allen Lane, 2001.

Purvis, June. *Emmeline Pankhurst: A Biography.* New York and London: Routledge, 2002.

——, and Sandra Stanley Holton, eds. *Votes for Women.* New York and London: Routledge, 2000.

Romero, Patricia W. *E. Sylvia Pankhurst: Portrait of a Radical.* New Haven, CT: Yale University Press, 1987.

Rosen, Andrew. *Rise Up, Women! The Militant Campaign of the Women's Social and Political Union.* London and Boston: Routledge and Kegan Paul, 1974.

Rubinstein, David. *Before the Suffragettes: Women's Emancipation in the 1890s.* New York: St. Martin's Press, 1986.

Smith, Harold L. *The British Women's Suffrage Campaign, 1866-1928.* London and New York: Longman, 1998.

Stowell, Sheila. *A Stage of Their Own: Feminist Playwrights of the Suffrage Era.* Ann Arbor, MI: University of Michigan Press, 1992.

Van Wingerden, Sophia A. *The Women's Suffrage Movement in Britain, 1866-1928.* New York: St. Martin's Press, 1999.

Whitelaw, Lis. *The Life and Rebellious Times of Cicely Hamilton.* London: The Women's Press, 1990.

Winslow, Barbara. *Sylvia Pankhurst: Sexual Politics and Political Activism.* London: University College London Press, 1996.